Frederick A. Abel

Mining Accidents and Their Prevention

With discussion by leading experts; also the United States, British and Prussian laws

regulating the working of coal mines

Frederick A. Abel

Mining Accidents and Their Prevention
With discussion by leading experts; also the United States, British and Prussian laws regulating the working of coal mines

ISBN/EAN: 9783337297930

Printed in Europe, USA, Canada, Australia, Japan

Cover: Foto ©Suzi / pixelio.de

More available books at **www.hansebooks.com**

MINING ACCIDENTS

AND THEIR PREVENTION

BY

SIR FREDERICK AUGUSTUS ABEL

WITH DISCUSSION BY LEADING EXPERTS

ALSO:

THE UNITED STATES, BRITISH, AND PRUSSIAN LAWS
REGULATING THE WORKING OF COAL MINES

NEW YORK:

THE SCIENTIFIC PUBLISHING COMPANY

1889

"ACCIDENTS IN MINES."

The following admirable paper on Accidents in Mines was originally read before the Institution of Civil Engineers, in London, by its distinguished author, Sir Frederick Augustus Abel, and with the discussion accompanying it is republished by the Scientific Publishing Company of New York by the express permission of the Institution of Civil Engineers.

The edition of the laws governing coal mining in every State and Territory of the United States, and those of Great Britain and Prussia, add a feature of great value—for these laws have never before been collected or published in accessible form.

THE SCIENTIFIC PUBLISHING CO., PUBLISHERS.

CONTENTS.

ACCIDENTS IN MINES.

PART I.

THE causes of accidents in mines, and the development of measures and applications for combating or avoiding them, have, for many years past, been the subjects of careful study and experimental investigation, at the hands not only of practical men possessing special knowledge and experience in connection with mines, but also of eminent authorities in science and its applications.

Since 1835 a succession of Royal Commissions and of Parliamentary Committees has collected and weighed the results of experience and the views and opinions of miners, mine-managers and scientific experts; legislative enactments consequent upon these successive official inquiries have, from time to time, effected important improvements in the condition, the working management and the supervision of mines, whereby the proportion borne by accidents to the number of men employed, and to the coal or minerals raised, has been gradually diminished. Much of the improvement which has been effected in the working and management of mines since 1850 has unquestionably been due to the appointment at that time of Government Inspectors of Mines, and to the provision by the Act of 1855, of certain important general rules for the conduct of mines, as well as of power for owners to frame special rules for the government of their mines, defining the conduct of the various workers " in a manner best calculated to promote the safety of those employed therein,"—such special rules being submitted to the Home Secretary, and becoming, after his approval of them, as legally binding as the clauses included in the Act itself.

But although great improvements had been effected, the necessity for more extended legislation was not long in being made manifest, and an Act was passed in 1860, after a protracted discussion, which embraced not only additional measures for improved ventilation and protection in other ways against accidents but also provision relating to the education of the children of miners, and to other matters tending to improve the condition of those connected with mines. The operation of the Act was moreover extended to ironstone mines of the Coal-Measures. It was attempted by some Members of Parliament, but without success, to act upon suggestions made by representatives of the miners, and to provide by this Act for the legal qualification of managers of mines, and for various other measures which became the subject of subsequent legislation, including the provision of two shafts to every mine. The inquiry into the great disaster in Hartley Colliery in 1862, involving a loss of nearly two hundred lives, of which a large proportion might most probably have been saved had the mine been provided with a second shaft, led to the passing of a short Act in that year which rendered the provision of two shafts compulsory.

The continued heavy mortality due to accidents in mines, in spite of the undoubtedly beneficial effects of the successive advances in legislation which have been indicated, led to renewed representations to Parliament, resulting, eventually, in the appointment of a Select Committee in 1866, and to the introduction of successive Bills between 1867 and 1872, which were, however, not passed. But early in the session of 1872, the Home Secretary, Lord Aberdare (then the Right Hon. H. A. Bruce) brought in a Bill, which by its provisions was a very considerable advance upon all previous measures relating to mines. This Bill became law as the Coal-Mines Regulation Act and the Metalliferous Mines Regulation Act for 1872, which Acts still regulate the working of mines. Several of the provisions established by these Acts had long been much advocated, especially in connection with coal-mines, chief among these being the condition that all persons acting as managers of mines must hold, from the Home Office, certificates of competency or of sufficient service to afford a guarantee of their fitness for the post of manager. The regulations regarding the use of powder, the employment of safety-lamps, the inspection for firedamp and other important matters were improved, the general rules for the conduct of mines were considerably amplified, and the powers of the owners to make special rules for the discipline of the mine were much strengthened.

That the progressive legislation in connection with mines, the sketch of which, just given, carries the subject to the first session of this year, has proved most beneficial in diminishing the proportion borne by the accidents to the number of persons employed in mines, and in improving the condition of miners generally, has been admitted even by those who have, since the legislation of 1872, been most prominent in pressing for further inquiries and further legislation.

In a speech made in Parliament by the late Mr. Alexander Macdonald, in June, 1878, it was stated that when, about 1850, the output of coal did not exceed 50,000,000 tons, the number of persons employed in mines being a little over 200,000, the deaths slightly exceeded 1000 in the year; while in 1877, when the output of coal was 134,000,000 tons, and the number of people employed was at least double that in 1850, the deaths were a little over 1200 in number. But it was warmly maintained by Mr. Macdonald that, on one hand, the benefits which should accrue from existing laws were far from being fairly realized, while, on the other hand, further and more stringent legislation was urgently needed in several directions. Although particular stress was laid, in the debate ensuing, upon the lamentable loss of life due to explosions in mines, as pointing specially to the necessity for great reforms, the important fact was several times dwelt upon, that certain causes of accident which attracted but little public attention gave rise, year after year, to a proportion of deaths far exceeding that due to explosions.

STATEMENT of PROPORTIONS of DEATHS from EXPLOSIONS in COAL-MINES, from FALLS of ROOF, and SIDES, and from OTHER MISCELLANEOUS CAUSES, to TOTAL DEATHS in MINES from ALL CAUSES, DURING the YEARS 1875–1885.

Year.	Total Number of Deaths from Accidents of all kinds.	No. of Deaths from			Results of some of the more Disastrous Explosions in each Year.
		Explosions of Fire-damp.	Roof and Sides Falling.	Other Causes	
					Explosion at / **Lives lost.**
1875	1,244	288	459	497	Swaithe Main Colliery, nr. Barnsley 143
					Bunker's Hill Colliery, Stoke-on Trent 43
					New Tredegar Colliery, Monmouthshire...... 23
1876	933	95	449	380	Llan Colliery, near Cardiff.... ... 16
					South Wales Colliery, Abertillery.. 23
1877	1,208	345	448	415	Blantyre Colliery............... 207
					Pemberton Colliery, near Wigan... 36
1878	1,413	586	469	358	Abercarn Colliery, Monmouthshire 268
					Wood Pit, Haydock............. 189
					Apedale Colliery................. 23
					Barwood Colliery, Kilsyth, near Glasgow....................... 17
1879	973	184	426	363	Dinas Colliery, Pontypridd. 63
					Blantyre Colliery................ 28
					Stanley Colliery, near Wakefield... 21
1880	1,318	499	462	357	Seaham Colliery............. 164
					Risca Colliery.................. 120
					Penygraig Colliery............... 101
					Leycett Colliery................. 62
1881	954	116	450	388	Abram Colliery, Wigan........... 48
					Whitfield Colliery, Tunstall....... 25
1882	1,126	250	468	408	Trimdon Grange Colliery, Durham 74
					Tudhoe Colliery, Durham......... 37
					Clay Cross Colliery, Derbyshire.. 45
					Baddesley Colliery, Warwickshire 23
					West Stanley Colliery, Chester-le-Street........................... 13
1883	1,054	134	469	451	Altham Colliery, Lancashire...... 68
					Wharncliffe Carlton Colliery, near Barnsley..................... 20
1884	942	65	482	395	Pochin Colliery, near Tredegar, Monmouthshire................. 14
					Naval Steam Coal Colliery, Penygraig 14
1885	1,150	341	439	370	Clifton Hall Colliery, Lancashire.. 178
					Mardy Colliery, South Wales..... 81
					Usworth Colliery, Durham........ 42
	12,315	2,903	5,021	4,391	

Deaths from explosions of fire-damp, 23·57 per cent. of the total deaths from all causes.

"   "   falls of roofs and sides, 40·77   "   "   "

"   "   miscellaneous causes,   35·66   "   "   "

The Table[1] on preceding page which has been compiled from the annual Reports of the Mine Inspectors for the years 1875 to 1885 inclusive, gives the total number of deaths due, in each of those years, to explosions, to the falls of roof or sides in mine workings, and to other causes classed together as miscellaneous.

It will be seen that the proportion of deaths from explosions, in the total number of deaths during these eleven years, is only 23.57 per cent.; the mortality due to this cause exhibits, however, considerable fluctuations which are, it need scarcely be said, due to the specially heavy loss of life caused by particularly calamitous explosions in some years. The maximum percentage of deaths from this cause in these eleven years was 41.6 (in 1878), and the minimum (in 1884) 6.9, while last year it was very nearly 30. On the other hand, the number of deaths arising from falls of roof and sides is not only almost always higher than that due to explosions, but it also exhibits comparatively small fluctuations; the number of deaths from this cause in different years is nearly constant (and the same may be said of the number of deaths from miscellaneous causes), but the proportion which it bears to the total deaths is raised or lowered according to the degree of severity of the accidents due to explosions. The highest percentage of falls in the last eleven years was about 47 per cent. of the total deaths, in 1881, and the lowest was about 33 per cent., in 1878, when the deaths from explosions considerably exceeded those in any other of the eleven years, but even in that exceptional year the deaths due to all other causes were nearly 59 per cent. of the total deaths.

It is not, however, surprising that the daily occurrence of fatal accidents, singly or in small numbers, in the ordinary pursuit of the miner's vocation, which combine to contribute to the majority of deaths in mines, should attract but little public attention; while the paralyzing moral effect exercised upon small communities, and the heart-

---

(1) Final report of Her Majesty's Commissioners appointed to inquire into Accidents in Mines, p. 6. London, 1886.

rending local misery and suffering which suddenly afflict many families, upon the occurrence of explosions of any magnitude or severity, command special sympathy, and elicit public expressions of regret and surprise that the resources of science and of legislative power should hitherto have failed to prevent, or even greatly reduce, the magnitude and frequency of such disasters.

In the Parliamentary Debate of June, 1878, the dangers attending the use of gunpowder and of naked lights in coal. mines constituted the most prominent features of the discussion, and it was after this discussion, in which Viscount (then Mr.) Cross, Secretary of State for the Home Department, took a prominent part, that the Council of the Royal Society was requested by the Home Secretary to suggest some men eminent in science who would be willing to serve upon a Royal Commission to deal with the subject of Accidents in Mines. The Commission was appointed in February, 1879, under the chairmanship of Professor (now Sir) Warington W. Smyth, and included Sir George Elliot, Bart., M.P., Mr. Thomas Burt, M.P., Sir William Thomas Lewis, and Mr. Lindsay Wood, men eminent for practical knowledge and experience in all matters relating to coal-mines and in the operation of existing legislation connected with mines; Professors Tyndall and Clifton, and Sir Frederick Abel, together with Mr. Smyth, constituted the Scientific Section of the Commission; Lord Crawford and Balcarres was, at his own request, afterwards appointed a Commissioner. In the warrant by which the Commissioners were appointed, they were directed to inquire and report whether the existing resources of science furnished any practical expedients not yet in use, which were calculated either to prevent the occurrence of accidents in mines or to limit their disastrous consequences. The first work of the Commission consisted in the collection of evidence on all matters bearing upon accidents in mines, from the Government Inspector of Mines, from experienced colliery proprietors and managers and mining engineers, and from a number of workmen specially selected by the Miners' Associations. This evidence was published in 1881, together with a preliminary Report of the Commission, which consisted chiefly of a summary of the facts and opinions elicited by the examination of witnesses.

Very considerable differences of opinion were found to prevail, even among those who combined great practical experience with considerable scientific attainments, in reference to several important subjects connected with the safe and efficient working of mines such as the circumstances under which the employment of naked lights in coal-mines was admissible; the safety of certain well-known miners' lamps, and the relative merits of others; the conditions under which gunpowder or other explosives may be used underground, and the possible influence of coal-dust in the development or extension of explosions. It was, therefore, in regard to these subjects more especially that the Commissioners considered it their duty to pursue experimental inquiries, and, as the consequent investigations progressed, their importance, and the necessity for further research, became more and more apparent, while the results obtained opened up new fields in which inquiry became indispensable, so that, although several of the Commissioners were almost continually at work in connection with these researches, it was found impossible to carry them sufficiently far to permit of definite conclusions being deduced therefrom until the commencement of last year.

The final Report of the Commission is dated 15th March, 1886; it embraces a number of very definite conclusions and recommendations, which have been based upon the results of exhaustive inquiry and experiment; but, although the Commissioners were repeatedly censured and most unjustly reproached by ignorant critics for not bringing their labors to an earlier termination, no important use has yet been made of their work. A Bill, prepared and introduced by the late Administration after the presentation of that Report, did not reach the Committee stage, but the measures it included were far from embracing the wide scope of improvement and advance in existing legislation, which appeared to be warranted by the results of primary importance included in the Commission's Report.

It has been contended that many of the minor classes of
accidents in mines, which combine to constitute a more
formidable total of deaths than even an unusual succession
of serious explosions, are, at any rate to a great extent,
ascribable to unavoidable sources of danger to which the
miner is exposed; and that, on the other hand, the causes
of explosions have long been well understood, and should
be readily guarded against by the exercise of obvious precautions. The soundness of neither of these contentions
can be admitted, for it is certain that the nature of some
of the most prevalent conditions favorable to mine-explosions has been only recently demonstrated beyond reason
able doubt, and that the extent to which precautionary
measures are feasible for avoiding, or for diminishing the
magnitude of, accidents arising out of the occurrence of
those conditions, is still within the region of experiment.
On the other hand, it is not difficult to indicate directions
in which carelessness, neglect of regulations or of prescribed precautions, or the permission of practices fruitful
of danger, have continued to contribute largely to the
number of accidents which the superficial inquirer may
regard as unavoidable. An examination of the statistics
furnished by the Mine Inspectors' Reports shows that the
accidents classed together as "miscellaneous" do not
exhibit a decrease, since 1851, at all in proportion to the
diminution of accidents due to other causes; but, as bearing upon this, it must be remembered that, during the
past thirty years, the methods of conveyance of the coal
or minerals from the workings to the pit-bottom have
undergone great changes; the transport of moderate quantities along the mine-ways, at a comparatively low speed,
by horse or manual-power, has given place largely to the
traction of large quantities at one time, by means of ways
fitted with ropes and chains worked by powerful engines;
the trains of wagons are hauled at comparatively high
speed along these engine-planes, travelling sometimes at
a rate of 8 to 10 miles an hour; and although the observance of precautionary measures, against the more obvious
kinds of accidents likely to occur in connection with this

underground haulage, are prescribed by the general rules
of the Act of 1872, and by the special rules of the districts,
the risk of casualties which it involves is comparatively
great, and appears to demand closer attention.

As an illustration of sources of underground accidents
of the miscellaneous class, arising out of practices which,
though they may be both dangerous and unnecessary, have
long prevailed here and there, and are difficult to eradicate,
the custom may be referred to, which exists in South
Wales coal-mines, of allowing boys to run in advance of
the horses and trams used for haulage, for the purpose of
opening and closing the air-doors. It was repeatedly and
forcibly pointed out by the late Mr. Wales, formerly Inspector for that district, that this practice is fruitful of
casualties and should be prohibited, a course which would
cause no inconvenience if boys were stationed at the air-
doors, instead of running with the trams.

The class of accidents connected with the shafts of a
mine, and included in the tabular statement under the head
of miscellaneous casualties, has been more successfully
grappled with in later years than any other source of
danger incident to mining operations. Thirty years ago
the list of casualties from the breakage of ropes and chains
used in shafts, from the occurrence of collisions, or the
falling of men and material from the surface, or from some
part of the shaft, was very heavy : thus in the British collieries and ironstone-mines, the average of the ten years
1850 to 1860 shows that one death resulted from these
causes among 1161 persons employed ; within the next ten
years, the number of persons was 2121 for one death ; the
years 1871 to 1880 gave an average of one life lost for 3557
persons employed; and the average of the three years following shows only one death from shaft accidents to 4718
persons employed. The introduction of guided shaft-
cages, the improvements effected in winding-engines and
ropes and pit-gear generally, and the increased care on the
part of officials and workmen, have all been instrumental
in bringing about this great improvement. As an illustration of the safety with which shaft-work is conducted, it

may be mentioned that, at the Navigation and Deep Duffryn Collieries in South Wales, 1200 men have been lowered and raised 430 yards, for an average of four and a half days a week for twenty and eighteen years, in the two pits, representing the passage up and down of nearly 6,000,000 of persons in that time, during which no single accident has occurred.

Occasional shaft-accidents through the fracture of a rope, or through over-winding, particularly in the earlier portion of the last fifty years, have led to the invention of many devices for guarding against such casualties. The first " safety-cage " which came before the public prominently was that of Mr. E. N. Fourdrinier, to whom a medal was awarded in 1851 ; its action depended upon the drawing-in of wedges between the guides and the framework of the cage, when a spring was released by the breaking of the rope. Catches devised for safety-cages are very numerous ; one, and perhaps the earliest class, depended upon the lateral projection of bolts intended to catch in a ratchet or ladder-way, which is fixed upon opposite sides of the pit ; in another class a similar result is intended to be attained by means of bars, which hang over the cage in the form of a chevron and terminate in strong teeth ; another variety operates by embracing the sides of the cage-conductors, by eccentrics or by toothed clutches, which are brought into grip through the liberation of a spring, when the tension is relaxed by the breaking of the rope. Some forms are designed to bring the cage gradually to a stand-still when relaxed by the fracture of the rope, instead of suddenly, as in the case of the contrivances already referred to. Thus, in the contrivance of Mr. Cousin, when the rope breaks, a catch is intended to clutch a second (or safety) rope, which passes over a pulley at the shaft-top, and has attached to one end a series of heavy weights, resting upon seats. When the rope is clutched by the action of the falling cage, the weights are successively lifted, and the descent of the cage is thus checked by degrees until it is brought to rest in the shaft. Another plan, intended to accomplish the same result, has been applied in connection with two cages, having a balance-rope passing from the bottom of one cage to the bottom of the other. The tops of the two cages are connected by a pair of side-ropes; these pass over pulleys resting on spring-pedestals, which are set on the pit-head frame and act as brakes when a weight comes upon them. The confidence in the certainty of action of many safety-clutches of the indicated types, entertained in the earlier days of their invention, does not appear to have stood the test of experience in many instances, and it seems to be even considered doubtful whether their adoption is not in some cases attended by the introduction of fresh sources of danger. There are many recorded examples of safety appliances having failed to come into action at the critical moment, even when automatic arrangements of the kind indicated have been supplemented by the provision of a brake-lever, under the control of an experienced operator; on the other hand, many instances are on record of clutches coming into action when not required.

Casualties, due to over-winding, have been reduced in number to some extent by the employment of "safety-hooks" designed to disengage the cage, if raised too high, leaving it either to be attached to the guides by the coming into play of one or other of the devices just referred to, or to become suspended by strong catches, in the pit-head frame. A safety-hook which has been employed by Mr. Bryham of the Rosebridge Colliery, and others patented by King, Walker, Ormerod, Ramsay and Fisher, operate in the latter way. Although opinions as to the value of safety-hooks are divided, there are many in use in collieries; but more reliable means of protection have recently been provided, in connection with the more modern winding-plant, in the shape of powerful steam-brakes which will bring a loaded cage to a stand-still within a few feet of travel, and which are even arranged to come into action automatically. These brakes can be fitted to existing plant expeditiously and without practical difficulty. A terrible calamity occurred on the 30th of December, 1886, at Houghton Main Colliery, near Darfield, when, from some accidental cause, the engine-man lost control over the winding-rope while a cage containing ten men was being hauled up; the cage was violently drawn up against the roof, and this was immediately followed by the breaking of the rope, when the cage and its contents fell to the bottom of the shaft, a distance of 530 yards. Had the winding-gear been provided with such an automatic brake arrangement, there can be little doubt that the lamentable result of over-winding would in this instance have been avoided.

Although considerable improvements were effected under the provisions of the Act of 1872, in the construction and places of the ladders which are still very largely used in the shafts of metalliferous-mines, especially during preliminary work, the casualties attendant upon their use still give rise to a somewhat high death-rate. On the other hand, the experience acquired in metalliferous-mines with the use of the so-called "Man-engine" compares favorably with the use of ladders, but there can be no question as to the advantages, both in point of comparative safety and of comfort to the men, secured by the use of winding-gear, wherever the nature of the shafts in this class of mines admits of it.

A comparison of the proportion borne by deaths from falls of coal and stone to the total deaths from accidents of all kinds, in coal-mines, during three successive decades ending with 1880, and in the years 1881, 1882, 1883 and 1884, would appear to demonstrate that deaths from falls of roof and sides in mine-workings constitute a larger proportion of the total deaths in recent years than they did thirty years ago:—

In the ten years ending	1860	the percentage was			37·6
" "	1870	"	"		39·1
" "	1880	"	"		39·7
For the year ending	1881	"	"		47·2
" "	1882	"	"		41·5
" "	1883	"	"		44·5
" "	1884	"	"		51·1

Last year's returns, examined in this way alone gave a more favorable result, the percentage being 38·1; but the number of deaths from explosions was in that year much higher than in the four preceding years. The percentage of deaths in the five years ending 1855 was 44·48. When, however, the proportion of deaths from falls of coal and stone in the three decades above specified is considered with reference to the number of persons employed in mines, it is found that a decided improvement has taken place in the death-rate from this cause,[1] yet there is no doubt that much remains to be accomplished before it is so far reduced that the majority of casualties of this class may be reasonably regarded as unavoidable.

The tendency to a sudden yielding or dislodgment of the roof or sides of a working is determined and regulated by a number of causes, such as the manner in which, and the conditions under which, seams, beds or veins are worked ; the position in, or inclination at, which they exist, and the character of material which composes the roof and floor of the mine. These several conditions vary so considerably, not only in different districts, but also in different seams in the same district and even in one and the same seam in a colliery, that the prescription of definite rules, to serve as safeguards against falls, is impracticable. In some places, faults, slips and joints, or cleavages, intersect the coal even up into the roof, and the latter may also be inter-stratified with comparatively loose masses or "balls" of ironstone, which may become suddenly detached from the roof, their presence having been unsuspected. It also often happens, in districts where seams of coal are comparatively close together, that great pressure, or thrust, has to be guarded against, from the sides in some instances, and in others from the rising or heaving of the floor.

It is obvious that such variable conditions present a formidable obstacle to anything approaching a trustworthy comparison of the different systems of timbering practised

---

(1) The annual average death-rate from falls of roof and sides during
  The ten years ending 1860 was 1·531 per 1,000 persons employed
    "   " 1870 " 1·304 " " "
    "   " 1880 " 0·935 " " "
the latter being a reduction of 40 per cent. on the average death-rate per 1000 persons employed, compared with the ten years ending 1860.

in different coal-fields. The employment of cast-and wrought-iron and cast-steel, in place of or in combination with timber, for propping and securing mine-workings has found favor here and there, but has not been largely substituted for ordinary timbering and arching. Cast-iron punch-props of various patterns were used in Yorkshire and the North about half a century ago, and are still met with in some mines, but do not appear to have presented any prominent advantages over timber. Wrought-iron has more recently been somewhat extensively employed upon the Continent and in some Welsh mines in main-ways, in place of timber frames or sets of timber; rolled-iron frames, generally elliptical, in one or more pieces, the joints being secured by fish-plates, placed at short intervals, the spaces between them being guarded by bars, generally of wood. This form of support is stated to have resisted pressure to which ordinary timbering or arching would have yielded. In the use of timber only, a decided advance in the direction of safety appears to have been made by the extension of the employment of so-called " nogs " or " chocks " of crossed pieces of timber instead of, or in addition to, single props, and by the more extensive and careful employment of packing or "building" of stone in worked-out places.

In a work lately published on the causes of accidents arising from falls of roof and sides, Mr. A. R. Sawyer, H.M. Inspector of Mines for North Staffordshire, has given detailed descriptions with illustrations of the mode of timbering and supporting the roof generally practised in that district, and, in showing how accidents from falls are brought about, has explained the nature of different precautions which, in his opinion, would lead to a diminution of their frequency in North Staffordshire. The seams worked in that district vary greatly in thickness and in inclination, and under these variable conditions almost every method of working in use elsewhere is represented there.

With reference to the inspection of mines, for the purpose of ascertaining whether the roof or sides are safe, Mr. Sawyer points out that the universal practice of tapping the

coal or stone with some heavy tool, and judging of its condition by the hollowness or deadness of the sound, and by
slight vibrations felt on placing the hand against the surface while the tapping is applied, although good, is not on
any account to be relied upon implicitly, especially in the
case of rock roofs and long-pieces. It has often been
stated by witnesses, at inquests on deaths from falls, that
the roof had been sounded shortly before the accident, and
considered perfectly safe. Many accidents would be
avoided if, in addition to the tapping test, the roof were
carefully inspected for the purpose of detecting natural dislocations, such as faults or slips, or defects developed by
the working, and if the bearing, the inclination and the
frequency of occurrence of slips were studied by the mining
officials, the timbering being regulated accordingly.

While improvements in the nature of materials and appliances for the support of the roof and sides in mine-ways,
and the methods of using them, must tend to the diminution of casualties from falls, there is no question that unre-
mitting, careful and intelligent inspection, and the continued devotion of skilled labor to the liberal provision and
maintenance of reliable supports, even where their necessity
may seem open to question, constitute the best safe-guards
against accident. The provision of special labor and supervision for the application and maintenance of timbering
of the mine generally, and for its removal from worked-out
places, where, if left, it might conduce to the breaking of
the roof, would seem to recommend itself to mine-owners,
as well as the provision of ample labor in shifts for driving
the working places as quickly as possible ; but as the timbering of the working places will generally be in the hands
of the miner himself, it is of the first importance that ample supplies of timber should be maintained in positions as
convenient as possible to the men, and that every facility
and encouragement should be afforded them to obtain
proper training in the operations of timbering and of otherwise protecting working places, and to prevent them from
grudging the expenditure of time and labor necessary for
carrying out this work thoroughly.

In workings where powder and certain substitutes for blasting cannot be employed with safety or advantage, and where, therefore, mechanical appliances have to be used for the bringing down of coal and stone, the risk of accident from falls must obviously be reduced by the employment of drilling and wedging or cutting appliances, which increase the ratio of work done to the time spent by the men in close proximity to the working-face. Of the numerous coal-cutting or kirving machines which have been devised, but few seem to have established such claims to efficiency and economy as to give promise of their extensive adoption. Some progress has been made in recent years in the employment of hydraulic pressure in the forcing down of coal; thus it has been applied by Mr. Chubb to the working of a range of pistons placed inside the hole,[1] and by Messrs. Bidder and Jones, and Grafton Jones, to the forcing of a long wedge into a hole in the coal.[2]

Compressed air has been applied with more success to the bringing down of stone : one of the most powerful and efficient machines for the purpose is that devised by Messrs. Dubois and François, called the *bossoyeuse*, which has been used for some years past on a considerable extent at coal-mines near Liège and at Blanzy.   Holes, grouped in a particular way, are first made by the compressed air-borer of those engineers ; so-called plug-and-feather wedges are then driven into the holes by a ram acted on by compressed air. The rock is thus rapidly broken in from one hole to another, and the expedition with which the rock is removed by this mode of working is said to compare favorably with blasting. A machine of analogous description to that of English and Beaumont, which has been used in the drift of the proposed Channel Tunnel, has recently been applied at the Bridgwater Collieries, to the boring out of a drift in the stone 7 feet 2 inches in diameter. One serious defect of this system, if applied in localities where fire-damp may

---

[1] Minutes of Proceedings Inst. C.E. vol. xxviii. p. 118.
[2] *Ibid.* p. 113.

occur, appears to be that, if the cutters come upon hard, gritty stone, sparks are abundantly given off. It is doubtful whether the risk of accident arising from this may be efficiently guarded against by keeping a jet of water playing upon the face of the stone.

In some of the Cleveland mines a rotary borer actuated by compressed air, which has been devised by Mr. W. Walker, is in use for preparing holes for powder-charges, and is said to effect great economy in time.

Considerable improvements have of late been made in hand-drilling machines, and their employment in combination with compound wedges of recent invention has greatly facilitated the getting of coal by hand. One of the most efficient is that of Messrs. Asquith and Ormsby, who by using an endless chain for working the drill are readily able to bore holes close to the roof ; an efficient modification of the plug-and-feather system of wedging enables them to work with considerable expedition in coal and stone.

Although the efficient support of the roof and sides in mine-workings, and the increased facilities for the expeditious performance of mechanical work connected with coal-getting, must contribute to the diminution of the death-rate from falls, it is evident that the provision of good illumination in the mine-ways and working places would be invaluable as a protection against accidents of this class. Vigilance on the part of the miner must often be of little avail, if, as is still very frequently the case, he is dependent upon a source of light, whereby to observe the first signs of an impending fall, which is insufficient to enable him to see distinctly in his immediate vicinity. The utter inadequacy of the light furnished by the safety-lamps hitherto most generally employed, *i.e.*, the Davy, the Stephenson, and the Clanny, has been the chief cause of the frequent yielding to the strong temptation to employ naked lights, even in regions where the possibility of an explosion from the presence of fire-damp is scarcely doubtful.

The importance of effecting improvement in the illuminating power of safety-lamps has been borne in mind by

2

many of those who have devoted skill and ingenuity to the attainment of greater security in the use of lamps in mines, where fire-damp is either prevalent, or where its sudden dis-engagement from coal or stone may occur at any time. One of the chief, and most laborious, branches of experimental investigation upon which the late Royal Commission entered was the determination, by trustworthy and searching methods of experiment, of the relative merits of the numerous varieties of safety-lamp which have been devised in recent years, and especially since the appointment of that Commission.

These and similar experiments and their results will be dealt with in Part II. of this Paper, it being desirable in the first instance to review the circumstances and conditions relating to the existence, in mines, of that great (in the eyes of the public, the chief) source of calamity, fire-damp, the gas which escapes, either gradually and almost continuously, or fitfully and in sudden outbursts, from coal, or from stone adjacent to coal-seams.

Fire-damp, as it comes off from so-called blowers and from freshly-cut coal, consists almost entirely of light carburetted hydrogen or marsh-gas, being mingled with only small proportions of nitrogen and of carbonic acid. The recent analytical investigations of Mr. J. W. Thomas, Dr. E. Von Meyer and others, have shown that, as would be inferred from the known laws governing the escape of gases on their passage through porous bodies, the portions which first pass from these into the air contain the highest proportion of marsh-gas, while those which are evolved at later periods contain comparatively high proportions of carbonic acid and nitrogen. The composition of fire-damp in one and the same mine may, therefore, differ materially, according as to whether the gas has escaped chiefly from blowers or from the freshly-cut coal faces; or whether it has been drawn out, or expelled to some considerable extent, from old workings by a diminution of atmospheric pressure, or by local disturbances, such as falls in the goaves or old workings.

It has long been well known that fire-damp exists, in a

more or less condensed condition, in coal, even some time
after it has been brought to the surface; its gradual escape
has constituted a fruitful source of disaster to coal-laden
ships and to steam-vessels carrying large provisions of coal.
But the conditions under which the gas supplies are confined in seams and in the contiguous strata, and the causes
of certain frequently recurring phenomena connected with
the escape of the gases from coal, are still but little understood. In many cases the gas finds vent gradually and
quietly, though evidently under considerable pressure from
the faces of the freshly-cut coal; in others its escape from
new faces is made manifest by a singing or hissing sound,
and, if the face of the coal be wet, as in the case of drifts
under the sea, it may be covered with minute bubbles.
Sudden and violent eruptions of gas occasionally even overpower for a time the most efficient ventilation, and are accompanied by the dislodgment and projection of large
quantities of coal, much of it in a disintegrated state.
The issue, in some localities, of powerful jets, or so-called
" blowers," from the coal, many of which have furnished a
continuous supply of gas for long periods, demonstrates
that fire-damp must exist in the strata under very high
pressures.

Experiments have been made at the instance of the late
Royal Commission by Mr. Lindsay Wood,[1] with a view to
obtain measurements of the gas pressures which may be
developed in cavities bored into the coal at from 750 to
1268 feet below the surface, in the Hetton, Elemare, Ap-
pleton, Boldon, and Harton Collieries, county Durham.
Holes, ranging from $1\frac{1}{4}$ inch to 3 inches in diameter, and
in length from 7 to 47 feet, were bored into the coal either
horizontally or at a small upward inclination. A pipe was
inserted into the hole, the extreme end of which was left as
a gas-chamber. To the projecting end of the pipe, which
was made tight by means of a long india-rubber washer,
was attached a Bourdon, or Schæffer and Budenberg

---

(1) North of England Institute of Mining and Mechanical Engineers. Transactions, vol. xxx. 1880–81, p. 163.

gauge. In several instances the pressure recorded by the
gauge considerably exceeded 200 lbs. on the square inch,
and occasionally exceeded 300 lbs.; in one instance (in
Boldon Colliery) it reached 461 lbs. The gas, having in
several of the experiments been allowed to escape freely
from the hole for some time, was found not to be proportional to the maximum accumulation of pressure; when
the pipe carrying the gauge was again fitted into it, the
pressure once more accumulated gradually to about the
former maximum. Among the observations made, one of
the most curious was the great difference in the maximum
pressures developed, respectively, in three holes bored to
different lengths parallel to and within short distances of
one another. Some experiments corresponding to the foregoing were carried out for the Commissioners in several
collieries in South Wales, the results of which were, generally, in accordance with those obtained by Mr. Lindsay
Wood; at the Celynan Colliery, Abercarn, where there have
been many sudden outbursts of gas, the maximum accumulation of pressure, in a hole bored to a distance of 47
feet 10 inches into very hard and compact coal, at a depth
of 1480 feet from the surface, was 430 lbs. on the square
inch, the gas being given off from the open hole at the rate
of only 0·3 cubic foot in twenty-three hours. A hole was
bored to a depth of 20 feet into a different heading in the
same seam, where the coal was very soft, and represented
in this respect the character of those parts of the seam in
which sudden outbursts generally took place in this colliery; the maximum pressure here recorded was 318 lbs. on
the square inch, but the gas escaped at the rate of 34·5
cubic feet in twenty-three hours. These experiments show
that the pressure of gas may vary considerably in one and
the same seam, in consequence of variations in the character and consequent permeability of the coal, and probably also of the roof and floor, and of the adjacent strata.

When fire-damp becomes distributed through the air in
sufficient amount, a mixture is formed which will ignite
with a more or less violent explosion when flame or a white-
hot body is approached, or immersed in it, the violence of

explosion, or rapidity of transmission of flame, being in proportion to the fire-damp in the air, and the proportion of gases, other than light carburetted hydrogen, which exist in the former. It has hitherto been accepted that a mixture of air and fire-damp, to be explosive, must contain the latter in some proportion not lower than 7 parts by volume in 100 parts of air; this having been arrived at, in former days, by experiments with mixtures of gas contained in small narrow tubes; but the late Commission found, during the experiments upon a comparatively large scale carried on with safety-lamps, that flame could be transmitted by a mixture of air and marsh-gas containing little more than 4 per cent. of the latter. It was experimentally demonstrated that the facility with which flame travels, through a mixture of air with comparatively small proportions of marsh-gas or pure fire-damp, is dependent upon the diameter of the channel containing it. Thus, a mixture of marsh-gas and air, containing 5·5 per cent. by volume of marsh-gas, could not be ignited in an ordinary eudiometrical tube by an electric spark, nor in a tube 1·75 inch in diameter by a lighted taper; but it was ignited, and burned round the flame applied, in a tube 3 inches in diameter. In this tube a mixture of air containing 6 per cent. of marsh-gas propagated the combustion readily; in some of the Commission's lamp-experiments at Llwynypia, in South Wales, a violent explosion was produced by the immersion of a Clanny lamp in a current of air containing about 6 per cent. of fire-damp, travelling through a channel, which had a section of about 13·5 inches by 10 inches; and there is no doubt that, in the more spacious passage of a mine, the power of mixtures of air with comparatively small volumes of fire-damp is still further developed. These observations of the Commission have received confirmation from the results of somewhat analogous experiments made in Germany by Professors Kreischer and Winkler.

The plan, hitherto pursued, for ascertaining whether the air in any part of a mine-way or working is contaminated to a dangerous extent with fire-damp, is to observe the effect of the air upon the carefully-trimmed and properly-adjusted flame of a safety-lamp, by preference a Davy, Clanny or Mueseler lamp. The first effect of a small proportion of fire-damp in air is to produce an elongation of the lamp-fire, which increases as the proportion of fire-damp rises, until a very feebly luminous bluish flame, due to the combustion of the gas in the mixture, makes its appearance outside the elongated flame. This so-called cap, or aureole, extends as the fire-damp increases in amount (presenting appearances which differ with different kinds of lamps), until, when the atmosphere becomes actually explosive, the gas-mixture burns at the air-inlet of the lamp; or if, as is the case with the Davy lamp, the air enters from all sides, the gauze cylinder becomes filled with the bluish flame, and the lamp-flame is extinguished with more or less rapidity.

Mr. William Galloway, formerly one of H.M. Inspectors of Mines, was the first to carry out a series of experiments, with the object of estimating the proportion of fire-damp in the air of a mine by the behavior of a safety-lamp flame, employing definite mixtures of air with a natural fire-damp, almost entirely marsh-gas, which was supplied by a "blower" in Llwynypia Colliery. More extensive experiments with the same object have since been made by Kreischer and Winkler, who employed accurately-prepared mixtures of pure marsh-gas and air, and made use of five different kinds of safety-lamps, two of which burned rape oil, two benzine, and one a mixture of the two.

Galloway's results led him to the conclusion that a practised eye could just detect 2 per cent. by volume of pure fire-damp in air, "an exceedingly faint cap, ⅛ inch high," being observed by him on the most carefully-adjusted flame of a Clanny lamp when immersed in air containing that proportion of marsh-gas. The results of Kreischer and Winkler were confirmatory of the broad result of Galloway's experiments; but they found that the readiness with which fire-damp could be detected, when present in air in small proportions, differed with different lamps and illuminating materials. An amount of 1 per cent. of gas was not at all indicated by a safety-lamp burning rape oil, while only the faintest traces of a cap were exhibited when benzene, or a mixture of benzine and rape oil, was used. With 2 per cent. of marsh-gas, only an indistinct cap was detectable on the flames of lamps burning rape oil, while the flames furnished by benzine and by the mixed illuminants showed distinct caps. They found that the Davy and the Stephenson lamps furnished less marked results than the lamps (of the Clanny and Boty types) used by them, so that their conclusions as to the minimum amount of fire-damp which can be detected, by means of a safety-lamp burning the ordinary illuminant, agree very well with Galloway's earlier results. Other authorities on these subjects have also instituted experiments in this direction, especially with the view of ascertaining which form of safety-lamp is preferable as a fire-damp indicator ; thus Mr. A. R. Sawyer has been led, by an extensive series of experiments ·with the Davy, Mueseler, and Marsaut lamps, to the conclusion that the second of these is distinctly superior to the others for testing purposes ; and Messrs. Mallard and Le Chatelier have also been led by experiment to prefer, as a gas indicator, the Mueseler to the Davy lamp, especially when certain modifications are made in it, whereby the flame is rendered more sensitive.

The results of Galloway and of Kreischer and Winkler, and those of the Commission which relate to the minimum proportion of marsh-gas needed to impart to the atmosphere in a mine explosive characters, or the power of propagating flame, appear to leave no doubt that a contamination of the air by fire-damp to an extent little, if at all, more than double the minimum amount which can be detected by a fairly expert observer by the only means hitherto employed (*i.e.*, by means of a Davy, Clanny, or Mueseler lamp), suffices to impart to it explosive properties. Moreover, as will be demonstrated later on, the existence of fire-damp in the air of a mine, to an extent below the minimum proportion which an intelligent observer of average experience can detect by means of the lamp-flame, is now known to become a source of great danger under conditions which are prevalent, though in different degrees, in a very large number of coal-mines. It is therefore a matter of great importance that some more delicate indicator of fire-damp than the flame of the miner's lamp should be provided, which, while being thoroughly trustworthy, shall not be complicated in action nor difficult of employment underground, by a properly instructed person. Much ingenuity and scientific skill have been applied to the production of sensitive and reliable fire-damp indicators, and instruments and appliances of great variety have been elaborated, which, however, have only in a few 'instances afforded promise of successful practical application. The great importance of this subject must be the Author's excuse for examining, somewhat in detail, the most prominent results of work done in this direction.

One of the most recent suggestions, which has received considerable attention in Germany, and may lay claim to great simplicity, has been to employ alcohol in place of oil as the fuel, in a very tall form of Davy lamp, having an Argand wick, the air-supply to which passes up through a properly-protected vertical channel in the centre of the vessel containing the fuel. There is a short conical chimney round the flame, and the height of the latter is so regulated as not to be seen above the top of the chimney. The author of this mode of testing, Mr. Pieler, states that so little as 0·25 of fire-damp is indicated by the production of a cap 1·25 inch in length; in experiments made for the Commissioners in the return-air of a mine, where other experiments had afforded indications of the existence of about 1 per cent. of gas, the cap shown on the flame was 3 inches in height. This form of lamp is a most sensitive gas-indicator, but, at any rate in its present form, its use is attended with danger and uncertainty; it is at once extinguished by a very moderate current of air, and, if introduced into an explosive fire-damp mixture, it will bring about an explosion in a few seconds.

The late Mr. Ansell was one of the earliest and most persevering workers in this field, having patented ingenious and apparently promising fire-damp indicators, more than twenty years ago, which were based upon Graham's classical researches on the diffusion of gases. If a vessel, partly composed of a porous body, such as gutskin, sheet india-rubber, or unglazed earthenware, and filled with atmospheric air in its normal condition, is surrounded by air containing an admixture of marsh-gas and at the same pressure as the contents of the vessel, the gas will diffuse through the porous body and pass into the vessel at a more rapid rate within a given time than the air will leave the vessel by diffusion ; hence the pressure in the latter will be temporarily increased, and this increase will be proportionate, approximately, to the amount of fire-damp in the surrounding air, so that the percentage present may be inferred by comparing the observed maximum pressure with those pressures known to arise when given percentages of marsh-gas exist in the atmosphere. Conversely, if the contaminating gas in the surrounding air is carbonic acid instead of marsh-gas, the tendency will be to temporarily reduce the pressure in the vessel. To render the increase of pressure apparent Mr. Ansell adopted several ingenious devices, such as enclosing an aneroid barometer in a small case, one side of which was made of thin porous earthenware, and arranging the indicator of the barometer so as to show the percentage of marsh-gas present in the air (on the assumption that the results are not disturbed by the presence of any other gases). In another instrument the distension of a small india-rubber bulb by the pressure, temporarily exerted, serves to close an electric circuit, and thus an alarum is rung, when the pressure exerted corresponds to the percentage of fire-damp to which it has been adjusted. Or, the interior of a vessel, partly composed of porous earthenware, is connected with one limb of a mercury siphon guage, the other limb of which is in communication with the air of the mine. Another form of indicator, on precisely the same principle, was brought out a few years ago by Mr. Libin. Indicators of this class only operate when first, or suddenly, exposed to the air to be tested, being obviously no longer available as indicators of a given proportion when the air within the vessel has once become contaminated with marsh-gas. To make these indicators of any value, it would be necessary that a supply of pure air should be carried about, to be applied to the instrument before every fresh observation. If a small store of compressed air were provided for this purpose, it would be essential that the supply introduced from it into the instrument should be at the same temperature and pressure as the air of the mine, since variations in these will give rise to conflicting indications with the instrument. Moreover, gases other than marsh-gas, or vapors, if existing in the air of a mine, as they invariably do, will also produce changes of pressure within the instrument; thus aqueous vapor produces similar indications to those of marsh-gas, while carbonic acid would, as already stated, operate in the opposite direction, tending therefore to mask the presence of marsh-gas; and ready means do not exist for determining how far the total increase of pressure indicated is ascribable only to marsh-gas, or how far it falls below that which should be produced by the existing contamination with that gas. Simple and sensitive as are these indicators, they are obviously unreliable for the foregoing reasons. Suggestions have recently been made, to apply the principle utilized in these particular forms of fire-damp indicator in conjunction with electric glow-lamps, so as to cause these, through the agency of the indicator and a shunt arrangement, to show the existence of fire-damp in the air by an alteration in the color, or the intensity of the light, exhibited. It need scarcely be stated that such an arrangement would be of no value as affording any trustworthy indication of the extent of contamination of the air by fire-damp.

Another class of proposed fire-damp indicator is based upon the ratio borne by the densities of mixtures of the comparatively light marsh-gas with air, to the proportions in which these gases are mixed, and upon the fact that, when a body is weighed in air, its apparent weight is equal to its true weight diminished by that of the air, or of a mixture of air with some particular proportion of other gas of different density which it displaces. These circumstances would appear to render it possible to determine the proportion of marsh-gas in the air of a mine, by previously ascertaining the weight of a particular body in air, in marsh-gas and in mixtures of those gases, and comparing the result furnished by a corresponding observation in the mine with the data thus obtained. Mr. Henry Reece, Mr. George Duggan, and Messrs. Chaloner and Della Bella submitted to the Commissioners proposals for determining the proportion of fire-damp in mine-air, by ascertaining its buoyant effect upon a body suspended in it. A portable form of balance indicator of this type has been constructed by Chaloner and Della Bella, whereby small variations in the density of the atmosphere can be detected, and which is arranged so as to be well protected from dust and from air-currents : but although this instrument would give correct information as to the percentage of marsh-gas in the otherwise pure air, and at a particular temperature and pressure, it is obviously impracticable to submit the results of observations, by such simple methods, to the indispensable corrections for the modifying effects due to the presence of other gases or vapors existing in variable quantities as impurities in the air, and to the fluctuations of temperature and of pressure occurring in the atmosphere of a mine. Hence an instrument of this kind possesses no practical value as a reliable fire-damp indicator.

Mr. G. H. Carleton, of the United States, has recently elaborated, in much detail, an ingenious plan by which he professes to render it possible to determine, with considerable accuracy, in an office above ground, the density of the air at selected stations in the mine. At each of such stations a delicate balance is to be fixed, and maintained in electrical communication with one in the office. But the successful and reliable application of such a system must be attended by formidable difficulties ; not only would it be almost impossible to maintain in a mine a series of delicate instruments free from disturbances, and to secure free access of the external air to them unattended by the deposit of sufficient dust accumulations to interfere with their accuracy ; it would also be necessary to provide for the abstraction of the aqueous vapor and carbonic acid

from the air before it passed into the balance. The fulfilment of these various essential precautionary conditions
would involve great complications, and could be, at the
best, but very imperfectly accomplished.

A very philosophical plan has been suggested, by Professor George Forbes, for determining the proportion of
fire-damp in the atmosphere of a mine, which consists in
filling, with the air to be examined, a tube fitted with a
piston, the position of which in the tube can be adjusted so
as to ascertain the length of the latter required, when
filled with the particular air, or fire-damp mixture, to give
the greatest resonance upon the approach to its open end
of a vibrating tuning-fork of a given pitch. The results of
observation of course need correction for variations of
temperature. The apparatus devised to accomplish this
result is, however, difficult to use, even by persons possessing a highly-trained ear. Mr. Blaikley, working in conjunction with Professor Forbes, has devised another
ingenious application of sound to the same purpose; the
method of observation consists in determining the want of
unison in, or the number of beats produced in a given
period by, the sounds which two vibrating reeds emit, the
one being freely exposed and the other being placed at the
bottom of a tube. · The length of the tube is adjusted so
that, when it is filled with pure air, the two reeds are in
·unison ; when the instrument operates in a vitiated atmosphere, the tube becomes filled with the air to be tested,
and as this air, when containing marsh-gas, is reduced in
density, the pitch of sound of the vibrating reed enclosed
in the gas-mixture by means of the tube is changed, and
beats are produced by the sounds of the two reeds. As,
in these acoustical indicators, the conclusion drawn,
respecting the composition of the air examined, rests upon
the relation between a column of gas which produces
sound of a particular pitch, and the density of the gas
tested, and as this density, besides being influenced by
temperature, is also subject to variation from the presence
of unknown quantities of aqueos vapor, carbonic acid and
other gases, the attempt to estimate the percentage of

marsh-gas in mine-air by them would be attended by complications which would render these instruments impractical.

The late Dr. Angus Smith suggested that an ordinary glass compression-syringe should be used as a fire-damp-detector. He found that the heat developed, by the sudden compression of a mixture of air containing 5 per cent. of marsh-gas, was generally sufficient to produce inflammation, and that a flash might be observed on the compression of a mixture of 2·5 per cent., provided a little platinum black were contained in the syringe ; but as an expert observer can detect that proportion of fire-damp with a safety-lamp, and as there is always a risk of fracture of the syringe by the heat of the combustion suddenly developed, this mode of testing is not to be recommended upon any ground.

A method of estimating fire-damp in air, which, if reliable, would recommend itself on the score of simplicity, has been suggested by Mr. Aitken ; it consists in passing the air through a cylinder enclosing two thermometers, one of which has its bulb coated with a mixture of platinum black and plaster of paris, which becomes heated if the air contains fire-damp, causing this thermometer to indicate a higher temperature than the one with the uncovered bulb. If this difference between the indications of the thermometers were proved to be proportional to the amount of marsh-gas in the air, this would present a ready method of examining the atmosphere in a mine ; but although satisfactory results are said to have been obtained with pure, artificially-prepared marsh-gas by this method, this does not appear to have been the case with actual fire-damp.

The proportion of fire-damp in the air of a mine can be ascertained approximately, by observing the contraction in volume of a measured sample of the air enclosed in a small vessel, after a platinum wire within the latter has been maintained electrically at a sufficiently high temperature to cause the inflammable gas to undergo combustion, and has then been allowed to cool. Several forms of apparatus have been devised for accomplishing this in a mine ; one of

them by Professor Monnier, as complicated as it is ingenious, is designed to be a fixture at different stations, and to
furnish records at intervals of one hour of the condition of
the air at those particular parts of the mine.   It does not
fulfil one of the chief desiderata, viz., sufficient portability
to allow of its being employed in any portion of the mine-
ways and workings.   Portable forms of apparatus for carrying out expeditiously this so-called eudiometrical examination of mine-air have, however, been devised by Mr. Coquil-
lon, Mr. A. H. Maurice and others.   The former states
that he has been able to detect as little as 0·25 per cent. of
marsh-gas in the air operated upon by his instrument ; but
Messrs. Mallard and Le Chatelier, in the Report of the
French Fire-Damp Commission, state that the indications
which it furnishes are below the truth.   The same criticism
appears likely to be applicable to the particular form of
apparatus designed by Mr. Maurice, at any rate if the testing operation is performed with the expedition essential in
a practically useful gas indicator.   It is not improbable
that further efforts in this direction may result in the provision of a eudiometrical apparatus, which will fairly answer
to the qualities demanded of a really useful fire-damp indicator, namely, that it shall be comparatively simple in construction and not difficult of use by a person of average
intelligence, expeditious in action, and not liable to get out
of order, and that it shall readily detect less than 1 per
cent. of fire-damp in air, and furnish concordant results
under like conditions.   Mr. J. W. Swan has quite recently
constructed a small and handy form of such a gas indicator,
arranged for use in conjunction with a miner's electric
lamp, which is now being submitted to practical trials.

The instrument, which has hitherto most nearly approached the fulfilment of these essential conditions, is the
fire-damp indicator of Mr. E. H. Liveing, in which he uses
photometrically the rise of temperature produced in a platinum wire, when this is heated in a mixture of fire-damp
and air.   A small oblong box is divided into an upper and
a lower compartment.   Inside the upper one are two spirals
of fine platinum wire, fixed one against each end of the

box, so that an extremity of one spiral faces that of the other, the two being four inches apart. One of the spirals is enclosed air-tight in a tube which contains pure air, the other one is enveloped by a cylinder of wire-gauze, through which the surrounding air has free access to the platinum ; the ends of these envelopes, or cylinders, which face each other, are of glass. In the lower compartment of the box is a small magneto-electric machine with which the platinum helices are connected, so that by turning a handle outside the box an electric current can be passed through both, whereby they are raised to a moderate red heat of equal intensity; but if the air, which has access through the gauze to one of the helices, contains more than 0·25 per cent. of its volume of firedamp, the brilliancy of this half will be heightened, and the brightness of its glow will be further increased as the proportion of fire-damp in the air rises towards that required to produce an explosive mixture. A simple photometric arrangement, applied in conjunction with the helices, affords a ready and rapid means of determining the actual percentage of marsh-gas in the air which enters the apparatus from the mine. A small wedge-shaped screen is situated between the tubes containing the spirals, so that each one, when glowing, illuminates only the side which faces it. The screen is attached to a slide-rod, adjustable from the outside of the box ; a scale, graduated from the results of experimental observation, is fixed in close proximity to the sliding wedge-screen, and these can be observed either with the lid of the box open or through a window which is let into the lid. When both the spirals are maintained in a glowing condition by working the electro-magnet, the position of the wedge-screen is adjusted by shifting the slide-rod, until the two faces are equally illuminated ; if the air in the box is free from firedamp, the screen will then be in a position midway between the spirals, but if marsh-gas is present in the air tested, the increased light emitted by the platinum spiral, to which the atmosphere has access, will necessitate the shifting of the screen to some position nearer to the spiral glowing in pure air, in order to produce uniform illumination of both sides of the screen, the position of which, with reference to the scale, will then indicate the percentage of marsh-gas contained in the air. The following tabular statement illustrates the delicacy of action of this indicator, and shows that the ratio of illuminating power of the two helices increases very rapidly with the increase in the proportion of marsh-gas.

Percentage of Marsh-Gas in the air.	Ratio of Illuminating Power of exposed Helix to that of the Helix in pure air.	Percentage of Marsh-Gas in the air.	Ratio of Illuminating Power of exposed Helix to that of the Helix in pure air.
0	1	2·50	6·00
0·25	1·23	3·00	8·55
0·50	1·52	3·50	12·70
1·00	2·24	4·00	19·30
1·50	3·10	4·50	31·00
2·00	4·28	5·00	51·40

The lowest percentage above given, 0·25, is readily detected by means of this instrument, and the brilliancy of the exposed helix in air, containing the smallest proportion of marsh-gas which an expert can detect by means of a safety-lamp is more than four times greater than that of the helix in pure air. Mr. Liveing has satisfied himself that, although by working the handle of the magneto-electric machine at different rates, the electric current sent into the spirals may vary in power, and they may become in consequence more or less highly heated, the results obtained are not affected thereby; as the brilliancy of a wire, in a gas mixture of given composition, is always proportional to that of the same wire in pure air under like conditions as to strength of current.

A source of inaccuracy which may, however, be avoided by attention to simple precautions, consists in the circumstance that, with the frequent use of the instrument in the localities in mines where the air may be decidedly vitiated by fire-damp (as in old goaves), the repeated heating of one of the spirals to a higher temperature than the other alters the physical character of the wire, so that the two coils are no longer raised to the same temperature when heated in pure air. To meet this the scale in the instrument can be slightly shifted, so as to alter the position of the zero; with this alteration the indicated percentages of marsh-gas, though not strictly accurate, are sufficiently correct for practical purposes. When the readjustment of the zero is no longer possible, in consequence of a considerable change in the exposed helix, a new one must be substituted for it, which can be easily and rapidly done.

For purposes of the daily inspection of mines, the instrument may be first adjusted above ground, and given to the fireman with the screen fixed in a position on the scale representing the limit which is considered a safe proportion of fire-damp. The operator has then only to fill the instrument with the air at the particular spot where the test is to be performed, to turn the handle until the wires glow brightly, and to observe whether the exposed spiral glows less or more brightly than the one in pure air. If the former, or if the two are alike, the mine is safe at that part; if the latter, it must be additionally ventilated before the workmen enter. Before shot-firing a similar method of inspection would be applied, the screen being probably set for a smaller percentage of gas. To ensure the box being filled with the air to be tested, the lid is opened and the air in it blown out, and the air may then be tested, leaving the lid of the box open; but if it is desired to test the air in some cavity, or near the roof, the lid of the box is kept closed and a flexible tube is attached to one of two entrance tubes with which the apparatus is fitted; the air is then drawn through the box for a short time by applying the mouth to the other tube.

The Royal Commissioners satisfied themselves, by experiment, of the delicacy and accuracy of this method of testing for fire-damp, by the repeated examination of mixtures of air with known proportions of gas, from 0·25 to 3 per cent., and a Committee, of which the Author was a member, appointed by the Admiralty to consider the steps to be taken for the thorough ventilation of the bunkers in H. M. ships, employed Liveing's indicator, with very satisfactory results, for controlling the composition of artificially-prepared mixtures of air and small quantities of gas in experiments in the ventilation of bunkers; for ascertaining

3

the extent to which gas was removed within given periods
from the bunkers by ventilation ; and for searching for fire-
damp in ships' bunkers, in which coal had been stored for
different periods.

Although, as has been pointed out, fire-damp is imprisoned in coal and the adjacent strata, under pressure, which
often is very high, its escape from the face of even comparatively soft coal, or from crevices existing in coal-seams, is
generally small in reference to that pressure, and, as the
gas-pressure probably maintains a fairly constant proportion
to the distance from the worked surface of the coal, the
escape of gas from the latter under fixed external influences
is fairly constant for, at any rate, considerable periods ;
these will be regulated by the character of the coal, and
the extent to which it is charged with gas. The rate of
escape may, however, be affected by variations in the pressure exerted by the superposed strata as the work pro-
gresses, and by fluctuations in the pressure, temperature,
and hygrometric condition of the atmosphere to which the
face is exposed. Some very interesting experiments, made
ten years ago by Mr. H. Hall, Government-Inspector of
Mines, in different fiery seams of coal, appear to have
afforded conclusive evidence of the considerable extent to
which the escape of gas may be increased by the rarefac-
tion of the air upon the face of the coal. One important
inference drawn by Mr. Hall from the results of these experiments was, that the issue of gas from the fall of coal
may be greatly increased when shots are fired, in consequence of the lateral diminution of air-pressure upon the
face of the coal, caused by the rush of gas which attends
the explosion. If a shot be fired in a face at the extremity
of a narrow heading, the pressure of air upon the surface of
the coal, forming the sides of the heading, will certainly be
reduced upon the rush of powder-products from the exploding charge along the heading, and a considerably increased
quantity of gas may, therefore, be drawn out into the air ;
and then, if a second shot be soon afterwards fired near the
position of the first, any flame which may be propelled into
the air by it might meet with a more or less violently

explosive mixture, or might, at any rate, be very greatly increased in magnitude, and be productive of dangerous results.

Some extensive experiments in a similar direction to those of Mr. Hall have been recently carried out in Austrian Silesia, in a coal-mine belonging to the Archduke Albert, at Karwin. The attempt has there been made to partially exhaust the air in an entire pit; and, although the barometer underground was only reduced 2·5 inches in consequence of the exhausting arrangement being connected by some leakage of air into the pit from neighboring-workings, an increase to an extent exceeding 80 per cent. was observed in the amount of gas passing into the air of the mine. In the locality where this experiment was conducted, the results were obviously vitiated to a considerable extent by the existence of goaves in the old workings, from which accumulations of fire-damp escaped abundantly on the fall of the barometer; another district of the mine, free from any connection with goaves, was therefore selected for experiment, where the reduction of pressure, by partial exhaustion of working, to the above extent, caused an increase by 44 per cent. of the proportion of firedamp in the air.

There is difficulty in reconciling the results of this and other experiments at Karwin with the observation that, when the barometer fell, from natural causes, to the same extent as the fall artificially produced, the increase in the proportion of gas in the air of the mine was far below the results of the exhaustion experiments.

The Royal Commission carefully examined into the existing information, including the foregoing experiments, which bear upon the influence exerted by variations in atmospheric pressure on the condition of the air in coal-mines in which fire-damp is prevalent. Where gas has accumulated in the goaves and cavities of old workings, there can be no question that a reduction of atmospheric pressure may, by causing the gas to expand, and pass out into the mine-ways, give rise to a dangerous condition of things. It is not impossible that, where a goaf is to a considerable extent open to air-spaces in the mine, a sudden change in atmospheric pressure may cause so large an escape of gas from the goaf as to render the air in the vicinity explosive, even before any distinct fall in the barometer has been observed. In illustration of this, it is stated by the Commissioners that, for a diminution of 0·01 inch of barometric pressure, a goaf of only 1 acre in area and average height of 3 feet may part with about 44 cubic feet of its gaseous contents. In mines where natural or very feeble additional ventilation is trusted to, such an effect of variation in atmospheric pressure in causing or promoting the issue of firedamp into the mine-ways, from accumulations, or from the face of the coal, may be of serious consequence : but the same remark does not apply to the majority of British coal-mines, which are now provided with ventilation amply sufficient to cope effectually with any such possible variations in the condition of the air in the workings.

Numerous striking instances have, from time to time, been quoted of the coincidence of explosions with, or their speedy occurrence after, unusual and abnormally rapid barometric depressions ; but an investigation of existing data on this head led the Commissioners to the conclusion that much of the evidence, in support of the general application of this view, is untrustworthy, and that systematic observations, such as those compiled by the Government Inspectors of Mines, by the North of England Institute of Mining and Mechanical Engineers, and other trustworthy authorities, practically established the absence of any general connection between colliery explosions and barometric changes. So many causes may combine, and in a variety of ways, to determine a dangerous condition of things in a mine—of which variations in atmospheric pressure constitute only one, and perhaps the best understood and therefore least to be feared—that the attachment of such importance to variations in the barometric pressure, as to lead to attempts prominently to connect this one possible concomitant cause with explosions generally, may be distinctly mischievous, as tending to divert attention from other sources of danger which may be much more potent.

For these reasons the Commissioners deprecated the adoption of any such official measures as the establishment of observatories in mining districts, or the issue of warnings to colliery districts, by the Meteorological Office, of approaching changes in atmospheric conditions ; and they express their conviction that safety in mines is much more likely to be ensured by the increasing vigilance of the officials and workmen, than by encouraging a sense of security which may be very misleading, as based upon an attention to such warnings.

The Author has already referred, incidentally, to the most serious forms which escapes of gas from coal and its associated strata take in mines. Of these, the continuous issue from a fissure or crevice of a more or less copious stream of gas, or blower, is the least formidable or difficult to cope with. Wherever seams partake of a fiery character, blowers occur at one time or another ; these vary in magnitude from the small escapes which are called " pipers," because of the hissing sound with which they issue from the freshly-cut face of the coal, to the powerful currents or jets of gas which burst out suddenly, continuing to furnish for weeks, months, or years, more or less copious supplies of gas, which fluctuate occasionally in quantity, and either suddenly cease or gradually die out. Thus the Wallsend Colliery was, for many years, noted for a copious blower, the gas from which was piped up to the surface and continued for a long period to be evolved at the rate of 120 cubic feet per minute. Similar examples might be quoted, but remarkable as is the occurrence of these supplies of natural gas, they do not compare with the stupendous quantities which are furnished by the petroleum districts of the Caucasus and of the United States. In the description of the Pittsburgh oil-and gas-fields by Mr. Andrew Carnegie, a well in the Murraysville District is stated to yield 20,833 cubic feet of gas per minute, or 30,000,000 in twenty-four hours.

The sudden and violent escape or liberation of gas, which appears to have accumulated locally under considerable pressure, is occasionally observed ; and in days past,

when ventilating currents in mines were of comparatively
feeble character, men in the immediate vicinity were sometimes suffocated by the liberated gas, which for a time existed in a but slightly diluted condition. Sudden outbursts
of gas, often very formidable in extent, have been much
more prevalent in fiery mines during the past thirty or
forty years than formerly, and appear to have increased in
frequency with the augmentation in depth of collieries.
When the violent eruption of gas takes place from the
seam of coal itself, a quantity of disintegrated coal is generally projected by the outburst ; thus, in one of a number of
instances cited in the Report of the Royal Commissioners,
an outburst in the "Black Vein" seam at Celynen Pit
(Newport Abercarn), occurred in November, 1880, during
the driving of an air-way 9 feet wide, when one of the men
working in the face of the drift was buried in the small coal
projected, to the amount of about 40 tons. The quantity
of gas suddenly thrown into the working has often been so
considerable as to overpower for a time the most efficient
ventilation. On the occasion of another outburst in the
" Black Vein " at Abercarn, so large a quantity of gas was
liberated that, although 12,000 cubic feet of air per minute
passed through the place where the outburst occurred, the
workings in the neighborhood were not cleared of fire-damp
to a safe extent until four days after the accident. In Belgium, the number of outbursts from coal-seams has been
very considerable of late years, and some of them have
been attended by disastrous results. Full details of the
most prominent, and a careful description of precautions
to be practised in districts where these outbursts are prevalent are given in a valuable essay on the subject by Mr. G.
Arnould.

It is not only from the seams themselves that these outbursts occur ; the pent-up gas has long been known to
break out occasionally from the roof or floor overlying or
underlying the coal. Several disasters, due to this cause,
which occurred at Shipley Collieries in 1851, and in the
years immediately following, first directed grave attention
to this form of outburst. The Midland Institute of Min-

ing Civil and Mechanical Engineers has published a narrative of the most serious eruptions of gas, which have occurred in this way, in the important seams of Silkstone and Barnsley. In some instances the issue of gas from fissures, created by its first escape, has continued, more or less abundantly, for a long period after the outburst and has then suddenly ceased. The Author, when serving upon the late Commission, inspected, in May, 1880, a long narrow fissure in the floor of one of the workings in Strafford Main Colliery, which had been produced by an outburst in 1877, and from which gas had continued to escape up to within a few days of the Commissioners' visit. Many outbursts of this class have occurred in the collieries of Risca and Abercarn, which have been the scenes of terrible disasters, traceable, at any rate in some instances, to extensive sudden outbursts of gas.

The causes of these extensive, and often long-continued, emissions of gas from coal have long been a fruitful subject of speculation. None of these have as yet served to throw light upon the origin of the great pressure under which the gas is imprisoned, as demonstrated by the force exerted by it in escaping (men being thrown down, and coal and stone violently projected by its outbreak). The actual measurements made of the pressure speedily accumulating in borings have, at any rate, demonstrated that any closed cavities possibly existing in coal-seams or the immediately adjacent strata, or becoming developed during the operation of mining, may, in comparatively brief periods, become charged with fire-damp under high pressure, by escape and transmission through the surrounding permeable and highly surcharged coal or stone. It is recorded in the " Narratives of Outbursts of Gas," published by the Midland Institute of Mining Civil and Mechanical Engineers, that gas which has suddenly invaded workings has come, in some instances, from a depth below them of over 50 feet, having shattered and upheaved several feet of intervening hard rock; and that in a bore-hole put down to the layer of shale and rock, from which the gas appeared to come, a pressure of about 9 atmospheres was recorded, which was still increasing.

Other illustrations were mentioned, by experienced witnesses before the late Royal Commission, of the formidable
effects of the pressure of gas in the vicinity of mine-workings, strong rock-roofs having been either actually forced
down or become much curved, and eventually recover-
ing their normal position when the gas-pressure had been
diverted in some other direction. Other witnesses described
the discovery or the formation of cavities of considerable
size and extent in coal, or in the shale above or below, which
in some instances had been found to contain gas confined
under apparently considerable pressure.

It is scarcely conceivable that a seam of even the most
compact coal should not include some comparatively
porous portions, within which the gas, developed by the
metamorphoses which have resulted in the formation of the
coal, will have accumulated under gradually increasing
pressure with the increased accumulation of superincumbent ground. When, in working the seam, the compact
and comparatively impervious portions of coal in the vicinity of such magazines of gas become so reduced in thickness as no longer to possess strength to resist the gas-pressure from behind, above, or below, the imprisoned gas may
suddenly burst through into the working, carrying with it
the porous portions, which become disintegrated by the
sudden escape of gas from them. But there does not
appear to be any foundation for the supposition that cavities pre-exist in coal, in sufficient magnitude to contain
such stores of gas that their emission may continue for
months. The steady maintenance of gas-supply in considerable abundance from the blowers, to which reference has
been made, remains therefore unexplained. On the other
hand, it seems probable that cavities of considerable extent
may be produced during the working of a mine, and in the
direction in which a working is being pushed forward, and
that such cavities, while escaping detection, may greatly
favor the sudden outburst of gas into the mine. The gas
with which a seam, or the adjacent strata of shale or porous
stone, may be highly charged will, so long as these
remained undisturbed, be perfectly retained by the imper-

vious character of the strata which separate it from the workings beneath. But if, by work done in an adjacent seam, the existing equilibrium between vertical and horizontal pressure upon the imprisoned gas be disturbed, the strata, intervening between it and the workings beneath, may yield more or less to the gas pressure from above, and to the lateral pressure or thrust caused by the superincumbent weight of the ground; a separation of the strata or a cavity may then be formed, and continue to open up in a line with the workings beneath. Such a cavity, extending in time to considerable distances in the direction of the workings, like a culvert or tunnel, may get charged with gas under pressure, ready suddenly to burst forth into the mine as soon as the intervening strata become unable at some point to resist the pressure exerted upon them. Cavities or channels of this nature would probably disappear altogether in time after the pressure of imprisoned gas had subsided, and the amount of the latter, which might be accumulated under a moderate pressure in such a channel even only a few tenths of an inch in height, but extending to the same width as the working, might suffice rapidly to fill the channel with an explosive atmosphere. If the distance between the accumulation of gas and the working be considerable, and the intervening strata be strong, an outburst when it occurs will be very violent, and the torrent of gas suddenly escaping may not be speedily diluted to a harmless extent, even by powerful ventilating currents.

A consideration of the development of these conditions, and their relation to those which prevail with the two important systems of working in coal-mines, the long-wall and the pillar-and-stall, led the Commission to the conclusion that, in mines where sudden outbursts of gas are liable to occur, the first-named system is decidedly to be preferred. Under any circumstances it appears highly important to keep the working-face of the seams continuous, avoiding the production of steps or angles, which must give rise to distortions of the line into which a channel (opened up as suggested) may be directed, to flexure of the strata, in several directions, and to consequent lines of weakness.

A careful examination of the physical characteristics and conditions of the strata, over-and underlying a seam which is being worked, is very important, as it may lead to a discovery of the existence of conditions, involving elements of obvious danger, which may possibly be met or mitigated. Thus, the formation of cavities of the nature suggested, would obviously be proportionate to the ease with which the strata separated from each other (at their "partings"); and the existence of a bed of porous gas-bearing stone, or shale, in contiguity to an impervious stratum, overlying or underlying the coal-seam, would certainly favor the rapid charging with gas of any cavities or channels which might be developed in the course of the working.

The possibility of taking measures for facilitating the comparatively gradual escape of fire-damp from gas-bearing strata, so as to relieve the pressure, which might otherwise give rise to a sudden outburst of gas, has received much serious attention. The driving of bore-holes into the coal considerably in advance of the working-face has been attended by good results, and the plan has also been to some extent adopted of driving bore-holes into gas-bearing strata which are contiguous to the mine-workings, but the time and cost of carrying out such operations to any useful extent, in localities where such strata are at a distance from the workings, preclude extensive recourse to this practice. In the case of accumulations of fire-damp in the old workings and goaves, and in cavities and recesses, which can be only to a slight extent, if at all, guarded against, or dealt with by means of the ordinary ventilating arrangements, the available remedial or preventive measures will vary with local conditions. In some cases special gas-drains have been provided in connection with goaves and other lurking-places for gas; in other localities it has been found beneficial to carry on air-way along the rise side of the workings. Even well within the experience of existing mining authorities, it was the custom, in some workings of limited extent, where extensive escapes of gas had not been experienced, to fire periodically the accumulated mixture of gas and air, and this course of proceeding has been occasionally advocated, even within a very recent period. So lately as 1879, the practice of keeping open lamps suspended in the higher regions of workings to burn the fire-damp was recognized by the authorities in Saxony, and it was not until after an official inquiry into a disastrous explosion, which occurred at Zwickau in that year, that this dangerous course was prohibited in mines where the use of the safety-lamp is prescribed.

The late Sir William Siemens brought under the notice of the Commission, in 1881, an invention of Mr. Körner, of Freiberg, for consuming the fire-damp in mines; it consisted in maintaining a mass of porous material, coated with spongy platinum or palladium, at a low red heat by a stream of vapor emitted from a petroleum lamp beneath it, and allowing the air charged with fire-damp to pass over this species of slow-combustion furnace. This arrange-ment was tried in some mines in Saarbrucken and West-phalia, and experiments were made with it by the Commis-sion in mixtures of marsh-gas and air; but its action was found to be only feeble, and its employment would cer-tainly be attended with danger, because small portions of the platinized material occasionally become very highly heated, and are then liable to inflame a gas-mixture. Other expedients for removing fire-damp have been pro-posed, chiefly of electrical or chemical nature; but not one of them is of a practicable character, and there is no prospect of success for this class of suggestion for dealing with accumulations of fire-damp.

With respect to the sudden invasion of mine-workings by large volumes of fire-damp, bursting forth under great press-ure, the most that can be hoped for, with existing knowl-edge, is some reduction in the frequency of such occur-rences, and the Royal Commissioners lay stress upon their conviction, that the only present safeguards, against such serious consequences as may result from their occurrence, are to be found in the provision of ventilation ample to cope with exceptional demands upon its powers, in con-stant watchfulness combined with strict discipline, in the provision of lamps which can be relied upon as perfectly safe where explosive gas-mixtures travel at high velocities, and in abstention from the use of powder, or of other explosives, except under conditions and precautions, which the experiments of the Commissioners have enabled them to indicate definitely, as calculated to insure safety.

With regard to the first of these safeguards, the provision of efficient ventilation, all who have paid attention to the working of coal-mines, cannot fail to be aware of the ample resources now at command at most collieries of any considerable magnitude. Furnaces erected at the surface for maintaining the circulation of air, and which were often very indifferent in their action and power, have during the past thirty years almost entirely disappeared; underground furnaces are now applied, which are capable of circulating volumes from 200,000 to 400,000 cubic feet of air per minute, and mechanical ventilators of various kinds have been developed during the past twenty-five or thirty years to such an extent that volumes of air ranging from 100,000 to 250,000 cubic feet per minute are maintained in circulation by them. It is only possible, within the limits of this Paper, to refer in a few words to the varieties of fans and other mechanical ventilators now in extensive use. Among the most effective and largest fan-arrangements are those of Guibal and Leeds, working in casings, and ranging in dimensions up to 50 feet in diameter, by 12 or 15 feet; the Waddle and Rammel fans, which are open at the circumference, and range up to 45 feet in diameter, and the quick, running fans of Schiele, ranging to 15 feet in diameter. Other forms of mechanical ventilators, such as those of Nixon, Roots and Cooke, are in favor in particular collieries; and numerous others, such as those of Pilzer-Harzé, Goffint, Winter, and Fabry, are more or less extensively employed in France and Belgium.

The liability to serious injury being inflicted by explosions upon ventilating-machines, if they are in immediate proximity to the shafts, renders it important to place them, and the engines which work them, at some distance from the up-cast, and to have a second engine in reserve in case of accident. Considerable benefits have been secured by the provision of special auxiliary ventilating appliances (such as those of Körting), actuated by jets of compressed air or steam, or by water under pressure; although not adapted to the efficient ventilation of extensive areas, they are very effective for local purposes, or in the event of accidents. By all the arrangements which have been referred to, ventilation is accomplished by drawing the air through the mine-ways to the surface; the opposite method of effecting ventilation, by forcing air down the downcast shaft of a mine, has of late been advocated by some, and although it has only met with limited application here and upon the Continent, it is applied, and very effectively, to the general ventilation of some extensive collieries in the United States.

The improvements accomplished, in the arrangements for rapidly passing large volumes of air through mines, have been accompanied by others of at least equal importance, with respect to the distribution of the ventilating-currents through the mine-workings. The course originally pursued, of simply passing a single current of air through the mine-ways, and leaving ventilation, in some of the localities where it was most needed, to be accomplished by diffusion, has to a large extent given place, and with incalculable benefit, to a division of the air-supply into distinct ventilating-currents passing along separate districts. By thus splitting up the ventilating-current, the air-courses are greatly shortened. Obviously the friction of the air against the sides, floor, and roof of the mine-ways, which varies as the square of the velocity of the current, is lessened by thus subdividing the current and reducing its velocity; hence, as the power applied to draw the air through the mine is largely expended in overcoming friction, a given volume of air can be made to circulate by the application of less power, if it be split up into different courses. The supply of air necessary for ventilating the working places in individual districts can moreover, be readily adjusted, when the current is thus divided up, by the application of regulators in the several air-ways, by which the resistance to the current in the different splits may be modified. The division of a mine, into separately ventilated districts, may also tend to minimize the disastrous effects of explosions; at times it has happened that, after an explosion in a particular seam or district, men have escaped uninjured from adjacent seams or districts, which were ventilated by separate splits. It is obvious that, in laying out the arrangements for thus distributing the air to different portions of extensive workings, local circumstances and conditions have to be well studied ; and that most careful consideration has to be given to such points, as the particular distances from the down-cast shaft where the several splits are to be taken from the air-current, the precautions for minimizing the leakage of air from the splits, the regulation of the volume of air to be passed into each district, and the arrangement of the several return air-courses, especially with a view to secure as much independence as possible, and thus to limit the disastrous effects of an explosion occurring in any particular district. The Papers which have been from time to time communicated to various Institutes of Mining Engineers, by some of the Inspectors of local mines, and others well known as authorities in mining, and the important discussions which they have elicited, have greatly contributed to advance to its present satisfactory condition the knowledge of the conditions to be fulfilled, and of the course to be pursued, in the efficient ventilation of mines.

The principle of dividing the air-currents as indicated, after being practically developed, with most beneficial results, in some of the larger collieries, gradually received general application both here and on the Continent. A lucid exposition of the present system of mine-ventilation in its connection with the methods of working pursued, is given in a work entitled " Explosions in Coal-Mines," recently published by two of H.M. Inspectors, Messrs. W. M. and J. B. Atkinson.

The extent to which the air in mines, where fire-damp issues from the freshly-cut coal-faces, is liable to be contaminated with gas, under the existing improved conditions as regards ventilation, has been carefully considered by

Messrs. Atkinson, and by others before them. Mr. Galloway, by his examination of Penygraig Colliery (after the
disastrous explosion of December, 1880), was led to the conclusion that the air-current circulating through the mine,
and receiving a small proportion of gas from each working-
place which it passed in succession, would, upon leaving the
place nearest the up-cast shaft, contain rather more than
2 per cent. of fire-damp a proportion which, considered by
itself, is perfectly harmless. Mr. E. H. Liveing made, by
means of his gas-indicator, a series of examinations for the
Royal Commission of the return-air as it passed along a
single return to the up-cast shaft at Boldon Colliery, in
May, 1884, and he found the proportion of marsh-gas in it
to range from 0·7 to 0·9 per cent. The object of the experiments was to ascertain whether the ceasing of work had
any rapid effect in diminishing the amount of gas passing
into the air from the working-places, and the observations
showed that the reduction in the amount of fire-damp in the
return-way was scarcely appreciable after two and a-half
days' cessation of work. It was also noticed by the examination of the air of two splits of the in-take, one of which
passed over a fresh face of coal, and the other over a face of
corresponding area, which had not been worked for nearly
twelve months, that the new face gave off 74 cubic feet of
gas per minute, while the old face yielded 33; so that, in
twelve months, the issue of gas from the face had only become reduced about one-half.

Messrs. Atkinson consider that the proportion of fire-
damp normally issuing from collieries where gas is prevalent, and escaping from such mines in the return-air as it
enters the up-cast shaft, may be fairly estimated at somewhat less than 2 per cent. of the air. They calculate that
one-half of this proportion of gas enters the air-current at
the working-faces, while the other half is acquired during
the passage of the air through the in-take and return air-
ways; and they estimate that the greater portion, or about
four-fifths of this, is derived from goaves and old pillars to
which the return air-ways are open, while the other fifth
may enter the air as it passes along the in-take, and chiefly

as it reaches the far end, where the slow but continuous ex-
udation of gas from the comparatively recently worked
coal and stone may still be proceeding. They point out
that, for the air-current, even in fiery mines, to be at any
time contaminated with fire-damp to any important extent
before it reaches the working-places, some outburst of gas
must occur, or some more or less permanent blower exist,
in the in-take or haulage road, and this can only be the case
where these roads have formed part of the working face.
They know of no instances of blowers having developed
themselves on main-roads which have been in existence for
some years, and although falls of stone have occurred in
such roads in the case of particular collieries which the
Authors have especially studied, these falls have not been
attended by the sudden liberation of any large volume of
gas.

   The inferences to be drawn from these various observations are that, with the improved mine-ventilation of the
present day, the air, even in fiery mines, cannot become
dangerously charged with fire-damp by the gas which escapes
from the freshly-wrought coal, and from the coal-faces
which are being worked, and that, for such a condition of
things to arise, a sudden and considerable liberation of gas,
or some considerable fall of coal or stone, accompanied by a
large escape of gas, must occur at, or at no very great distance from, the working-places. In not a few of the more
recent coal-mine disasters, the origin of which have been
enveloped in mystery, the explanation has been sought on
the assumption that some sudden and considerable outburst
of gas must have occurred at the time of shot-firing, and at
a sufficient distance from the place where shots were fired,
to allow of an explosive mixture being formed by the escaping gas with the air in the workings, and which must
have become ignited by the firing of another shot. The
presumptive evidence in favor of this hypothesis has, in
most instances, been of slender or doubtful character. Of
late, another explanation of the propagation, and even of
the origin, of at any rate a large proportion of explosions,
which was suggested long ago but was received for long

with doubt or distrust, has been promulgated; this has found increasing favor, as serving to account for disasters in mines where experience has been adverse to the conclusion that they could be ascribable, with any degree of probability, to an unlooked-for contamination of even some small portion of the air in the mine by fire-damp, to an extent to impart explosive properties to it.

The careful examination into the effects produced by explosions in mines, and of the condition of things prevailing in such mines, coupled with the results of many elaborate researches and series of experiments, some of the most recent of which have been carried out on a scale fairly representing the conditions which obtain in mine-workings themselves, have led to a very general realization of the existence of an important element of danger additional to, and possibly sometimes even independent of, the presence of fire-damp in the atmosphere of a mine. The discussion of this important branch of the subject is reserved for the second part of this Paper.

4

PART II.[1]

In summing up, in the first part of this Paper, submitted to the Members of the Institution last May, the information extant relating to the possibility, under the existing improved conditions as regards the ventilation of coal-mines, of a contamination of the air by fire-damp to an extent to constitute *per se* an element of danger, the Author pointed out that, in well-ventilated mines, such contamination could only arise from a sudden and considerable liberation of gas in the form of a blower, or from a heavy fall of coal or stone, accompanied by a large escape of gas, occurring at, or in the vicinity of, the working places; but that, in mines where fire-damp occurs, and goaves and cavities of old workings exist to any considerable extent, where moreover the natural ventilation is only supplemented by comparatively feeble additional ventilating resources, a sudden fall in atmospheric pressure may be attended by the escape into the mine-ways of gas, to even a dangerous extent, from the accumulations which exist in those lurking-places, such escape being liable to occur even before a distinct fall of pressure has been indicated by the barometer.

Mr. Henry Harries has recently called attention to the fact that many colliery explosions have occurred during or immediately before anti-cyclonic disturbances, and, connecting this with the greater prevalence of mine-explosions during the winter months when the range of pressure is greatest, the barometer being usually high, he argues that the downward movement of the earth's surface, under increasing pressure, tends to force the gases pent up in coal and adjacent strata into the workings of deep mines, and that such movement may also give rise to the formation of minute fissures in the seams or strata through which the gases

---

[1] Part II., read 15 Nov., 1887.

will pass into the workings with great rapidity. The Author has pointed out that the Royal Commission on Accidents in Mines was led, by a careful examination of systematic observations made or compiled by various trustworthy authorities, to conclude that, while certain coincidences of fall or rise of barometer with mine-explosions may be selected to support particular views or theories, no general connection has been established between colliery-explosions and barometric changes.

That gas-escapes from goaves, which are liable to accompany a sudden fall of barometer, constitute a not unimportant source of danger in coal-mines, was established by the concurrent testimony of many competent and experienced witnesses examined by the Commission. Mr. W. Morgans, of Bristol, who has given the subject much consideration, is strongly impressed with the view that colliery-explosions are in many instances either actually due to, or are greatly increased in extent and severity by, the condition of the deserted workings or goaves, in mines where fire-damp is prevalent—a view which cannot but be shared by all those who have given attention to the condition of old workings in coal-mines. These goaves, which continue to extend in area as a coal-seam is worked away, are formed by filling up, or packing, the old working-places or gobs with the rubbish produced in working the seam. When this is thin, and the roof and floor are of a character to close in upon the packing by settlement and swelling up, the goaf may become so compactly filled up as to contain little or no spaces where gas can lodge. But where thicker seams are worked, the old workings are very rarely filled up more than partially, the available débris being insufficient for their complete packing. The more or less irregular subsidence, in large masses, of the roof overlying the cavities, is a natural consequence, and this is frequently attended by the formation of interstices in the upper part of the goaf, in consequence of the irregular form, and the hardness, of the dislodged blocks of stone ; these spaces, as well as the caverns created by the fall of the roof over the goaves, form a system of cavities in which large volumes of gas may lodge, and which are often inaccessible to inspection or to anything approaching effective ventilation. The low specific gravity of fire-damp tends to maintain these upper spaces or cavities in the goaves charged with the gas occluded by the coal or adjacent strata. These facts were well established by the concordant evidence of many experts, collected by the Commission, as was also the very great difficulty, if not impossibility, on the one hand, of accomplishing more than an exceedingly imperfect or partial ventilation of goaves, and, on the other, of effectually drawing off the gas from goaves by special drain-arrangements, or of sealing the goaves so as to prevent the formation of explosive gas- and air-mixtures within them, especially when powerful ventilating currents sweep along different sides of extensive goaves at somewhat different pressures.

Mr. Morgans directed the attention of the late Commission to a possible connection of accumulations of explosive gas-mixture in goaves, adjacent to workings, with disastrous explosions, which certainly merits careful consideration. He pointed out that the settlement of those portions of worked-out strata overlying only partially packed goaves must give rise to the formation of considerable cracks and fissures, and that these may extend to, or close to, the coal or stone which is being worked at no great distance off; such fissures may become filled with explosive gas-mixture by the diffusion into them of some of the gaseous contents of the goaves from which they start, and may therefore convey flame from a fired shot to the magazine of more or less explosive gas-mixture, between which and the shot they serve as an explosive fuse or train. He refers to the fact that the examination of mine-workings upon which old goaves abut, after the occurrence of explosions, has led to the observation of instances where pack-walls, which have been so consolidated by pressure from above and below as to resemble the solid stone in hardness, have been found blown out into the road or working, which he regards as conclusive evidence of the development of great pressure

by gas-explosions within the goaf, and as supporting his
view that explosions may have originated in the goaves as
indicated by him.

Mr. A. H. Stokes, one of Her Majesty's Inspectors of
Mines, in some Notes upon the Report of the Royal Commission on Accidents in Mines,[1] comments upon that part
of the Report which deals with the possibility of danger
arising from gas-accumulations in goaves, and considers
that, what at first may appear a dangerous state of things,
arising out of the existence of extensive imperfectly packed
goaves in a mine, is considerably modified by facts which he
states as follows:[2] "It is very seldom, in long-wall working, that a goaf of 1 acre in extent, and having an average
height of 3 feet, can be found standing open; and old
workings should either be kept ventilated and examined, or
stowed up when abandoned. In the second place, large
and ably managed collieries are now so well ventilated, that
any excess above an average of the gases given off, due to
barometric fluctuations, is carried away unnoticed." It
need scarcely be stated that these remarks do not affect the
validity of the views advanced by Mr. Morgans. The fact
that extensive goaves can seldom be found which are standing open, and the assertion that they should be either
stowed up, or kept ventilated, affords no proof that they
may not be magazines of gas or of explosive gas-mixtures,
or that they are generally dealt with in one of the two ways
indicated as proper methods of dealing with them, while,
on the other hand, evidence to the contrary, and to the
effect that the conditions essential to safety are difficult of
fulfilment, was given by competent witnesses examined by
the Commission. The statement that efficient ventilation
removes "any excess above an average of the gases," which
may be given off by goaves upon a sudden reduction of atmospheric pressure, is scarcely of a nature to controvert the

---

(1) Transactions of the Chesterfield and Midland Counties Institution of
Engineers, vol. xv., p. 93.
(2) Transactions of the Chesterfield and Midland Counties Institution of
Engineers, vol. xv., p. 117.

fact that a large amount of gas may be discharged suddenly into mine-ways under the conditions pointed out by the Commission.

There is no doubt that, at any rate, many of the most extensive and disastrous explosions have occurred in mines (*e.g.*, at Abercarn, Dinas, Risca, and Swaithe Mine), containing extensive goaves which, where they have been only partially filled with débris, may have served as lurking places for large accumulations of gas, which the ventilating arrangements were powerless to deal with. While the roads and working-places of such mines may have been reported safe, as the result of the prescribed daily inspection, extensive accumulations of gas, or of explosive gas-mixture, may have existed in the vicinity of these places, ready for escape into the adjoining open spaces, upon a sudden change in atmospheric pressure. Such gas-escapes might either be fired through fissures or large cracks connecting them with the part of the seam or stratum where shots are being fired, or exploded when reached by the flame of a shot fired in the neighborhood, this flame being probably increased in volume, or propagated so as to reach to a gas-laden goaf, by coal-dust employed in tamping the shot-hole, or by inflammable dust raised by the firing of the shot. To this extent Mr. Morgans admits that dry coal-dust in a mine is an element of danger, which, however, he regards as only of secondary importance as compared to the perils entailed by the existence of imperfectly-packed goaves in a mine.

That coal-dust does very greatly add to the dangers and increases the disasters caused by the existence of fire-damp in mines, and that it may even, under certain special conditions, give rise to disastrous explosions, which but for its presence would be impossible, are facts now so conclusively established that the dangers have been officially recognized and to some extent, at any rate, dealt with, in the Coal-Mines Regulation Act of 1887, the passing of which must be admitted as ranking amongst the most useful of the work which Parliament has accomplished in the recent Session.

Eighty years ago Mr. J. Buddle, who was at the head of

the Newcastle Coal Miners during nearly the first half of this century, directed attention, in a published account of an explosion in the Wallsend Colliery, to the destructive effects produced, at a distance from the point of first explosion, by the ignited dust; and fifty-nine years ago Mr. Robert Bald pointed out[1] that the blast of flame from a fire-damp explosion might ignite the coal-dust deposits which covered the floor of many coal-pits in or near the working-places. It was reserved for Faraday and Lyell to demonstrate, in their Report to the Home Secretary on the explosion in Haswell Colliery in September 1844, that coal-dust may be instrumental in greatly extending and in increasing the disastrous effects of fire-damp explosions in mines.[2] The Author had occasion, in his opening Address to the Society of Arts[3] in the Session 1885–86, and three years previously in a Discourse delivered at the Royal Institution,[4] to refer to some salient points in the history of the development of knowledge regarding the part played by coal-dust in mine-explosions, and this interesting subject is more exhaustively discussed in the final Report of the Accidents in Mines Commission: it will suffice for the purposes of this Paper to very briefly review the course of experimental inquiries, pursued upon a small and upon a large scale, by many investigators since the publication of the Report of Faraday and Lyell, which failed at the time, and for many years subsequently, to receive the attention it merited.

The extension of the destructive effects of coal-mine explosions by dust was dealt with, as an original observation, by the French Government Mining Engineer du Souich; ten years after the publication of that Report, and since 1875 the connection of coal-dust with mine-explosions has continued to be the subject of scientific and practical inquiry in France, England, Germany, and Belgium. In

([1]) The Edinburgh New Philosophical Journal, 1828. Vol. 5, p. 101.

([2]) Inst. C.E. Tracts, 8vo., vol. 284.

([3]) Journal of the Society of Arts, vol. xxxiv., p. 21.

([4]) Royal Institution of Great Britain. Notices of the Proceedings, 28 April, 1882 Vol. x., p. 88.

France, the observations of du Souich, Verpilleux, and Vital, have been followed by more extended investigations which Mallard and Le Chatelier carried out in connection with the French Mines Commission. In England, Gallo-way, Hall, and Clark, Marreco and Morris, the North of England Institute of Mining and Mechanical Engineers, the Chesterfield and Midland Counties Institution of Engi-neers, the Author, and others, have pursued experimental investigations upon more or less parallel lines, and, in a few instances, upon a comparatively large scale, so as to approximate in conditions, at any rate in some respects, to those which obtain in a coal-mine. More recently a system-atic series of experiments upon a very extensive scale has been carried out in Germany by the Prussian Fire-Damp Commission at the König Mine, in the District of the Saar, and the results there obtained have furnished conclusive evidence, on the one hand, of the possibility of coal-dust being the sole inflammable agent instrumental in the pro-duction of a coal-mine explosion, and, on the other hand, of the exceptional character of the conditions essential to bringing about such a result.

The fact that, in the complete absence of fire-damp (or other inflammable gas) in the air, a sufficient coal-dust deposit in the immediate vicinity of a working, or the employment of coal-dust as the tamping of a shot-hole, gives rise to considerable elongation of the flame projected by a blown-out shot, has been abundantly demonstrated by the various experimenters ; but it was very difficult to base reasonably acceptable deductions, as regards the way in which coal-dust may behave, under those conditions, in mine-workings and ways where the *perfect* freedom of the air from fire-damp is demonstrable, upon the results obtained by experiments in models of mine-workings of only small dimensions, and with arrangements very favora-ble to the thick suspension of dust in the air.

Only a few experiments upon a scale approaching the conditions which obtain in underground workings had been attempted when the Prussian Fire-Damp Commission was provided by that Government with the resources and arrangements necessary for practical experiments. That Commission speedily and amply confirmed the facts already established by experimenters in England and France respecting the power of coal-dust to increase and to propagate, generally to a comparatively limited extent, the flame from a blown-out shot, in the atmosphere of a mine quite free from inflammable gas; and they found, with most varieties of dust, that when the shot-hole was tamped with clay, 50 feet was about the maximum limit of distance through which the flame would be transmitted, while that limit was increased to about 70 feet if the shot-charge were tamped with coal-dust.

Among the numerous descriptions of coal-dust experimented with upon a large scale by the Commission, there was, however, only one variety, from "Pluto" mine, which combined the properties of very high inflammability, very fine state of division, and comparatively low specific gravity, to such an extent as to cause it to furnish explosive effects, approximating to those produced by a fire-damp-and air-mixture, when a blown-out shot was fired in a gallery of similar dimensions to a mine-way, upon the floor of which the dust was thickly distributed, the air in the gallery being free from fire-damp.

Similarly, in experiments previously carried out by the Author in a mine-gallery at Chatham, with a dust obtained from Leycett Colliery which resembled the so-called "Pluto" mine-dust above referred to, and which, in a series of experiments upon a smaller scale, with many varieties of dusts, had shown itself to be especially sensitive or inflammable, results were obtained approaching the exceptionally violent ones furnished by the latter. In the Prussian and Chatham experiments, the atmosphere in the galleries was known to be absolutely free from inflammable gas. In some much earlier experiments made by Messrs. Hall and Clark, in an adit which was driven from the surface into a seam of coal, and the atmosphere in which was stated to be "practically" free from fire-damp, results of the same character as those above referred to were obtained, by spreading out a very fine coal-dust and firing a powerful blown-out shot at the far extremity of the adit.

Messrs. Atkinson, who, in their recently published work give the results of very careful enquiries made by them into the data regarding the behavior of coal-dust suspended in air,[1] and into several disastrous explosions in which they consider that coal-dust has played a prominent part, point out that the dust existing in one and the same mine-way varies greatly in regard to its ready inflammability and to the readiness with which it becomes diffused through the air, and that the dust deposited upon the sides, top-timbers and ledges in a dry, dusty mine-way, to which they give the name of " upper dust," is much finer and more inflammable than the " bottom dust " which covers the floors of such places more or less thickly, and which is frequently mixed to a considerable extent with dust produced by the grinding action of the horses' feet upon the bottom stone of the seam.   Referring to the broad statement made by Mr. Galloway, that 1 lb. of coal-dust is the minimum required to form an inflammable mixture with 160 cubic feet of air, they point out that, upon this basis, in an area of 40 square feet, 1 lb. of dust is required for each length of way of 4 feet, and that, on dry and dusty haulage roads, a quantity of dust in excess of this proportion often exists as " upper dust " only, which has been raised at the working-places or from the floor-dust, during the passage of men and horses and of the trucks, much fine dust being shaken out from these, and deposited by the dust-laden air as it travels along.[2]

They also point out that while dust accumulations on the floor are necessarily removed from haulage roads in dusty pits from time to time, the deposits of " upper " dust are not interfered with.   Messrs. Atkinson state that the coal-dust which collects in the higher parts of haulage roads

[1] " Explosions in Coal Mines."   By W. N. and J. B. Atkinson.   1886.
[2] It may be here mentioned that, in the Prussian experiments just referred to, the proportion which the coal-dust strewn upon the floor bore to the area of the mine-way was greatly in excess of the above, being 1 lb. to 1 lineal foot of the gallery.

becomes more inflammable than fresh coal-dust, and they incline to ascribe this to some chemical or physical change which it undergoes, possibly to the absorption of oxygen by the dust. In all probability, the increase of inflammability is due in part to the very complete desiccation which the upper deposits of dust, extended in thin layers over large surfaces in the warmest parts of a dry mine-way, must undergo, and partly to a still further disintegration of the powder, consequent upon the "weathering" of the particles. Moreover, the extremely finely-divided and very inflammable deposits of "dant," or so-called "mother-of-coal," which exist in more or less abundance in the horizontal "partings" of coal-seams, is separated to a large extent from the coal-masses during the working and the underground haulage, and may sometimes constitute no inconsiderable proportion of "upper dust."

It would appear, therefore, that the exceptional character, as regards extremely fine division, extreme dryness and high inflammability, essential in coal-dust to enable it, when sufficiently distributed through the air, to transmit flame with great rapidity, may be presented by a class of dust which exists in dry and dusty mines, and is distributed over the workings of such mines to a greater extent than was formerly credited; that the propagation of flame by such dust, mixed in due proportion with air, may proceed with a rapidity approaching the transmission of explosion by a gaseous mixture; and that, even in the complete absence of fire-damp, an almost explosive combustion of dust may, under these conditions, possibly extend to distances which are only limited by a falling off in the abundance of the dust-supply, or by considerable changes in the area of the workings reached by the flame. In a very dusty mine, there is likely to be a considerable deficiency of oxygen-supply for the combustible material, and this, combined with the gradual progress of the flame along a dust-laden atmosphere (as contrasted with the rapid transmission of explosion by a gas-and air-mixture), must give rise, on the one hand, to only a partial burning, or even to only a charring of some of the dust particles, and, on the other, to the development of inflammable gas and vapors by the distilling action of heat upon some portion of the dust, the production of which may assist in promoting the propagation of flame.

Secondary, or back-explosions in mine-ways, of which the existence of distinct indications has been observed by Galloway in his careful examination of the effects produced by some disastrous explosions in mines where coal-dust had evidently played an important part, have been noticed in the course of the experiments of the Prussian Commission, and were also observed by the Author in some of his coal-dust experiments; they appear to be due either to gaseous combustible matter which has been developed from the highly heated coal-dust remaining unburned, or to gaseous products generated from them immediately after the first explosion; in either case, an explosive mixture would be formed at once upon the inrush of air, and would be fired by either incandescent or burning matter.

The possible action of coal-dust in connection with mine-explosions has been so far considered on the assumption that fire-damp may be altogether absent, the dust itself being the sole inflammable agent instrumental in taking up, carrying on and developing to large proportions, the flame from a shot. The experimental results which serve to support the opinion entertained by some, whose views are entitled to great consideration, that certain coal-mine explosions have been practically caused by coal-dust, and are not ascribable directly or indirectly to fire-damp, are open to the criticism that those results are more or less exceptional in character, or that they have been attained under conditions which do not approximate to those likely to occur in a mine, more especially as regards the amount of dust suspended in the air, or the facilities created for its being raised in very large quantities at the time of, or by, the firing of a shot. It is urged that the various items of evidence, in support of what has acquired the name of "the coal-dust theory," collected in dusty mines after an explosion, such as, the deposition, and mode of deposition, of coked-dust upon timbers, ledges or floors in mines, and the appearance of burning or frizzling presented by dead bodies of men and horses after an explosion, though they furnished undisputable evidence that coal-dust had either played a more or less important part in the catastrophe, or had at any rate contributed to a considerable extent to the production of some of the effects, afford no proof that the presence of fire-damp in the air of the mine, even if only in proportions so small that its existence has been unsuspected, or, the unexpected local invasion of workings or mine-ways by some small proportion of fire-damp, may not have been the cause either of the origination of the explosion, or of its propagation, supposing its initiation to have been possibly due to coal-dust only.

It has been pointed out in Part I of this Paper that, up to the present time, the only method pursued of examining the air of a mine for fire-damp is that of observing its effect upon the carefully-adjusted flame of a safety-lamp, and that the most skilful and experienced observers are scarcely enabled to detect, by this mode of testing, the presence of 2 per cent. by volume of pure fire-damp in air. A working-place, or mine-way, may, therefore, be pronounced by a skilled inspector to be free from gas, and safe for the operation of blasting, when it actually contains at least 2 per cent. of fire-damp. Now, although the existence of gas to that, or even to a decidedly larger, amount in the air of mines which is free from dust, or in a locality where no dust can be raised and suspended in the air by a disturbance of any kind, involves no danger, the presence of a very inflammable dust, even only in small quantities, in air containing such a proportion of fire-damp, or of a less inflammable dust thickly suspended in the slightly contaminated atmosphere, will render the mixture of air, gas, and dust susceptible of explosion by the flame from a blown-out shot. The reciprocal influence of coal-dust and of fire-damp in bringing about explosive effects under conditions, as regards the proportions in which they exist in air, when *either* would be harmless if the air contained *it* alone, is not only interesting but constitutes the chief element of danger of dust in a mine. Some varieties of inflammable dust

which will not convey flame to any great distance if exposed to its action when thickly suspended in air free from
fire-damp, and travelling at a low velocity, will produce
explosions under the same conditions, if the air contains
only 1·5 per cent. of fire-damp; on the other hand, a mixture of gas and air bordering in composition upon that
which will just ignite upon the approach of flame, is instantaneously fired by a lamp-flame if it contains only very little
dust in suspension. It was found by the Author that even
a dust which is perfectly non-combustible, provided it be
very fine and porous, will determine the instantaneous ignition of such gas-mixtures, an observation which explained
why, in a series of experiments with a variety of coal-dusts
differing from each other in physical characters as well as in
the proportions of inflammable matter which they contained, certain dusts, comparatively poor in the latter ingre-
dient, were found to rank among those most prone to
develop explosions in air containing small proportions of
fire-damp.

It will be evident from the foregoing, that there is no
need to assume that coal-dust, broadly speaking, is liable to
give rise to explosions in mine-workings which are *absolutely free* from fire-damp, in order to accentuate the danger of allowing any accumulation of dry dust to exist in
workings where shots are fired, or of suffering considerable
deposits of dust to accumulate in any mine-workings or
mine-roads.

Neither are the serious dangers arising from the existence of dust-accumulations in collieries likely to become
more impressed upon the mining public by the contention,
which has been frequently maintained with much pertinac-
ity in the public prints and in official publications within
the last few years, that particular explosions have been
examples of "pure dust explosions," when all that could be
said in reference to the asserted freedom of the air in the
mine at the time of the explosion from fire-damp, has been
that the mine was "practically free from gas" (as indicated,
of course, by the only method of testing in use, the safety-
lamp, which allows from 2 to 3 per cent. of gas to exist in

the air unnoticed); or, that there were "no accumulations of gas." The circumstance that safety-lamps were used in mines which furnished these supposed illustrations of pure dust explosions, showed that fire-damp was known to exist in the coal which was being worked, and the most careful and experienced inspector would not venture to assert that a small proportion of fire-damp might not exist in the air, in the workings, which he had no means of detecting, or even that some accumulation of gas might not exist in inaccessible, though not hermetically sealed, cavities in the goaves. And, in all the quoted instances, the small proportion of gas, the very probable existence of which, at any rate, cannot be denied, may have been the determining cause of the propagation of the explosion by the dust through the mine workings. The formidable nature of dust as an agent of destruction is surely not in the least affected by the admission that the small proportion of gas generally essential to its operation as an explosive agent was, in all probability, there present. Let its absence in such collieries have been demonstrated at any time by Liveing's Indicator or by some other equally reliable means, instead of being assumed; there would then be reasonable grounds for the assumption that a "pure dust explosion" may possibly have occurred, but the danger of allowing accumulations of dusts to remain undisturbed in mines would not be emphasized thereby.

Messrs. Mallard and Le Chatelier, in the Report of their coal-dust experiments,[1] combat the view that coal-dust has played a chief, or even a prominent, part in certain disastrous coal explosions which by some observers have been mainly, if not entirely, attributed to that agency. They point out that all such explosions of any magnitude have occurred in mines in which fire-damp exists; they contend that the possibility of coal-dust, in the complete absence of fire-damp, giving rise to an important explosion, can only be established by the occurrence of an explosion in a

---

[1] Recherches expérimentales et théoriques sur la combustion des mélanges gazeux explosifs. 8vo. Paris, 1883.

dusty mine in which the total absence of fire-damp had been conclusively demonstrated, and they refer to the fact that no explosion has arisen in lignite-mines, which are free from fire-damp but very dusty, the dust being of highly inflammable nature, as a demonstration of the impossibility of dust alone giving rise to extensive explosions. On the other hand, their own experiments have confirmed those of the English investigators, who demonstrated that the propagation of flame by coal-dust is promoted by the presence of fire-damp in the air in proportions insufficient to produce explosive mixtures *per se*, and that even non-combustible dusts will determine the ignition of a gaseous mixture, which in their absence is not inflamed. Results which Messrs. Mallard and Le Chatelier have themselves arrived at are, therefore, opposed to their argument that the influence of fire-damp upon the inflammability of dusts, and *vice versâ*, is much less important than it has been believed to be by others, and that coal-dust does consequently not play that prominent part in mine explosions the frequent exercise of which has been conclusively demonstrated. The validity of their contention, that no coal-mine accident of importance can be attributed with any claim to probability to the action of coal-dust, can scarcely be maintained against the results obtained with coal-dusts, in the absence of fire-damp, by Galloway, Marreco and more recent experimenters, and especially by the large-scale experiments of the same class carried out by Hall and Clark, by the Author, and by the Prussian Commission. That the effects of transmission of flame by coal-dust in the absence of fire-damp, though they may be very formidable if produced on an extensive scale (and the Saarbrücken experiments sufficiently indicated this probability), would be decidedly different from, and inferior in violence to, those produced by a fire-damp explosion, or by an explosion of fire-damp, coal-dust, and air, was pointed out by the Author in his Lecture at the Royal Institution in 1882; the comparative suddenness of the gas-explosion would produce greater destruction and less burning effects than the comparatively gradual explosion, or rapid burning, of a mixture of coal-dust and air, or of such a mixture in the presence of a small proportion of fire-damp. But, so far as regards destruction of life, there can be no question that an explosion in which coal-dust is prominently concerned, must, whilst being quite as disastrous as a fire-damp explosion, assume a far more terrible character as regards the sufferings which it entails upon the victims.

The foregoing sketch of the nature of the dangers arising from the accumulation of dust in mines will, it is believed, sufficiently demonstrate the necessity for the measures relating to this subject insisted upon by the Royal Commissioners in the summary of their Report.

They point out that the constant removal of accumulating dust from the workings of dry mines, to such an extent as to guard against the raising of any dense cloud where shots are fired, could scarcely be so thoroughly accomplished as to constitute by itself an effectual precaution;— that the employment of hygroscopic or deliquescent substances (such as sea-salt, chloride of calcium or chloride of magnesium), in conjunction with water, has not been shown, by practical experience, to afford trustworthy means of maintaining dust in a safely moist condition (especially in warm dry mines through which powerful ventilating currents pass), and, that the application of water, unless very efficiently carried out and within a brief period of the firing of powder-shots, would not be an effectual safeguard against the development of explosions through the agency of dust. While admitting that such an application of water may be not unfrequently attended with practical difficulties, they insist upon the exclusion of the use of powder from such localities unless the removal of dust from the workings, as far as practicable, is combined with copious watering of the floor, face, roof, and sides, shortly before the shots are fired.

The practice of watering in dusty mines appears to have extended considerably, and it is maintained that the practical evils or inconveniences, which were expected to result therefrom, have not proved to be generally so serious as was anticipated by many. It need scarcely be urged, after what has been stated with regard to the comparatively very

5

inflammable nature of the dust which, in dry mines, lodges upon the sides, roof, upper surfaces of timber, etc., that watering, to be efficient, must not be simply limited to the floors, but that it is most important to water the coal-face, and the upper parts of workings in the close vicinity of the shot which is to be fired. Very efficient and portable appliances exist by the employment of which a thorough wetting of upper dust can be accomplished with a comparatively small amount of water. In illustration, the Author may refer to a very efficient portable compressed-air hand-engine (Vinning's anchor-engine) of about the size of the ordinary extincteur, which is expeditiously and easily charged, and distributes the water with considerable force in the form of spray, which can be directed upon the dusty surfaces so as thoroughly to drench them, with the minimum amount needed for that purpose.

In carrying on shot-firing, the concussion and blast produced by the shot and the breaking up of coal by it give rise to a considerable amount of dust, independently of any that may pre-exist in close proximity to the shot-hole. In order therefore to guard against the addition to possible danger in consequence of the raising of dust, in places where a number of shots are to be fired at one time in proximity to each other, it is either necessary to fire such shots simultaneously, or to allow a sufficient interval between the firing of the individual shots to give time for the dust raised by the effects of the explosion to subside or to be carried away by the ventilating current.

The only possible way, other than the removal of dust and application of water, by which the dangers arising from the getting of hard coal, or the removel of stone in the vicinity of coal in the presence of coal-dust and fire-damp, can be avoided, would be, as pointed out by the Commission: the discovery of thoroughly reliable means for preventing the possible occurrence of "blown-out shot;" the adoption of particular explosive agents, or of particular methods of using such agents, which will deprive a blown-out shot of its danger by guarding against the possibility of a projection of flame, or of highly heated solid matter by the shot ; or lastly, the substitution, for explosive agents, of some similarly efficient method of bringing down coal and stone, which is free from the special dangers attending the use of such agents.

Various methods and appliances have been proposed from time to time with the view of preventing the occurrence of blown-out shots ; but neither the employment of highly resisting tamping materials, nor the attachment of heavy weights to tamping rods, and other contrivances of this class, have realized any approach to success in this direction. One of the latest devices for preventing blown-out shots, submitted to trial by the Commission, but without success, was a so-called blasting plug, devised by Mr. Humble, which consists of a perforated spindle corresponding in length to the tamping required, and having a screw-thread at each extremity ; a conical brass nut with a broad base is screwed upon the lower end, a long cylinder of somewhat rigid vulcanized india-rubber is slipped over the spindle, and a broad-based nut is screwed down upon it, over the upper extremity of the spindle, so that the india-rubber cylinder or tube, which fits loosely into the shot-hole, into which this arrangement is inserted, may be expanded by screwing down this nut. The firing-fuse is passed through the hollow of the spindle. In long holes, the single india-rubber cylinder is replaced by several shorter ones, with intervening nuts in the shape of double cones, which, when the upper screw-nut is tightened, bring pressure to bear upon the individual cylinders. Several trials of these plugs showed them to be ineffectual in preventing the occurrence of blown-out shots, while their costly nature, even if they were fairly successful, would have constituted a grave obstacle to their extensive adoption.

Formidable danger frequently attends the employment of blasting-powder in coal-mines, on account of the flame which generally attends, though to a very variable extent, the firing of a shot, tamped in the usual manner; and especially on account of the larger volume of flame which is projected to a considerable distance, either when a blast-hole is overcharged, or when the preponderating strength of the material operated upon, gives rise to what is termed a "blown-out shot," the tamping being projected from the hole like a shot from a gun. These sources of danger were recognized long before any views were advanced regarding the possible connection of coal-dust with mine-explosions, and the precautions enacted for ascertaining the absence of any important contamination of the air at the working-place with fire-damp before shots were fired, and for reducing to a minimum the number of lives subject to possible danger when shot-firing was carried out, are well known.

Proposals have, from time to time, been considered by the Inspectors of Mines and others, for either abolishing the use of powder in fiery mines or for greatly restricting its application, by the imposition of more or less stringent conditions. When the Royal Commissioners gave this subject their attention and collected evidence bearing upon the dangers of shot-firing in mines and the possibility of dispensing with the practice, they were led to the conclusion: that the abolition, or even the very considerable restriction of shot-firing, as practised under the existing laws, would be incompatible with the working of a large number of pits, except at a prohibitive pecuniary outlay. Realizing most fully, on the other hand, the dangers frequently attending the use of powder in coal-mines and the extreme difficulty of effecting any important diminution of those dangers, they devoted much attention to the question whether it might be possible to discover any powder-substitute, or any method of using such substitute, which would secure immunity from danger due to the presence of coal-dust and fire-damp in the localities where blasting had to be carried on.

From time to time assertions have been made as to the supposed comparative safety of different explosive agents, more or less analogous in composition to blasting-powder. The validity of such assertions is not difficult to put to the test by chemical examination of the particular explosive preparations, and it may be confidently maintained, from the experience which the Royal Commission and the

Author individually acquired of preparations of this class, that there are but very few practically useful explosive agents of the gunpowder type which possess any advantage in point of comparative safety over ordinary black or blasting-powder.[1]

The employment of powder in the compressed form, which has of late years become very extensive, presents important advantages in point of convenience and general safety of handling, but does not in any way affect the dangers in reference to use in coal-mines, inherent in an explosive agent, the employment of which is liable at any time to be attended by the production of considerable volumes of flame. Attempts were made, in the earlier days of the history of gun-cotton, to apply that material as a blasting agent in coal-mines, but the circumstance that its explosion is attended by the development of a large proportion of carbonic oxide, renders it inapplicable in this direction, as its explosion (even by detonation) is liable, on that account, to be attended by the production of a considerable volume of flame. Finely divided gun-cotton may be readily incorporated with the proportion of a nitrate (saltpetre, or barium nitrate) necessary for the complete oxidation of its carbon, the generation of carbonic oxide being thus prevented or reduced to a minimum, and such preparations as nitrated gun-cotton, tonite or potentite, produced by compression of mixtures of this class, have found favor to some extent in drift work, or in the blasting of stone over-and under-lying coal-seams, as being more powerful than powder; but their explosion is by no means unattended with the possibility of the development of flame. In this respect, nitro-glycerine preparations are undoubtedly superior; this explosive agent contains a proportion of oxygen slightly

---

(1) The name "Carbonite" has been given to one of the most recent of this class of preparations, stated by its makers, Buchel and Schmidt of Schlebusch, to be a safe explosive for use in fiery mines. Consisting as it does of saltpetre, barium nitrate, nitrobenzol and cellulose, its explosion would not be unattended with flame, and its use, therefore, is not likely to secure immunity from the dangers rising from blown-out shot.

in excess of that required for the complete oxidation of its constituent carbon, hence its perfect explosion is unattended by the development of inflammable gas. The most common form in which nitro-glycerine is commercially applied as a blasting-agent is the so-called dynamite, a mixture of the liquid explosive with from one-third to one-fourth its weight of a very porous siliceous earth, known as kieselguhr. When dynamite is exploded by detonation (the only efficient way of employing the so-called "high explosives") the heat developed by the metamorphosis of the nitro-glycerine raises to a bright red or white heat particles of the mineral matter (kieselguhr) with which the liquid is mixed; hence the detonation of this form of preparation is always attended by the appearance of sparks in the dark. But if even the undiluted nitro-glycerine is exploded in a shot-hole, the high temperature has the effect of raising to incandescence particles of the tamping employed, or of the coal or stone exposed to the highly-heated gases and vapors developed, so that under any circumstances, sparks would be liable to be projected on the firing of a nitro-glycerine charge. The same holds good with any of the nitro-glycerine preparations known in commerce, such as lithofracteur, blasting-gelatine, or gelatine-dynamite; moreover, flame in more or less abundance may be produced by the explosion of some nitro-glycerine preparations, the composition of which includes proportions of inflammable materials.

That the heat to which very finely divided solid particles may be raised, by exposure to the highly heated products of detonation of nitro-glycerine preparations, is sufficient to determine the ignition of an explosive fire-damp mixture, has been amply demonstrated by experiment, and it is even possible that sparks sufficiently hot to produce that result may be carried to some distance by the blast of heated gases projected by a shot, and thus reach places at some distance from the shot-hole where gas may have lodged.

The Author's long connection with the study of explosives, and their application to every variety of use, naturally

led to his special devotion, as a Member of the late Commission, of much attention to this branch of its investigations; and the first idea bearing upon the occurrence of
casualties in coal-mines which suggested itself to him, at
the outset of the labors upon which the Commission em-
barked in 1880, was to apply the principle of most complete explosion, or detonation, of one or other of the so-
called "high explosives" (chemical compounds highly susceptible of sudden metamorphosis into gaseous products or
vapors), in conjunction with the method first devised by
him in 1873, and communicated in that year to the Royal
Society,[1] of distributing the operation of the force, developed by small charges of the explosive, over a considerable
area, through the agency of a comparatively large volume
of water, by which the charge is enveloped.

The principle of suddenly transmitting the force of
detonation of a charge of explosive uniformly in all directions, by *completely surrounding with water* the charge to
be detonated, had already been successfully applied by
him to the conversion of an ordinary shell into a projectile
operating with the destructive effects of a Shrapnel-shell,
and to several other purposes, and it occurred to him that
by applying the same principle to the charging of a shot-
hole, the effect might be not only to modify the destructive
action of a high explosive, and thus to attain a comparatively moderate splitting or rending action instead of powerful disintegrating effects, but also to accomplish the extinction, through the agency of the water envelope, of any incandescent particles or sparks, and perhaps flame, projected
by the exploding charge, the water being thrown forward
together with them, in a finely divided condition. It soon
afterwards came to the Author's knowledge that Dr. McNab
had previously put into practical execution the idea of extinguishing the flame of a *powder*-charge, projected from a
shot-hole, by inserting a cylinder filled with water over the
charge, and confining it by a small amount of tamping.
The application of water in this way, in conjunction with

---

[1] Proceedings of the Royal Society of London, vol. xxii., p. 160.

powder, was also expected by Dr. McNab to effect an important economy of time in blasting operations, by diminishing the persistency of the smoke through the solvent action of the water thereby enabling men to return to work in a comparatively short space of time after the firing of shot. The latter result appears to have frequently been attained to a useful extent, but experience showed, on the other hand, that sufficient reliance could not be placed upon the extinguishing effects of water, thus applied in conjunction with powder, being sufficiently exerted to afford reliable security against the ignition, by the flame from a blown-out powder-shot, of an explosive gas-mixture, or of dust thickly suspended in air containing a small proportion of fire-damp. A series of experiments conducted for the late Commission indicated, however, that water-tamping, as first suggested by Dr. McNab, used in conjunction with a *high explosive*, such as dynamite, afforded very considerable, if not absolute, security against accidental explosions, under the conditions just now specified.

This method of using water appears to have been abandoned by Dr. McNab in favor of a mode of operating substantially the same as that proposed by the Author, experimented with by him and Mr. Smethurst at the Garswood Hall Collieries, near Wigan, in November, 1880, and published in the spring of 1881.

An exhaustive series of experiments was instituted, chiefly in South Wales, for the late Commission, with a view to ascertain whether perfect security against ignition of explosive gas-mixtures, and of coal-dust thickly suspended in air containing a small proportion of coal-gas or fire-damp, was secured by the application of high explosives in conjunction with water in the way suggested by the Author, the charge of explosive being enclosed on all sides by water, with or without the additional use of superposed tamping. The methods of experimenting, which were of a searching character, and also included trials in mine-workings themselves, are described in detail in the final Repor. of the Commission ; the results appeared to justify the conclusion that the so-called water-cartridge, employed in conjunction with a high explosive, could be relied upon to afford security against accidental explosions during shot-firing in the presence of explosive gas-mixtures, or of very inflammable coal-dust thickly suspended in air containing some small proportion of fire-damp. The results obtained for the Royal Commission by the Author and by Mr. W. Galloway have been confirmed by experiments of a similar nature pursued by others in this country, by experimenters in Saxony, and by members of the Prussian Fire-Damp Commission. In the course of these various experiments it has been found that the particular form of dynamite to which the name *gelatine-dynamite* has been given,[1] on account of its physical characteristics, is especially suitable for employment in conjunction with water. Unlike ordinary kieselguhr-dynamite and similar preparations, its most important constituent, nitro-glycerine, is not displaced from it by even long immersion in water, so that it retains its explosive properties unimpaired under these conditions, and may, in blasting operations, be placed quite unprotected either in a shot-hole which is filled with water, or in a cylinder full of water, of suitable dimensions for insertion into the hole. In constructing a water-cartridge there is not the least necessity for employing any device for keeping the explosive in such a position that its circumference is surrounded equally on all sides by the water; it suffices simply to insert the charge, with its waterproofed fuse or wires, attached, into the blast-hole direct (if the latter is in perfectly solid stone or coal and in a suitable position), or into the cylinder of thin sheet metal, varnished paper or membrane, which is filled with the water; it is best, however, to insert the charge nearly to the bottom of the water, so as to utilize the tamping effect of the greater part of the column. The liquid is retained by a wooden or cork plug, through which the fuse or conducting wires pass, and tamping is applied over this after insertion of a tuft of hay or other suitable padding material.

---

[1] Gelatine-dynamite, like blasting-gelatine and some other modifications of the latter, is the invention of Mr. Alfred Nobel, to whom is due dynamite as well as the initiation of the technical use of high explosives, applied through the agency of detonation.

The work done in coal by a high explosive, through the agency of a column of water which encloses it (or "water-cartridge "), is different in character to that accomplished by the same charge used in the ordinary manner. Instead of exerting a crushing action immediately round the charge, whereby much small coal is produced and no large amount of displacing work performed, the force being distributed over the whole area of the water-column ; its action is thereby greatly moderated, and the coal is brought down in large masses, the work done extending over at least as large an area as that of the best powder-shots.

In applying this system as a safeguard against accidental ignition of coal-dust or fire-damp-mixtures, the quantity of water used should at least amount to four times the volume of the charge employed. It has come to the knowledge of the Author that, in a colliery where a serious explosion recently occurred, so-called water-cartridges were in use, in which, when the charge of explosive had been inserted, very little room was left for water. From the published account of the evidence given at the inquest, it appeared to have been affirmed that Abel's water-cartridge had been used, at great expense, and it was left to be implied that the calamity was due to confidence being falsely placed in the safety to be ensured by its employment.

The mode of surrounding the blasting-charge of high explosive with water on all sides, which constitutes a "water-cartridge," was made public by the Author in the early days of the Royal Commission, and soon afterwards he repeatedly furnished to persons interested in mining simple instructions and patterns to serve as guides for the application of this system of blasting.

The practical development of the principle of applying water in conjunction with high explosives cannot fail to be fruitful of improvements in the mode of operation, as indeed it has already been ; thus, in order to avoid a loss, or diminution, of the safeguard furnished by the water, from the escape of the liquid through channels or fissures in the shot-hole or through leaks in the water-cylinder or cartridge, it has been proposed by Messrs. Heath and Frost to dissolve sufficient size or glue in the water, warmed for that purpose, to make it solidify on cooling in the case or shot-hole to a sufficiently stiff jelly to prevent such escape. Again, the experiments carried out for the Commission with water-cartridges led to the observation, that a consid-erable proportion of the water was driven forward in a body instead of being dispersed in a very fine state of division, by the force of a blown-out shot, and a suggestion was con-sequently made for the employment of the water in a differ-ent manner, which was worked out by Mr. Galloway with most successful results, so far as related to the extinction of flame and sparks from a blown-out shot. By distributing the water through a very porous body (such as sponge or moss), and thus effecting an initial interruption of con-tinuity of the mass of liquid placed over the shot, its thor-ough dispersion in a very finely divided condition is en-sured, and its extinguishing power is greatly increased. It was found, in a number of experiments at the Dowlais works, that in holes of 2 inches diameter the placing of 9 inches of loose tamping of moss, soaked with water, over a 4–oz. charge of dynamite sufficed to prevent the ignition of dust-laden air containing coal-gas by the blown-out shot, and that such a shot, produced with 2 1–2 oz. of dyna-mite, the charge being covered with only 4 inches of loose moss- and water-tamping, failed to fire an explosive gas-mixture. A number of comparative experiments demonstrated that the water-cartridge was on an equality with moss- and water-tamping in preventing the ignition, by blown-out shots produced with dynamite, gun-cotton, tonite and gelatine-dynamite, of a dense cloud of highly in-flammable dust suspended in air containing a small proportion of coal-gas (the cloud, produced under the same conditions being invariably inflamed by an ordi-nary blown-out dynamite shot); but they proved that the water-cartridge did not afford that absolute security against the ignition of an explosive gas-mixture by a blown out dynamite shot which, so far as a number of consecutive experiments showed, was attained by the comparatively simple moss- and water-tamping, which can be applied without difficulty even in holes having an upward inclination.

The water-cartridge, employed with various high explosives in such a way as to produce blown-out shots in the presence of coal-dust and gas, has been made the subject of official experiment in Prussia and Saxony, and apparently with results as satisfactory as have now been obtained in different mining districts in this country; it may be considered to have been conclusively established that the application of water in the shot-hole in one or other of the ways indicated, in conjunction with the use of high explosives, affords most important security against accidents in blasting stone or coal in mines where dust and fire-damp co-exist.

It may be well again to emphasize the fact that neither the water-cartridge, nor water-tamping applied in the manner in which it has been found so thoroughly efficient in conjunction with high explosives, affords any safeguard against explosions arising from the presence of fire-damp or of coal-dust associated with fire-damp, in mine-workings where blasting is carried on, if *powder*, or any explosive agent analogous in its composition and mode of explosion to powder, be employed in conjunction with them.

Suggestions have been made to use, in conjunction with powder, or as tamping over the charge, certain solid preparations which will evolve gases or vapors, when exposed for a sufficient period to heat, capable of extinguishing flame, the idea being that the heat developed by the explosion of the charge would accomplish the desired results, and that the dangers arising from blown-out shot might thus be guarded against;[1] but the authors of these suggestions have not realized the importance of time as a factor in the establishment of chemical changes by the action of heat, and the consequent impossibility of gases and vapors being evolved, in the desired manner, within the exceedingly brief period

[1] Tamping mixtures, containing hydrated crystallized salts, chalk, alkaline bicarbonates, ammonium salts, etc., have been proposed, some of them quite recently, with this object in view.

during which the materials applied are exposed to heat. The Commission, at the Author's suggestion, had experiments carried out for the purpose of ascertaining whether condensed (liquefied) carbonic acid could be applied, in suitable tamping vessels, in conjunction with high explosives, as an extinguishing agent, but the results were not sufficiently encouraging to warrant perseverance in this direction of experiment.

Some attention has been attracted, since the publication of the Commission's final Report, by a safety blasting cartridge brought forward by Dr. Kosmann of Breslau, which depends for its action upon the rapid development of hydrogen under high pressure from very finely divided zinc by the action of sulphuric acid (enclosed in one compartment of a compound vessel of glass). The acid is intended to have access to the zinc after the apparatus has been fixed into the shot-hole in such a way that the gas, which is said to speedily attain a high degree of compression, shall exert its force upon the stone or coal. The cost of each shot is stated to be only small. but the description scarcely warrants the view that the arrangement is a practically efficient one, and no account of successful experiments with it in actual blasting operations have yet reached the Author.

Various proposals to apply compressed air to the getting of coal have been put forward, among which was one by Mr. Samuel Marsh of the Clifton Colliery, Nottingham, to the practical development of which Mr. Ellis Lever devoted much trouble some years ago, but no really satisfactory results appear to have been attained with it.

The considerable increase in volume which caustic or quick-lime rapidly undergoes during the slaking process (or its conversion into hydrate by union with water), was already many years ago regarded as a source of powder which might be available in lieu of powder for the bringing down of hard coal; but repeated attempts to utilize it met with no practical success, until Messrs. Sebastian Smith and Moore, about six years since, made two important steps in advance. In the first place, by reducing freshly burned fat lime of high slaking power to powder, and converting this into cylinders by applying powerful pressure, they obtain the lime in an exceedingly compact form which enabled them to utilize the full diameter of a drilled shot-hole, and which rendered the material much less liable to deterioration from air-slaking than if kept in its natural state, in lumps, containing fissures. In the next place, Messrs. Smith and Moore apply the heat rapidly developed in the loaded hole by the slaking of the lime-charge simultaneously throughout its entire length, to the generation and superheating of steam on a somewhat considerable scale, whereby the force exerted by the expanding charge of lime is importantly supplemented.

The idea of compressing unslaked lime into cartridges appears to have been entertained by Messrs. Hughes and Jones three years before Messrs. Smith and Moore ; but its practical development has certainly rested with the latter, and this is in great measure due to the ingenious, simple, and very efficient arrangement adopted by them for ensuring the application of water to the compressed lime almost simultaneously throughout the entire length of the charge. Mr. A. H. Stokes, therefore, in his comments on the Commission's estimate of the value of Messrs. Smith and Moore's plan of using lime, has scarcely done justice to his powers of appreciating the merits of such practically good contrivances as not unfrequently lead to the successful application of processes, or operations, the germ of which may have been for some time created, but has remained dormant for want of development in a practical form. There is much in the somewhat remarkable comments of Mr. Stokes, brought before the Chesterfield and Midland Counties Institution of Engineers, on the statements of the Royal Commission regarding the lime-cartridge, that would appear to merit close examination as emanating from one of H.M. Inspectors of Mines ; but those comments hardly bear the stamp of dispassionate criticism, and it may suffice, in illustration of this, to mention that, when pointing out that the Commissioners, in their impartial examination into Smith and Moore's system of getting coal by means of lime-cartridges, stated certain facts not favorable to its successful application under particular circumstances, Mr. Stokes thinks fit to preface the extracts from the Report by the words "the Commissioners themselves admit."[1]

The Author, in company with other members of the late Commission, witnessed on two occasions a series of operations with lime-cartridges in the Shipley Collieries, Derby, where they have been in constant use since 1882. The preparation and charging of a number of holes at one time was expeditiously carried out, and the joint action of the holes in bringing the coal down in large masses was very satisfactory, the charges generally performing their work up to the back of the holes. The time occupied by the action of the lime ranged from ten to forty minutes from the time of wetting the charge, but the men were able to return to their work directly the coal had fallen; the latter was brought down almost entirely in large masses, and the work in such coal (the "deep hard" seam) as is met with in the Shipley Collieries appeared, from the figures furnished to the Commission, to be carried on with advantage in point of economy over blasting. The results which have since that time been obtained with the lime-cartridge in a number of English mining districts appear, on the whole, to have been favorable to the efficiency and economy of the system of working. Several collieries in Staffordshire and Yorkshire now employ the lime-cartridge, and the Author understands that it has also been in use in collieries in Lancashire and Nottinghamshire. That its application should not be attended with the same success in soft and in very hard coal as in massive coal of medium hardness is to be expected, and seams in which many fissures occur are not likely to be worked successfully by the system, as the force due to the generation of steam by the slaking of the lime must be lost in many instances.

The inconveniences attending the distribution, after the

---

(1) Transactions of the Chesterfield and Midland Counties Institution of Engineers, vol. xv., p. 134.

blasting operation, of the hydrate of lime, which retains
feebly caustic properties, through coal, must no doubt be
occasionally felt by miners, though it is difficult, in reference to the strong views of their serious nature by Mr.
Stokes, to understand why they are supposed to be especially felt in damp mines, or why a material which bricklayers continually handle with impunity, and without the
protection of their hands " by leather and rags," should be
so violent in its action when it comes into contact with the
miner's hands, as to necessitate the protection of the skin
from being " eaten away."

It is essential that, especially in damp mines, the cartridges should be kept in tightly-closed cases until just
before they are required to charge a hole with; but this is
scarcely more inconvenient than the necessity for keeping
explosives, under similar conditions, in their properly closed
receptacles.   Statements which are unquestionably exagger-
ated have been made regarding dangers attending the use
of lime-cartridges. A so-called blown-out shot with lime
causes the latter to be more or less violently scattered about
in the vicinity of the shot-hole, and should men be in the
immediate neighborhood it is very possible that their eyes
may suffer from such an accident, but there is no possibility
of an explosion being brought about by the blowing out of
the lime, or by any other circumstance which may attend
the use of the lime-cartridge. A series of experiments
made under the Author's directions at Woolwich Arsenal,
with the object of determining the maximum heat developed in the interior of a lime-cartridge as applied in coal
getting, and the direct measurement of that temperature in
several ways, showed that its extreme did not exceed about
600° Fahrenheit, and was therefore insufficient to inflame a
gas- and air-mixture, or to ignite any inflammable material
with which the lime-cartridge might possibly come into contact in actual practice.

The conclusion of the Commission, that " in some coal-
seams the lime-cartridge will perform work quite equal to
that accomplished with powder, at no greater cost, and with

absolute immunity from risk of explosions," was arrived at after very careful inquiry, and is well worthy of the attention of colliery-proprietors.

Before quitting the subject of the removal of coal and its adjacent strata by disruptive agents, a few words should be said regarding the means employed for firing shots in coal-mines. It is obvious that the efficiency of any measures adopted for diminishing the risk of accidental explosions, consequent upon the employment of blasting agents, may be counteracted to a great degree by igniting the fuse, employed in firing the shot, either by means of a lamp-flame, a match, or a highly-heated wire, or by a liability of flame or very highly-heated gases to be projected into the air from the open end, or to burst through the covering of that part of the fuse which projects from the shot-hole. It is satisfactory to know that the original makers of the miner's fuse, Messrs. Bickford Smith & Co., are now manufacturing a special fuse for use in fiery mines, which, so far as the Author's experiments with it allow of his speaking with confidence, appears free from any liability to allow of the escape of fire from it into the air of the mine. Some special forms of safety-lamp have been recently constructed, with arrangements for allowing the fuse to be inserted therein and ignited without risk, so that the application of fire or a red-hot body to the fuse in the open air may be dispensed with. Devices have also been constructed to be fitted like a cap over the projecting end of the fuse, and containing an igniting arrangement which may be set into action from the outside, and will prevent the escape of fire into the surrounding air.

The application of electricity to the firing of shots, with the development of which the Author has been connected since, in the days of its infancy, the subject was jointly pursued by Sir Charles Wheatstone and himself, has for a long time past been so perfected as to render the operation

---

(1) Since completing this Paper, the Author has had an opportunity of seeing a new and very efficient safety-fuse especially adapted for coal-mines, which has been devised by Mr. Alfred Nobel.

G

simple, safe, and, in the long run, but little more expensive
than firing by means of the so-called safety (or miners')
fuse. In addition to its safety, the firing of the shot being
accomplished out of contact with air, and within the charge
itself, it presents the important advantages that the operation of firing is performed at a distance and precisely at any
desired time, and that it may be postponed at any moment should doubt suddenly arise as to the safety or ex-
pediency of carrying out the operation. It, moreover,
eliminates all risk of a premature explosion, and, if a shot
fails to be fired, it may at once be approached without
risk. The application of electric arrangements admits,
besides, of the simultaneous or the more or less rapidly
successive explosion of a number of shots, at accurately
predetermined intervals, by the adoption of very simple
arrangements. The operations connected with electric
firing are very simple, and the Author has found no
difficulty in obtaining their ready execution at the hands
of miners of average intelligence. For these various
reasons, and while admitting that there are circumstances,
such as the difficulties connected with electrical firing in wet
mines, which preclude the possibility of a general adoption
of this mode of dealing with shots, the Author strongly
urges that the use of electrical arrangements for shot-firing
in fiery mines should, as recommended by the late Commission, be encouraged wherever it is practicable.

One of the most important subjects connected with the
prevention of accidents in mines still remains to be dealt
with, namely, the necessity for devoting especial attention
to the sufficient and safe illumination of roads and working-
places in mines.

There is no subject connected with the working of coal to
which, since the days of Davy and Stephenson, more study
and ingenuity have been continually devoted than to the
improvement of the miners' lamp. The history of the first
development of the safety-lamp has been so frequently
before the public that its discussion here would present no
feature of interest. One important matter should, however,
be referred to, relating to the employment of the historical

lamps of Sir Humphrey Davy and George Stephenson, and the but little less popular lamp of Dr. Clanny, the three kinds of lamp which have been in general use in this country until very recently. In the very moderate ventilating air-currents to be met with in coal mines, for some time after these lamps were first introduced, and which but rarely attained a velocity of 5 feet per second even in the air-ways of a mine, while there was but very little motion of the air in working-places, these lamps were really safe. In recent years, however, the great improvements in the ventilation of mines have completely changed the condition of things in the mine-ways and working-places, as regards the velocities of air-currents there met with. Even in the stalls of pillar workings, air-currents having velocities of over 5 feet per second are now to be found, while in long-wall workings the air passes the coal-face often at velocities of 10 to 15 feet per second, and the currents in the main-ways frequently range in velocity between 20 and 25 feet. Conditions may, moreover, arise, such as, on openings being made between two air-ways, when lamps may be exposed to currents travelling at a rate of 30 to 35 feet per second. It has long since been demonstrated that these great changes in the velocities with which air travels in, at any rate, a large number of coal-mines, have deprived the Davy and the Clanny lamps of the quality of safety which rendered them valuable to the miner, because, if they are exposed for short periods to currents of air (charged with fire-damp) which are travelling at velocities now frequently met with, they are liable to communicate fire to the gas- and air-mixture which surrounds them. This had been demonstrated, at any rate in the case of the Davy and the Clanny lamps, before the experiments of the late Royal Commission, by the results of experiments with lamps carried out by the Midland Institute of Mining Civil and Mechanical Engineers at Aldwarke Main Colliery in 1883 and 1884, under the superintendence of Mr. C. E. Rhodes and Mr. Joseph Mitchell, M. Inst. C. E., by other Societies, by Mr. Smethurst and by individual workers. The dangerous character of these lamps, as well as the liability of the

Stephenson lamp to bring about explosions when exposed
to powerful currents of fire-damp mixture, was so thoroughly
demonstrated by the earlier of the Commissioners' systematic experiments, and appeared at the same time to be so
little known at the date of their experiments (1880) that
they thought it right at once to direct the attention of the
Secretary of State for the Home Department officially to
the insecurity of these lamps.   The action taken thereon by
the Home Office led to the warning of the Commissioners
being withheld from the mining public; but, during the
Committee stage of the new Mines' Regulation Act, the
effect of that warning, repeated in the final Report of the
Commission, prevailed, and words were introduced into
the General. Rule relating to safe construction of miners'
lamps, excluding "unprotected" Stephenson, Clanny, or
Davy lamps from being embraced under the definition of
safety-lamps.   Those important words were struck out by
the House of Lords' Committee, upon the ground, as stated
by the defender in the *Times* of this action of the Lords
(speaking apparently with official authority), that they were
superfluous.   The context of that rule, however, clearly
shows that this was by no means the case, and the writer
was evidently not cognizant of the fact that air-currents
vary greatly in velocity in different parts of one and the
same mine, so that, although an unprotected Davy lamp
might be safely carried in "that part of a mine" where it
was to be "for the time being in use," the miner carrying
it might, in passing to and from that part with this lamp,
have to traverse air-ways, where, in the possible event of an
incursion of gas, the conveyance of the lamp might be attended with danger, on account of the comparatively high
velocity of the air-current against which it has there to be
carried.   The rule, as it now stands, does certainly not
guard against this possible great danger; while, if the use
of unprotected Davy, etc., lamps had been prohibited, the
only hardship incurred by their owners would have been
the necessity for having them converted into *protected*
lamps, which can be effected at a small outlay, and whereby
they are changed from dangerous into comparatively very

safe lamps. The clause adopted by the Commons would therefore certainly not have operated as a " most vexatious restriction upon mine-owners," as urged by the defender of the Lords' amendment ; indeed, the alteration of the Davy to a protected lamp was long ago extensively carried out voluntarily by some mine-owners who had very large numbers of that lamp in use.

The systematic experiments of the Royal Commission included trials of more than two hundred and fifty lamps in explosive gas- and air-mixtures, travelling at velocities which ranged from 400 to 3,200 feet per minute. The inflammable gas used was of three kinds: fire-damp furnished by a powerful blower in the 9-foot Wigan seam at Garswood Hall Colliery ; a copious supply of fire-damp furnished by a blower in the sandstone, about 60 yards above the 6-foot seam of the Rhondda Valley, situated in Llwynypia Colliery ; and illuminating gas manufactured in the Royal Arsenal, Woolwich. The majority of the experiments were carried out in a long model gallery, similar in construction to the apparatus used by the various other experimenters already referred to. Special arrangements were adopted for insuring the maintenance of a uniform gas-supply to the apparatus, and a thorough mixture of the gas with the air-current as they entered the gallery together. The preparation of the lamps for trial and the mode of taking observations were also made the subjects of careful arrangement, so as to insure that the results obtained with different lamps were strictly comparative.

While the latter portion of the Commission's lamp-experiments was in progress, at Woolwich, a large number of lamps of different kinds, sent in by competitors for a prize offered by Mr. Ellis Lever, were submitted to the same tests as applied by the Commission, and with the use of the same apparatus; as two of its members, Mr. Burt and the Author, formed also part of the body of judges, the results obtained were kept thoroughly comparative with the Commission's experiments, and therefore formed a very useful addition to the data available for study. It was difficult to bring those experiments to a conclusion, as, up to the very last, fresh specimens, which were either modifications of particular lamps already tried or lamps presenting new features, were sent in for trial. The results of these extensive experiments (including special tests of considerable severity which were applied to some of the most promising lamps) showed that at the time the Commission brought its experimental work to a close, early in 1886, many varieties of miners' lamps existed, which, when in thorough working order, would afford almost complete safety if carried even in a highly explosive atmosphere, moving at the maximum velocities ordinarily met with in the air-ways of well-ventilated mines. Some of the lamps even resisted currents passing at over 3,000 feet per minute during the brief periods for which it was practicable to submit them to this severe test. At such high velocities very slight imperfections, which do not affect the safety of a lamp at moderate velocities, are likely to become sources of danger. On the other hand, the exposure of a lamp to currents of extremely high velocities is likely to be only of very rare occurrence and short duration.

When a lamp of the Davy, Clanny, or Stephenson type is introduced into a current of an explosive fire-damp and air-mixture, the flame is almost immediately extinguished, and the gas-mixture burns within the lamp. In some lamps, the air-supply to which is meagre, the inflamed gas-mixture sometimes also ceases to burn in a very short time, but as a rule it continues to burn until extinguished accidentally, or until flame is communicated to the explosive atmosphere which surrounds the lamp, either by some portion of the latter becoming heated to bright redness, or by the glass breaking, or by the flame being driven through the gauze from some accidental cause. In some kinds of lamps, such as the Stephenson under certain conditions, both the lamp-flame and the ignited gas-mixture are almost instantaneously extinguished. If this occurs at high as well as low velocities (which is very rare) such a lamp obviously ranks high in point of safety; but it does not of necessity follow that a lamp in which the gas-mixture continues to burn is unsafe. So long as no portion of its structure is raised to incandescence, or so long as the glass, if the lamp has one, remains intact, there is no danger attending the burning of the gas-mixture. For these reasons it is obviously of the greatest importance that the part of the lamp within which the gas burns should be protected from the mechanical action of the current.

A large number of the lamps of recent construction have, like the Clanny and Mueseler, glass cylinders, which form the lower portion of the case surrounding the lamp-flame. From the point of view of efficiency as illuminating agents, such lamps are obviously superior to others of the Davy and Stephenson types; but they are open to objection on the score of the uncertainty of safety which the glass presents, partly because the latter may become cracked from various causes, independently of rough usage, such as irregular heating or cooling, by the burning of the gas-mixture within the lamp in close proximity to the glass, or by the lamp-flame impinging on the glass when the lamp is tilted, the accidental dropping of water upon the heated glass, etc. In such cases the establishment of an aperture of sufficient size to allow flame to pass may occur at any time. The difficulty which may be experienced in maintaining a thoroughly tight union between the ends of the glass cylinder and the metal-bearing surfaces is another possible cause of doubtful safety in lamps of this class. A too rigid closing up at those parts is liable to lead to the cracking of the glass, but if the joints are unduly loose, these are liable to become an obvious source of danger, which will be very greatly increased if the glasses are at all chipped at the bearing surfaces, or are not ground very fairly parallel. Washers should also intervene between the glass and metal-surfaces, and the omission of them may give rise to danger. The experience of the Commissioners showed that washers of asbestos mill-board are far superior to those of leather or of india-rubber in point of efficiency and durability, and washers of that material have now come into very general use.

Numerous lamps have been constructed with double glasses, the air-supply, before it reaches the flame, being brought down the annular channel formed by the space between the two glasses, the possible passage of flame through which is generally prevented by the application of wire-gauze diaphragms. These lamps, when perfect, are very safe, but the inner glass is exceedingly liable to be cracked or fractured by the action of the lamp-flame, and in that case the lamp becomes altogether altered in character and is liable to explode. Moreover, the difficulty of putting the lamp together, so as to ensure its perfect safety at starting, is obviously much increased by the use of two glasses.

The safety-lamp of Belgian origin, called the Mueseler, attracted great attention not many years ago, and has since been somewhat extensively used in some English collieries, besides being the Belgian official lamp and used in other parts of the Continent. It is derived from the Clanny lamp by the insertion, into the gauze cage or cap, of a central conical chimney, which is supported by an attached annular diaphragm of gauze, seized between the lower end of the gauze cap and the upper end of the glass cylinder. When this lamp is burning, and in a vertical position, the air requisite to feed it passes, under ordinary conditions, through the lower part of the gauze cage, in through the gauze diaphragm, and down to the flame, the products of combustion escaping up the chimney. But if the lamp is tilted so that the heated gases and vapors from the lamp-flame strike upon the gauze diaphragm, instead of passing up the chimney, the feeding of the lamp with air at once takes place down the chimney instead of through the diaphragm, and as the products of combustion are then immediately carried down from the upper part of the lamp on to the flame, the latter is extinguished almost directly, and more rapidly in proportion as the bottom of the chimney is closer to the flame. Hence the Mueseler lamp requires very careful handling to prevent its being accidentally extinguished, and this has prevented it from becoming popular in this country. Moreover, the high reputation for safety with which the Mueseler lamp was introduced to the English mining world were in a measure destroyed by the results of experimental observations before the Commission commenced its lamp-investigations. Even slight departures from the officially prescribed dimensions of the chimney in the Belgian Mueseler lamp (and in English-made lamps there have been considerable variations in this respect) will give rise to a complete difference in the behavior of the lamp, consequent upon an alteration in the mode of feed of the air, and, while the Belgian lamps are, as a rule, extinguished almost directly after their introduction into an explosive current, others of the general Mueseler pattern have been found to explode readily, even if the current is only travelling at a moderately high velocity.

Reference has already been made to the importance of affording that part of a lamp, through which the gas-mixture is likely to burn if it is introduced into an explosive air-current, protection against the mechanical action of the current. The partial inclosure of the Davy lamp in a glass cylinder (as in the jack-lamp) is an illustration of this kind of protection, which has been recently afforded still more effectually by completely inclosing the lamp in a tin can provided with one or more windows. Again, the upper part, or gauze, of the Clanny lamp has been protected by a metal jacket, or *bonnet*, as in the case of Smethurst's and Ashworth's lamps, which are comparatively very safe, and of the Marsaut lamp, one of the very safest and most efficient of recent lamps, in which, besides the jacket or bonnet, the single-gauze cap of the Clanny lamp is replaced by two or three somewhat conical caps of gauze, fitting closely one within the other at their bases, and gradually separating towards their upper part. By covering the gauze cap of the Mueseler lamp with a jacket or bonnet, and arranging for the entrance of air through holes in the horizontal flange to which the base of the bonnet is fixed, it becomes almost impossible to get a gas-mixture to burn in the upper part of the lamp; it may, however, possibly burn above the gauze diaphragm, and in that case the glass is liable to become cracked. The Morgan lamp, which was

one of the safest lamps submitted to the Commission, is of
the bonneted Mueseler type, but presents several original
points of detail.

The results arrived at, in experiments with safety-lamps,
by the several Mining Institutes, by the Commission, by
Mr. C. E. Rhodes, of the Aldwarke Main Colliery, by Mr.
Marsaut, by the French Commission, by Messrs. Kreischer
and Winkler and others, present many points of practical
interest which it is impossible to discuss within the limits of
this Paper; the Commissioners' experiments, which have,
perhaps, been the most systematically pursued and studied,
have demonstrated that, among many lamps exhibiting a
high degree of safety, there were some which failed to be
practically useful, on account of their becoming extinguished so readily as to require the greatest care in carrying and handling, while others failed on account of deficiency in illuminating power, and others again were of so
complicated a structure, consisting of so many parts that
they were very difficult to put together in a safe condition,
and to keep in working order. The Commission specified
lamps by Morgan, Mann, Purdy, and Soar, as ranking high
in point of safety and other good qualities, while four
lamps more especially, namely, the Marsaut lamp, Gray's
lamp, that of Evan Thomas of most recent construction,
and the bonneted Mueseler lamp, combined in a pre-eminent degree the quality of safety, under all conditions of
service, with simplicity of construction, and good illuminating power as compared with that of lamps hitherto in
general use. Since the publication of the Commissioners'
experiments, improvements or simplifications have been
made in some of the varieties of lamps tested by them, and
the Author has, from time to time during the past year,
been requested to examine lamps brought forward as
novel, some appearing to possess features of considerable
promise, which, however, it has not been in his power to
test. The Mining Engineers' Associations in different
parts of the country, and such trustworthy experimenters
as Mr. C. E. Rhodes, will, it is to be hoped, continue to

pursue the valuable lamp-testing experiments which they have instituted, from time to time, before and during the work of the Commission, so that the merits of new lamps may be practically and impartially determined.

The provision of appliances for closing the air-inlets or outlets, or both, in bonneted forms of safety-lamps, must be alluded to as an additional measure of safety which can readily be supplied, and has already been provided in some instances, as in the bonneted Mueseler of Mr. Stokes, and the bonneted Clanny of Mr. Mercier. By such arrangements the lamp can be extinguished at once if there appears any danger of the glass being cracked by the burning of gas within the lamp. Arrangements have also been devised for automatically closing the inlets and outlets of lamps, when a temperature in some part has been attained which is likely to lead to danger. The closing mechanism, in most instances actuated by a spring, is held either by a string, or by a wire or strip of readily fusible metal, which is applied in that part of the particular lamp likely to become highly heated. The burning or charring of the string, or the melting of the metal wire or strip, releases the spring, which brings the closing appliance into operation. In a new, and apparently very good lamp of Mr. Clifford's, a loose perforated diaphragm, one side of which consists of fusible metal, is placed over the gauze diaphragm, which closes the top of the air-shafts. Should this become heated, the melting of the fusible metal causes the perforations to close up, and, the current through the lamp being thus interrupted, the flame is extinguished.

The closing or locking of safety-lamps before they are issued to the miner for use, in some way which renders an attempt to open them difficult of success and easily detected, is a wise precaution against the temptation to smokers to get at the lamp-flame. Although it is stated that the practice of opening lamps has much diminished in late years, the not unfrequent carrying of matches into mines scarcely warrants the conclusion that the dangers involved by the exposure of a flame in mine-workings are yet generally recognized or sufficiently dreaded by many miners.

Only on the 23d of last September, a paragraph in the *Times*, referring to an explosion at West Cannock Colliery, in South Staffordshire, stated that "pipes and matches were found in the injured men's clothes, the regulations being thus violated," and "that the pit was rather fiery, only locked safety-lamps being allowed to be used in it."

Until comparatively lately, the mechanical locks, with which lamps were mostly fitted, were of little or no use as a security against the lamp being opened, because a very simple key could readily be extemporized for undoing them. Many attempts have been made to provide greater security by arranging for the application of a magnet or an air-pump to withdraw a bolt which secures the two parts of the lamp together, but it has generally been found that these bolts could be withdrawn, by a little dexterity, without those appliances. One which appeared efficient to the Commissioners, and could not readily be tampered with, was a magnetic lock by Wolf. Some locks are so arranged that the unfastening of the lamp draws down the wick, the flame thus becoming extinguished, but most of them are liable easily to get out of order, so that they do not move the wick. A very simple and efficient lock has been recently devised by Mr. Mercier; it is in the form of a bolt, the complete withdrawal of which is necessary before the lamp can be opened, while its partial withdrawal draws a hood over the lamp flame, and at once extinguishes it. In another lamp of quite recent construction, devised by Mr. Eeli J. Palmer, of Toronto, the unscrewing of the oil-reservoir at once brings an extinguisher over the wick.

One of the best and most simple means of preventing a lamp from being opened, and which has come into extensive use, is a rivet-plug of lead, by which two projecting sockets on the upper and lower parts of the lamp are riveted together, the oil-vessel being thus connected with the lamp. The two faces of the plug, after the riveting is completed, are stamped with some mark or letter, which is changed from time to time; unless the stamping is adopted, it would not be difficult to remove the plug and replace it without detection. The mode of applying the rivet-plug

and the position where it is applied varies; thus, when
used with Ryder's patent lock it is applied horizontally,
which allows of the stamped ends of the rivets being easily
inspected. The so-called "protector-lamps" are also supplied with these rivet-locks, although the additional security
thereby provided is scarcely needed, as the particular arrangement of the wick-tube in the lamp, combined with
the nature of the fuel used in it, renders any attempt to
open the lamp without the extinction of the flame almost
impossible. An objection to the highly volatile character
of the illuminant used is, however, that its flame is so
slightly adherent to the wick, as to be readily extinguished
by a jerk; on the other hand, this sensitiveness of the
flame is an element of safety, as, if an explosive gas-mixture
enters the lamp the flame is often extinguished even before
there is time for the gas to become ignited. The uniform
light given by these lamps, consequent upon the nature of
the illuminant and the construction of the burner, secures
to them advantages in addition to those due to their comparative safety; on the other hand, the employment of so
highly volatile a liquid as petroleum spirit, especially upon
the somewhat considerable scale arising out of the use of a
large number of the lamps in connection with a colliery,
involves risks of accidents in stores and lamp-rooms, which
necessitate the adoption of special regulations in its storage
and use; hence it is to be regretted that the manufacturers
should have deemed it expedient to give to the petroleum
spirit supplied for use with the protector-lamps, a name
which cannot be called otherwise than misleading, inasmuch as the designation *colzaline*, under which it is sold,
certainly would lead the uninitiated to believe it to be
at any rate related to colza oil or rape oil in its character
and properties, instead of being a very volatile and therefore highly inflammable spirit.

It has been already stated that some recent forms of
miners' lamps, the construction of which secures a high
degree of safety, present the serious defect of giving but
little light. This is due either to the tortuous character
of the channels through which air has to be supplied or the

products of combustion have to escape, or to the great
cooling action of the mass of metal through which the
products have to pass away, whereby the circulation or
draught necessary for the maintenance of a proper air-
supply is greatly diminished. The light furnished by the
Davy and Stephenson lamps, even when freshly lit, is so
poor that the superior light furnished by the Clanny and
Mueseler lamps gave these a great advantage as effective
illuminants, especially as, after burning for three or four
hours, they still furnish as a rule more light than the Davy
or Stephenson lamps. One of the objects which have been
aimed at, as very important in improving safety-lamps, is
to increase the illuminating power, which, in the Davy and
Stephenson lamps, is only equal to between 0·1 and 0·2 of a
sperm candle when they are first lighted, or directly after
they have been freshly trimmed; while, the Clanny and
Mueseler lamps give, when freshly lighted, between 0·5
and 0·4 of a candle, which is very fairly maintained during
a shift, with proper attention to the lamp. It is, however,
scarcely matter for surprise that, for the reasons given just
now, the illuminating power attained in new forms of lamps
has very rarely exceeded, and not often attained, the results
furnished by the Clanny and the Mueseler. The difficulties
attending the achievement of any important improvement
in the form of burner and of wick are obviously great, as
any attempt to render the wick more suitable for the
advantageous burning of the illuminant, and to introduce
improvements in the trimming arrangements, have to be
circumscribed by the conditions which safety dictates. The
employment of flat and broad wicks, instead of the simple
cylindrical solid wick of small diameter, has been attended
with some improvement in the light-giving power with the
use of suitable oil, but such wicks are apt to smoke, and the
flames to fall rapidly in illuminating power. The Marsaut
lamps, in which loosely-plaited, flat, thin wicks of 0·5 inch
in breadth are used, have furnished the best results in this
direction; although their illuminating power appeared,
from the Commission's experiments, to be little, if at all,
superior to that of the Clanny lamp (the highest result at-

tained was 0·7 candle, while other lamps gave 0·4 to 0·54 candle) ; but they were found to maintain a very uniform length of flame for a comparatively considerable time. In the photometric experiments of the Commission, the protector lamps of the Davy and Stephenson types (burning petroleum spirit, *i.e.*, " colzaline ") gave more light than similar lamps of ordinary construction burning rape or seal oil, while this was not the case with the protector Clanny Mueseler, and Marsaut lamps. The original luminosity was, however, much more uniformly maintained by them than by the corresponding lamps burning rape or seal oil ; indeed, the luminosity of the protector lamps was often found to increase slightly with long-continued burning, which was probably due to the lamp reservoir getting slightly warm, and thus yielding a somewhat more copious supply of illuminant to the wick.

Comparative photometric experiments, made with lamps of one and the same description, burning different oils or mixtures of oils, the treatment of the several lamps and flames being carefully recorded have shown that seal oil is unquestionably superior to good refined rape oil or colza oil in regard to the maintenance of the flame at a fairly uniform height, and therefore in regard to uniformity of light given during lengthened periods, without having recourse to trimming. The results of a series of experiments with mixtures of these oils, and of mineral (petroleum or paraffin) oil, in various proportions, demonstrated that an admixture of petroleum oil of a flashing point of about 80° Fahrenheit (Abel-test), and therefore a safe oil, with rape oil and with seal oil, in the proportion of 1 part by measure to 2 parts of either of the two oils, furnished (especially with seal oil) a superior illuminating agent for miners' lamps, burning uniformly and with very little charring of the wick, or separation of lamp-black. The experiments showed that the two constituents of the mixed oil appeared to be burned in equal proportions throughout the duration of the life of a lamp-charge, and as regards the practical question of cost, the very considerably lower price of petroleum oil causes this improved mixed liquid illuminant to be cheaper than

the pure vegetable or animal oil.   The Author was recently
informed by the Messrs. Peace of Tyldesley Colliery, near
Manchester, that these results have been confirmed by practical experience. ·

The Commissioners direct attention to some points relating to the condition and nature of the wick used in miners'
lamps, which considerably influence the duration of efficient
burning of a lamp.   Thus they point out that the capillary
action of a wick is much interfered with if it be tightly
twisted or plaited, and if it fit very tightly into the wick-
holder ; that a wick should always be dried before a fire or
in an. oven shortly before use, as the free passage of the
illuminant is impeded by the presence of moisture in the
wick-fibre, and that, if a wick is used for a long time, or
allowed to remain soaking in the oil for a long period, its
feeding action becomes reduced by the deposition of solid
or semi-solid impurities collected from the oil, so that it is
conducive to the efficiency of the lamps to fit them only
with short lengths of wick, and to change the wick frequently.

The admitted possibility of some injury or defeat of construction, or of the putting together, of a lamp, being so
minute or difficult to discern as to escape the most experienced eye, and being yet sufficient to cause the lamp to be
dangerous, renders the provision of some reliable means
of testing a lamp in gas, before it is issued to the miner, a
most important precautionary measure.   The testing of
lamps in gas, in some way or other, has been adopted here
and there for several years past ; but the Royal Commissioners, impressed by their own somewhat extensive experience of the great difficulty frequently to be encountered
in detecting minute imperfections in lamps which have
given rise to explosions, insist, in their final Report, upon
the absolute necessity of providing a gas-test for safety-
lamps at all collieries where they are in use, and of sub-
mitting every lamp to the test before it is allowed to be
taken into the mine.   They point out that such gas-tests
as are here and there provided, although better than none
at all, are not by any means trustworthy, and they give

indications as to the nature of testing arrangements which in their opinion will afford satisfactory results. Unfortunately, the necessity for bringing their labors to a conclusion before they could devote sufficient time to all the numerous branches of their inquiry, precluded their carrying the subject of lamp-testing by gas to a definite practical issue ; but there is little doubt that this important subject will be thoroughly worked out ere long by one or other of the associations, or individual experimenters, who continue to labor in the direction of increasing the safety and efficiency of illuminating appliances for mines.

When the late Commission entered upon its labors, some of the members looked forward, perhaps somewhat too sanguinely, to the pleasure of recording, at no distant day, the successful application, in practical ways, of electricity to the illumination of mine-roads and workings. That it was only able, upon completing its Report six years later, to describe achievements which could scarcely be considered much more than the germs of the future utilization of electricity in these directions, may have been disappointing ; yet it was evident, even then, that the electric light had an important future before it in mines.

Its application to the illumination of the pit-bottom and the immediately adjacent portions of the mine-roads obviously presented no practical difficulty, while even this limited utilization of the light, combined with its employment at the surface and in the buildings attached to a colliery, appeared likely to secure advantages in regard to efficiency of illumination, convenience, and comparative safety. The first experiments on the employment of the light underground were carried out by Mr. R. E. Crompton at Pleasley Colliery, near Mansfield, in 1881 ; glow-lamps were applied in some parts of the road, and conducting wires were carried up to a working face, but the trials were not pursued very far. Attempts were made to apply the light where the work of cutting coal was proceeding, by connecting portable lamps with the main conducting wire (fixed against one side of the haulage-road) by means of

7

light leads, allowing plenty of slack; but this arrangement
proved unpractical, on account of the obvious liability of
their injury by falls of coal or stone, and of men to get
their feet entangled in them, to the probable damage of
the wires, and injury or fracture of the lamp.   Trials of a
similar nature were made soon afterwards at Earnock Colliery, where glow-lamps were also applied to some extent
along the roadway of the mine: but they were not continued for any great length of time.   At Risca Collieries an
extensive electric-light installation was established at about
this time, and has continued in operation with very satisfactory results.   Arc-lights are applied at all the screens and
sidings, and glow-lights in the shops, offices, and cabins, as
well as at the pit-bottom, and to a distance of 100 yards
along the main haulage-road, and the work at these parts
is now carried on to great advantage with the aid of this
very effective illumination.   The National Colliery and the
Abercarn Colliery speedily followed the example of Risca,
the lighting installations there adopted being counterparts,
of that worked out at the latter place; the Harris' Navigation Colliery has also, for some years, been provided with
electric light to the same extent, both on the surface and
underground.

The impossibility of guarding against injury or fracture
of such light insulated wires as could alone be applied for
connecting movable lamps, for use at the working-places
with main conductors leading to the dynamo-machine at
the surface, soon rendered it evident that the success in
providing the miner with a safe and efficient electric light
could only be attained by the production of a perfectly self-
contained lamp, not too heavy or bulky to preclude its
being carried about underground, and capable of maintaining a supply of light equal to that furnished by efficient
safety-lamps, during the entire period of a working shift.
When Mr. Ellis Lever offered a prize, in 1883, for the best
safety-lamp, two or three attempts at self-contained electric lamps were brought forward, but they could not be
said to have afforded any encouragement to the hope that
some practical success in this direction was imminent.

The subject was, however, earnestly attacked by Mr. J. Wilson Swan, and, before the Royal Commission concluded its labors, Mr. Swan was able to submit a secondary-battery lamp, of sufficiently small and suitable dimensions to be called really portable, though considerably heavier than was desirable (it weighed between 9 lbs. and 10 lbs.) ; when freshly charged and fitted with a glow-lamp of suitable resistance, it gave a light which was maintained for several hours at between 2 and 3 candle-power, and still furnished a light of about $1\frac{1}{2}$ candle-power at the expiration of eleven hours. Since then Mr. Swan has made further improvements in this lamp, which, with its strong wooden cylindrical case and compactly-arranged storage cells, weighs now only about 7 lbs., while the power and duration of the light furnished by it are about the same as in the earlier form of lamp. The Author is informed by Mr. G. W. Wilkinson, of Risca, that the lamp has been modified in some of its details, from time to time, in accordance with what were found to be essential requirements, in the course of its practical trial in that colliery ; thirty of them, supplied by the Edison-Swan Electric Light Company, have been in use at that colliery for three months, having during that period been employed in connection with every variety of underground work. When brought to the surface at the end of a shift, they were recharged with the aid of a simple charging table, in connection with the dynamo of the general installation, this operation being carried out by one of the lads of the colliery. The weight of the lamp was not objected to by the miners, and it was found to furnish ample light for all purposes at present fulfilled by safety-lamps, up to the expiration of sixteen hours, although its brightness had become considerably reduced ; at the expiration of the three months, the batteries did not afford any evidence of a diminution of efficiency, and although they were submitted to the rough treatment incidental to their employment on the haulage roads, no instance of fracture or cracking of the stout glass which incloses the small glow-light, nor of injury to the glow-light itself or to any part of the instrument, occurred during the whole of the trial period. In fact, excepting the small expenditure of power in re-charging the lamps which, with a large installation like that at Risca, was of no practical account, the lamps cost nothing for maintenance; a mere trifle was expended in wages in their preparation for use, and in these respects they obviously compared most favorably with even the simplest kinds of safety-lamps. Mr. Wilkinson feels himself justified from this thorough practical trial in considering that, if the miners' Swan lamp can be supplied at a cost of even somewhat more than double the price of the most expensive efficient safety-lamp of latest construction, and will remain efficient for twelve months, it will repay its cost in that time for the reasons above given.

The London and South Western Coal Company, the Abercarn Steam Coal Company and the National Steam Coal Company, have recently decided to have recourse to the exclusive use of these lamps in their collieries, and three thousand will shortly be supplied for that purpose.

Mr. Swan, who is continuously active in elaborating improvements in the general efficiency of the lamp, and additions to its value in coal-mines, has endeavored to make a modification of it, for inspecting purposes, in which a gas-indicator forms part of the lamp. He succeeded in the first instance in constructing, upon the side of the lamp, a small form of indicator upon Liveing's principle but has abandoned this in favor of a eudiometrical indicator, by means of which he hopes that an inspector will be able, in a very simple and expeditious manner, to ascertain whether the air in different parts of a mine is equal in purity to a given standard. The objections to the eudiometrical method of examining the air of mines have been discussed in another part of this Paper; a practical trial of some duration, underground, to which this addition to the Swan lamp will shortly be submitted, may determine how far those objections interfere with its practical value.

While Mr. Swan has attained the results just indicated, others have also not been unsuccessful in approaching the fulfilment of the conditions essential to the production of a serviceable miners' electric lamp. Mr. James Pitkin has constructed a portable and efficient variety of secondary battery, and has made a near approach towards the production of a good miners' lamp. The results which he now attains in regard to light furnished, and maintenance of the light, are fully equal to those obtained with the Swan lamp, and the weight of the experimental lamps which he has constructed is scarcely greater than that of some of the more recent forms of safety-lamps, being between 5lbs. and 6 lbs. An efficient reflector concentrates the light of the small glow-lamp used, so as to effect strong illumination in any particular direction in front of the lamp. The latter requires modification of construction in several essential matters of detail, before it can be considered a practically serviceable lamp, and the duration of its efficiency, under practical conditions, has still to be determined upon a sufficiently extensive scale ; this is, however, already in progress at Tyldesley Colliery, where, by the kindness of Messrs. Peace, the Author and some other members of the British Association recently had an opportunity of seeing some of these lamps in use underground.

Several attempts had been made before the completion of the Royal Commission's Report, to produce primary batteries of different kinds, in a portable form, of sufficient power to maintain a practically useful light for the purposes of the miner. One of the first to attain somewhat promising results in this direction was Mr. Trouvé, though the maintenance of power of the battery used by him was insufficient to serve any useful purpose underground. Mr. T. Coad submitted a primary battery lamp in 1884, which appeared to afford some promise of success, though neither the maintenance of power, nor the dimensions of the battery, constituted an approach to the fulfilment of practical exigencies.

The liability of an explosive gas-mixture to be fired by the fracture of an incandescent glow-lamp within it, was experimentally demonstrated at an early stage of the attempts to apply the electric light in mines. But the possibility of danger arising from the use of glow-lamps in mine-ways and workings has been reduced to the remotest contingency by the arrangements adopted in the Swan electric-lamp. The miniature tubular glow-lamps are very difficult to break ; they are moreover hermetically inclosed in exceedingly strong and carefully annealed hemispherical glass covers, which are not likely to be fractured by very rough usage, and which may therefore be considered thoroughly efficient protectors of glow-lamps. With a view to ensure absolute safety in connection with the use of the glow-lamp, Mr. Coad adopted the ingenious device of inclosing carbonic acid, under pressure, within the protecting glass. In the first instance, he proposed to fill the space within that glass with water, super-saturated with carbonic acid, and there was immersed in the carbonic acid solution an arrangement, whereby the circuit from the battery to the glow-lamp was to be at once broken if by the fracture of the glass the gas-pressure within was relieved. In a more recent form of his lamp which has been brought forward by Mr. Wilkin, a stop-cock arrangement is applied, through which the space inclosed by the glass shade may be charged with gas under pressure, by means of a small force-pump. When this pressure is established, the glow-lamp is set into action, and when the gas-pressure is relieved by the fracture of the glass or the opening of the stop-cock, the light is instantly extinguished. A similar arrangement has recently been brought before the public by Mr. Baily. For the ingenuity of the idea much credit is due to Mr. Coad ; but it appears to the Author doubtful whether, with the practically absolute security afforded by the very stout hemispherical glass-protecting shades, there is the least necessity for adopting this extra precaution, which, besides adding to the cost, detracts from the simplicity in preparation and use of electric hand-lamps.

Some special forms of primary battery have been proposed for the provision and maintenance of a light suitable for a miners' lamp. Thus Mr. Schanschieff has constructed a small sulphate of mercury battery, which he is applying to this purpose, and which has furnished, in regard to maintenance of power, more promising results than those attained by the batteries used by Trouvé and Coad.

Early last year the Author had submitted to him by Mr. Blumberg some experimental lamps, in which the source of electricity consisted of a combination of small cells of Skrivanoff's modification of De la Rue's battery ; the elements are zinc, and silver foil coated with chloride of silver, the exciting liquid being a solution of caustic potash. The smallest of the lamps submitted weighed only 4½ lbs. ; it furnished at starting a light equal to 1 candle-power ; the luminosity fell only very gradually, and at the expiration of eight hours the light was but little superior to that of an ordinary Davy lamp. The Author has not had an opportunity of seeing the most recent form of this lamp, which is now, he believes, undergoing thorough practical trial ; but the result quoted, which was decidedly in advance of any other furnished by primary batteries, afforded great promise of a future for this variety of miners' lamp. The first cost of the battery itself may be somewhat heavy on account of the silver which enters into its construction, but as the value of the metallic silver, resulting from the reduction of the chloride during the operation of the battery, is always recoverable, the replacement of the elements is not costly.

The re-charging of the small primary batteries for miners' lamps is, of course, a somewhat more troublesome operation than the restoration of power of the secondary-battery lamps ; on the other hand, the employment of the latter necessitates the provision of a generator. The great advantages secured, however, in connection with the necessities of a colliery by the provision of an electric-light installation, for general purposes, and for the efficient illumination of the pit-bottom and adjacent roadways, render their extensive adoption very probable. The average life of secondary-battery lamps has still to be ascertained, and the results accruing from the very extensive trials about to be made of them in South Wales will be awaited with much interest, as they will determine how far the original cost of these lamps, which at present will in many instances be prohibitive of their adoption, is compensated for by their durability, added to the very trifling expenditure upon their preparation for use and their maintenance. Meanwhile, there are now most substantial grounds for the confident belief that the problem of the successful and thoroughly safe application of electric light, in connection with every class of underground work, is in course of speedy and complete practical solution.

Although this Paper far exceeds in dimensions those originally contemplated by the Author, it has dealt, and that but imperfectly, with only the most important branches of the subject of accidents in coal-mines, their causes, and the means for preventing them, or, at any rate, for reducing their disastrous effects. The consideration of some parts of this important subject, such as accidents due to irruptions of water in mines, has been left untouched, and the results of much valuable work connected with the investigations of the causes of mine-explosions, which have during the last few years been assiduously and successfully pursued in this and other countries, have been discussed to an extent quite inadequate to their high importance. If, in reviewing those results generally, the Author has overlooked or failed to do justice to, the fruits of patient toil of zealous workers who have labored individually or collectively, with the object of reducing the perils to which a most important class of the community is constantly exposed, it is from no want of appreciation of their importance, but rather from an imperfect knowledge of all that has been accomplished in this direction.

To those who have thus earnestly labored in this country, it must be a source of much satisfaction to know that, to some small extent, at any rate, the workers in British coal-mines are now about to reap the benefit of the knowledge which has been accumulated since the Mines Regulation Act of 1872 came into force. While the second part of this Paper was being prepared, the Coal-Mines Regulation Bill of 1887 has become law, and it will be cheerfully acknowledged, by all directly interested in the subject, that a great amelioration of the laws relating to the working and management of coal-mines has thereby been effected,

even although those who have labored to attain such amelioration may incline to the opinion that there are directions in which bolder innovations might have been
accepted, with regard to matters directly relating to safe
working in fiery and dusty mines, concerning which very
definite conclusions were put forward by the late Royal
Commission, based upon the results of comprehensive
enquiry and experiments by its members and by many
others.

That the publication of those conclusions has, however,
borne good fruit, may be illustrated by reference to many
clauses in the " General Rules " prescribed by the new Act,
such as those which relate: to the provision of dumb-drifts
in connection with ventilation of mines by furnaces; to the
placing of mechanical contrivances for ventilation in positions where they will not be injured in the event of an
explosion; to the provision of supplies of timber in suitable places underground, convenient to the workmen , to
the regulations of a precautionary nature with regard to
the preservation and manipulation of explosives, the charging of bore-holes, etc.; to the restrictions placed upon the
use of gunpowder; and to the indications of the means to
be employed for dealing with dry and dusty localities, and
for blasting coal in such places where the use of powder is
prohibited. The regulations which existed in the former
Act regarding the employment of locked safety-lamps have
been improved, and an important check has been given to
the practice, which has prevailed in some places, of working with mixed lights, to which most serious attention was
called by the Commission. The conditions which shall
determine the safety of lamps to be used in mine-ways and
workings are clearly laid down; but the clause, as altered
in the House of Lords, has, in the Author's opinion, and
for the reason which he has given, been much weakened in
regard to the protection from explosions afforded by it, by
the omission of that part of the clause adopted by the
Commons' Committee, which specifically prohibited the use
of " *unprotected*" Davy, Clanny, and Stephenson lamps in

any place in which there is likely to be any such quantity
of inflammable gas as to render the use of naked lights
dangerous.[1]

The inspection of a mine, for the purpose of determining
whether "*any*" inflammable gas is present, is still prescribed to be performed with a locked safety-lamp, which
fails, in even the most skilled hands, to afford indication of
the presence in the air of any proportion under 2 per cent.
of fire-damp, and even nearly 3 per cent., according to some
authorities. The careful examination by the Commission,
of the merits of a considerable number of fire-damp detectors, showed that there was at any rate one description of
instrument, easy of manipulation, by which small quantities of fire-damp, even considerably below 1 per cent., can
be rapidly detected, while another class of detector was
likely soon to be sufficiently perfected for practical use
with similar results. It is now generally accepted that
even less than 2 per cent. of inflammable gas in the air of a
mine, may, under certain conditions, constitute a source of
considerable danger ; moreover, it is admitted to be desirable that more accurate means of ascertaining the extent of
contamination by fire-damp of return air-currents should be
provided than are afforded by the safety-lamp test. It is,
therefore, to be regretted that some allusion to a probable
future prescription of the use of trustworthy fire-damp
detectors could not have been inserted in the Act, as an
inducement to managers of mines to familiarize themselves
with such instruments as Liveing's Indicator, and to workers in these subjects to develop other testing-apparatus,
which already present the germ of future usefulness.[2]
Again, it was certainly most desirable to encourage the use
of a gas-test in the inspection of safety-lamps, upon the

(1) *Ante*, p. 71.
(2) In illustration of work which is being done in this direction it may be mentioned that the Count Montgelas is obtaining promising results by combining
an ingenious system of testing for gas and of underground signalling, elaborated by Mr. T. Shaw, M.E., of the United States, with improvements made
by Mr. Sugg in the specific gravity gas indicators, referred to in Part I. of this
Paper.

necessity for which great stress was laid by the Commission, but no reference is even made to the desirableness of its provision.

Taken as a whole, however, the "General Rules" embraced in the new Act, constitute a most important advance upon those of the Act of 1872; they cannot fail to contribute greatly to the diminution of the number and disastrous nature of coal-mine explosions and other mine-accidents, and their adoption constitutes a rich, and, it will be admitted, well-merited reward to those who have labored long, earnestly and disinterestedly for the advancement of knowledge of the causes, and for the application of that knowledge to the prevention, of Accidents in Mines.

DISCUSSION.

MR. BRUCE, president, said that the subject of the Paper was of great importance, and it was one on which the Author was a distinguished authority. The questions brought forward for discussion were the various causes of accidents in mines, falls in the roofs, dangers in hauling up and letting down cages in the shafts, and dangers from the variations in the barometric pressure and the presence of fire-damp. The object should be to ascertain what could be done in the way of lessening those accidents from the roofs and the shafts, to decide what was the value to be ascribed to the difference of barometrical pressure at different times, how best to detect fire-damp and discover the extent to which it was present, how far coal-dust added to the danger, what was the safest way of using explosives, what were the safest explosives to use, and the best means to be employed for getting coal when explosives could not be used ; also to consider the nature of the lamps to be employed in mines. Those appeared to him to be the points chiefly requiring consideration.

SIR FREDERICK ABEL said that his Paper, long as it was, presented so many imperfections, there being several subjects on which he might have touched, such as inundations in mines and other minor causes of accidents, that he wished to be allowed to make a few supplementary observations before the discussion commenced. He desired especially to refer to one important topic, because it might be alluded to in the course of the discussion, namely, the measures for dealing with casualties in mines. The Royal Commissioners were greatly impressed with the desirability of some system being instituted, whereby more effectual and generally applicable arrangements for dealing with casualties might be secured, and they pointed out two or three steps that might be taken by mine owners and

SIR FREDERICK ABEL.

those interested in mines, quite apart from any action of the Government in the matter.   They referred, for example, to the importance of having ambulances, stretchers, and appliances ready for immediate use at every mine, and also of having centres where apparatus of a more special character might be kept, so as to be available at short notice in the event of serious accident ; as, for example, the Fleuss apparatus, the employment of which rendered the user independent of the external air.   They further pointed out how important it was that men should receive some amount of training in the use of simple appliances for saving life, or at any rate for dealing with accidents ; and also in simple means of dealing temporarily with wounds or other casualties.   It was very satisfactory to note that in the Mines Regulation Act a clause had been introduced which prescribed that ambulances, stretchers, splints and other such appliances should be kept at mines; and also that no sooner had the Act been passed than the St. John's Ambulance Association, which did an important work in this country, set about actively to endeavor to introduce a system of training miners in simple operations useful in dealing temporarily with casualties when they occurred. He had referred to the Fleuss apparatus ; he might also allude to others which had been brought forward from time to time to assist in the exploration of mines after accidents.   There were different kinds of respirators, of which one or two of a very efficient character had been exhibited, notably one from Prussia, devised by Mr. Loeb, a respirator which enabled an explorer to go a short distance into a mine and remain there, this respirator being connected by means of a pipe with the external air.   Mr. Fleuss had also furnished a very powerful and useful self-contained lamp of high illuminating power for exploring purposes ; and, of late, electric lamps of comparatively high illuminating power, much higher than those which would probably come into use as substitutes for miners' lamps, had been brought forward, and would, no doubt, prove very valuable in explorations.   He had in the Paper

SIR FREDERICK ABEL.

dealt with the subject of the great advance made within
the last two years, he might say within the last twelve
months, in the development of self-contained electric lamps
for mines.   As the latter part of his Paper was necessarily
gone over rather cursorily, he might be permitted to refer
briefly to the question of primary batteries.   In reference
to secondary batteries he had pointed out the great advance
that had been made, especially by Mr. Swan, and the promising efforts made by Mr. Pitkin.   He had also seen that
evening a capital lamp of the same type exhibited by
Mr. Urquhart, which was of comparatively small weight,
and appeared to furnish a very satisfactory light.   With
regard to primary batteries, he had mentioned one or two
that seemed to promise good results, notably that brought
forward by Mr. Blumberg, the chloride of silver battery,
and a single liquid battery in which sulphate of mercury
was used, viz., the battery of Mr. Schanschieff.   He had
lately seen an important advance made by Mr. Schanschieff in the development of his battery, which combined
very low internal resistance with high electromotive force :
the experimental observations, which he and others had
made with lamps in which this battery was used, indicated
that it afforded very great promise of furnishing the miner
with a light and comparatively cheap electric lamp.   He
had himself found that a lamp of that kind, weighing 5 or
6 lbs., gave over half a candle light at starting, at the end
of five hours four-tenths, and at the end of ten hours (more
than the time of an ordinary shift) it gave a greater illuminating power than an ordinary Davy lamp.   Those results
were very satisfactory, but no doubt they might be further
improved upon.   Both the Schanschieff and other primary
batteries, such as the Eclipse lamp, were comparatively
cheap in regard to maintenance ; thus, the cost of the
Schanschieff lamp just referred to had been found to be
somewhat less than 1d. per hour.   There was, of course,
the one difficulty, that they had to be charged at every
shift, but the charging could be reduced to as simple an
operation as that of filling an ordinary lamp with oil, and

PROFESSOR ARNOLD LUPTON.

he did not think that it would stand prominently in the
way of the introduction of primary electric lamps.   It was
evident that the question of the application of electricity
to portable lamps, for general purposes in mines, was on
the way of being achieved with success.

PROFESSOR ARNOLD LUPTON suggests that, the Royal
Commisioners sit in permanence ; he said, "let those men
of scientific attainments, and practical mining engineers,
be always sitting in London, so that any one who had an
invention or idea might bring it before them ; let it filter
through their minds, and then let the information be made
public.   It would be much better to enlighten and guide
the public in that way than to order them.   He hoped that
so far as the intelligence of the meeting could affect the
future legislation of the country it would be in favor of
allowing mining engineers to manage their mines in the
best way they could.   The inspectors of mines used their
great experience and position to guide or help the management.   He considered they did great good ; it was not the
living hand of the Inspector to which objection could be
taken, but the dead hand of a law about ever-changing
mechanics to which he objected.   The Author had alluded
to the question of gas issuing from goaves.   The danger of
a goaf depended upon the depth of the mine and the age of
the goaf.   In the case of a deep mine and an old goaf of
large area, there would not be any hollows or places in which
gas could accumulate.   He had never seen a hollow in
driving through old workings in the goaves in a deep mine ;
it was only on the verge of the workings, where the goaf
was new and the subsidence of the strata had not had time
to crush and fill up every hole and interstice, that any
opening could be found where gas could accumulate.
The Danger depended upon whether this was ventilated or
not.   In working mines, on the system of bringing back
and having no air-road through the goaf, there might be a
danger of a large quantity of gas accumulating, which, with
a fall of the barometer, or some other cause, might come
out and help to produce an explosion ; but if air-roads were

PROFESSOR ARNOLD LUPTON.

taken through the goaf, and it was properly ventilated, there was comparatively little danger. He was pleased to observe the statement in the Paper, that the ratio of accidents in mines had been diminishing. This was true. In 1856 one life was lost for every 64,700 tons of coal raised; but in 1886 one life was lost for every 188,800 tons of coal raised. Thus the death-rate was now only about one-third, a diminution most remarkable, and he thought in the highest degree creditable to the owners, managers, inspectors, officials of all degrees, and to the workmen. The amount of coal raised had very rapidly increased; with that increase new dangers had arisen, and mining engineers had hardly acquired the amount of experience which enabled them fully to cope with all the dangers that were met with. Some accidents occurred through overwinding, through the cage being drawn up too far. Many mechanical engineers had set to work to devise means for preventing overwinding by disengaging hooks, so that the rope might be separated from the cage and not be drawn over the pulleys. Now, if he were in a cage suspended in a shaft, the last thing he should want to happen would be to be separated from the rope. Of course if he were just going over the pulley it would be a desirable thing, but he would rather go over the pulley than go down to the bottom of the pit. It had unfortunately happened that just when the safety apparatus was most wanted it had generally failed. When winding up at a slow rate it acted effectually; but if it was wound up fast through some mistake of the engine man it was generally smashed to pieces. That showed how much a safety apparatus could be relied upon to prevent accidents. Many different kinds of hooks were used, and he thought that his observations would apply to all of them. Safety-hooks were not regarded as of high value by continental mining engineers, who preferred safety-cages, which in their turn were despised by English engineers. Thus safety-cages were adopted almost universally on the Continent, while safety-hooks were almost universally adopted in England. That was a matter which should be taken into consideration by those who were inclined to pass regulations for the working of coal-mines. He thought an automatic contrivance, to regulate the speed of winding and stop the engine if it went too far, was much better than a disengaging hook; he had seen such an apparatus in France and also in England. He wished to ask the Author whether any measurements could be thoroughly relied upon to give the maximum gaseous pressure existing in the coal, considering that there were great practical difficulties in driving a bore in coal a sufficient distance, and then plugging it up so as to prevent the escape of any portion of gas. Allusion had been made in the Paper to the means of testing for gas in mines other than safety-lamps, such as Ansell's indicator. He believed he was present at the first practical test ever made in a mine with that instrument twenty years ago, and it was then a failure. It was evident that there was gas in the mine before the indicator showed it. He had carried a modified form of the indicator in his pocket, but had generally found it fail. The Author had alluded to the cheap way in which the electric fuze was now made. He had himself used thousands of those fuzes, or fuzes that bore his name, which he had bought in London, and the only fault he had to find with them was their cost. If they could be reduced from $2\frac{1}{2}d$. to $\frac{1}{2}d$. each a great boon would be conferred upon the mining community. The Royal Commission attached great importance to the testing of safety-lamps before they were allowed to go into the mine. He had tested safety-lamps for many years, and the method he adopted was to take a lead pencil, push it through the gauze, and make a hole $\frac{1}{4}$ inch in diameter, so as to render it a thoroughly unsafe lamp, and then put it to the test; such a lamp often resisted a test in still gas. He thus tested the testing apparatus to see whether it would give him the assurance that he could not put an unsafe lamp into the mine after it had been through the apparatus. That was the difficulty. What he wanted was a testing apparatus that had been thoroughly tested, so that he could apply it to testing

8

PROFESSOR ARNOLD LUPTON.

lamps. Until he had that he should prefer a safety-lamp that had been subjected to ten thousand practical tests, and then, when he knew the lamp was right, he would trust the eye and skill of the lamp-man and those who saw it put together, so as to feel sure that he had a practically safe lamp. With regard to a very important question, that of coal-dust, the Author had dealt with it in a masterly way, as he did all such questions. He believed that his experiments upon coal-dust, as well as those which he had reported in connection with the Prussian Fire-damp Commission, had established without doubt the possibility of what might be called a pure coal-dust explosion ; but as a mining engineer Professor Lupton would rely more upon the evidence found in the mines that had exploded. When he went into a mine and found an explosion originating in an intake air-road close to the pit, and that the explosion had gone through the intake roads, and not into the return roads, or working places where gas might be expected to be exuding from the coal, confining itself (though it had penetrated the workings of three or four seams) to the roads where gas would not be expected, and simply taking place where there was oxygen and coal-dust, he thought that was evidence going a long way in support of the pure coal-dust explosion theory. But the Author had asked what was the use in theorizing about a pure coal-dust explosion unless the air had been first analysed, and it was certain that there was no gas? Now there were places in mines where, if a chemist should say that he had analyzed the air and found fire-damp, he should be inclined to dispute the analysis. He should say "That coal was hewn twenty years ago, cut up into pillars, and roadways have been draining those pillars of gas for twenty years : there is an overwhelming supply of fresh air continually rushing along, and are you going to tell me that there is any coal-gas there? Because, if you do, let me ask how much coal-gas I may expect further in ? If in 200 yards a main intake air-road will give an appreciable percentage, how much may I expect when I have gone through 20 miles of roads—not an uncommon

PROFESSOR ARNOLD LUPTON.

length in one mine? How much fire-damp may I expect
in the return air that has passed through all that?" It was
a simple question of rule of three. Allowing for the
greater quantity of gas that came out of the workings
nearer the face, it was not so simple; but the case was
strongly in favor of the theory that there was no fire-damp
in the intake air-road close to the pit—not 1 per cent., not
0·1, or 0·01, or even 0·001 per cent., and if he came down to
0·001 per cent. he thought the Author would agree with
him that if an explosion occurred, and if it was a question
between fire-damp and coal-dust, it must be a pure coal-dust
explosion. He had recently studied the subject, and he
had done so by the aid of information given him by the
Author and also by Messrs. Atkinson. Referring to the
coal-dust question, he thought the mining engineers of the
country owed a great debt of gratitude to Mr. William
Galloway, mining engineer, of Cardiff, to whom in a great
measure the bringing forward of the subject was due. His
investigations, experiments, and persistent demonstrations
had elicited a great deal of knowledge upon the subject.
He had always in his own mind connected Mr. William
Galloway with the coal-dust theory. He brought the subject before the Royal Society in 1876, and was the first
mining engineer in England who drew attention to its
importance. His investigations of many mines proved, he
thought, almost beyond the possibility of doubt, that
there had been large colliery explosions which might be
correctly described as pure coal-dust explosions. Of course
there had been many others which might be described as
fire-damp and coal-dust explosions, and there had been
others which might be called pure fire-damp explosions.
But of late years most deaths had been produced not by
pure fire-damp explosions, but by fire-damp and coal-dust
explosions, and by pure coal-dust explosions.

The means of laying the dust were now well ascertained
and largely practised in different parts of the country. A
short time ago he visited several collieries in South Wales,
one of which was the Ynishir Colliery, managed by Mr.

PROFESSOR ARNOLD LUPTON.

John James Thomas. Under his energetic management
a length of about 3 miles of pipes had been laid through
the workings, carrying water at a pressure of 70 or 80 lbs.
on the square inch, in pipes 1½ inch or 2 inches in diameter.
At intervals of 25 or 30 yards he had stand-pipes, 4 feet
high, with little jets sending out water in a fine spray, which
were caught by air-currents and damped the mine. In that
way the whole mine was damped, and when that was done
the formation of dust was stopped. No harm was done to
the roads by the water-spray ; the duration of the timber
was increased, the temperature of the mine was lowered,
and the horses had a good supply of drinking-water at hand
in the pipes. Even if the whole intake road was damped
it was not likely that there would be much dust in any part
of the mine. That plan was carried out by Mr. Archibald
Hood at Llwynipia and at other collieries in South Wales.
In some places there were not merely jets of water at high
pressure, but of water and compressed air, the compressed
air carrying water out in a fine spray into the mine, so that
no puddles of water were formed which might cause injury
to the road. This was the invention of Mr. Martin of
Dowlais. There were several other ways of damping mines.
Perhaps one of the most ingenious was that of Mr. Stratton,
in the Pochin pit, Tredegar Collieries. He turned the
exhaust steam of an engine into the downcast shaft, and it
had the effect of heating the air and damping it at the same
time. It was well known that it was impossible to damp
the air unless it was heated, and Mr. Stratton did both at
the same time. He succeeded in damping the whole of the
mine by putting steam into the intake air in the downcast
shaft. It did very well in spring, summer, and autumn, but
in winter it was not sufficient, because it would not heat the
air enough, and in winter therefore the steam was supplemented by water-carts for laying the dust. This method of
damping the air by steam was only applicable to mines of
moderate depth, and consequently low temperature, say
under 65° Fahrenheit, because it would make deeper mines
too warm. The steam had done no harm to the roads or

timber at the Pochin pit, and it made the mine much pleas-
anter.   He would only say that it would be interesting to
calculate what would be the probable effects of an explosion
in a coal-dusty mine.   He should measure the effect by the
amount of oxygen in the mine, because he assumed that
wherever there was coal-dust there was more than enough
for chemical combination with the oxygen.   He had made
one calculation in the case of a large colliery which had
exploded, and the combination of oxygen and coal-dust,
assuming that all the oxygen in the air-ways where the
explosion occurred was burned, was equal to an explosion
of 90,000 lbs. of gunpowder, or of 4 lbs. for every lineal foot
of the roadway.   He did not pretend to say that was a
trustworthy calculation ; he merely used it as an illustration,
and would rather put it interrogatively to the Author, or to
some other chemist.

Mr. C. TYLDEN-WRIGHT said all persons interested in
mines, and in the working population, owed a deep debt of
gratitude to the members of the Royal Commission, who
had undertaken a Herculean task.   The work had occupied
them seven years, and it was a standard work for every one
connected with mines throughout the country.   The Commissioners had given an immense amount of detail which
would be of great service, and absolutely without fee.   He
regretted, however, that the present discussion had not
taken place before the Bill was considered in the House of
Commons, because in that case the coal-owners would have
been spared the trouble of combating many amendments
that were introduced, which were certainly of an extraordinary nature.   It was proposed to form "harbors of refuge"
underground, which were to be hermetically sealed from
the surrounding atmosphere, to be explosion-proof, and to
be erected in different parts of every colliery.   It was also
proposed that there should be two engine-men in every
engine-house,—he supposed for the purpose of occupying
one another's attention.   Another proposal was that wherever gas was found in a mine, no underground furnace for
ventilating purposes should be used for twelve months.

Mr. C. Tylden-Wright.

The effect of that would have been to close absolutely the
largest collieries in the country. Again, it was proposed,
and he was sorry to find that the Author to some extent
endorsed it, that all safety-lamps should be tested with gas.
He might not be aware that there were hundreds of collieries in the country that had no gas-mains within miles of
them, and how, in such cases, safety-lamps were to be tested
by means of gas it was difficult to say. The public had to
thank the common sense of the Home Secretary, and the
calm judgment of the House of Lords, that coal-owners
had been saved from the harrassing legislation proposed by
certainmembers of the House of Commons. The Bill was
in some respects one of the most stringent ever passed, but
in others it was thoroughly workable and practicable, notably with regard to the use of explosives in mines. Whereas
there was formerly a great restriction put upon the use of
gunpowder and explosives if gas had been found within
three months, that time had now, without any risk whatever, been reduced to forty-eight hours, which was a very
great improvement. No one understood the use of powder
so well as the Author, who was *facile princeps* in everything
connected with explosives ; but he wished to tell him that
for the purposes for which an explosive was wanted in mines
no nitro-glycerine compound had been yet invented equal
to gunpowder, and if he would devote his talents to the
adoption of powder in some water-cartridge, he would do the
greatest service to the coal-owning interest.

With regard to safety-lamps, he had been greatly surprised and pleased to see the admirable collection of electric
lamps produced for exhibition. They had their disadvantages, and safety-lamps of the old type must, he thought,
always be used. One of the disadvantages was that they
were all apparently of the nature of a bull's eye lamp, only
throwing the light on one side, which he considered a fatal
objection to a lamp underground in a pit. Again, the cost
was, he thought, eight times that of an ordinary protected
or unprotected Davy lamp, and what the effect would be of
dropping them on the ground, which was a frequent occur-

rence in mines, he could not say ; but he imagined that they would not long survive. Again, some of the lamps weighed 5 or 6 lbs., whereas an ordinary safety-lamp would only weigh from $1\frac{1}{4}$ to $1\frac{1}{2}$ lb. In that respect, therefore, he thought that the old safety-lamps were likely to hold their own for some time. They would also probably do so in other ways, because the electric light was absolutely useless in testing for gas. One might walk into choke-damp with an electric light and fall to the ground without the light affording the slightest indication of danger, but with a safety-lamp the danger was at once apparent. The Author had raised a question on which he was bound to join issue with him with reference to " protected " and " unprotected " lamps. The House of Lords had met with very unmerited abuse for having altered the Bill, as it left the House of Commons, to the state in which the Home Secretary had originally drawn it. Nothing could be more definite with regard to the use of lamps than the present clause : " Wherever safety-lamps are used they shall be so constructed that they may be safely carried against the air current ordinarily prevailing in that part of the mine in which the lamps are for the time being in use, even though such current should be inflammable." The Author seemed to think that the part of the mine where the lamps were in use applied only to the working place where the man happened to work. His own view was that it was wherever the working man happened to take the lamp, and that the lamp must be perfectly safe in that particular place. He therefore thought that the House of Lords was perfectly justified in striking out the words which were hastily added in the Committee of the House of Commons, saying that unprotected Davy lamps should be prohibited. He thought it would be a great pity for the name of Davy to be under, however small, an amount of obloquy by being expressly prohibited in mines. He came from a district in South Staffordshire where the Davy lamp was looked upon as the most delicate and best practical apparatus for testing for gas. He would

MR. C. TYLDEN-WRIGHT.

not say that it was the best for working throughout the shift in gaseous pits ; but the condition of mines in that and some other districts was not generally gaseous ; they only wanted examining by a safety-lamp, and then naked candles were used for the work.

There was also a proposal, to which the author had alluded, that " detaching hooks " should be enforced. He did not know how many accidents had happened from the want of them during the last fifteen years. In South Staffordshire not a single life had been lost from their not being used in working pits. As to the rest of England, eleven lives had been lost from over-winding during the last year, of which ten were lost where detaching hooks had been employed. There was one other matter to which he would wish to refer connected with the safe working of mines, and that was inspection. It might be thought that coal owners were most unscrupulous, and workmen most incompetent to take care of themselves, from the number of inspectors supposed to be necessary. There were (1) the Government inspector and his staff of assistants, of whom he would wish to speak in nothing but praise; (2) Inspectors of weights and measures, who were compelled to test every machine at least twice a year; (3) Boiler inspectors, as provided by the Bill presented to the House of Commons by the President of the Board of Trade ; (4) School Inspectors; (5) Inspectors on behalf of workmen. The House of Commons altered the Bill so that any person who might have worked a month or so in a pit twenty or thirty years ago, might be sent by the men as often as they liked, to make this official inspection. He need not say that the experienced and trained managers of the pits, than whom a finer class did not exist, objected most strongly to taking such men through the most dangerous parts of the workings. The House of Lords did no more than bare justice to the colliery officials when they restricted the examination to actual working miners. He trusted mining legislation was now at rest for many years.

Mr. EMERSON BAINBRIDGE said he would name one or two points, which had been omitted by the Author, and there were one or two others on which he joined issue with Mr. Tylden-Wright. Reference had been made in the Paper to the increase of accidents due to a fall of the roof, but no cause for it had been assigned. He ventured to suggest that it was due to the fact that the seams which had the best roofs, had, year after year, gradually become exhausted. The coal now produced in the various mining districts of the country from coal seams, had, in many cases, roof which was not so good to manage as formerly, and, therefore, was more liable to cause accidents. In reference to the various means of breaking down coal, the Author had spoken of several mechanical wedges, but he thought he was right in saying that, in nearly all cases, the wedges referred to were not now used. As a matter of fact, there was scarcely a single wedge, perhaps with one exception, that was now able to hold its own as a means of breaking down coal. The cause was much the same as that which had been the means of limiting the use of the lime-cartridge.

The Author had warmly defended the lime-cartridge, and with good cause; but the fact that it was not used on a large scale, in more than about a dozen collieries, was rather against the idea of its being a success. The want of success was due almost entirely to the fact that it was difficult to get combined, a face of coal which would break down easily, a roof which would separate freely, and a coal which would break off well, conditions which were generally required, whether the wedge or the lime-cartridge was used, both being slow means of applying force to break down coal. There was one wedge now in use with great success in Belgium and the north of France. It consisted of two long, steel wedge-pieces, which were placed in the shot-hole, the thick end inwards, and a third long wedge was driven between the two. The wedge was not employed in England on a large scale, but in France and Belgium it had been largely adopted. The objection to it was,

MR. EMERSON BAINBRIDGE.

that whilst with the lime-cartridge or any other means of
breaking down coal simple ordinary explosive force was
applied, with the wedge a considerable quantity of "elbow-
grease" was required, and a man had to take five or ten
minutes in striking the centre wedge in order to get the
coal broken down.   No mention of that wedge, or of any
wedge in practical use was made in the Paper.   As to the
question of safety-lamps, it might be a bold thing to say,
but his impression was that there had been a great tendency to over-legislation, and to making restrictions upon
means of mining which had never been proved to be the
causes of any accident.   In all the accidents of the last
thirty years, it would, he thought, be impossible to find
five cases where an accident by explosion had been actually
proved to be due to the use of such lamps as were condemned by the new Act.   But in spite of the new regulation, which perhaps would cause nearly a million lamps to
be altered, he was sure that every manager of a mine, who
knew what a serious thing an accident was, would welcome
the results of such important experiments as had been
made by the Royal Commission.   He was glad that the
Author had passed a merited encomium upon Mr. C. E.
Rhodes for his endeavor to test lamps, which he had done
on a large scale in Yorkshire; but the moment a lamp was
now put to a test, the idea was to have it tested at a current of 50 or 60 feet per second, which was an impossible
velocity in any mine in existence.   The ordinary velocity of
an underground air-current was not more than 10 or 15
feet per second, and he ventured to assert that if a lamp
would stand safely double that, or 30 feet per second, it
might be considered, for most mines in the kingdom, practically and perfectly safe.   It was not, therefore, necessary
to fall back upon the elaborate designs of safety-lamps,
some of which had been mentioned by the Author, and
many of which were very complicated and costly.   He
might be permitted to give a sketch of a lamp which he
was now endeavoring to bring out, and which had been on
the previous day tested by Mr. C. E. Rhodes, as a lamp of

MR. EMERSON BAINBRIDGE.

very simple construction, and which stood a 30-foot per second test by actual experiment. It was a bonneted Clanny lamp. First of all, the bonnet with holes in it at the top allowed the escape of carbonic acid gas; next, the gauze allowed the admittance of the fresh air into the lamp, the shield bonnet being a necessary addition. This lamp had been proved by experiment to stand a velocity of current of 30 feet per second, instead of exploding, as did the ordinary Clanny, at about 8 feet. The ordinary safety-lamp which stood severe tests had eight or nine parts, but the lamp he had designed was so arranged that the glass was fixed in the top of the lamp; the top or bonnet part unscrewed, so that when the top was removed the gauze could be examined and cleaned; the bottom part was also unscrewed to trim the lamp and the glass was, therefore, left untouched, and could be left for six months, instead of as was usual with the ordinary Clanny lamp, being removed every day.

In speaking of the means of preventing accidents, the Author had referred to cages which were caught by self-acting catches, but he had failed to mention what appeared to be the most important invention of all. Perhaps he had not heard of this, as it was that of a working man who had been for twenty years trying to bring it before the mining public. Mr. Calow had invented a method of having a safety-cage so arranged, that the grip attached to the cage, which, if the rope broke, prevented it from falling down the shaft, only came into action when the cage actually became a falling body. In all other "cage-catchers," he believed that the catch itself was dependent upon the loosening of the winding-rope, but by means of a simple spring, Mr. Calow's was so arranged that the moment the cage became a falling body, the grips caught and stopped it.

The Author had referred to substitutes for gunpowder and Mr. Tylden-Wright had stated that no substitute had yet been found for gunpowder as an explosive which seemed to answer the purpose. It had been his good fortune during the last few months to come across an ex-

MR. EMERSON BAINBRIDGE.

plosive of that character. In June last, he was engaged to go to Germany to report upon an explosive known as "roburite." He was told, that in Germany, there were some mines that had a stratum of 4 or 5 inches of gas constantly floating under the roof, that he might go down one of them, take this new explosive, put it in an ordinary blasting hole, and fire it off, and there would then be no danger of any flame appearing! He need hardly say that he declined the experiment, but said that in a mine where there was no gas, he should be prepared to try it. He made the first experiments in July, for safety, in a quarry, where the roburite was tested under very trying conditions. He had first gunpowder, then dynamite, and then roburite, placed in small heaps, and covered with about 1½ inch of sand. The experiment was tried at nine o'clock at night, and when the gunpowder exploded there was a very large illumination; when the dynamite exploded there was a large flame; but when the roburite was exploded by a detonator, there was not the least spark. He then proceeded to try the same experiment underground, and on the following day he placed, in the presence of twenty persons, a cartridge of roburite into a hole in the coal and the shot was fired, but there was no spark. He then tried, for the first time with this explosive, an experiment with a blown-out shot, which, as the Author had stated, had probably been the main cause of nearly all the most serious explosions that had happened in this country; and if anything could be done to prevent the disastrous effects of blown-out shots, one of the main causes of accidents by explosion would disappear. A charge of roburite was put into a hole, a small "stemming," of about ½ inch, was put next to the charge, and a detonator was applied. The charge was then fired, and he had the satisfaction of seeing that the "blown-out shot" did not produce the least spark. If, therefore, roburite turned out to be, practically and economically, a good thing, it would prove a very important agent in future for mining. He also discovered in Germany that there were two other explosives, one named carbonite, and the other securite, which appeared to have similar action. The Author had spoken of carbonite with some degree of doubt, but Mr. Bainbridge thought that one or all of those explosives would be a very important means for putting an end to the risks attending the use of gunpowder, and to the danger of blown-out shots. A well-regulated mine, however, as a rule, ran very little risk of serious accident from the latter cause.

At present, instead of leaving every man to fire his own shot, as was done years ago, a well-managed mine had a number of men called shot-firers, who attended to that matter and nothing else. They gained experience as to the size of the hole, as to the amount of gunpowder required, and as to whether the explosive was exactly regulated according to the work to be done ; and, of course, if those things were well balanced there was little fear of blown-out shots taking place. As a point of economy, it might be mentioned that whilst the lime-cartridge, the water-cartridge, and wedges required a hole about 2 inches in diameter, an explosive like roburite acted perfectly well with a hole $1\frac{1}{4}$ inch in diameter. Colliery managers in Germany reported that in using this explosive, there was an increase in the quantity of large coal produced.

Mr. WILLIAM MORGANS stated that he was unable to agree with the views of the last speaker as to the testing of safety-lamps. It was necessary that lamps should withstand higher velocities than the ordinary currents met with in mines, because they might be exposed to sudden outbursts of gas. Turning to the subject of explosions, if the manager of a colliery was wise, he would attach due importance to both coal-dust and fire-damp accumulations in mines. By all means, let the moistening of coal-dust be carried to any extent desired, but let not the danger of fire-damp accumulations be overlooked, which, though rarely seen in working-places, were often found in adjacent goaves or contiguous old workings, and unfortunately so by the sanction of the law. One speaker appeared to feel very positive

MR. WILLIAM MORGANS.

that more explosions were due to coal-dust than was generally realized, but so far as Mr. Morgans could judge, it had
become the fashion to apply the coal-dust theory too commonly. Not only had there been a disposition to subordinate the evils of fire-damp to those of coal-dust, but the
active pursuit of the coal-dust theory had engendered a disposition to ignore fire-damp altogether. This had done
harm by diverting attention from a long standing danger.
It was to be hoped that the height of enthusiasm respecting coal-dust was reached in the case of the Altofts explosion. Fire-damp was known to occur in that colliery, but
the explosion was attributed to coal-dust alone. The official report afforded reason for considering that fire-damp
was the backbone of that explosion, and that it occurred
mainly in the disturbed roof strata, where gas was often
found in cracks and partings over intakes, as well as in
other ways. Those who believed in explosions of coal-dust
alone must find some better example than Altofts, which
belonged to the armory of their opponents, because fire-
damp was given off in that colliery. As yet there was not
a single example to be brought forward of a colliery explosion in any of the dusty workings in this country which
were free from fire-damp, notwithstanding that blasting was
extensively carried on in them day by day. Consequently,
explosions of coal-dust could not be regarded as anything
more than supplementary to explosions of fire-damp. Experiments might be pointed to in opposition to this view,
but experience would be found arrayed against those experiments. The thanks of the mining community were due
to Mr. Joseph Dickinson for recently taking a step to divert the pursuit of coal-dust extremes to a safer course.
In his Report on the Udston Colliery explosion, he subjected the coal-dust theory (which appeared to have been
ridden rather hard by some witnesses) to criticism, and suggested alternative views, giving fire-damp its due promi-
nence, and directing attention to the gas in the stoopings or
goaves. On p. 19 of his Report, the following paragraph
occurred : " The mine being dry and dusty, and the coal a

MR. WILLIAM MORGANS.

Splint coal of a highly inflammable kind, gives plausibility to the supposition that the explosion was aggravated by dust.   The evidence, however, showed that the main roads were the most dusty part of the mine, and not the rooms. It was, however, in the rooms not cut through and least dusty, that there were the greatest signs of coking, extending not quite up to the face, and not in the main roads, some of the principal coking being in rooms which were not at work."

Notwithstanding that light had been made of the danger of goaves, the authority of many inspectors of mines and of the late Royal Commission and of the Author was against him.   When he gave his reasons, it was clear that they would have to be greatly modified to harmonize with facts and with experience.   As regarded the ventilation of goaves, he thought the day had passed for appealing to that impracticable idea.   To ventilate the inaccessible ramifications of goaves, caused by the collapse of the broken roof strata over the excavated parts of a thick seam, was a physical impossibility.   What was euphoniously called the ventilation of goaves would be more correctly described as the ærating of goaves.   Unfortunately goaves could be ærified and brought to an extremely dangerous condition; and it could be shown that in ordinary cases it was impossible, if once goaves were permitted to exist, to prevent them from assuming that threatening character.   The most dangerous goaves were found in collieries where thick fiery seams were extracted and little rubbish remained to occupy the wastes; and it was in collieries answering to that description that the examples of the greatest explosions which had happened in this country must be sought.   It was the practice of allowing the roof to be crushed down in large masses which was the great mischief.   The fallen debris, by filling up the excavated plane of the seam and getting compacted therein, was very misleading in giving an idea that the goaves were closed, but the dangerous goaves were the cavities and ruins of the broken roof strata overhead and out of sight.   Goaves were by no means con-

MR. WILLIAM MORGANS.

fined to the plain of the seam. When the dislodged masses of roof strata were very hard, the interstitial spaces and arched cavities were a long time closing, and they formed gas-holding goaves, often many acres in extent, bordering on the workings. These magazines of fire-damp were in direct communication with the colliers, not only at the edges of the goaves, but through many joints and fissures developed in the roof, in consequence of not providing it with adequate support in the goaves. The strain thus set up in the roof converted what would be a safe top into a dangerous one, and increased the accidents by falls, which were the most prolific cause of fatalities in mines. This was an important port of the goaf question which should be mentioned, although he was now more particularly dealing with explosions. The remedy for the evils consisted in adequately stowing the goaves with rubbish, but he would not here enter upon the commercial considerations beyond expressing his convictions that, apart from the saving of life and limb, great pecuniary benefit would accrue to the coalmining industry and to the nation at large were the remedy applied. People must first be convinced that goaves were the cause of great disasters in mines.

A good test of the existence of dangerous goaves in a fiery colliery was the effect of barometric changes upon the condition of the return air. Whenever a rapid fall of the barometor caused a great increase of fire-damp in the return air, it might be concluded that the colliery was beset with dangerous goaves. This test had been incidentally confirmed in a Paper " On the Effect of Atmospheric Changes upon the Development of Fire-damp," read before the Manchester Geological Society, on the 1st of December, 1885, by Mr. J. S. Martin, H. M. Inspector of Mines,[1] dealing with experiments made in the Gabriel Colliery, near Karwin, in Austro Silesia. But whilst the presence of dangerous goaves could be detected during a decided fall of the barometer, they remained an element of risk in a col-

---

[1] Transactions of the Manchester Geological Society. Vol. xviii. p. 351.

MR. WILLIAM MORGANS.

iery under all barometric conditions, because gas might be suddenly expelled from them into the workings by a subsidence of the roof strata when the barometer was rising, or it might be exploded in the goaves by blasting elsewhere, or by some accident at any time independently of atmospheric conditions.

The views referred to by the Author on the goaf danger appeared in a little book on the " Solution of Colliery Explosions." In it Mr. Morgans had endeavored to strip the question of some of the glamor with which it had been surrounded ; but the chief point in view was to direct attention to a factor in colliery explosions which aggravated the goaf danger, and had been overlooked. That was the dangerous character of cracks and fissures in the roof strata (1) as affording means of ærifying fire-damp in goaves ; (2) as introducing unrecognized risk in shot firing, whereby gas might be ignited in an unseen crevice at or near the seat of the cartridge or charge ; and (3) as constituting avenues for the communication of the flame of an explosion from a working place or other point of origin to a goaf, and from one goaf to another over extensive ranges throughout the mine, without necessitating that the flame of the explosion should pass entirely through the ventilated ways and roads. The view thus indicated attributed the extension of the most violent and wide-spread colliery explosions to the firing of gas in the goaves and in the passages developed in the disturbed roof strata overlying the roads and workings of the mine. It accounted for the large falls often seen after explosions by the forcing down of the roof-beds, owing to the pressure of the explosions in their partings and joints. It explained the occurrence of conflicting blasts, or back explosions, bursting down into the roads at different points, and of apparently simultaneous explosions at parts of the workings very remote from each other, and other problems which could not be cleared up by the coal-dust theory. It suggested that the principal zone of the explosion was not necessarily in the plane of the workings, but ofttimes in the gas-charged goaves and roof strata overhead ; and that

9

Mr. William Morgans.

the courses of the explosion, instead of being restricted, as by the coal-dust theory, to the ordinary roads, were frequently to be traced in the disturbed strata immediately above.

One of the most conspicuous features of extensive colliery explosions had been the traces of violence, and of burning or charring, in widely separated districts or portions of the mine. To account for the transmission of the flame from one district to another had been an object for investigation for a long time. Investigators appeared to have confined their attention to the overt ways of the colliery; while the dangerous system of communication opened by covert ways overhead had been overlooked. It was impossible to account for the presence of fire-damp in most of those overt ways, since they were known to be abundantly ventilated. In this difficulty the coal-dust theory had been promulgated, and had done duty ever since. But it had certainly been accepted in some instances subject to the somewhat narrow view that an explosion must always pass through the roads forgetting the fact that it might often pass above and cross over the roads.

Dangerous goaves were not commonly found in thin seam workings, because the comparatively low wastes were usually so well stowed by the rubbish at hand as to prevent the wreck of the roof strata, and there was hardly a case on record of an explosion of magnitude in workings of that description, however dry, dusty, and fiery they might be. But workings in the thicker seams, where goaves were formed, owing to the insufficiency of the rubbish provided for stowing them, furnished the scene of almost every extensive colliery explosion on record, and all of the most disastrous and wide-spread explosions of the thirty-two on the Author's list had been confined to fiery seams of from 6 to 9 feet thick, or, in other words, to those precise conditions under which the most capacious and dangerous goaves were found to exist. Were not these grave facts which called for serious reflection? Was it not time that the investigation of the highly important goaf agency should be undertaken? It had long been neglected; it presented many features which demanded searching enquiry. Now that the Author had directed attention to the dangers of gas-holding goaves, it was to be hoped that the day was not far distant when they would be made a subject of thorough examination. At present, in some mines extensive surfaces of dust were watered whilst huge volumes of fire-damp were warehoused.

He readily joined in the expression of thanks due to all who had taken a prominent part in directing attention to coal-dust. Mr. Galloway had been more fortunate than many men in having his efforts freely recognized, and every one would feel glad to acknowledge the capacity he had shown. But the labors of other workers must not be forgotten, of men on the French, Prussian, and English Commission, and especially of the Author of the Paper now under discussion. In pointing out that the violence of explosions, where coal-dust was a prominent factor, would be far less pronounced than when fire-damp was the chief agent, the Author had, he believed, supplied a very valuable key. Mining engineers could never lose sight of their indebtedness in the first instance to Faraday. Whatever experiments might indicate, actual experience had so far taught them that there was very little in the coal-dust question beyond what Faraday disclosed and put upon record, although its importance might have been in danger at one time of being forgotten. Had the goaf agency received a tithe of the attention which had been devoted to coal-dust, the prevention of accidents in mines would have made much greater progress.

Mr. SYDNEY F. WALKER said he was rather surprised to find that the Author had not referred to electric signals as one source of the avoidance of accidents. It was perhaps a humble one, but he believed that it had saved many a broken leg, and possibly a good deal of damage to the road. With regard to casualties it was surprising that there were so few telephones in use in the working of mines. The

Mr. Sydney F. Walker.

amount of injury that a man received after an accident
varied very closely in proportion to the time taken by the
doctor in getting to him.   If the telephone were at work,
or could be attached to the existing signal wires, establishing a communication between the workings and the surface
a message could be sent that a man was hurt, and how, and
a good deal of valuable time might thus be saved.

With reference to the question of electric lighting, he
had under his own superintendence twenty installations at
different collieries, pit-bottoms, sidings and main roads; but
in no case had they been taken to the face to the coal.   In
one instance the farthest lamp was a mile distant from the
dynamo.   He would only refer to the matter in regard to
the question of cost.   There was no difficulty in maintaining the lamps day and night, and the cost came out at from
one-fourth to one-twelfth of the cost of gas.   In the case of
one-twelfth the gas was made at the colliery.   The main
point dealt with in the Paper, in regard to the illuminating
of collieries, was the lighting of the face of the coal.   He
thought that the eventual method of lighting the face of
the coal by electric light would be similar to that adopted
for the main roads, namely, from the supply mains.   His
experience, like that of every electrical engineer, was that
no matter what light was displaced, immediately the electric
light came on the ground the user was not satisfied with
the same amount of light that he had before.   No matter
whether a small candle was in use in a Cornish mine or a
large argand lamp in a lighthouse, a great deal more light
was wanted.   That was shown, he thought, by the avidity
with which the electric lamps exhibited in an adjoining room
were taken up, on account of the extra light which they
gave.   But it was impossible to go far in that direction
with a portable lamp, as the weight increased very rapidly
in proportion to the degree of light.   If, therefore, more
light was wanted, and both the collier and the colliery owner would very soon appreciate the advantages of more light,
it would become a question of providing it in another way.

MR. SYDNEY F. WALKER.

Then it should be borne in mind that at the same time the education of the collier was going on among the rising generation.

There were science schools in the villages, and miners were getting accustomed to the use of electricity and electric lighting in all parts of the mines, and when they discovered that by connecting the wires of a lamp, which possibly they carried in their pocket to their work, properly protected, they could have the light they needed, and that if the connection was broken they would have no light; when they arrived at that point there would be no serious difficulty in working from supply mains, properly and carefully fixed. Of course the grave danger would be the spark at the moment of connection; but it was by no means necessary that the final connection should be made in contact with the atmosphere. Many simple kinds of apparatus could be arranged to make the final connection out of contact. He might also mention that, from some experiments made by Mr. Mordey and himself, it had been proved that it was not a spark *per se* which ignited the gas, but a spark of a certain energy, and that that degree of energy did not exist at the end of a connection with a single lamp.

As to the question of primary versus secondary lamps, he agreed with the Author that the operation of charging any properly-designed primary lamp would be quite as simple as the operation of cleaning and re-filling existing lamps. He thought, therefore, if a portable electric lamp came into use, that the primary lamp offered the greatest advantages in the present state of knowledge possessed by electrical engineers and by colliers. A secondary battery lamp looked more simple, but it was not so in operation. If there were five hundred lamps to connect in the colliery, there would be at least two thousand connections, the greater portion of which would be hidden. The case was not on all fours with the mechanical arrangement of emptying out liquids and putting them in again. Connections might go wrong at any time without anything to show it. Then again, how was the current to be obtained? The Author had sug-

COLONEL PAGET MOSLEY.

gested that it could be got from the existing dynamo at
the colliery; but, in his opinion, to work from the existing
dynamo would entail a considerable amount of complica-
tion, because it would entail a series multiple arrangement,
which would be out of place at a colliery. He also most
strongly condemned all switches, resistances, and automatic cut-outs aud circuit-breakers for work in a colliery.
Strength and simplicity were wanted, nothing else.

COLONEL PAGET MOSLEY observed that it had been stated
in the course of the discussion that the lime-cartridge
system was quite unable to get coal from where the parting
between the roof and the coal was not a good one ; or, at
all events, where the circumstances were not exceedingly
favorable to the operations of any dislodging power. He
had had on many occasions ocular demonstrations of the
working of the lime in the collieries at Shipley, where the
system was first brought out. The top was there of a particularly sticky nature ; indeed, there was practically no
parting at all in a great part of the colliery ; so much so
that, when wedges were formerly employed to dislodge the
coal, after the wedges had dislodged as much coal as could
be got by that means there still remained a layer of 2 or 3
inches of very hard sticky coal, which had to be hacked off
the roof with picks, but the lime got the entire seam
down without leaving any coal on the roof. He regretted that Mr. Sebastian Smith, the inventor, was unable to be present, or he would have been able to give
many more instances of the lime acting perfectly well in
coal where the roof was of a very sticky nature. That had
been evidenced also by the reports of managers in collieries
where lime had deen tried on many occasions. The system only wanted fair play, and the fact that it was not
more largely adopted at present was perhaps in some measure due to the comments which were made by Mr. Stokes,
one of the Government Inspectors, on the conclusions at
which the Royal Commission had arrived with regard to
the lime process in a paper read before the Chesterfield
and Midland Counties Institution of Engineers. Those

comments were characterized by the Author as not being quite of a dispassionate nature; but ever since the system was brought out at the collieries at Shipley, Mr. Stokes had opposed it. He should have imagined that, as one of the Government Inspectors Mr. Stokes would have done all he could to encourage a system which, the Commissions stated, would in some seams perform work, quite equal to that done by powder, at no greater cost, and with absolute immunity from risk of explosion.

MR. HENRY HALL remarked that the Author was not a mining engineer, but men outside the profession would often hit upon expedients that men inside it might fail to see. The principal points for discussion were, in his opinion, the method of lighting mines, and the method of blasting. With regard to lighting, he contended that too much stress had been laid upon the necessity of procuring a large amount of light from the lamps. The Author had recommended glass lamps, but these, he thought, were subject to many more dangers than the old-fashioned lamp which had gauze round the flame. A glass lamp was often broken by heat, and it might also be broken by being dropped on stone, or by anything falling on it. More than a dozen glass lamps would be broken in a colliery against one gauze lamp. It was pointed out in the Paper that falls of roofs would be less frequent if the men had a good light. He did not himself believe that such accidents ever happened from a collier having a bad light. The collier judged of the state of the roof by sounding it and listening, and he could do that whether he had a good or a bad light. As to blasting in mines, if the water-cartridge was as safe as had been represented, it would no doubt prove to be the greatest blessing that had ever fallen to the lot of miners. But there were certain points which needed some precaution. The water envelope was a weak contrivance, and it had to be used in a rough way. A thousand shots might be fired in one day by all kinds of hands: and if it was something that the colliers could manage to make dangerous, some of them would be sure to effect that object.

COLONEL J. D. SHAKESPEAR.

With reference to dust, he did not think that any explosion had happened in a mine of importance where there was no fire-damp. Still, there could be no doubt that the presence of coal-dust did greatly aggravate explosions. A good deal had been said about tests for gas. Certain instruments had been recommended as likely to be useful for that purpose. The difficulty that he and others had met with was not that they could not find the gas, but that when found they did not know how to deal with it. Even if much finer tests were available the difficulty would not be removed. He had used some of the apparatus suggested, but he had always to fall back upon the ordinary Davy lamp. He believed it was possible to test gas with a Davy lamp better than with any other instrument. Liveing's instrument had been recommended, but he was very unsuccessful in its use. It appeared that the handle had to be turned at a certain fixed speed, and if it was not turned at that speed the effect was not always constant. There was one point, which, he thought, might have been entered into more fully by the Royal Commissioners. They might have given some information as to the explosive force of certain quantities of fire-damp. Officials found large volumes of gas here and there, but thought nothing of it, and said that it was not dangerous. It was difficult to say how much gas was dangerous. His own opinion was that a very small quantity, if it was really at the most explosive point, was very dangerous; but he had never come across any law on the subject.

COLONEL J. D. SHAKESPEAR objected to the idea that coal-dust exploded; all it did was to get hot in the flame of a lamp and then, from being in minute particles, it might be driven through the wire gauze by the ventilating current, and if at a white heat it would ignite any fire-damp present, whether in large or in small quantities. If coal-dust really exploded, coal-cellars would have been wrecked years ago. As to shot-firing its evil consequences were the concussion it gave to surrounding strata. With respect to the gunpowder and water-cartridge he contended that the gases, from the ignited powder, instantly overcame the extinguish-

ing influence of the water which the inventor vainly hoped
it might exert.   Much ingenuity had been expended on
electric safety-lamps, but he considered their intense brilliancy unsuitable to the hewer, since they cast a white beam
that in the extreme darkness of the surroundings materially
dazzled his sight.   Rather than a dazzling speck of light
close to him, a cutter of coal needed a diffused, soft light.
On Tyneside, gas had been found to escape from the surface
of the coal at a tension of 600 lbs. per square inch ; and at
Chester-le-Street, Mr. Lindsay Wood had found the tension
to be 464 lbs. per square inch, compared with which 50 lbs.
per square foot, the force of wind in a hurricane, was a
trifle.

Mr. STEPHEN HUNBLE observed that reference had been
made to an accident which was attributed to the failure of
the apparatus connected with a detaching hook.   At the
Houghton Main Colliery, where the accident occurred, the
depth of the shaft, from pit-bottom to the girders on which
the catch-plate was fixed, was about 570 yards.   The engines
were 1,000 HP., and under steam forty seconds, and at the
time of the accident the steam-brake had not been applied ;
consequently the force at which the cage went into the head-
frame had been computed to be equal to a dead shock of 90
tons, which that part of the head-frame was not capable of
sustaining ; and although the hook detached the rope, the
force of the overwind was so great as to tear away the bolts
holding the catch-plate to the girders, which with the hook
and cage dropped to the bottom of the shaft.   Here the
hook and catch-plate were found intact, and subsequently
put into use again.   Ten men lost their lives, but the accident was not attributable to the hook, and at the inquest
the evidence proved that the hook acted perfectly well, and
that the deaths occurred from the inadvertence of the
engine-man in overwinding.   At the neighboring colliery
of Messrs. Briggs, Son and Co., only a short time previously
a similar case of overwinding had occurred, and there the
hooks saved the lives of ten men ; and only that morning
he had received, from another neighboring colliery, a letter

Sir George Elliot.

which had been spontaneously written by Messrs. Pope and Pearson, stating that "during the six years we have had your 12-ton hooks in use at our Silkstone pit, where we work 1,000 tons per day, they have given every satisfaction. In a recent case of overwinding, the only one we have had, the action of the hook was all that could be desired."

SIR GEORGE ELLIOT, Bart., stated that he had had something to do, in consultation with Lord Cross, with the constitution of the Royal Commission on Accidents in Mines. It was thought that at a time like the present, when intelligence and education and all sorts of practical skill were combined, it would be well to have a hybrid Commission, including what he might term philosophers and practical men. The Commission was accordingly constituted on those lines, and its members had worked together very earnestly; their Reports supplied a vast amount of information which was worthy of the study of every young mining engineer, and of discussion at every mining institution in the country. He might mention that he had taken part in the formation of the first mining institution in Durham, as well as the first mining institution in Wales. He had also suggested, in a Presidential Address in 1868, that the Durham Mining Institution of Engineers should be connected with the Durham University, in order that they might have the assistance of the professors there, and the many collateral advantages co-operation with a University would supply. He had also suggested an alliance between the great mining institutions of the country and the Institution of Civil Engineers, which he hoped the present President would do his best to bring about, mining engineering and everything connected with it being closely associated with civil engineering. He was unable to go fully into the great question of how to lessen accidents in mines, to which both as an employer of labor, and as an active public man, he had given much anxious thought; but as he had been a member of the Institution nearly forty years, had been a member of the Royal Commission, and had been long and largely associated with mines, he felt it a duty not to let the opportunity pass of testifying before his brother professional men the keen and abiding interest he took in this vitally important subject.

Sir Warington Smyth said he proposed to make a few remarks upon the Paper, taking the various subjects in the order in which they had been presented. He should indeed be acting the part of an unnatural parent if he had any quarrel with, or were to be unduly critical of, the Paper, seeing that the Author, being no doubt aware of the repugnance with which the greater part of the public looked upon Blue Books, had put their joint report into a readable form ; and he hoped that much good might come of people taking up a book that was more convenient to read than the Blue Books, which they were so apt to thrust on one side. The Paper dealt with the whole of the subject which had been, after a very long period of thought and labor, brought before the Government as the Report of the Royal Commission. Some additional points, however, had been introduced at the beginning and in the course of the Paper, upon which alone he thought it necessary to say a few words. He agreed so thoroughly with the great bulk of the Paper, which was in fact mostly in the words of the Commission, that he had very little to say on those points which his friend and colleague had made so much his own, namely, explosions, blasting, and safety-lamps.

But since reference had been made to the history of legislation on the subject of mines from the year 1835, he could not help suggesting that it had not been legislation alone that had done the great good which had been undoubtedly accomplished. He had observed, throughout the whole country, the totally different tone which now actuated those who performed their duties as managers of mines ; and he found that the great exertions made by Mr. Nicholas Wood and others in the North, the establishment and active working of the Institutes of Mining Engineers, which began at Newcastle, and had since been caried out in almost all the important mining districts, had contributed quite as much if not more, to the safer condition of mines than any legislation

SIR WARINGTON SMYTH.

that had been passed.   He saw that instead of holding aloof
from one another as people did formerly, instead of attending
exclusively to their own occupation, men now met together to
discuss all the difficult points, to make long series of experiments, and to discuss them in the most fair and friendly
manner.   He saw that they had been upon the right road,
and that what had been accomplished in the Report of the
Royal Commission was really contributing to confirm them
in keeping that right road.   He allowed there was much
that the Commission had accomplished which was not new,
but which others had been previously driving at, and he
hoped that the authority conferred upon some of the statements made had proved a source of additional confidence
and satisfaction in those Institutes, and in the men who
composed them.   There was also another remark which he
desired to make in connection with the introductory part of
the Paper—that whilst there was a very strong feeling entertained by a part of the public that legislation could do
everything that everything was to be referred to some Act
of Parliament and some particular clause, and that a greatly
increased Government inspection should be introduced for
the purpose of rendering mines more safe, he must say
from his own experience he held that nothing could be more
pernicious or mischievous than the idea of substituting, for
the daily and hourly inspection of the agents in the mines,
any Government officials.   When it was remembered what
an extensive mine was, the miles of workings that had to
be gone through in order to examine the whole place
thoroughly, and that they had to be inspected every day by
a series of, it was to be hoped, very competent persons, any
notion of sending a Government official down even once
a week was preposterous, and might produce the worst
effects, in removing responsibility from those who were
constantly amongst their men and placing it on outsiders.

On what did the safety of a colliery depend? It depended
from hour to hour, it might be almost said from minute to
minute, upon the care and attention which were bestowed
upon every portion of it by the subordinate officials, who had

in the first place to go round the whole of the workings to see that they were safe, and then from time to time to visit the men at their respective places of work.   A man might go through a colliery and find everything perfectly safe, and in five minutes afterwards there might be a blower bursting out, and the whole condition of things might be changed. Or some careless person might go through a ventilating-door and leave it open instead of shut, and in five minutes after the Government Inspector had been there, the whole place, instead of being safe, might be in a condition of extreme danger. It was the same with regard to lamps and many other particulars with reference to collier-ies.   He held, therefore, that any idea of substituting an outside inspection for that daily and hourly care, which had to be expended upon the mine by subordinate agents, over-men, deputies, firemen, or whatever they might be called, was altogether out of the question.

The Author had pointed out the satisfactory results, which had been obtained during the last thirty years, in the great diminution of accidents from most causes—from explosions and from accidents by machinery in shafts. Undoubtedly an enormous advance had been made in that particular direc-tion, an advance which he thought was not exceeded in any other country.   But from other points of view the retrospect was not so satisfactory.   The Paper had stated the fact, that, of the average number of deaths which had occurred for several years past, 23 per cent. only were attributable to explosions, while over 40 per cent. were due to falls of ground or of the coal or mineral itself, and in other cases to falls from the roof or the sides made of other material, miscellaneous accidents forming about 35 per cent. The last two items had in one case been somewhat diminished, not greatly, and in the other case they hardly seemed to have diminished at all.   He would therefore say a few words upon both.   The accidents and the numbers of the deaths resulting from explosions and their consequences were extremely fluctuating.   Of course, where at one partic-ular colliery one hundred or two hundred men were car-

SIR WARINGTON SMYTH.

ried away at one fell swoop, such an occurrence would very much disturb the run of the numbers. But the accidents from falls of ground to which men were always subject, though they had some small fluctuations, kept at a very uniform level. The same thing occurred in regard to accidents from falls of ground in metalliferous mines, and also in the mines of Prussia, Belgium, and France.

The Author had very properly opposed the contention of some persons, that causes of explosions having long been well understood should be readily guarded against. It was sometimes stated, both in and out of Parliament, and sometimes in speeches, which were to be greatly deplored from their violence and misstatements, that all accidents of that kind were preventable. He very much objected to that term. The same thing might be said with regard to all the accidents of life—" If you had avoided doing such and such a thing you would not have slipped down on the pavement, you would not have been thrown from your horse, or upset in a boat." No doubt there were many colliery accidents the origin of which could be traced and reasoned upon, but it was by no means the case that they were always preventable. There were so many ways in which the accidents took place, as shown by the annual reports of the inspectors, that although their origin might be explained, they could scarcely be called preventable. For example, with the very best ventilation and the best safety-lamps, if gas broke out suddenly, accidents might be occasioned from various causes. There were safety-lamps for giving better light fitted and guarded with glass, but glass was a substance of a very uncertain nature, and, however carefully it might be fitted and examined, it might sometimes be so chipped that the flame might pass. Again, there were well authenticated instances in which a mere blow, by a pick on some quartzose material had inflamed the gas which was present perhaps in small quantities. He did not assert that any very serious accidents had occurred in that way. There was, however, the analogous case of the sparks produced by the steel mill in former days before the general introduction of safety-lamps.

SIR WARINGTON SMYTH.

Explosions on a considerable scale had actually been traced to the action of those sparks falling into a gaseous mixture from the action of the steel mill. And, if that were the case, the stroke of a miner's pick might in many cases, as it assuredly had in some, have been the cause of an explosion. He mentioned that matter because there was no working without a pick or a bar, and if they were capable of producing dangerous sparks only once in five hundred thousand times, that was a source of accident akin perhaps to others that might be mentioned.

With regard to shaft accidents, he was happy to agree with the Author that they had diminished in a most remarkable degree, and that the safety with which men were now conveyed to and from their work by means of machinery was really wonderful. It was, however, often proposed that the means at present in use should be supplemented by various other contrivances, and the subject of parachute for safety-clutches had often been brought into notice. Various ingenious contrivances of the kind had been exhibited, and he supposed it might be said that there were not less than fifty or sixty different contrivances for that purpose. But, considering the rapidity of the winding now needed in the coalfields of the North, he had a strong sympathy with a number of thoughtful mining engineers who considered that, by adding an apparatus of that kind, they were merely introducing a new source of danger. Nor could he help recollecting that in two remarkable cases of late years there had been fitted to certain shafts apparatus of that kind, considered to be the very best that could be obtained.

He was at the Botallack Mine a few years ago, when the subject of lowering the men to their work and bringing them up again was discussed by the agents. He told them that he had very strong suspicions about the apparatus, although they showed him that they had an automatic contrivance, which was sure to clutch the rails in such a way as to make it certain that if the rope broke the cage would be sustained. The shaft was an inclined plane about 400 fathoms

SIR WARINGTON SMYTH.

in length, and dipping at a steep angle.   They then resolved
in order to avoid every sort of risk, to employ a man who
should be thoroughly practised in dealing with the safety-
clutch by means of his arm.   He was to go down and come
up with every batch of men.   He was a very careful man,
and he went regularly up and down with the apparatus, the
rest of the "gig" being filled with miners.   But on one unfortunate day in 1863 the chain broke and the cage fell
away.   The clutch was unavailing, the automatic apparatus did not act, the man who had his hand upon the lever
which was to work it was either paralyzed, or lost his presence of mind, or something else occurred which prevented
its use, and all the men were smashed to death at the bottom of the shaft.   Then there was another case which occurred only two years ago at Duke Hardenberg Colliery, in
Westphalia, where no fewer than twenty-five men were
dashed to pieces at the bottom of the shaft in consequence
of the breakage of the rope, and the safety apparatus, which
had been approved by every one up to that point,.failing to
act.   He believed that there were gentlemen present, who
would bear him out in saying that they had not a sufficient
trust in any of the varieties of safety-cages at present introduced, to make use of them, instead of adopting the ordinary plan of getting the best plant they could, and constantly
looking to its being in good action.   He need not refer to
other causes, but he might mention that in several districts
of England, to his certain knowledge, there had been a number of safety appliances of that kind attached to some of
the collieries. Mr. Fourdrinier attached them to a number
of collieries which he saw about the year 1850, and more recently some ingenious kinds of apparatus had been applied
at other pits ; but it was a very significant circumstance that
they were now all taken away.   After owners had incurred
the expense of fitting out pits in that manner there must,
he thought, be some very strong practical objection to their
remaining, if they had all been removed in a few years.

   The importance of a good light in collieries and other
mines was a subject upon which the Author had properly

SIR WARINGTON SMYTH.

enlarged. That mining engineers were not asleep about those matters might be seen from the various experiments that had been made, and the various, lighting apparatus now on trial in different places. He would merely refer to one example. He had been struck, during the last two or three years, with the excellent progress made in the sinking of a very difficult shaft in the Foxdale Mine in the Isle of Man. This shaft had been sunk about 206 fathoms, a large proportion of it being in exceedingly hard granite, so that it would have taken a very long time to have proceeded upon the old plan; air compressors were introduced, and the whole boring was done by machine borers. High explosives were used in the shape of tonite, and a telephone was carried down to give instantaneous messages to and from the men. Four electric lamps were used at the bottom and four at the surface, so that the men could go on night and day. After 10,000 lbs. of tonite had been used in that way, he was glad to receive a report from the agent to say that, in that long-continued sinking, there had not been a single accident. He thought that that said a great deal for high explosives, as well as for the completeness with which all the other matters had been carried out. In fact, the agent stated that as long as tonite had been used—a period of five or six years—there had never been a fatal accident.

The Author had laid emphasis upon the different varieties of emission of fire-damp. Upon that subject he would only say, that, whilst doubt had been cast upon the alleged emission by sudden outbursts occasionally overpowering all possible ventilation at the time, the Royal Commissioners, during the progress of their examinations and their report, had had sufficient evidence to show, with the utmost clearness, that those accidents were unfortunately too common, having occurred over and over again, in connection with the increasing depth and other circumstances. He was himself not in a condition to throw the least doubt upon such statements, for he had once the misfortune of being at the bottom of a shaft in Abercarn Mine. Fourteen persons

10

were assembled at the bottom, when the floor suddenly began to heave. The men had only naked lights with them, but there was a supply of air from a compressor through a pipe a few feet above. After the first two or three heaves, there was a sudden upbursting of gas and water, violent enough to extinguish the whole of the lights. The kibble was signalled for instantly, it was lowered gently in the dark, and all the men were sent up in batches. It was found that, from the agency of the compressed air, in about an hour and a half the whole of the gas had been carried off ; but there were marks in the bottom of the heaving up of the ground, while at the same time an advance bore-hole was being made 3 feet in depth below the bottom, and yet the gas and water had been able to burst up the shale floor. He was not likely to forget a scene of that kind, and he therefore attached due importance to the phenomenon, which was now vouched for by so many able and trustworthy managers.

With reference to the remarks of Mr. Morgans as to the liability (about which not much was known) of open spaces existing sometimes, not for a very great height, but over a large area through the workings, the Royal Commission had paid some attention to that subject ; but he might say in addition that there could be no doubt that it was the source of considerable danger. A few years ago a terrific explosion took place in the Risca Pit. It was found that the explosion from a shot took place in the midst of a very strong current of fresh air, and those who had seen the place could not but adhere to the opinion that gas must have been about somewhere, that there must have been open spaces in communication by means of the cracks constantly made as the roof came down. There might have been such a communication as would have allowed some flame to pass through and thus ignite the gas. That, however, was a point, he thought, that required further investigation on the part of mine managers.

With regard to blown-out shots, there could be no doubt that they had been the origin of a great many accidents of

SIR WARINGTON SMYTH.

late years. Why should those shots be blown out? It arose mostly from mistakes in charging, or in applying them, or in not sufficiently cutting away the ground below or at the side to take fair advantage of the direction in which the shot was likely to blow. Such accidents were far less frequent in metalliferous mines. Why should that be the case? He believed it was simply because the men, instead of putting in a charge at right-angles to the face of work, were accustomed to weigh carefully every place in which they had to put a hole. They considered the physics of the subject, the direction of the joints, the surface of the face and the nature of the material, and then they put in the shot to correspond with those joints, taking care, by means of a little heavy pick-work, to break away the rock in such direction as to be able to take advantage of the line of least resistance. He thought that in collieries sufficient attention was hardly paid to that point; and, therefore, if shots were to be carried on, as they must be in a great proportion of the collieries, the plan referred to by the Royal Commission of taking up the Author's original idea of blowing a mass asunder, by means of a comparatively small charge of high explosive immersed in water, promised to be of the very highest value in collieries as well as perhaps in some other mines. When it was called to mind that the Author brought forward that principle in the year 1873 before the Royal Society, and then experimented upon it in the presence of his friends and colleagues at the Garwood Pit, in Lancashire, and remembering the results produced as compared with the results of other charges, it was somewhat amusing to find people now quarrelling over the patent rights for what the Author had opened out for the benefit of the public. The experiments were not simply made in the sight of the few persons present, but they were published by Mr. Smethurst for the advantage of the public in the year 1881. The only satisfactory point about it was that, while people were disputing over their patents for some little modifications, so much attention was being paid to the subject, and that a long

Sir Warington Smyth.

series of most valuable experiments had been made, especially those carried out in North Staffordshire with the
assistance of Mr. Sawyer, Her Majesty's Inspector in the
district.   He thought, if the Royal Commission had done
nothing else, it had done a valuable thing in starting and
furthering that view which was likely to lead to so much
good.

As to the question of the lamp, he thought he must join
issue with the Author in his onslaught, first on some of the
lamps, and secondly on the House of Lords.   There were
many districts in the country where no gas had been
perceptible from generation to generation.   Why should
lamps be forced upon people in such districts?   Why go
further (as had been done for some time past) than have a
law that, in fear of any gas accumulating, a man should go
round the whole of the works with an ordinary Davy lamp
in his hand, and test for gas.   It had been objected that an
ordinary Davy would not stand a current of explosive air;
but in the collieries to which he had referred, which were
scattered broadcast throughout the land, as in the Forest of
Dean, South Staffordshire, and other districts, gas was
never noticed, and it would be very hard upon the people
there to say to them: "You must not have a Davy or a
Clanny lamp; you must take some new patent lamp capable of withstanding the effect of a strong current."   In
many of the collieries there was no strong current, but
only just enough to bring the air quietly along.   He
thought that the present clause was a very fair one, that in
no districts should lamps be used which had not the authorization of the Secretary of State for the Home Department.   At the same time he was very glad to be able to
confirm the statement, that there were now several lamps
quite capable of standing against any current likely to be
brought against them.

Reference had been made by a previous speaker to the
enormous pressure under which gas issued from the body
of the coal, but he thought that that point was a little mis-
understood.   Besides having lamps capable of resisting any

SIR WARINGTON SMYTH.

currents likely to be produced in a mine, it would also be desirable to have lamps free from the objections made to the more complicated ones, that they were not so convenient to test for gas as the ordinary Davy. The simple Davy had been very largely used, but he had been assured by a very competent authority, Mr. Lindsay Wood, that the Cased Davy, or Tin-Can Davy, the lamp placed in a cylinder in which a good part of the front was glass, was capable of testing for gas just as well as the open Davy, and that it was a thoroughly safe lamp for all ordinary conditions. He stated that his firemen were now using it, and that they could see the effect of the gas flame within just as well as they could with the ordinary Davy. At the same time he might mention that Mr. Sawyer had very carefully made a long series of experiments, which he had published, and he held that he could test for gas more satisfactorily by means of a Mueseler lamp than by any other. The glass of most modern lamps had been objected to by many old stagers, who were competent to give an opinion; but a still greater objection was that most of them were covered with a cap or bonnet, which gave a greatly increased heat to the lamp, and concealed everything above a certain plane in which the light was given out. He could not help thinking that that was a very serious matter. It tended to make miners wish to pull the cover off, as it prevented them from seeing what was doing in the lamp and whither they were going. They had to look to their feet to see that they did not run against a pulley, and at the same time to their heads to see that they did not strike against the beams. It was very important that light should be given freely on all sides, so that the men might be able to look both up and down.

The question of the setting and drawing of timber was a most serious matter. It would be remembered that by far the greatest proportion of accidents happened under circumstances where protection could only be hoped for by setting the timber suitably and in good time. Lack of skill and promptitude, and a want of coolness and courage, were the

SIR WARINGTON SMYTH.

circumstances under which many men lost their lives from not setting up timber at the proper time and in a proper way. But in collieries they stood on *terra firma;* there was a more or less horizontal plane to prop from, and everything was comparatively simple. When, however, those conditions were reversed, as in a metallic mine, where, instead of a solid horizontal ground, the deposit on which the working took place stood upon end, nearly perpendicular, and the men had to stand upon movable platforms, or upon thin pieces of plank, or some slippery ledge, then it was that skill, experience and courage on the part of the men were needed in an extra degree. It was under those circumstances that so many accidents occurred, which could not always be prevented. They were due to the fact that when men were underground they were subjected to the action of gravitation, tending to make everything fall about them. It was for that reason that he passed to the final subject, upon which he proposed to make a few remarks. It was impossible to begin that sort of experience too young. Unless men went early to mining, and got accustomed to use the pick and shovel and shooting-gear, they never became familiar with it ; and therefore it was not to be wondered at that many working men now-a-days complained, amongst other things, that people were put in charge of a working place who were not capable of protecting either themselves or their mates. Men taken from agriculture, or other fields of labor, after a certain age never learned the thing properly, but were a source of constant difficulty and danger. When, therefore, he saw men like Mr. Pickard, the late miner's agent at Wigan, an excellent collier, and scores of others, who told him that they had gone into the pit at ten years of age, and had passed though all the successive stages of the work, he believed that those men, to say nothing of their thews and sinews, formed a much better class of men than those who were brought up to the age of fourteen or fifteen to hold nothing heavier than a slate pencil or a pen. It was the constant wielding of their mining implements, and the skill acquired in setting timber, that made men cool afterwards and prompt to assist one another, and to act in such a way as might tend to reduce the number of accidents occurring from falls, somewhat in the same proportion as that in which they had been happily reduced, in other branches of mining over which scientific agencies could exercise a greater control.

MR. A. R. SAWYER proposed, owing to the great amount of matter brought forward, to confine his observations to a few points only, namely, those to which he had lately given his greatest attention. As the Author had been good enough to allude to his book on 'Timbering,' he might be permitted to read a few lines from Chapter IX., "Accidents in Mines arising from Falls of Roof and Sides," pp. 18 and 19, which were of importance at the present time, when special rules were being made under the new Coal Mines Regulation Act :—" From many years' observation of the nature of accidents from falls of roof and sides, the writer is of opinion that the best way to reduce the number of these accidents is to establish rules for timber setting at every colliery, prescribing definite maximum distances, and other matters in connection with timbering and packing. All rules in connection with timbering must be based on the method of working, the nature of the roof and the inclination and thickness of the seams. These differ considerably, even at the same colliery, and at times in the same seam. These rules should be made by the manager, to the best of his ability, in conformity with the experience which he gains of the seam, and should be liable to alteration at any time in accordance with altered conditions or evidence of insufficiency. The enforcement of such rules would not only ensure regularity, but would indicate to fresh workmen the best and most approved manner of keeping themselves safe in seams in which they may perhaps have had no experience. Only maximum distances can, of course, be prescribed. It will frequently be necessary to set timber over and above the requirements of the rules. The erection of these additional supports must be left to the discretion and judgment of those immediately em-

MR. A. R. SAWYER.

ployed, who alone are cognizant of the momentary changes which the roof and sides present." It was therefore most important, as the Author had pointed out, that the men should be properly trained in the operations of timbering, and it was with a view to assist them in acquiring information, bearing on the subject, that he brought out the book. As many men, however, and these often well qualified men, had been killed by falls owing to over-confidence as from ignorance, and he thought that such rules would restrain the over-confident, as well as instruct the inexperienced. If rules were thought too binding, the requirements might be presented in the form of advice, as had been done at the Dukinfield and other collieries.

He thought it was idle to try to establish a connection between barometrical variations and colliery explosions. He was perfectly satisfied that a barometrical depression would cause gas to issue out of old workings containing it, but the gas need not necessarily be ignited, and so no explosion need follow. If, as used more generally to be the case formerly, this gas had to pass over a furnace, and was not sufficiently diluted by mixing with air before reaching it, an explosion would certainly ensue; so that the connection which it was sought to establish was dependent on another factor, namely, the presence or absence of flame. Two explosions, the causes of which he had had to inquire into, occurred at the same colliery within a short space of time from that very cause. A dumb drift was then constructed; and although gas still flowed out of the old workings invariably with a descending barometer, no explosion had since taken place nor could any take place. Many explosions were due to causes which would have existed under any barometrical variation. Approaching barometrical depressions were soon detected by observant firemen, as outflows of gas were sure to show themselves at some point or other in most collieries, if not before, at least quite as soon as any barometrical indication. At some collieries the men were withdrawn when a barometrical depression reached a certain point. The quantity of air passing

MR. A. R. SAWYER.

through the workings should possess a sufficient margin to cope effectually with an increased quantity of gas due to barometical depression.   He had noticed that some explosions, presumably caused by a blown-out powder-shot, had occurred when the barometer was very high and the thermometer very low.

In a Paper on " The Temperature and Moisture of Air-Currents in Mines,"[1] he had pointed out from observations made at the Dukinfield and other collieries, that the difference between the quantity of vapor in a cubic foot of air on the surface and in the return was greater the lower the temperature was on the surface, and he thought that on very cold days the air, by taking up moisture during its passage through the mine, owing to its temperature being raised as it proceeded along the workings, might have a drying effect on the coal-dust and make it more susceptible to ignition by the flame of a blown-out shot.

With regard to the supposed great sensitiveness of the Mueseler lamp, he would say that the Mueseler lamp was much liked by those who had become accustomed to its use, and the men who had once become accustomed to it were as wedded to it as they once were to the "Old Davy." This lamp could be tilted long enough to examine the roof without being extinguished, and if preferred, he had found Mr. Brooks' reflector a convenient and effective adjunct for that purpose.   He invariably carried his own Mueseler lamp during inspections, and had seldom known it to be extinguished under ordinary circumstances, even in steep mines, although once in his hand he did not give it any further thought.   The proper handling of it became instinctive.   As a rule, especially in fiery mines, even Mueseler lamps should be bonneted, but the bonnets should be easily movable to facilitate an examination of the gauze by the fireman.

With reference to lamp glasses, experiments made by Mr. Haines, Assoc. M. Inst. C. E., Secretary of the North

(1) Transactions of the North Staffordshire Institute of Mining and Mechanical Engineers, vol. viii. p. 8.

Mr. A. R. Sawyer.

Staffordshire Institute of Mining and Mechanical Engineers, and himself, showed that a cracked glass was not necessarily unsafe. In several of these experiments the lamp glass was cracked by the gas flame, which continued to burn within the lamp without any bad effects. Even where these cracks extended to all parts of the glass the pieces were kept in their places by the top and bottom rings, and in no case allowed the flame to pass, showing the necessity of well-fitting top and bottom rings. Though these experiments were reassuring, as showing that no immediate danger was to be apprehended from a cracked glass, especially when the crack was a perfectly vertical or diagonal straight, clean fracture, yet the moment a glass cracked the light should at once be put out, as a piece of the glass, if detached by a three-cornered crack, might fall out by a subsequent knock on the lamp. In these experiments lamps were also tilted at an angle of 45°. In the Marsaut and Clanny, with an ordinary flame, the glass cracked after from thirty seconds to one minute, while the Mueseler was extinguished before this could occur, which spoke in favor of the Mueseler type of lamp.

With regard to the clause, in the new Coal Mines Regulation Act, concerning the conditions which shall determine the safety of lamps, he believed it would be found in practice to meet all the requirements of those who would have preferred a more specific prohibition of certain lamps. The sense in which it was understood in his neighborhood was all that could be desired, and these unprotected lamps were rapidly disappearing in all fiery mines. The safety of an unprotected gauze lamp, when it was carried against an inflammable current of the smallest velocity, depended entirely on the rate at which the person who was carrying it was travelling, and this varied much and could not be regulated. An explosion occurred the other day which was attributed to a Davy lamp, which was being carried by a collier, who was hastening in a direction contrary to that of an inflammable current, which at that place had a velocity of only 2 feet per second ; so that this showed that an un-

MR. A. R. SAWYER.

protected gauze lamp might not always be safely carried in an inflammable current of even the smallest velocity. He had made a table showing graphically the different sizes and shapes of "blue caps" produced by different percentages of gas in the air, and this was now put up in a conspicuous position at most of the North Staffordshire Collieries, and was serviceable in educating firemen and colliers with regard to the importance of even small caps.

With regard to coal-dust; the explosion which fully convinced him that coal-dust, with possibly the faintest trace of fire-damp, was sufficient of itself to cause an extensive explosion, through ignition by a badly-placed powder-shot, was the one which occurred at the Great Fenton Colliery in 1885. It was fully described in the Inspectors' Reports for that year. He had made numerous experiments with the water and the gelatinous cartridges, and placed the result of his observations before the North Staffordshire Institute of Engineers recently,[1] though these experiments began in May, 1885. He had come to the conclusion that if properly manipulated they were perfectly safe, but he thought it important to warn firemen and shot-firers that much depended on themselves to ensure perfect safety, and that this warning would become the more necessary later on, when the novelty of these cartridges had worn off, and when from their introduction fewer explosions occurred, thus having the effect of lulling them into a false sense of security. He saw these cartridges in use in the mines of North Staffordshire almost daily, and they had now been in use some years, with the satisfactory result that for that time such a dangerous coalfield had been exempt from explosions. The manner in which the gelatinous compound of Messrs. Heath and Frost's cartridge was blown out with a blown-out shot was interesting. From microscopical examinations made by Mr. C. M. Stuart, Fellow of St. John's College, Cambridge, it appeared that the front portion of it was honeycombed with bubbles of hot gases,

---

[1] Vol. viii. p. 266 *et seq.*

MR. A. R. SAWYER.

and was much dispersed or spread, but some portion of it, presumably from the back of the cartridge, was evidently only sucked out in small lumps, without spreading. It would be well to know whether, by the hot gases being so subdivided, much the same result was not obtained with this compound as with moss. A number of experiments which he had made with it pointed to this conclusion.

With regard to the lime-cartridge, he would bring forward the experience gained by Mr. Bridgett, Manager of the Chatterley Coal and Iron Co.'s Collieries at Bucknall, which he could fully corroborate from personal and frequent observation. The Author had referred to the variable thicknesses and inclinations of the seams of coal in North Staffordshire. The Bucknall Mines had an inclination of 30° and a thickness of from 4 feet to 5 feet. Owing to their being in part extremely fiery, powder had been entirely dispensed with by Mr. Bridgett, and he had found lime-cartridges particularly suitable for getting the coal. Since the introduction of the high explosives with their safe surroundings, he had adopted them in one of the seams which was a particularly difficult one to get with lime, owing to the coal adhering strongly to the roof. In an ordinarily dry mine he had never heard of any complaints from handling the coals with the slight deposit of hydrate of lime, but the falling of the coal was accompanied by the distribution of some portion of it in the air in the form of fine dust. This was only a slight objection in a well-ventilated mine in which it was immediately carried away, but if the ventilation was defective it might remain suspended in the air for some time, and that was objectionable. He believed a person might be killed by the discharge of a blown-out lime-shot if he stood immediately in front of the hole after the lime was wetted. The dangerous moment was from one minute to two minutes after the lime was watered; if the stemming was strong enough to hold the lime then, it would hold it during the whole of the time that the action was going on. The heat produced during the slaking process was no doubt very great, but it

MR. A. R. SAWYER.

was hardly sufficient to ignite gas. He had himself charged a hole in a very fiery colliery, with gas abounding in the place, without its being ignited, and this confirmed the Author's view of the matter.

The cost of the lime-cartridges as compared with the new cartridges was found to be slightly less, when the greater amount of round coal produced was taken into account. In steep mines the districts were more circumscribed than in flatter mines, and as the new cartridges required special persons to charge and fire them safely, and in some cases even to make them up at the face, more men would be needed for that work; whilst with the lime-cartridges, which were manipulated by the stall men themselves, the cost entailed by special shot-lighters was dispensed with. Comparing the lime-cartridges with explosives generally, there was a constant temptation with the latter, as Sir Warington Smyth had pointed out, to neglect the holing and cutting of the coal. It was sought to make the explosives do what should be done with the pick. This at some collieries conduced to make the men slovenly in their work, and it was from this cause that so many explosions had occurred from badly placed and fast shots, as he had pointed out lately in a Paper on blown-out shots.[1] With lime-cartridges there could not be such a temptation, as it was absolutely necessary to properly cut and hole the coal if it was to be removed by that means. In some seams it would then be found that, if properly cut and holed, the coals would come down without the intervention of the lime. Many accidents had occurred almost immediately after a shot had been fired, the roof or side having been shaken by the concussion of the explosive, whereas if the lime-cartridge had been in use, the piece of roof would, probably, have kept its place long enough to enable the workmen to remove the coal and set the necessary props. With explosives, props were also frequently knocked out, which was seldom the case where lime-cartridges were

---

(1) Transactions of the North Staffordshire Institute of Mining and Mechanical Engineers, vol. viii. p. 209.

Mr. A. R. Sawyer.

used, and this was particularly important with a bad roof.
Danger from missed shots with explosives could occur
from two causes: (1) where the mode of lighting the
charge was by means of a fuse there was danger from
returning to the shot too soon; it was well known that a
shot might go off from twenty to thirty minutes after it
had been lighted; and (2) all missed shots, whether lighted
by means of a fuse or by electricity, were dangerous owing
to the charge being necessarily and rightly left in the
coal, according to the Act, until it was blown down by
another shot. and then recovered by breaking up the coal.
Where high explosives were used, a blow on the detonator might cause the charge to explode, and in the case of
powder a spark produced by the tool might cause it to
explode with fatal effects to those engaged in the work.
An instance had occurred to his knowledge in which a
powder-shot missed fire, and the piece of stone which contained it was displaced by another shot. Whilst this
piece was being split up the powder exploded and killed
the unfortunate workmen. These were accidents which of
course could not occur with lime-cartridges.

He had recently made several experiments with Mr.
Mould's patent coal-getter. There was no time to describe its construction further than to say that it was a
hydraulic machine, the water necessary for its action
being contained in the machine itself, and that, contrary to
other such machines, its action was outwards. The experiments which he had witnessed had been satisfactory when
the getter was properly applied, and he believed that the
principle of its action was the right one. He considered it
very important that none of these safe methods of removing coal should be discountenanced in any way, and that no
one should be deterred by the difficulties which the want
of practice in the first instance necessarily entailed, as these
difficulties were frequently overcome by further experience.
With regard to the prevention of explosions, he was particularly anxious that the lime-cartridge and mechanical coal-
getters should receive all the encouragement possible, as

they were absolutely safe. The high explosives, with their safe surroundings though perfectly free from danger when properly used, were more or less dependent on human treatment for their safety and though he was quite satisfied that the risk of an explosion was very greatly reduced where they had taken the place of powder, it would be desirable to have some other method of coal-getting to resort to, in case future experience were to show that these cartridges failed either from misuse or from a neglect of the ventilation, owing to a belief in their infallibility under any conditions. In conclusion he would express his sense of the indebtedness of the mining community to the late Royal Commission for its very arduous labors, and to the Author in particular for his valuable communications. The steadily diminishing death-rate in the North Staffordshire coalfields from one hundred and three persons killed in 1880, to twenty-six killed in 1886, could not but have been promoted by the stimulus given to the question of safety by the Commissioners' labors, and they were sure to bear still further fruit in future.

MR. A. GILES, M. P., hoped it would not be allowed to go forth from the Institution that its members advocated the employment in mines of boys under ten years of age. It would be remembered that an Act of Parliament was passed last session providing that no boy under the age of twelve should be allowed to go underground.

MR. R. BEDLINGTON said that some explosions might be due to other causes than those that had been mentioned. He remembered a case of several men timbering during the night, and a fall ensuing while they were at work the concussion put out their lamps. The fireman coming up found the heading full of gas. He turned on one side and waited for some time, and then the gas disappeared. He went up to the men who were in the dark and found that there was no appearance of gas. If there had been an explosion in that case there would have been nothing to show how it occurred. He remembered another case in which there was a rupture making an opening in the floor. The

MR. R. BEDLINGTON.

gas came from the seam below in large volumes, and overcame the ventilation for a considerable time, but after
a while the issue of gas ceased. So in many cases it was
difficult to account for explosions that took place. There
might have been a sudden emission, but there was no
subsequent appearance of gas.

As shown in the Paper the loss of life from explosions
was 23·17 per cent. ; and although the source of only one-
fourth of the total loss of life, public attention was drawn
much more to this class of accidents than to others, because
of the great number of lives lost at one time. When an
explosion took place the proportion burned to death was
very small, seldom reaching 10 per cent. The great loss of
life was due to suffocation. This arose from the air-doors
being smashed, and the course of the ventilation being
stopped through the greater part of the workings, the air
taking the shortest course to the upcast. Where fans were
used, they should as far as possible be fixed in positions
that would not be affected by the rush of air after an explosion. In several cases they had been so damaged as to
be useless for some time after an explosion. With ventilating furnaces the ventilating power was not much affected
by an explosion. Assuming that the ventilating force was
continued, the weak points were the air-doors. To lessen
the risks from suffocation after an explosion, it appeared to
him that the following arrangement might be adopted.
Let the return air-way be at the top of the range, and the
system of ascensional ventilation be carried out as far as
possible. The splits of air should be as numerous as the
total volume would permit of, so that each split was sufficient to properly ventilate the area assigned to it. The
coursing of the air would then be as follows :—Passing
from the downcast along the intake, No. 1 split would be
coursed through the panel, or district, it had to ventilate,
and then pass into the return air-way on the rise, the
quantity allowed being regulated by a wall near the entrance
to the return, strongly built in mortar, with an opening of
the proper size. The same thing should be done with the

Mr. R. Bedlington.

other splits. If an explosion took place in No. 1 split, and if the doors were broken within that area, the air would still pass through in the most direct course, and would continue in the other districts. At present, when an explosion took place, nearly all the ventilation was cut off from the workings owing to the smashing of the air-doors, and so the men were suffocated. In many cases the men were able to run some distance, but at last they dropped down.

He was not yet convinced that dust alone would cause an explosion. If it did, explosions would be very frequent; but without contesting the matter he allowed that where much dust was about a gas explosion was aggravated by it. It was therefore desirable that the dust should be damped, and also for the reason that it was so injurious to health to breathe it. The temperature of the mine also would be cooled by the damping. A good system had been adopted of laying pipes from the pumping lift, along the level headings into the working places, with fine sprays at the requisite distances. The dust was thus damped and the temperature reduced continually without attendance. No doubt there had been many improvements in safety-lamps, making them safer in strong currents; but he thought that the electric lamp, such as Swan's, Pitkin's, etc., would be the safest of all to work by. At present they were heavy and expensive, in future he trusted these objections would be modified; yet the Davy lamp would be generally used for examinations by the firemen.

The greatest loss of life arose from falls of roofs and sides, being 40·77 per cent. In the South Wales coal-basin there were dangers in working coal which were not met with, or not to such an extent, in other districts. He thought the roofs there were generally weaker than in most districts. The slips in the coal ran into the roof, and so caused a breach of continuity. Slants, threads, bells, and large nodules of ironstone also occurred. The principal seams of coal in South Wales ran up to a thickness varying from 5 feet to 9 feet, and the thicker the coal the more

11

MR. EDWARD COMBES.

danger there was in working it. This was especially the
case where the seam consisted of two or more veins with
partings of shale. As the collieries became deeper the
pressure increased, and it became more difficult to support
the roofs, etc. The only means that could be adopted were
careful timbering, double timber and props, with close
packing of goaves to sustain the roof, holing props where
the coal was being holed, and props against overhanging
parts of the coal. The question of timbering had been well
considered by the managers and workmen in Wales, and
their opinion generally was that it was best for the collier
to timber and secure his working place, and not depend
on deputies. Such was the evidence before the Royal
Commissioners. A collier was always present during the
working hours, noticing the varying condition of his working place, and could promptly do what was necessary to
make it safe. Of course for general repairs timberers were
kept. It was surprising that so much as 35·66 per cent.
of the loss of life was due to miscellaneous causes. Over-
winding was of rare occurrence at the Welsh collieries, and
great credit was due to the enginemen. At some collieries
the appliances for the prevention of overwinding were fixed,
but a majority of the managers thought it was best to
depend on careful men, good machinery, and brakes. It
was hardly necessary for him to speak of the great importance of good ropes, with a great margin of strength. Of
late years mechanical haulage had been largely adopted,
and there was now more liability to injury of persons than
when the slow haulage by horses was employed. The man-
holes, or refuges, were now 10 yards apart, instead of 20,
and therefore it was hoped the danger would be lessened.

MR. EDWARD COMBES, C.M.G., wished to point out a
class of accident to which no allusion had been made either
in the Paper or in the discussion, and his object in speaking
was simply to invite the attention of the Author to the
subject. In goaves or old workings large volumes of carbonic acid gas, or choke-damp often accumulated, and
when any extensive fall of the roof took place, this deadly

agent was, sometimes, by the consequent compression of the air, forced into the workings with fatal results to the miners, who were immediately suffocated. In some Australian mines, where no fire-damp existed, this had been a fruitful source of accident, and had several times come under his notice. The question, he was aware, was one of ventilation ; but it was rather a difficult one, inasmuch as with a rolling floor in a worked-out part of the mine, the levels would vary so much, that in the lower portions the heavy choke-damp would find space in which to accumulate. Even when completely isolated, unless the brattices were made exceptionally strong, a heavy fall might cause sufficient pressure to blow them out and force the gas to positions where men were employed. This danger would escape the notice of any Government inspector. He therefore endorsed what Sir Warington Smyth and others had said with regard to the constant and careful inspection by responsible employees of mining companies, as affording better protection than the periodic inspection by Government officers.

Mr. GEORGE SEYMOUR said he wished to speak rather as a metalliferous than as a coal-mining engineer. Although the Paper, on which the discussion was founded, was in every respect an admirable one as regarded accidents in collieries, the Author had, after all, only taken one side of the question, since he had made no allusion to the frequent accidents and grave loss of life which occurred from time to time in metalliferous mines. It was, of course, true that the number of men employed in the latter amounted to but a fraction of those employed in collieries, and that consequently the output from coal-mines was vastly greater ; but, nevertheless, metalliferous mines had in days past contributed enormously to the wealth of the country, and still continued to do so, notwithstanding foreign competition ; whilst the value of the metallic, as compared with the carbonaceous products, was in itself to a certain, although limited, extent, an equalizing factor as regarded the relative importance of the output in such instances. The

MR. GEORGE SEYMOUR.

accidents in coal mines were, consequently, to-day, ton per ton, far more numerous than in metalliferous mines; but a hundred years ago this was not the case.   The proportion of accidents in 1886 in English coal-mines from falls of rock was 48 per cent., and in metal mines 32 per cent., so that, after all, the difference was not very great.   Falls of roof in collieries were naturally more numerous than in metalliferous mines, since in the latter instance the workings were more or less vertical, whereas in the former there was what might be termed an almost constant horizontality of roof, and consequently a greater natural liability to falls, attended frequently by most disastrous results.   Whilst, owing to the generally vertical character of the workings, and the greater hardness and cohesion of the rock, such accidents were rarer in metalliferous mines; still they were not of unfrequent occurrence, and a few years ago four men were killed in Cornwall through an enormous rock falling upon them in the "winze," or underground shaft, in which they were working.

The most fertile causes of accidents in metalliferous mines were, however: 1. Explosions, due to carelessness in tamping or injudicious handling of explosives; 2. Falls from ladders or man engines.   The latter cause was one which rarely occurred in the deep American mines, owing to the custom almost universally prevalent in that country of raising the men by mechanical means.   It should, however, be borne in mind that the workings in this case were planned and laid out *ab initio*, with a view to this method of development; whereas in the Cornish mines, many of which had been worked for centuries, the tortuousness and irregularity of the shafts rendered such a mode of haulage impossible, whilst the expense of sinking perpendicular shafts through hard rock to a great depth could not reasonably be entertained.   It was not an unusual thing for a Cornish miner to walk 5 or 6 miles to his work, climb down from 300 to 400 fathoms on ladders, work an eight-hours' shift on a close end, and then climb back to the surface, carrying a heavy load of tools to be sharpened.

MR. GEORGE SEYMOUR.

Under these circumstances, the frequent occurrence of accidents of this description was not a matter for surprise. So long, however, as the present system remained, such accidents were inevitable. As regarded accidents in collieries, he would express his opinion that it was quite unnecessary, as contended by Mr. Morgans, that in order for a lamp to be safe, it should be able to withstand the velocity of current produced by an outburst of gas. Should such extreme safeguards be insisted upon, in all commercial undertakings, there would be a serious limit to enterprise. Seldom, if ever, had an explosion taken place when safety-lamps were used at the point and at the time of an outburst. In order to get an explosion with a safety-lamp—say such as Mr. Bainbridge had described—in the immediate vicinity of an outburst, three conditions were indispensable: 1. The outburst ; 2. An explosive atmosphere caused by the explosion ; 3. A lamp in the exact position where the speed of the expelled gas would strike it with velocity greater than 30 feet per second. It was exceedingly improbable that a combination of such conditions would occur simultaneously; and if colliery managers were expected to anticipate such coincidences, their attention would have to be diverted from objects far more conducive to the safety of the men and material under their charge.

In conclusion, he wished to remark that, although the Author had devoted several pages to the question of gas indicators, experience had demonstrated that these were of but little practical use. The inspection of all fiery mines was now virtually continuous, and the true check upon danger was such a constant examination of the different parts of the mine, as would render the existence of a small quantity of gas in any particular locality of very little if of any importance. The manager of the fiery mine would watch not so much for the returns which carried away the gas yielded by the mine, but would aim, by constantly and vigilantly watching the working faces, at conveying such a regular and sufficient current of air round the faces in question, as would cause the returns to consist of air containing a safe and regular quantity of gas.

MR. HENRY HARRIES said that the Author had stated, that the Royal Commission had come to the conclusion that no general connection had been established between colliery explosions and barometric changes; but in the preceding paragraph of the Paper, and in two or three other places he had observed that a fall of atmospheric pressure might be attended by an escape of gas to a dangerous extent. The discrepancy was only another instance of the differences of opinion existing on the question of the emission of fire-damp in connection with barometrical fluctuations. Although, however, there was some confusion on the question, it would be conceded that the vast majority of both miners and the general public had great faith in the idea that explosions were experienced only with a low barometer. He had carefully examined the occurrence of explosions in connection with weather changes, not dealing with the variations at individual stations, as had been the custom hitherto, but taking into account the distribution of pressure all over the country and throughout Western Europe. He had taken European and American explosions, and instead of finding that they were experienced only with a low barometer, he had found that they seldom occurred at such times, but mostly under opposite conditions. A great deal of the prevalent opinion was due to the practice of newspaper reporters and writers, who appeared to be imbued with Mr. Buddle's opinion with regard to explosions, and generally ascribed disasters to a deficiency of pressure, whereas a little enquiry would disclose the facts to be otherwise. That, however, was not peculiar to this country, for he found in a leading French coal-trade journal the statement that fire-damp explosions were almost invariably coincident with a marked diminution of pressure. A disastrous explosion at Quaregnon, near Mons, in March last, was commented upon in the Belgian press as having taken place with a very low barometer. Mr. Lancaster of the Brussels Observatory took up the question, and pointed

MR. HENRY HARRIES.

out, in *Ciel et Terre*, how misleading the newspapers were upon the subject. The explosion was one of a series which took place during the march of a large anti-cyclone from the Atlantic. The first explosion was in the Rhondda Valley on the evening of February 18th. Then on the arrival of the anti-cyclone in the south of France on February 23d, there was the Riviera earthquake. On the morning of March 1st, when the centre of the anti-cyclone had reached Central France, the Chatelus mine, near St. Etienne, exploded, and ninety lives were lost. Then, moving northwards, the anti-cyclone was directly over the district where it was stated in the Belgian press that the barometer was low, whereas it was about 30·5 inches. It was not until a week afterwards that the barometer descended at Brussels to 30 inches. The Author had given a list of the principal explosions that had taken place in the eleven years 1875–1885. Mr. Harries had gone through the list with the distribution of pressure for each day, and he had found that instead of following what was supposed to be the general rule, only six out of the thirty-two had taken place when the barometer was at 29·5 inches or below ; in other words, only 18·75 per cent. occurred with a low barometer, while the deaths in the same amounted to 17·4 per cent. of the total loss. Even out of the six with a low barometer it was observable that three occurred when the barometer was rising rapidly. On the occasion of the great disturbance in January 1884, the barometer had risen 0·75 inch in twelve hours, when the Naval Steam Coal Colliery at Penygraig exploded, another, but slight, explosion taking place on the following day at Rowley, the mercury still rising. With the remaining twenty-six disasters the barometer ranged between 29·8 and 30·7 inches. Time did not permit of his entering fuller into the details of each explosion, but he might mention that in the present year, when the Walker Colliery accident occurred, five weeks ago, the barometer was at 30·3 inches and rapidly rising. The Udston explosion, in another anti-cyclone, had been heralded during the increasing pressure by less disastrous accidents at Darcy

MR. HENRY HARRIES.

Lever and Wigan. Last year three out of the four principal cases took place under similar conditions. The Pochin accident in 1884 occurred when the barometer was at 30·3, and on the next day in Belgium, when twenty lives were lost at the Wasmes mine, the barometer was at 30·4 inches. In the Leycett explosion of 1880, the barometer was at 30·65, at Seaham it was at 30·1, at Penygraig, December 1880, 30·4, and at Mardy at 30·7 inches. The increase of pressure which set in at about midnight of December 3, 1875, was accompanied by the New Tredegar explosion on the 4th, the Llan on the 5th, and Swaithe Main on the 6th. There did not appear to have been any disaster with the exceptionally low pressure of December, 1886. Miners were after all but human, and, if they believed that accidents could only occur at certain times, they were apt to think that at other times they could do very much as they liked in spite of all regulations to the contrary. He had endeavored, in a communication to *Nature* on the 8th of September last,[1] to explain this frequency of explosions with the prevalence of anti-cyclonic distributions of pressure, by the production of evidence from independent sources, showing that the enormous changes in the weight of the superincumbent atmosphere caused a straining of the earth's crust, to such an extent as to favor the issue of gas from the strata at a time when, theoretically, the escape of gas should cease. Professor G. H. Darwin had calculated that, with a range of 2 inches of barometric pressure, the surface was from 3 to 4 inches nearer the centre of the earth when the mercury was high than when it was low; but in the past few years the range of the barometer in this country had been close upon 3·75 inches, so that the level of the British Isles would vary by about 7 inches. It would be absurd to contend that a fall of the barometer did not affect the gas in goaves and waste places; the knowledge of the fact secured careful attention in almost every mine, and this might account for the small number of ex-

---

(1) Vol. xxxvi, pp. 437, 438.

MR. WILLIAM COCHRANE.

plosions which took place with low pressure. The worst disasters were those which occurred when the danger was least expected, and if the perusal of these remarks could lead to a more careful study of the subject, and tend to reduce the liability to explosions, the time devoted to the present discussion would have been well spent.

His remarks on the coal-dust question must necessarily be very brief. Much had been said on the subject in recent years, and all agreed that if the dust was an agent in explosions, it was most dangerous when it was driest. This being so, the question resolved itself into a consideration of the hygrometric condition of the atmosphere. Professor Lupton's remarks forcibly illustrated this, the moistening of the dust being comparatively easy in the warm atmosphere of spring, summer and autumn, but very difficult in the cold, dry air of winter. In Mr. Sawyer's Paper on "The Temperature and Moisture of Air-Currents in Mines,"[1] it was shown that dry and dusty mines were drier, and the dust more inflammable, on cold days than on warm days; and, where blasting operations were permitted, the experiments accounted for the increase in the number of explosions in the winter months. Now, a dry atmosphere, when it was most difficult to damp the dust, was a characteristic of anti-cyclones, and rendered the dust inflammable. Cyclones were accompanied by an excess of moisture in the air. This was an additional reason, therefore, for paying more attention to periods of high barometer than had hitherto been thought necessary. Taking all the explosions, great and small, it seemed that at least 75 per cent. took place with a high barometer, but he did not say that they were directly due to it.

MR. WILLIAM COCHRANE wished to state the result of experiments with which he had been connected in 1875 and 1876, when the first steps were taken in this country, after certain indications given by Mr. Vital in the *Annales des*

[1] Transactions of the North Staffordshire Institute of Mining and Mechanical Engineers, vol. viii, p. 8.

Mr. William Cochrane.

Mines, that small coal-dust, *per se*, was explosive without the possibility of admixture with carburetted hydrogen. Probably every one would be impressed by the perusal of the Paper with the idea that a slight admixture of fire-damp was necessary for an explosion. He did not know what would be called an explosion, but if, as in an experiment which he conducted with Professor Marreco, in January, 1876, in the laboratories of the Physical Science College at Newcastle-on-Tyne, a detonation and the projecting of two small cast-iron weights from the top of a model drift, one going uncomfortably near his head, and the other across the experiment room, were to be called an explosion, it certainly took place, with the use of small coal-dust alone, there being no possibility of having gas anywhere near where they were operating. A Davy lamp gauze formed the roof of the model drift on which the dust coal was placed, a small Guibal fan formed the air current, and by rapping the side of the model drift, the coal-dust fell, and a small pistol was fired into the drift. The result was an explosion, which ripped up the model and destroyed the Guibal ventilator employed to maintain the air current. That showed that there was no necessity for the presence of even the smallest percentage of gas, which had been so much dwelt upon, and which the Author concluded was necessary.

CORRESPONDENCE.

MR. JAMES ASHWORTH remarked that in general arrangement the Ashworth-Clanny lamp was similar to the Clanny lamps he sent to the Mines Accident Commission in May, 1882, known in the report as Clanny's Nos. 17, 18, and 19, which were the first completely shielded lamps tested by the commission ; but the details of construction had been so greatly improved, that instead of the illumination produced by the wick flame being respectively 39, 64, and 56 per cent. of a standard sperm candle, the present lamp gave 79 per cent. as tested by Mr. Betley, of Wigan Mining School. Attached to the screw ring which kept the glass in position, and at right-angles to it, was a thin metallic cylinder reaching nearly up to the level of the top of the wick-tube, and perforated by four holes at its base ; the top of the oil-vessel was made of tin or some metal which was a bad conductor of heat. By this arrangement of parts air entering the lamp was brought down the combustion-chamber close to the side of the glass, through the holes in the new ring and over the top of the oil-vessel, thus keeping both the glass and the oil-vessel cool, and also supplying an air-feed to the flame in the best way to secure perfect combustion. The Ashworth-Mueseler, A type, was a combination of his gauze chimney Jack-Davy lamp (called Ashworth No. 2 in the Mines Accident Report), and his shielded Clanny. Its principal novelty was in the substitution of a chimney, consisting of a slightly conical gauze cylinder with a truncated conical metal base, to which this gauze and the horizontal gauze disk were attached, for the metal chimney of the standard Mueseler. Besides being a safer form of chimney, its construction enabled him to increase the illumination of the wick flame, and to reduce the liability of the lamp to become suddenly extinguished when thrown on one side. The B type only differed from the A

171

MR. JAMES ASHWORTH.

type in being provided with a second shield (No. 4 of the Mines Accident Report) placed between the outer one and the cylindrical gauze, perforated near its base with a row of inlet holes, and having a conical outlet.   The outlet was gauged to permit the products of combustion to escape easily under normal conditions; but when fire-damp exploded or burned within the lamp, the outlet was insufficient, and the whole of the interior of the shield became so full of carbonic acid gas, that the inlet air was fouled and all light within the lamp was extinguished at once.   This type had been tested by Mr. Rhodes, of Rotherham, by Mr. Morgan, with his blow-pipe apparatus, at a pressure of $1\frac{1}{2}$ lb. per square inch, and lastly by Mr. Clifford, in a horizontal current of upwards of 100 feet per second, without any failure.   For officials and firemen, this type of lamp was furnished with a "shut off" on the inlet holes, which, when closed, compelled the air of the mine to enter by the holes near the top of the outer shield, and thus to indicate the condition of the air within about $1\frac{1}{2}$ inch of the roof. As soon as the wick flame indicated the presence of gas, the "shut off" was opened to admit purer air, and to avoid the risk of an excessive quantity of gas extinguishing it.

The Hepplewhite-Gray Davy lamp was an adaptation of the Gray inlet tubes to the shielded Davy lamp, the shield having a conical outlet similar to that of the Ashworth-Mueseler B, and was fitted with Ashworth's patent for making practical examinations for fire-damp.   In the Hepplewhite-Gray of the Clanny type the inlet tubes were protected from dirt falling down by a horizontal ring, which screwed on the body of the lamp, and formed a "shut off" of the most absolute kind.   The shield was fitted with a conical outlet to prevent down currents, and to act also as a Mueseler chimney, and was protected from dirt and the direct action of the ventilating currents of the mine by the perforated top on which the "shut off" screwed.   The slightly conical gauze inside the shield was not exposed to any dusty current, and as its only duty was to form another

MR. JAMES ASHWORTH.

protection to the outlet, its dimensions were very small. Its base was furnished with spun copper rings which clipped the top of the truncated conical glass. This form of glass was extremely strong : first, to resist particles of coal or dirt which might be thrown against it, through presenting two inclined planes to ease the direct action of the blow ; and secondly, in its adaptability to resist sudden expansion or contraction, because the increase of the diameter of the small end by heat was less than that of the large end, therefore the increase in length was compensated for by the increase in the larger diameter without perceptibly increasing the perpendicular height of the glass. A screwed ring secured this glass in the ordinary way, and was followed by a ring with rectangular openings covered by a strip of gauze, which ring, when screwed close up, left an annular space at the foot of the inlet tubes, and allowed the entering air free ingress to the wick flame through the strip of gauze. One or more of the inlet tubes of the Hepplewhite-Gray lamps were furnished with Ashworth's arrangement for making practical tests for fire-damp, consisting of a hole near the base of the tube, and covered by a slide. It had been discovered, that theoretically the Gray arrangement was the best for obtaining accurate indications of the state of the mine close up to the roof ; but practically it was wrong, as when gas entered the tubes it was compelled to pass through the lamp before any fresh air could enter. Thus, in most instances, the wick flame was extinguished, and the lamp rendered useless for making further examinations until relit. When testing with the new arrangement, the slide was pushed up, and the hole in the tube left wide open ; thus gas could enter by three tubes from the extreme top, and fresh air from the base of the other ; and, supposing that gas did thus enter, it was consumed on one side of the flame whilst the flame itself was maintained by the current of fresh air on the other side. If, on reaching the highest point of the mine, in this way no gas was found, the official gradually closed the hole with his thumb, or with the shutter, and if no trace of fire-

MR. J. B. ATKINSON.

damp was then found, it was certain that the place was absolutely clear.   He made all tests for gas with the wick
flame at its normal height.   Thinner strata and smaller percentages of fire-damp could be detected with the Hepplewhite-Gray fireman's lamp than with any other shielded lamp.

MR. J. B. ATKINSON observed that the Author had devoted much attention to mine accidents, and his high scientific attainments had been of great service to the mining
community.   But he thought the Author had not yet realized the full importance of the influence of coal-dust in
colliery explosions.   In stating this it might be remarked
that, with no precautions against the existence of fire-damp
in the passages of a mine, disastrous fire-damp and air explosions would be frequent ; but considering that all the
endeavors of mining engineers in the past had been devoted to the prevention of such occurrences, and that these
efforts had produced a direct effect in promoting accumulations of coal-dust over long distances, and that in dry
mines coal-dust in dangerous quantities was much more
ubiquitous and continuous than fire-damp, it was a matter
of no surprise that the part played by coal-dust in mine
explosions was much more disastrous than the part played
by fire-damp.   Several considerations in favor of the belief
that coal-dust was often the main agent of destruction in
mine explosions, and of the view that explosions might
originate from, and be propagated by, coal-dust under
certain conditions, in air free from any fire-damp other
than a trace, were advanced in the book " Explosions in
Coal Mines," referred to by the Author.   As some of
the facts and opinions advanced therein were new, and had
not been noticed by the Author, he would venture to refer those interested in the question to the book itself.   On
the 13th of March, 1884, a disastrous explosion occurred in
the Pocahontas coal-mine, Virginia, U.S.A., involving the
loss of one hundred and fourteen lives.   From a report
published in the " Transactions of the American Institute
of Mining Engineers,"[1] it appeared that fire-damp was un-

---

[1] Vol xiii. (1885) p. 237.

MR. J. B. ATKINSON.

known in the mine, which, however, was very dry and dusty. The report gave as a condition leading to the explosion "the probable existence of small quantities of fire-damp slowly given off from the coal;" but it also stated that "the existence of fire-damp in the Pocahontas mine is the disputed point," and nothing was advanced to prove its presence. The Author's statement that explosions ascribed by some to coal-dust and air alone was open to the criticism, that "experimental results which serve to support" such opinion, "are more or less exceptional in character, or that they have been attained under conditions which do not approximate to those likely to occur in a mine," might be opposed by the following considerations. In the many miles of roads in dry mines where coal was led by engine power against rapid currents of air, causing the formation of deposits of coal-dust of the finest and most inflammable character, in positions where the explosion of a shot must dislodge quantities of it, and where the speed of the air sustained it as a cloud, occasionally, conditions even more favorable than any yet provided in experimental researches, for the ignition of the dust, in air free from fire-damp might be attained.   When it was found that shots fired in such roads were the rarest class of shots fired in a mine, and when it was further found that the firing of such shots was often accompanied by an explosion, was it unreasonable to conclude that what had been observed in experiment had occurred in practice ; and, while not maintaining the absolute freedom from fire-damp of the air (although many mine-managers would maintain it), yet to admit that, so far as evidence could be obtained, the air did not contain sufficient to have any influence on the result? Instead of its being an assumption, as the Author considered it, to maintain that the air in an intake air-way was so free from fire-damp as to be perfectly safe, so far as it was concerned, whether coal-dust was present or not, the assumption was in supposing fire-damp in definite volume to be present in the absence of any evidence.   The fact that 2 per cent. of fire-damp must be present, before it

Mr. J. B. Atkinson.

could be observed by the safety-lamp, afforded no presump-
tion that a definite volume under 2 per cent. was present in
an intake air-way where an explosion had occurred. As
the lamp in such situations afforded no test, other considerations must be the guide, and it might be stated that the
probable amount of fire-damp normally present in intakes
was more susceptible of estimation than that present in
other parts of the mines. He differed from the Author in
the opinion that, in the passages of a mine, the combustion
of coal-dust in air was gradual, and attended with less violence than the combustion of fire-damp and air, or of a mixture of fire-damp, coal-dust and air; his experience pointed
to the reverse being true, with the following exceptions,
which he thought might go far to reconcile divergencies of
opinion :—(1.) Where the coal-dust was coarse and confined
to the floor, as in working places at the face and roads adjoining, the violence developed was small, even if, as must
often be the case in such situations, a definite but small
amount of fire-damp was present in the air. (2.) Where
coal-dust in a fine dry state existed more or less on all the
surfaces of a haulage road, from 50 to 80 yards from the
point of origin of an explosion of coal-dust, with air free
from fire-damp other than a trace, no great violence was observable, and probably the passage of the flame had been
gradual. (3.) If over a long distance in a confined passage
in a coal-mine, a thoroughly diffused mixture in the most
explosive proportion of fire-damp and air existed, then,
probably great violence would be produced on its ignition.
It was difficult to point to any great explosion where even
the probability of the last condition could be asserted. In
the return air-ways of a coal-mine, it might be expected
with far greater probability than in the intake air-ways, but
great explosions did not affect to any considerable extent
the former class of roads. The speed of flame, or rapidity
of combustion of a homogeneous gas and air-mixture, probably reached its maximum within a short distance of the
point of ignition, while the reverse was probable in the case
of a coal-dust and air mixture; if this was true, no experi-

MR. W. N. ATKINSON.

ments had yet been made on a scale of sufficient magnitude to test fully the phenomena of explosions of coal-dust and air. As to the nature of the combustion of coal-dust in air free from fire-damp, he would venture with great diffidence to make a few remarks. As a factor, possibly contributing to violence, it might be mentioned that, contrasting a fire-damp with a dust explosion, in the case of the former, if of the most explosive mixture, one-tenth of the amount of oxygen would be replaced by fire-damp ; while with the dust the road was filled with air, the amount of oxygen limiting the amount of combustion ; there was in this way an advantage for the dust. The possibility of a further supply of oxygen existing in the fine dust on the upper parts of a haulage road was worth attention. The combustion in the case of coal-dust might be either that of the gas expelled from the dust, or, if the particles were very minute, possibly the solid matter might be consumed ; but in either case, the finer the dust, the more rapid would be the combustion. Supposing the combustion to be that of gas expelled from the dust, then the Author's discovery of the power of finely-divided, even non-inflammable bodies, of promoting inflammation would further help to increase the rapidity of combustion.

Mr. W. N. ATKINSON remarked that various theories had been promulgated in order to account for the occurrence of explosions in coal-mines. Amongst them were blowers or sudden outbursts of gas, the accumulation of fire-damp in goaves, or abandoned workings ; the influence of atmospheric disturbances ; movements of the earth's crust, or earth tremors ; and the presence of coal-dust. It might be pointed out that the only one of these possible causes known to have been present in all extensive explosions, of which there were sufficient records to enable a judgment to be formed, was coal-dust. Sudden outbursts of gas were known to occur sometimes; but many explosions had been attributed to them when no evidence existed that such an outburst had taken place, and where, even if the outburst had occurred, it would be impossible to ac-

12

Mr. W. N. Atkinson.

count for the result by it alone. Extensive explosions had happened in pits where there was no goaf, and in some cases where there were no abandoned workings. The most careful study revealed no sustained connection between large explosions and meteorological conditions, although it was well known that the movement of fire-damp in goaves and open spaces was governed to an appreciable extent by atmospheric pressure. The usual opinion was that the period of greatest danger from fire-damp was when the barometer was low, and that was probably correct, when modified by the knowledge that the gas was more sensitive to changes of pressure than the mercury. The "colliery warnings," now periodically given in the public press, appeared to indicate that the periods of high atmospheric pressure were considered the most dangerous, but on what grounds was not apparent. The possible influence of earth tremors on explosions had not been sufficiently studied to allow of any positive conclusion on the subject; it was as yet an entirely speculative question. With regard to the influence of coal-dust, it might be pointed out that no extensive explosion had taken place, in recent times, under circumstances which precluded the possibility that coal-dust might have been the chief agent in operation; and the same held good so far as could be judged from the records of explosions in former times. The conclusions arrived at as to the cause of colliery explosions, when the influence of coal-dust was not taken into consideration, were vitiated for that reason. It was a recorded fact that in many recent cases the explosions were confined to those passages in the mines which contained much coal-dust, and did not traverse any roads which were free from coal-dust; even, although the roads containing the coal-dust were the intake air-ways, and the roads free from it and not traversed by the explosions were the return air-ways. Indeed, cases were known where the explosion was actually confined to the dusty main intakes, and did not penetrate to the working faces, or affect the return air-ways. This was so at the Seaham Colliery explosions in 1871 and 1880; at Tudhoe Colliery

MR. W. N. ATKINSON.

explosion in 1882; at Mardy Colliery explosion in 1885, and at the Altofts Colliery explosion in 1886. In all ·the above cases, except Mardy, shots appeared to have been fired in the main intakes coincidently with the explosions. At Mardy the explosion was probably initiated by the ignition, by a naked light, of an accumulation of fire-damp, in a cavity in the roof where the stone had fallen, to the height of nearly 30 feet. It would probably not be difficult to prove by means of Liveing's indicator, or the Pieler lamp, that the large volumes of air passing along the main intake air-ways of such collieries did not contain even the very minute quantities of fire-damp which these instruments were capable of detecting. The recently passed Act for the regulation of mines did not provide for the systematic damping of coal-dust in dry mines, so that, so far as the law was concerned, they might remain in the same state in that respect as they were before. The Act, however, provided that precautions should be taken to prevent the ignition of coal-dust either by gas or by explosive substances. For the purposes of the watering required by the Act, which was limited to the locality where shots were about to be fired, it was desirable that some efficient means should be introduced for distributing the water effectually. The Anchor engine referred to by the Author appeared to have this object in view, and a more detailed account of it would be interesting. Another method might be by the application of a small pump, or fire-engine, worked by hand and fitted to an ordinary water-tub; the water being forced through a flexible tube, and delivered in the form of spray. What was required was a means of applying the water with facility and precision to any part of a drift, whether roof, bottom, or sides. Efforts were now being made at several collieries to damp the dust in a systematic manner; but sufficient experience had not yet been obtained to indicate the most efficient way, which would probably vary according to the conditions existing at different collieries. In some cases small pipes containing water under high pressure were laid along the dusty haulage roads, with cocks at suit-

MR. W. N. ATKINSON.

able distances apart, to which a hose-pipe was fixed. In this way every part of the passage could be literally washed. In other cases short branch pipes were taken from the main range into the centre of the drift, and the water was allowed to escape, against the air-current, in the form of fine spray, through a minute aperture. The distance to which the spray thrown out in this way would effectually damp all parts of the passage did not appear to be great, and if too much spray was thrown out at one place the bottom got too wet there. This might be obviated by having sprays at more frequent intervals, and only allowing every second or third one to be in operation at the same time. This system had the advantage of being self-acting, and requiring little attention. Efforts had also been made to cause the ventilating current itself to damp the dust, by raising its temperature and saturating it with moisture when it entered the mine. Methods for mechanically distributing water carried in tubs had been devised by Messrs. Archer and Robson, and by Mr. J. A. Ramsay. The proper use of the water-cartridge with high explosives in blasting greatly reduced the risk of igniting gas, or coal-dust, but at an increased cost. In the North of England it had not been found suitable for getting coal. The compressed lime-cartridges had been tried at several collieries in Durham, but their use had been discontinued. Under favorable conditions (which were, perhaps, not very general) the method seemed to be a good and safe one for getting coal. It was of little use for stone-work. It might be mentioned that on more than one occasion, where the paper in which the cartridges were wrapped was put into the cartridge-hole as stemming, the paper was ignited by the heat evolved from the lime, and was found smouldering when the coal fell. It was unnecessary to put paper, or other inflammable material into the holes. In one case a man was severely injured by a blown-out lime-cartridge shot. Trials were about to be made in Durham of some of the recently invented explosive substances said to produce no flame, or at any rate, to be incapable of firing gas or

coal-dust.   If such a substance could be found with explosive properties similar to gunpowder, and capable of being
used in shot-holes of the same size as was necessary for
gunpowder, it would be hailed with delight; for none of
the new methods of coal-getting approached the use of gunpowder for general applicability, convenience, and economy.

MR. BENNETT H. BROUGH remarked that the results of
the investigations described by the Author deserved careful
attention, not only from coal-miners but also from metal-
miners.   For, unfortunately, fire-damp was not confined to
collieries.   In a number of cases it had been met with in
mines of lignite, of salt, and of metals.   Indeed, the first
fatal fire-damp explosion recorded took place in 1664, not in
a colliery but in a salt-mine at Hallstadt, in Austria.   An
illustration of the disastrous effects of a fire-damp explosion
in a metalliferous mine had been afforded by the lamentable
accident at the Mill Close lead-mine, in Derbyshire, on the
3d of November last, when five men lost their lives, and
others were injured, by the ignition of fire-damp, caused by
firing a dynamite charge.   The deposit of lead ore at that
mine occurred in dark limestone beds immediately below
the Yoredale shale that separated the limestone from the
millstone grit.   This shale, whenever it occurred in beds of
25 to 35 fathoms in thickness, always gave off a little gas.
Probably this gas had collected in the fissured limestone,
and becoming ignited by a shot, forced down the rock
masses upon the unfortunate miners.   The mouth of the
great adit level which drained many of the Derbyshire
mines, known as the Hill Carr Sough, was in the vicinity of
the Mill Close Mine.   This adit or sough passed through
the shale for 2 or 3 miles, and with a candle at the end of
a stick, up to a very recent date, visitors used to light the
thin stream of gas along the roof.   This would flash along
almost the whole length of the level.   The gas was now exhausted, or was found in very small quantities, but, when
new ground was cut, there was a decided emission of gas.
Similarly, outbursts of fire-damp had been observed at the
Van lead mine, near Llanidloes, at the Silver Islet Mine in

MR. T. FORSTER BROWN.

Lake Superior, at Monte Catini in Tuscany, and at several
of the Saxon metalliferous mines. Inaccurate mine survey-
ing was a frequent source of accident, which was dwelt on
neither in the report of the Royal Commission, nor by the
Author. A glance through the reports of H. M. Inspectors
for a number of years would show that several of the accidents therein recorded were obviously due to a neglect of
the variation of the magnetic meridian, to which mine plans
were usually drawn. Thus, Mr. T. Evans recorded an accident in 1875 at a small colliery in Nottinghamshire, where
the men holed into some old workings. The disaster was
caused by the men working according to plans one hundred
years old, which showed a barrier of 100 yards. Another
accident from holing into old workings was recorded, in
1878, by Mr. J. Dickinson. The men were working, without any bore-holes in advance, and thus an inundation was
caused whereby two lives were lost. In that instance there
was a correct plan of the former work, but, by a mistake in
the surveyor's office, a wrong direction had been set out.
Now that the means of constructing accurate mine plans
were more abundantly taught, such accidents would, it was
to be hoped, be of rare occurrence.

MR. T. FORSTER BROWN observed that the thanks of the
community were due to the members of the Royal Commission for the practical turn which they had given to the
direction in which increased safety in working coal-mines
could be secured. With regard to explosions of fire-damp,
thoroughly efficient damping of the coal-dust would add
immensely in reducing this risk. At large collieries with
which he was associated, extensive lines of water-pipes had
been lain along the main haulage roads, with a water-
pressure of 100 lbs. per square inch, and with outlets giving
off fine spray at intervals of about 40 yards apart, with most
beneficial results. Not only had the dust been damped,
but the temperature had been reduced. At Harris Navigation Colliery the temperature had by this means been reduced 6°. Mr. Henry Martin, of Dowlais, had introduced
a considerable improvement by combining water under

MR. T. FORSTER BROWN.

pressure in pipes with compressed air, which enabled the moisture to be more finely disseminated throughout the passages of the mine.   Upon the question of shot-firing, at the suggestion of Mr. Galloway, two or three years ago, blasting gelatine tamped with wet moss had been adopted as an explosive with good results, and so far no flame had been observed to pass.   The next great desideratum no doubt was a safe lamp, giving an effective light.   Several of the improved lamps of the present day would resist a strong current; but apart from the question of danger from explosion, a considerable reduction ought to be expected in the loss of life due to falls from the roof and sides, if a thoroughly good light could be introduced into fiery collieries.   This difficulty, however, seemed to be approaching a solution by means of the electric lamp.   Mr. Swan had devised an excellent electric lamp, which in turn would be improved upon, and Mr. Forster Brown anticipated the speedy invention of a thoroughly efficient self-contained electric lamp.   With such a lamp it would be practicable to light the main hauling roads with fixed lamps, and to reduce the number of riders upon the sets, and in that way diminish the risks upon the haulage roads.   He had adopted in many cases in the main haulage roads, where compressed air was available, a system of engines at each end of the main planes, doing away in that way with the tail ropes, and simplifying the operation of hauling.   With well-lighted haulage roads of sufficient width, and laid with heavy rails, the risks of injury and loss of life ought to be reduced to a minimum. The system of long-wall working, as practised in South Wales, as compared with any other mode of working was attended with the least risks; and having regard to the fact that, up to within 150 yards or 200 yards of the face of the workings, the ground settled on the goaf up to the surface, he did not go quite so far as to consider the goaves a source of accumulation of gas.   It must be so, more or less, with regard to the width of the goaf, which had not settled down; but when the face advanced to the rise, the gas flowed out to the face, and in the case of the

MR. S. B. COXON.

workings going to the dip, the tendency would be to accumulate in the goaf. With regard to shaft accidents, the difficulty was to avoid increased complications. Taking the case of the Harris Navigation Colliery, where the load was 19 tons, running at the rate of about 30 miles an hour, in the middle of the pit, the guides being iron rails, less weight would not suffice to obtain a reasonable output from such a great depth, and any apparatus in the shaft for counteracting a breakage of the rope would be extremely difficult to invent, and the cure would probably be worse than the disease. The course to adopt was, in his opinion, to have every part of the machinery of ample power, the engine well balanced, an automatic steam-brake attached, an efficient system of signalling from top to bottom and bottom to top, and detaching hooks below the pulleys.

MR. S. B. COXON, during the spring of the year 1887, by permission of the Imperial German authorities representing the Department of Mines, had the good fortune to witness a series of experiments on the properties of so-called high-class explosives ; these were conducted by the mine inspector of the district at the Government experimental works adjoining the König mine, Neunkirchen. As these works had been erected to enable the Fire-damp Commission to carry out tests on a scale approximating to the conditions met with in coal-mines, the Government had spared no expense in rendering them complete in every detail. The works consisted of a tunnel 51 metres long by 1·70 by 1·20 metre, strongly built to resist the force of explosions, and strengthened by iron girders, hoops, and stays. The top of the tunnel was provided with large safety plugs and doors, which yielded to the effects of explosion, and formed, so to speak, so many safety-valves. At frequent intervals small squares of strong glass were let into the sides of the tunnel, to enable the observers to watch in safety the behavior of shots in the various mixtures of fire-damp and coal-dust in which they were tested. The fire-damp was piped from a blower in the mine, and was received by a suitably constructed gasometer, from which it was easily admitted into

MR. S. B. COXON.

the explosion chamber in such quantities as the experimenter might require; but, as a rule, the testing mixture consisted of 10 per cent. of mine gas CH_4, and about 15 kilos of
finely pulverized coal-dust scattered over the drift, a large
proportion being held in suspension by the air in the chamber.   The shots were fired by electricity.   The staff was
well supplied with instruments, and possessed all that was
necessary to carry out their experiments with scientific accuracy.   The Government Inspector, Mr. Fabian, illustrated
the effects of blown-out shots in an atmosphere containing
coal-dust in a fine state of division without any mixture of
fire-damp.   The charge consisted of 230 grams of ordinary
black blasting-powder.   When the shot was fired a tremen-
dous explosion took place; all the safety plugs and doors
were blown out, and flames, accompanied by clouds of
smoke, burst through every opening.   After the explosion
a layer of fine coke-dust was found deposited on the floor
and sides of the tunnel.   This experiment was twice
repeated with like results; the explosions appeared to be
almost as violent as when mine-gas formed part of the mixture.   It might be well to mention that the coal-dust was
from the Pluto mine; it was friable, bright and bituminous,
in appearance not unlike the duff from the gas coals of the
Durham coal-field.   There could be no doubt that in these
experiments the explosions were instantaneous, and no
mere elongation or extension of flame.   He thought it
might not be without interest to place on record his experience of an explosion at a colliery under his management
some twenty-five years ago, which appeared altogether due
to a blown-out shot firing the dust in suspension in the
mine.   The circumstances, briefly stated, were as follows:—
A drift was being driven between the down- and up-cast
shafts for the purpose of erecting an additional ventilating
furnace.   The coal being friable, a quantity of dust became
mixed with the ventilating current.   After the drift had
been carefully examined for gas, not only by a Davy lamp,
but also with a naked light, a shot was fired, but having
been unskilfully placed, it was blown out; the result was

Mr. S. B. Coxon.

an explosion which burned severely a number of men who were working near the downcast shaft. The air-current, in volume over 150,000 cubic feet per minute, was checked, the separation doors were blown open, and the effect of the blast was felt at the bank. In this particular case not the slightest indication of gas was apparent, nor was any observed either before or after the explosion. No fall had taken place, nor had anything occurred to interrupt or derange the ventilating current. After a careful investigation of all the circumstances, the conclusion arrived at was that the accident was caused by the blown-out shot igniting the coal-dust. Granting that the examples given were faithfully represented, the lesson was of easy application, and would show that there was a strong probability that coal-dust had played an important part in many accidents, the proximate causes of which had been enveloped in mystery. It was to be feared that so long as ordinary blasting-powder was used in coal mines, blown-out shots would be an ever-recurring source of danger. It would, however, appear that the time had arrived to take a new departure by substituting other blasting compounds. A cartridge had recently been invented that was quite flameless, and which had undergone the most severe tests in mixtures of firedamp and coal-dust. Perhaps the most noteworthy test to which this cartridge had been subjected was in 10 per cent. of mine-gas and finely pulverized coal-dust. A number of experiments were made in this highly explosive mixture, and in no case was it fired. Not less remarkable was the fact that when this cartridge enclosed dynamite or blasting gelatine, these powerful compounds ceased to emit flame without any apparent loss of strength. Photographs had been taken at the instant of firing, which might be cited as truthful and scientific testimony to the value of this discovery. It was not surprising that mining engineers, having the management of extensive and dangerous collieries, had long been seriously impressed with the risks daily incurred by treating the ordinary Davy as a safety-lamp. It was well known that these lamps, when exposed to inflammable

MR. S. B. COXON.

mixtures, would pass flame in currents of a comparatively low velocity. A large colliery required a ventilation of from 200,000 to 300,000 cubic feet of air per minute, consequently many of the splits must of necessity attain high velocities. It was difficult to imagine a greater source of danger than when a loaded current at a high speed impinged on the unprotected gauze of the Davy type of lamp. Many of these lamps would fire an inflammable current if the velocity reached 8 or 10 feet per second. It was not necessary here to emphasize the danger from such a condition of things. Another fruitful source of danger arose from falls in goaves, which in deep mines generally contained accumulations of fire-damp. When fractures occurred in the superior strata, and the roof fell, the contents of the fissures were driven into the working-places, and not infrequently filled the lamps of the workmen with inflammable gas; this contingency should be guarded against with the greatest care; indeed, there were many reasons why the attention of mining engineers should be directed to other sources of light and safety. Happily electric lamps pointed to a solution of the difficulty, and in what direction the end in view might be most easily attained. There could be little doubt that in the electric lamp there was the nearest approach to absolute safety, whilst the superior light would add much to the comfort of the collier, and tend in no slight degree to ameliorate the disagreeable nature of his vocation. A judicious selection of the kind of battery to be used was of the first importance, as, given the proper battery, the form and arrangement of the lamp were matters of detail. It might be of interest to show how closely electricity approached oil in point of economy. The result of several weeks' consecutive testing showed that the Schanschieff lamp (primary battery), yielding a light of 2-candle-powder, cost only $\frac{7}{8}d$. per shift of eight hours. This was a single fluid battery of high electro-motive force and low resistance. The cells consisted of zinc and carbon, the solution being a basic sulphate of mercury. The action was remarkably constant; there was no danger from spark-

MR. C. LE NEVE FOSTER.

ing ; the lamp gave off no gas nor fumes of a disagreeable odor ; there was nothing in either the construction of the lamp or the nature of the solution to produce a risk of explosion. The weight of a four-cell lamp was 4 lbs. 6 oz. and the three-cell was only 3½ lbs. These lamps might be changed as easily and in a shorter time than it took to trim a Davy lamp.

Mr. C. LE NEVE FOSTER, in reference to deaths from accidents and disease in metal-mines, said he had pointed out on more than one occasion, in his official reports, and in papers read before the British Association and the Statistical Society,[1] that the ore-miner had very nearly as dangerous an occupation as the collier, and that in some metalliferous districts, such as Cornwall, the average death-rate from accidents was higher than in coal-mines. In other words, as has been frequently shown, though the fact was scarcely rooted in the public mind, fire-damp was not the miners' worst enemy. Nay, he would go further, and almost look upon it as a blessing in disguise. If it had not been for explosions in mines, there would have been less stringent regulations for their safety. The numerous dangers, which caused only one or two deaths at a time, would have been less carefully guarded against by statute, and ventilation would not have received that strict attention which was now an absolute necessity. Though not killed by explosions, the colliers would have had their lives shortened, by breathing vitiated air, like their brethren in Cornwall. In considering the well-being of a class of workmen, such as miners, it was necessary to look at the mortality from disease as well as the mortality from accidents. It had been shown by Dr. Ogle[2] that, in spite of accidents, the death-rate of coal-miners was not high. In order of comparative mortality, coal-mining stood 30th in the list of ninety-four occupations which he cited, whilst mining in Cornwall was as low as No. 91 ; that was to say, only three

---

[1] Journal of the Statistical Society, vol. xlviii. p. 277.

[2] Supplement to the 45th Annual Report of the Registrar-General of Births, Deaths, and Marriages in England. London, 1885, pp. xxvi. and xlix.

of the ninety-four trades exceeded tin-mining in deadliness. His late colleague, Mr. Frecheville, called attention to this fact in his report for 1885, and ascribed this high mortality to inadequate ventilation, and excessive climbing of ladders from deep mines. He quite agreed with Mr. Frecheville in this opinion, and he had stated in his official reports that these evils, together with others, demanded an amendment of the statute of 1872, which regulated the working of metalliferous mines.

Mr. W. GALLOWAY stated, in reference to the quantity of air necessary to the combustion of 1 lb. of coal-dust, that in January, 1876, a month after the completion of his first experiments, with definite proportions of fire-damp and air, and with undetermined quantities of coal-dust, he wrote in a Paper, published in the Proceedings of the Royal Society in the following March, that "It is always possible, however, that if coal-dust could be made fine enough, and were thoroughly mixed with dry air in the proportion of about 1 lb. to 160 cubic feet of air, the mixture might be inflammable at ordinary temperature,"[1] and so on. He arrived at 160 cubic feet of air by taking 12 lbs., the weight of air necessary for the complete combustion of the fuel given at p. 280 of Rankine's "Steam Engine," 1861 edition, and calculating its volume at ordinary pressure and temperature. It had appeared to him that if complete combustion of the elements of the coal-dust could be assured, without any surplus of oxygen, the best possible results would be obtained, and that might be explosion in a confined space. In a subsequent Paper published in March, 1879, he stated that "The proportion of coal-dust which gave the best results, was much larger than might at first sight be thought necessary, namely, about 1 oz. of dust to a cubic foot of air for all mixtures of gas and air, ranging between one of gas and twenty of air, and one of gas and forty of air. Also, in one of the experiments, with the return air of a mine, which I propose to describe in this place, the air

---

[1] Proceedings of the Royal Society of London, vol. xxiv. p. 369.

MR. MAX GEORGI.

requires to be literally black with dust before it will ignite."[1] The last mentioned results were afterwards corroborated by Messrs. Mallard and Le Chatelier.

Mr. MAX GEORGI, of Zaukerode, thought that hardly sufficient importance had been attached by the Author to the subject of auxiliary ventilation. On the continent, with the pillar-and-stall method of working coal generally employed, auxiliary ventilation was of very great importance. In driving narrow bords, and occasionally, in consequence of dislocations of the seam, or of great pressure of super-incumbent strata, it was difficult or impossible to pass a ventilating current of air through the workings. However rapidly the air was forced through, the ventilation must always, at times, be left to be accomplished by diffusion. When there was a violent outburst of mine-gas, diffusion would, under certain conditions, be insufficient to prevent the formation of explosive gas-mixtures, or of an air-mixture liable to cause a coal-dust explosion. The latter mixture, however, was formed more easily at the working face if a small shot was fired; the reason being that the volumes of gas acquired greater velocity, and the coal-dust produced by the shot, or lying in the drift, was whirled with greater violence to and fro. If this agitation of the coal-dust could not be prevented as long as blasting was permitted, all measures for avoiding accidents must aim at drawing the coal-gas away from each working place, or of mixing with it sufficient fresh air to prevent the proportion of gas exceeding a dangerous percentage. The colliery rules, promulgated by the Saxon Government on the 25th of March, 1886, insisted, paragraph 113, that those points, where men were at work, and where the ventilation was accomplished by a current of air, must be kept free from fire-damp by auxiliary ventilation. This might be effected either by the main ventilating current, or by an auxiliary air current produced for the purpose. In the former case, if brattices were not to be employed, the main

MR. MAX GEORGI.

air-current must be further subdivided, splits being formed
by means of pipes. The more the main current was inter-
rupted and limited in this way, the more would its total
effect be diminished, thus detrimentally affecting the whole
of the ventilation in favor of certain working places.
When, on the other hand, recourse was had to auxiliary
ventilation for several working places, the application of
the main ventilating current should be entirely avoided, or
be limited to certain cases. The most simple, the most
convenient, and the most successful method was the employment of compressed air, whether blown direct, or by a
Körting blower or similar jet, into the ventilating pipes.
Inasmuch as compressed air not only transmitted power,
but also had a ventilating action, it far excelled steam or
water-power for working blowers of the injector type.
When available, either of the latter might be used more
advantageously for driving a ventilator, turbines acting
directly on the axle of the ventilator being especially suitable for the purpose. Dynamos were also extremely valuable for this purpose, especially where the source of power
was at a distance from the place where the power was
utilized. As a rule, all these machines were so arranged
that, by blowing, they brought to the working place air
free from gas. Recently, contrivances had been suggested
for exhausting the gas, each working place being connected
with a branch pipe, to suck the air from the highest point
where the gases usually collected. The gas thus obtained
would be conducted separately to the surface, where it
might be advantageously used for heating boilers. Although this method was excellent in principle, it remained
to be seen whether good results would be obtained in practice; since there must be a difficulty in keeping a long
length of pipes air-tight, and at the same time regulating
the exhausting action. Auxiliary ventilation was also of
importance for mines containing carbonic acid gas. Although the immediate danger of accident was slight, as the
presence of this heavy gas was generally indicated sufficiently early, by the extinguishing of the miner's light ; still

MR. W. S. GRESLEY.

there was no doubt that a slow but constant poisoning by carbonic acid gas was the cause of premature marasmus, and that the irritation of the respiratory organs by carbonic acid gas was the cause of the diseases of those organs, from which so many miners had suffered. This was a danger to which, perhaps, as many miners had fallen victims as to fire-damp, and to combat it no method seemed more efficacious than auxiliary ventilation combined with good total ventilation. Although the employment of the water-cartridge was a security against the danger of fire-damp in colleries, it was, however, necessary to bore holes deeper than would otherwise be wanted, so that there was a great practical drawback to their use. This disadvantage was obviated by an invention by Messrs. Müller and Aufschläger, who incorporated with the explosive itself the water necessary for extinguishing the flames of the shot. He alluded to the so-called fire-damp dynamite (*Wetterdynamit*). This invention consisted in mixing salts having a high proportion of water of crystallization with the dynamite; for example, about 40 per cent. of soda with ordinary dynamite, or of alum with gelatine-dynamite. Soda gave with gelatine a substance as hard as stone, and was consequently unfit to be used with gelatine-dynamite. This proportion of loosely combined water acted in a manner quite different to hygroscopic water, which completely destroyed the blasting power of gunpowder as well as of dynamite. The safe nature of the flame of the fire-damp dynamite, especially of soda-dynamite, had been proved by experiments made by the Prussian Government authorities. It was now only necessary to consider its practical value in coal-getting, and of this trials were in progress.

MR. W. S. GRESLEY said, with reference to the instruments employed for indicating the effect of atmospheric pressure upon the gas pent up in the goaves of coal-mines, that he had found nothing superior to the ordinary U-shaped water-gauge, used as he understood, for the last five or six years in the Seaham Colliery, Durham, as employed for ascertaining the friction or "drag" on ventilation. He had used this instrument for the last few years in a colliery in which the whole of the present workings were in main-road pillars, on either side of which were extensive areas of "wastes" or old workings, containing fire-damp. These old places were sealed up by stoppings constructed of clay. The water-gauge had one leg connected to a pipe which passed through one of these clay dams into the old goaves, the other leg being open to the atmosphere. The practical use of this gauge was that its fluctuations, being eight to ten times as great as those of the mercurial barometer, showed more clearly what the atmospheric pressure was at the time of observation. The water-column appeared to move as much as from six to twelve hours sooner than the mercury, thus enabling those in charge of the workings to know what to expect, and to exercise special care in cases where coming stormy weather was indicated. He placed confidence in the water-gauge readings, far before those of the ordinary barometer, as a " Colliery-warning " Indicator.

MR. J. A. LONGDEN remarked that, at the Blackwell collieries, there were three hundred doors to regulate the air in the mine. Boys were not employed as trappers; and evidently it would be impossible to obtain three hundred boys to do this work. During the nineteen years he had been practically managing collieries he had only had one boy killed, and that was through the horse starting while the boy was coupling the wagons together. He thought that, if the causes of boys' deaths were arranged under different heads, it would be found that many more were killed through accidents whilst coupling wagons together than from the cause assigned in the Paper. He had used safety-hooks ever since they came out, and had reason to be thankful for having done so. Winding-engines at collieries now drew a weight of 7 tons and upwards a distance of 400 or 500 yards in not much more than half a minute. This meant that the engine started, attained a velocity in some cases of 50 miles an hour, and stopped in thirty seconds; and this was going on incessantly for nine hours every day. If, through any accidental sticking of the valves, the engine

13

Mr. J. A. Longden.

became unmanageable, as had happened a few times, no automatic brake would be of the slightest use, and the velocity at which the immense weight came up the shaft would smash the timbers away to which the disengaging-hook plate was attached, and thus cause a similar accident to that at Houghton Main.

Safety-clutches had been tried in connection with wire guides, but nothing yet had been found of any service for high velocities with great weights where wire guides were used. It was surprising that hardly ever, if ever, was there any collision in the shafts, considering that, if the chairs were put opposite one another in the middle of the shaft, they could be made to hit each other by simply pulling one of them with one hand. The great diminution in the number of deaths through falls of roofs and sides, namely, 40 per cent., comparing the ten years ending 1880 with the ten years ending 1860, seemed remarkable, taking into account the much greater depth at which mines were now worked, and that the working faces were so much further away from the bottom, which of course meant considerably more road to maintain, and much more road for the men to travel through to get to their work and back again every day. He had tried coal-getting by wedges, but found that in a soft seam, when the wedge expanded, it simply lost its effect by squeezing the coal, and did not fetch it down. No doubt wedges would do their work in a hard coal; but the misfortune was, that when the wedges fetched down a block weighing several tons, the coal had to be broken up for loading for removal from the pit. This involved nearly as much labor as if it had not been got down at all. No doubt that, for economy, nothing had yet been produced better than gunpowder. His impression was that many accidents in the past had been the result of using " germans " or straws, instead of safety fuzes. He had tried these straws, and found that, when the shot took effect, the lighted end flew back in the goaf several yards, so that, in his opinion, they were highly dangerous. Whilst he should rejoice to see a satisfactory testing apparatus for gas, it

MR. J. A. LONGDEN.

must not be forgotten that, in well ventilated mines the only gas to be found was in the breaks in the roof, which penetrated sometimes 3 or 4 yards. The method now adopted was for the fire-trier to stand on the top of a tub and thrust his lamp, on the end of his yard-stick, into the fissure as far as he could reach. Any method which did not enable him to reach the same altitude would be practically inefficient. With respect to outbursts, he was glad to notice that the Author spoke highly of the long-wall system. He considered it the safest method of working, so far as outbursts of gas were concerned. Explosions had been far fewer, and attended with far less deadly results, where the long-wall method had been adopted, than with any other system. He had heard of a goaf being 20 acres in extent without any support. The natural effect of this was that either the floor or the roof would give way, and cause a cavity which would be filled with gas, and as soon as the floor or roof finally burst, the gas which had been penned up in the cavity would be given off. He was of opinion that this was how some of the most serious outbursts of gas had originated. With the long-wall system of packing every few yards, and the roof gradually falling behind the face, this was an impossibility. Compressed lime, he was afraid, must be considered a failure. When he tried it, the lime charred the coal for several inches round the hole, and spoilt the character of it, so that the coal had to be cut out as unmarketable. The same objection applied to compressed lime that he had before indicated in the case of wedges; it brought down a great weight of coal in a block, which had subsequently to be broken up. The difficulty of illuminating mines by electricity, where wires were connected with batteries at the bottom, arose from the falls of the roof and sides, which would be constantly putting the men in darkness. The objection to the self-contained electric lamp was that the miner would still need a safety-lamp with him to examine if there was any gas in the face. He was one of the Committee in connection with the Chesterfield Institute

MR. A. R. SENNETT.

which conducted a series of experiments on coal-dust. One particular dust, from the north of England, was highly explosive without the addition of any gas whatever. On the other hand, none of the dusts from the neighborhood of Chesterfield were nearly as explosive, and the dust from Blackwell Colliery could not be fired under any circumstances. But what constituted the inflammability in dust? No doubt some coal-seams yielded dust much more liable to explode than others. There seemed to be an inclination just now to attribute to coal-dust more importance than in the estimation of many mining engineers the case deserves. If some Committee could take up the question of the relative risk of explosion, from various dusts under varying conditions, he thought valuable information would be elicited as to the danger in working some seams and the almost total absence of danger in working other seams of coal. He should like to ask the Author his opinion concerning the origin of fire-damp. It had been held by many mining engineers that fire-damp could not exist except in the neighborhood of coal-seams, and that it was not generated by shale or bind. The late explosion in Derbyshire at Wass's lead-mine, which, he supposed, was in the limestone below the Coal Measures, brought forward this question again.

MR. A. R. SENNETT stated that the safety-lamps chiefly used in Germany were the Mueseler, the Säarbrucker (Boty), the Westphalian, and the Wolf Benzine. The flame of the lamp was in each case enclosed in a glass cylinder, it evidently being considered that the extra risk from breakage was more than compensated for by the extra candle-power obtained. Safety-lamps of any form might be made use of, provided they fulfilled certain requirements drawn up by the Rhenish Mining Board. The control was vested in this Board and five other similar Boards for the various districts, all of whom would shortly issue the conditions they required the lamps to fulfil. Mr. Hasslacker, the Secretary of the Accidents in Mines Board, had informed him that little or nothing had at present been done in lighting mines

MR. A. R. SENNETT.

by electricity, and that no satisfactory portable electric lamp, either primary or secondary, existed. Neither were fire-damp indicators, either as indicators or as recorders, made use of. On this the Board was of opinion that so long as oil lamps were employed the former were scarcely necessary, as it was considered that the lamps themselves acted sufficiently well as indicators. Belgium also was divided into districts controlled by inspecting engineers, the requirements of the lamps being modified according to the nature of the coal. With regard to electric lighting and portable electric lamps in fiery mines, Mr. Sennett felt that it should not be assumed that lamps were absolutely safe, unless provision was made that short-circuiting of the terminals could not take place in the event of the lamp being accidentally broken. The bulb of the incandescent lamp should, of course, be so enclosed that the miner could not detach it in the mine and thereby produce a spark. Also, there should be no switch nor other gear external to the lamp, or open to the atmosphere of the mine, which the miner could move or tamper with, or which might be accidentally moved. The requisite alteration of the connections for charging and discharging should be performed automatically, so that no skilled attendance should be required in connection with the lamps. Mr. Sennett had constructed a lamp to fulfil these requirements about five years ago, one of which was shown. It was intended to sustain a light equal to about 5 candles for fourteen hours. It was far too heavy and bulkly for convenient use, if the accumulators then obtainable had to be used. The contrivances for extinguishing the lamp and arranging the contacts for re-charging the accumulators, for putting the lamp again in circuit and connecting up for discharging, were all contained in an air-tight compartment of the lamp, without any movable connection with its exterior. When the lamp was first put together, compressed air was passed through the plug at the top of the lamp, which was provided with an ordinary oil-skin air-valve, to retain it when the syringe was removed. The effect of the compressed

Mr. A. R. Sennett.

air was to cause the corrugated sides of a small metallic box to collapse, and thereby establish contact through the lamp. The lamp would then continue to burn, but should the glass cylinder become cracked or broken, or the lamp otherwise damaged, the lamp was switched out of circuit, and all connection with the terminals disestablished. When the lamp needed re-charging it would be brought to bank and placed on the charging-table. The action of an electro-magnet beneath the charging-table would cause the lamp to be switched out of circuit, and the accumulators would be put into connection with two studs at the bottom of the lamp, and which came into contact with the charging terminals of the table. When the lamp was required for use, on its being taken off the table, it immediately became lighted, and all connection with the aforementioned studs was broken. He was not aware if the Commissioners considered it safe to employ incandescent electric lamps in the ordinary way, in portions of mines likely to contain an explosive mixture. If this were so, it appeared to him that in positions where a fall of roof was likely to occur, the danger of firing the mixture by the spark on breaking contact, when the cables were torn asunder, would be greatly minimized by employing, instead of two separate leads (one—one+), a single cable enclosing both leads encased in an insulating material much more elastic than copper, so that the wires might be broken and the sparking take place before the envelope was broken. This should be in conjunction with automatic gear at the bank, that the circuit might be simultaneously broken there, so that no electrical difference of potential should exist at the fractured ends. And further, the insulation between the leads might be plastic, so that in the event of a large mass of coal or other material falling on the cable, and there being danger of the latter having its leads laid bare, the plastic insulator would yield, and short-circuiting take place within the insulating envelope, and by suitable gear at bank the short-circuiting might cause the cables to be instantly disconnected. Much labor and responsibility was entailed

MR. M. H. N. STORY-MASKELYNE, M. P.

in connection with safety-lamps, on account of the necessity of unlocking, lighting, and re-locking the lamps at bank before they were taken down the shaft. While in Belgium recently he had seen an ingenious lamp, invented by Mr. H. Pieper, of Liège, which obviated this. It was an oil lamp, and similar to other lamps in which a glass cylinder was employed. The wick, however, was furnished with a platinum spiral, to which could be conveniently attached the terminals of an accumulator or primary battery, by means of which the lamp was lighted. It was also provided with an arrangement whereby the light would be extinguished were an attempt made to remove the oil-reservoir, etc., from its glass and gauze case.

Mr. M. H. N. STORY-MASKELYNE, M. P., wished to refer to a matter which appeared to be vital to the success of any good miners' lamp in which glow-lights would have to be employed. Only incandescent lamps could be used underground if electricity was to be the means of illumination. A lamp, weighing only 4 lbs. 2 oz., had been exhibited, with which he had a good deal to do in carrying it to its present position of excellence. It had been tried under every condition proposed by the mine managers of the North, and had withstood every ordeal to which it had been exposed. But for a practical application, on a commercial scale, of the principle involved in this or any other electric lamp for the use of miners, it was absolutely essential that their public use should not be barred by extortionate conditions to be imposed by any of the patentees of the manufacture of glow-lamps. Mr. Maskelyne therefore desired to direct attention to the state of the law in this regard. By the Act of 1883 (Patents, Designs, and Trade Marks Act), clause 22, this difficulty was entirely met. A patentee was bound to grant licenses on reasonable terms, and, failing his doing so, the Board of Trade might order the patentee to grant licenses on such terms as to the amount of royalties, security for payment, or otherwise, as the Board, having regard to the nature of the invention and the circumstances of the case, might deem just, and any such order might be

MR. ARTHUR SOPWITH.

enforced by mandamus.   It would be an outrageous thing if a patentee, having the monopoly of the manufacture of glow-lamps, were, by unnecessary delay in their supply or by demanding exorbitant terms for their use, or for the license to manufacture them, to prevent the great boon of a really safe electric lamp being supplied to the miners at a reasonable cost.   The persons who, with himself, were sanguine enough to believe that the problem of supplying such a lamp had been solved, were resolved that the clause in the Act should be immediately put in force, if this difficulty should be found to impede their efforts to supply such an economical and efficient electric safety-lamp.

MR. ARTHUR SOPWITH remarked that the Author had alluded to the utter inadequacy of the light given by certain safety-lamps, including the Clanny, and this statement could not, he thought, be materially modified in the case of any of the lately improved types of lamps, more especially as the bonneting or shielding of the gauze affected the upward diffusion of light.   As the safety of many lamps, even under extraordinary conditions in an explosive mixture of gas, was practically assured, it followed that any decided improvement must be looked for in the form of increased illumination rather than in the way of greater immunity from explosions.   Although there might yet be some little margin for providing a more efficient light, in the present types of lamps, it would appear that practically a limit had been reached in the illuminating power of oil safety-lamps, and it must be accepted that electric lighting was the only system from which material benefit could be expected.   An experience extending over a considerable time with half-a-dozen Pitkin lamps (which had been in the hands of the colliers and therefore subjected to rough treatment in the working face), was fairly favorable as regarded working efficiency, and at any rate sufficiently so as to afford grounds for believing in the ultimate success of such a system of lighting.   Necessarily there was much to be done before the practicability of using portable electric lamps, economically and on an extensive scale, could be determined.

MR. ARTHUR SOPWITH.

It must be considered, however, that while the light of primary or secondary-battery portable lamps was, relatively to ordinary safety-lamps, an adequate one, it was necessarily limited by the requirements of lightness in weight and long-continued action in the cells, and any considerable increase in the illumination of workings must result from the adoption of large accumulator cells, and the use of leads and branch wires. Whether it were desirable or not to aim at an illumination of mines which might more or less approach a luxury, he did not consider the Author was justified in so arbitrarily dismissing the system of having attached wires to lamps, on the mere ground that they could not be protected. The various details connected with the easy removal, and at the same time protection, of the wires in the workings could hardly have been determined by the trials alluded to, and the matter had, he thought, received insufficient attention. That the system was applicable to working faces must, in the absence of prolonged trials, be taken as a mere opinion, but it was based upon consideration of details in workings where great difficulty was experienced from falling roof and heavy timbering. The statement, made by the Author, as to the obvious liability of the men to get their feet entangled in the leads, presupposed the use of lamps without any order or method; but it must be considered that the necessity of frequent removal of lamps, or alteration in leads, was reduced by the increased amount of light obtainable. Thus 8-candle-power lamps placed 12 yards apart gave a comfortable working light throughout a stall face. In the case of long-wall working (to which alone he had confined his attention in respect to this system of lighting) there seemed little difficulty in protecting the leads and branch wires and lamps; the former could be run along the foot of the cog or pack wall, and the latter against the face of the wall, and so not only completely out of the way of the men, but in a practically secure position. Moreover the routine of lighting presented little trouble. As the working was carried out right and left from the way end, the leads could be gradually extended to the limit of

Mr. Arthur Sopwith,

this stall, say 30 yards on either side. After each "drift," or holing was worked off, no more labor was entailed than the coiling up of the lead and letting out 6 to 7 feet of the main cable, laid along the road from the accumulators, to cover the advance of the face. Apart from the broad question as to whether the introduction of wires should be admissible into fiery mines, there were many difficulties to overcome before the system of lighting with wires attached to lamps could be recommended; but the special difficulty, mentioned by the Author, was in all probability not so insuperable as he implied. Although it was quite probable that the use of leads and branch wires might be proved to be inapplicable as a universal system, the partial lighting by such system might be a useful adjunct in working faces, and it appeared important that the consideration of the protec-tion of, and practical way of economically and efficiently dealing with, cables or branch wires in a mine should not be lost sight of. Apart from the more difficult and intri-cate question of bringing electric lighting into use at the actual working face, he would direct attention to the facil-ities that existed in collieries for the economical extension of electric lighting in respect of main cables. This referred to the use of old iron or steel ropes for such purpose. At Cannock Chase Colliery some 4000 yards of old rope had thus been utilized, and in one instance a cable had been laid having only a resistance of $\frac{1}{25}$ ohm for 1400 yards, a condi-tion of profuse cable that would not have been thought of if copper cable had been in question. In any extensive system of lighting in by-roads and stations, the importance of cheap cable was evident. Approximately the relative values of old iron ropes and bare copper cable were, after allowing for difference in conductivity, as 1 to 5, and he could point to conditions where the difference was consider-ably greater. Some of these ropes had been laid together in a trench on the surface and only insulated with coal-dust and tar, so that little trouble was involved in insulating them in a dry mine. In fact, iron ropes laying side by side on the ground in an underground road, and extending over a distance of 140 yards (single distance) had been found to show no appreciable leakage.   The practical experience gained in laying down the cables alluded to, in trenches on the surface, in wet shafts and in roadways underground, and the economy and efficiency of the rough methods adopted in insulating, tended to prove that the problem of extensive lighting underground did not present such great difficulties as might at first be anticipated.   He knew of no obstacle, beyond the cost and as yet unproved certainty of any prolonged life of cells, to very large extensions of electric lighting underground, and he was by no means sure that the question of lighting the actual face of a working was yet disposed of.

MR. A. L. STEAVENSON observed that the fact that " miscellaneous " accidents had not apparently diminished since 1851, was satisfactorily accounted for, in face of the large quantities of minerals now dealt with, and the high-pressure speed at which all the operations were carried out.   He thought not merely the Government regulations, but the increased intelligence and care of the workmen, deserved credit, in that these accidents had not increased.   On the other hand, the shortening of the hours of labor resulted in the miner working at a higher rate of speed, which perhaps accounted for the " deaths from falls of roof and sides " constituting a larger proportion of the total deaths in recent years than they did thirty years ago.   To provide against these accidents, although forming 76 per cent. of the whole, not much benefit could be expected from the labors of the Royal Commissioners or scientific men ; but these labors had afforded great help in all matters relating to explosions of gas or dust, and especially as to explosives and safety-lamps, and to these subjects the Author had naturally devoted the most of his address.   It was very instructive, with existing views of the dust theory, to look back at the particulars of explosions in former years, practically never fairly accounted for, say, for instance, the Seaham explosion in October, 1871.   Every witness agreed that the explosion occurred at a given point on the main

Mr. A. L. Steavenson.

intake. The man who fired the shot survived to say he went about 30 yards out of the way of the shot, and both shot and explosion came together (stone was being blasted at night); he said, "There was no possibility of any gas where we were exploding as there was sufficient air to drive a windmill;" in fact, 78,000 cubic feet of air per minute were passing this point. The result was that the explosion was assigned to a sudden outburst of gas. Twenty-six persons lost their lives, and in this case, as in almost every one of the explosions in the North of England, dust alone was the only explanation which met all the difficulties which cropped up in the inquiry. Before leaving this particular case he would refer to the Author's allusion to a second or back explosion (p. 14, of the report of Mr. Willis, Inspector of Mines). Witness, a coal-miner, said, "Altogether I heard two explosions after Hutchinson's shot;" the first was a heavy explosion, but the second was not so severe. He had himself observed the evidence of a second explosion, when examining the workings after the explosion at Tudhoe Colliery. Baulks of timber, as thick as a man's body, were broken in two, in clearly opposite directions, and although he did not at that time believe in the dust theory, no doubt it was the proper explanation of that accident—from a shot which had been fired on the main intake. With the Author's objections to shot-firing in coal, he entirely concurred, and for these and other reasons he had promoted the use of the coal-wedge. At Tursdale Colliery sixty-four miners were now using it, with a great improvement in the proportion of large coal, and, of course, absolute freedom from danger; and, as the cost of using the wedge compared favorably with that of high explosives and of water-cartridges, it appeared to him to almost entirely obviate the necessity for using them in coal; their necessity had, in fact, ceased to exist; this referred not merely to long-wall working, but to the system of board and pillar. To the fact that water, when used with high explosives, would obviate their sudden and crushing effects, he could not at present assent, but would take an early opportunity

MR. A. H. STOKES.

of testing it in Cleveland Ironstone, where a slow rending action was an absolute necessity. His experience of the water-cartridge had not been large, but hitherto had been very unfavorable, on account of the cartridges bursting during insertion. With respect to the flame from a blown-out shot, he had found that not only was the tamping blown out, but the large grains of powder also, in a state of incandescence. . The greater prevalence of mine explosions in the winter months, especially during intense frosts, might, he thought, be accounted for by the dryness of the air robbing the dust of its moisture in the main air-ways. The distilling action of the heat of explosion upon coal-dust, which of course produced gas, had not received the general attention it deserved; it met the objection, still raised by many persons, to the possibility of dust alone affording an explosion. In none of the experiments upon coal-dust did he find the question of the fineness of the dust sufficiently appreciated. Whether the dust from that or the other colliery was most explosive, seemed to him to be entirely dependent upon the fineness of the particles. He had employed the Liveing Indicator ever since its first invention, and considered that in the hands of the colliery manager, or good overman, it was a very valuable invention; but it was not suited to the hands of every rough experimenter; the test was a delicate one, and must always have careful, and to some extent skilful, manipulation.

MR. A. H. STOKES thought the Author, p. 45, appeared to question his remarks published in a Paper read before the Chesterfield and Midland Counties Institution of Engineers, namely, that the excess of gas given off from goaves upon the sudden reduction of atmospheric pressure was carried away unnoticed. The Author had given an illustration, showing that for a diminution of 0·01 inch of barometric pressure, a goaf of only 1 acre in area and average height of 3 feet might part with about 44 cubic feet of its gaseous contents; but he had not mentioned the number of cubic feet of air in the ventilating current, which would probably have swept past the goaf during the fall of 0·01

MR. A. H. STOKES.

inch of the barometer. However, supposing the barometer
to have fallen 0·01 inch in five minutes—a very sudden fall
—probably in most collieries there would have passed by
the goaf 25,000 cubic feet of air in five minutes, and certainly 44 cubic feet of gas in 25,000 cubic feet of air would
escape unnoticed. The references in Mr. Stokes' Paper
were solely to accumulations of gas, and not to out bursts;
and he considered the Author's remarks, referring to
" the majority of British coal-mines, which are now provided with ventilation amply sufficient to cope effectually
with any such possible variations in the condition of the
air in the workings," scarcely in unison with the criticism
passed upon the comments named by the Author, pp. 51
and 52. The ventilation of a mine should always be far
in excess of what was required, and beyond the reach of
constantly recurring barometrical changes, having a surplus
of air which would be more than sufficient to meet such
emergency ; and any mine in which the rise and fall of the
barometer was the balance of safety should be considered
unfit to work. With regard to the lime-cartridge and the
" remarkable comments " published in the Transactions
of the Chesterfield and Midland Counties Institution of
Engineers, at the time those comments were penned he
fully believed, from experiments which he had seen, that
the lime-cartridge was a failure in the parts of a mine where
such an appliance was most needed, namely, at the gate
ends, or brushing, in the roadways ; and at the present day
he believed there was not a single coal-mine in the whole
of the Midland district using the lime-cartridge, except
Shipley Colliery, where the cartridge was made. The use
of the lime-cartridge was not free from danger, as could be
seen by reference to the accidents from its use, recorded
in the Annual Reports of Inspectors of Mines. He would
also like to direct attention to the great difference between
" bricklayers continually " handling " with impunity " mortar which had been thoroughly slaked and left without
heat, and the collier handling caustic lime in the process of
being slaked. He could only repeat the assertion, pre-

viously made, that the colliers loading coals in damp mines, where the lime-cartridge had been used, had to protect their hands from the effect of the unslaked lime; and even workmen in hot and dry mines, and perspiring freely, found the moisture of their hands caused the lime-dust to wear and eat away the skin, unless protected; and he repeated this assertion from actual investigation and from seeing and hearing the colliers themselves. Personally, he would like to have seen the lime process an unqualified success, for all and every case where explosives were used in mines; but he yet feared, in its present state, its successful application was only very limited for coal-getting or other mining operations.

SIR FREDERICK ABEL, in reply upon the discussion and the correspondence, said he would in the first instance notice the criticisms of Mr. Bainbridge, that the subject of wedges had been incompletely dealt with by him; of Mr. Sydney Walker, that he had not discussed electric-signalling appliances; and of Mr. George Seymour, that he had confined himself to the consideration of accidents in coal-mines, to the exclusion of metalliferous mines. He would point out that, in the concluding part of the Paper, he had disclaimed any attempt even to deal completely with the comprehensive subject of accidents in coal-mines, having confined his subject to the most prominent only of the causes of accidents in collieries, and to the knowledge of those means by which their disastrous effects might be diminished. It would have been presumptuous in him, as an amateur in the study of mechanical appliances connected with this subject, to have criticised in detail the relative merits of different systems of wedges for coal-getting, or to have done more than give the conclusions arrived at by his colleagues on the Royal Commission and himself, from the evidence collected respecting the value of detaching hooks, of safety-hooks or clutches, and of other mechanical devices to guard against shaft-accidents. He might point out, however, that although he had not dealt separately with sources of accidents which might be

SIR FREDERICK ABEL.

peculiar to metalliferous mines, he had, in the first part of his Paper, incidentally discussed the subject of the employment of ladders, cages, and man-engines, in mines of that class to which Mr. George Seymour had referred. While concurring in Mr. Walker's view that the adoption of electric-signalling appliances in mines was attended with important advantages in underground work, he could scarcely regard them as being directly connected with the subject of prevention of accidents, and he had therefore omitted their examination.

It had been stated by Mr. Lupton that the danger of a goaf as a lurking place for fire-damp and air-mixtures " depended upon two things, the depth of the mine and the age of goaf ;" but, surely, the possibility of danger from goaves was also closely connected with the question of the extent to which the old workings, where these goaves had been formed, were originally filled up, and the consequent degree of liability to the formation of large cavities, by the subsidence of large irregular masses of hard stone, which would not become filled up, in course of time, as assumed. Mr. Lupton dismissed the question of danger arising from accumulations of gas in goaves in a very facile manner, by saying that if the goaf was " properly ventilated, there was comparatively little danger." But it had been pointed out in the Paper that the great difficulty of dealing with the ventilation of goaves, in an effectual manner, constituted a most important and obvious source of danger ; and that the possibility of connections being established between gas-laden cavities in the interior of goaves, and localities situated at no great distance from them where shot-firing was carried on, was also a probable element of danger in connection with imperfectly packed goaves, which merited grave consideration. This view of the importance of giving serious attention to the possibly intimate connection of goaves with many coal-mine explosions, had been confirmed by Sir Warington Smyth's remarks on this head ; and the observations of Mr. William Morgans, who had done good service in carefully examining into this subject, were well

SIR FREDERICK ABEL.

worthy the consideration of Mr. Lupton. With respect to the inquiry made by that gentleman, as to whether there appeared to be any connection between the depth of a mine, and the pressure of gas in the coal of that mine, the results of the pressure-measurements referred to in the Paper as having been made in several coal-mines in the North of England and in South Wales, did not indicate any connection of that nature; thus, in one particular mine, the pressure of gas in a hole bored into the coal, at a depth of 2400 feet, was 150 lbs. per square inch; while in another hole in the same mine, at a depth of only 900 feet, the pressure was 280 lbs. In a second instance, a pressure of 430 lbs. was recorded in a hole at a depth of 1480 feet, while in a hole in the same mine 20 feet deeper, a pressure of 318 lbs. was indicated. It was also found that the direction of the hole, with reference to the cleavage of the coal, had no influence upon the gas-pressure indicated; and that, as mentioned in the Paper, several holes bored to different depths parallel to, and within a short distance from each other, gave very different maximum pressures of gas.

It had been suggested by Mr. Henry Hall that the late Commission should have given information as to the explosive force capable of being exerted by definite quantities of fire-damp; he stated that it was difficult to say how much gas was dangerous, and that officials treated the discovery of large volumes of gas here and there, during inspection, as being of no moment, saying that it was not dangerous. The Author could only reply that any statements, with regard to the explosive force capable of being exerted by different volumes of pure marsh-gas, would be of no practical value in reference to the possible destructive effects which roughly estimated accumulations of fire-damp of unknown composition, in admixture with unknown proportions of air, might exert. The information, now widely disseminated, regarding the effects of dust (existing almost everywhere underground) in adding to and carrying on fire-damp explosions, should, however, suffice to warn those entrusted with the inspection of mine-workings, that sur-

14

SIR FREDERICK ABEL.

rounding circumstances must indeed be most exceptional
which would warrant the treatment with indifference of a
considerable volume of gas, found in any part of a mine.

The observations of Mr. Lupton, with regard to the part
played by coal-dust in mine-explosions, were good illustrations of the nature of arguments advanced by ardent advocates of the view that coal-dust alone was the cause of
many explosions. There was some originality, however,
in the view that if the results of analysis of the air of a mine
in particular places demonstrated the existence in it of a
small quantity of fire-damp, there should be an inclination
to discredit those results, because Mr. Lupton's arguments
demonstrated, to his satisfaction, that no gas whatever
ought to be found there. Other observations in the course
of the discussion illustrated the diversity of views, still
entertained by competent authorities, as to the sufficiency
of the evidence, experimental and inferential, which had
been advanced or collected in favor of the view that explosions originated with, and were carried on by, coal-dust in
the complete absence of fire-damp. Thus, Mr. Morgans
had pointed out the insufficiency of evidence in the case of
two explosions which had been ascribed to coal-dust alone,
and Mr. Henry Hall, an eminent inspector of mines, who
(without any detraction from Mr. Galloway's merits) had
been the first to make experiments with coal-dust, upon a
scale nearly approaching in magnitude the condition of
things existing in a colliery, while stating his conviction
that explosions were greatly aggravated by the presence of
coal-dust, had, at the same time, expressed his belief that
no explosion had occurred in a mine of importance where
there was no fire-damp. On the other hand, Mr. Sawyer
had referred to a case in which, in his opinion, an extensive
explosion had been caused by coal-dust, with probably
only a "trace" of fire-damp in the air. The opinion as to
the probable amount of fire-damp present was, of course,
based upon the application of the usual (lamp-) test, which
failed to detect less than 2 per cent. of gas, in the hands of
experienced observers. This was an instance of the indefi-

nite kind of information upon which the assumptions that no fire-damp was concerned in particular explosions in dusty mines were always based, and which was not of a nature to combat the validity of the very definite statements advanced by the French authorities, Messrs. Mallard and Le Chatelier, namely, that all explosions of magnitude, in which dust had evidently played an important part, had occurred in mines in which fire-damp existed; and that no explosion had been known to occur in lignite-mines, which were quite free from fire-damp, although they were very dusty, the dust being highly inflammable. Mr. Bedlington had, in the Author's opinion, expressed the rational view with regard to the coal-dust question, when he stated that, while he was not convinced that dust alone would serve to account for explosions of magnitude, which should be of very much more frequent occurrence if such were the case, he admitted that, where much dust was present, explosions were greatly aggravated thereby.

In the opinion of Mr. J. B. Atkinson the Author had not realized the full importance of the influence of coal-dust in colliery explosions. A perusal of the Paper would, however show not only that the Author had there given the fullest weight to the facts and views contained in the Messrs. Atkinson's instructive work on Explosions in Coal-mines, but also that, after summarizing, he believed in a thoroughly impartial manner, the existing evidence and views regarding the part played by coal-dust (which he had to discuss in much greater detail in that part of the Royal Commissioners' Report which dealt with this subject), he had laid the greatest stress upon "the serious dangers arising from the existence of dust-accumulations in collieries," and upon the great importance of not "allowing any accumulation of dry dust to exist in workings where shots are fired." He had only argued (and in this action he was supported not merely by the writings of Messrs. Galloway, Atkinson, and others, but also by the observations which had been made during the discussion of the Paper), that the "serious dangers" liable to arise "from

SIR FREDERICK ABEL.

the existence of dust-accumulations in collieries," could certainly not become more impressed upon the mining public by the contention that particular explosions had been examples of "pure dust explosions," when all that could be said in reference to the asserted freedom of the air in the mine, at the time of the explosion, from fire-damp, was that it was practically free from gas, or that only traces of fire-damp existed, or ought to have existed, in the air of the mine. Certain experiments of Mr. Hall, of Professor Marreco (to which Mr. William Cochrane referred), of the Author himself, and most recently of the Prussian Fire-damp Commission, had demonstrated beyond doubt that explosions, of a more or less violent character, might be brought about by coal-dust possessing particular characteristics, in the complete absence of any trace of fire-damp, and this had been clearly pointed out by him in the Paper; but those experiments also demonstrated as conclusively that a combination, in coal-dust, of the characteristics of extreme fineness of division, high inflammability and peculiar physical structure or condition, essential for the production of explosive effects and for very rapid transmission of flame, was very exceptional. Thus the "Leycett" dust, used in his experiments, the "Pluto" dust (and one other), with which the Prussian Fire-damp Commission obtained, at Neunkirchen, violent explosive effects in the absence of fire-damp, such as described by Mr. S. B. Coxon, were exceptional dusts among a great variety of fine, dry coal-dusts experimented with, many of which exhibited comparatively very little, or no tendency to propagate flame rapidly and to a considerable distance, in the complete absence of fire-damp, even when they were much more thickly suspended in the air than there would be any probability of their being in actual practice. The statement made in the communication from Mr. J. A. Longden, of Alfreton, a member of the Committee of the Chesterfield Mining Institute, by whom a most important series of coal-dust experiments had been carried out, afforded valuable confirmation of the truth of these observations. He stated that, amongst the very large number of dusts experimented with, there was "one particular dust from the North of England," which "was highly explosive, without the addition of any gas whatever. On the other hand, none of the dusts from the neighborhood of Chesterfield were nearly as explosive, and the dust from Blackwell Colliery could not be fired under any circumstances." Mr. Longden concluded, from the results of his special practical and experimental experience, that "there seemed to be an inclination just now to attribute to coal-dust more importance than, in the estimation of many mining engineers, the case deserved." Mr. J. B. Atkinson's criticism of the Author's statement that experimental results, of more or less exceptional character, or obtained under conditions which did not approximate to those likely to occur in a mine, was answered, not only by the foregoing facts, but also by the illustration which Mr. Galloway's communication furnished, of the unpractically exceptional combination of circumstances which had attended some of the experiments made in support of the so-called "pure coal-dust theory," when, with the return-air of a mine, the freedom of which from fire-damp was not maintained, the air required to be literally black with dust before it would ignite.

In order to favor the pure coal-dust theory, it became necessary (as was done by its advocates), while admitting that fire-damp existed in the air of most mines, to dismiss it in special instances, as a "trace" (which it was assumed to be upon theoretical considerations), and therefore, of no account as a factor in the origination or the development of explosions. This was a method of dealing with it not warranted by the results of experiments, nor by the fact that it had hitherto been the custom to consider the air of a mine free from all but "traces" of fire-damp, when it had not furnished indications of gas by means of the safety-lamp test, but which might nevertheless contain at least 2 per cent. of gas. Mr. W. N. Atkinson's statement, that "it would probably not be difficult to prove by means of

Sir Frederick Abel.

Liveing's indicator, or the Pieler lamp, that the large volumes of air passing along the main intake air-ways of such collieries did not contain even the very minute quantities of fire-damp which these instruments were capable of detecting" suggested an obvious direction in which the advocates of the pure coal-dust theory could seek for positive evidence in support of their views. At the same time, the Author would not desire to suggest that further labors in this or other directions, with the object of supporting particular theories regarding the precise manner in which coal-dust operated as an element of danger in mines, would serve the least practically useful result; for while, on the one hand, both the possibility of serious explosions being caused in mine-ways and workings, where the air might be assumed to be absolutely free from fire, by the existence in abundance of coal-dust, possessing certain essential characteristics, and also the very exceptional occurrence in coal-mines of a sufficiently abundant supply of dust possessing those characteristics, had been thoroughly demonstrated, the serious dangers arising, in other ways now well known, from any kind of dust-accumulation in coal-mines, had, on the other hand, been not only conclusively established and elucidated, but had also become fully recognized by the mining community and officially, and means both practical and effectual had been prescribed for avoiding or diminishing those dangers. He considered that, in the present state of knowledge, it would have been unreasonable to provide, in the recently passed Act, for the systematic damping of coal-dust in all parts of dry mines, which Mr. W. N. Atkinson seemed to think should have been done; but that the prescription of precautions, to guard against the ignition of coal-dust during shot-firing, must certainly be regarded as one of the most important improvements effected by that Act; and it had been very satisfactory to have learned, in the course of this discussion, the nature of several efficient means of damping coal-dust in mines which had already been elaborated and applied, and which were obviously susceptible of further important development.

SIR FREDERICK ABEL.

It had been stated by Mr. J. B. Atkinson that his experience pointed in a direction opposed to the accepted fact, mentioned by the Author, that the combustion of a mixture of air with a finely-divided inflammable solid was gradual in comparison with that of a mixture of inflammable gas and air; but Mr. Atkinson had unfortunately not given the nature of his experience. On the other hand, he had mentioned several conditions under which he conceded that the Author's statement would hold good, and the argument advanced in favor of his view, upon which he appeared chiefly to rely, was embodied in the statement, that while the " rapidity of combustion of a homogeneous gas- and air-mixture probably reached its maximum within a short distance of the point of ignition," the "reverse was probable in the case of a coal-dust and air-mixture." The Author would venture to ask whether this statement did not point to the conclusion that the transmission of flame by the gas-and air-mixture was the most rapid of the two?

It was to be regretted that the labors of some of those who had contributed to a recognition by the mining public of the dangers of coal-dust, had, by developing in those workers a tendency to place it in a pre-eminent position among the elements of danger existing in collieries, led to a depreciation by them of the dangers due to sudden outbursts of gas, which had been so forcibly, but certainly not too seriously, dwelt upon by Sir Warington Smyth, and also by Mr. R. Bedlington, and to the accumulation of gas in, and its emission from, or possible explosion in, goaves, which Mr. Morgans had so lucidly discussed. That such was the case, however, must be evident to those who would peruse some of the observations elicited by the Paper. Without assenting to the remarks, made by Mr. Stokes, which tended to the dangerous inference that the possible escape of gas into the main-air from accumulations in goaves could not be matter for serious consideration, he feared that many mine-owners and managers would not consider that the conditions to be fulfilled by the ventilation of a mine, as laid down by Mr. Stokes, were such as they should be compelled to comply with.

SIR FREDERICK ABEL.

The particular source of accident to which Mr. Edward
Combes had directed attention, namely, the occasional
escape into workings of choke-damp, or carbonic acid gas,
from goaves or other lurking places, had received the consideration of the late Commission ; but no other means
could be suggested of guarding against its dangers than the
constant careful inspection of localities liable to be invaded
by escapes of the poisonous gas, the presence of which
fortunately was indicated by its effects upon the flame of a
lamp or candle before it could exert its deadly action. The
maintenance of powerful air-currents, in localities liable to
be infested by it, was an obvious precautionary measure,
and the observations of Mr. Max Georgi on the importance
of supplementing the regular system of ventilation by a system of auxiliary ventilation, and on the course of action
taken by the Saxon Government in reference to this important additional safeguard, well merited consideration in
especial regard to the dangers of choke-damp.

Sir Frederick Abel did not think that the remarks made
by Mr. Harries, in support of his view that accidents were
most prevalent during anti-cyclonic disturbances, needed
any addition by him to the observations made in the Paper,
in respect to the extent to which importance could be
attached to the various views advanced regarding the connection between atmospheric disturbances and coal-mine
explosions. Mr. Sawyer had made some very cogent remarks, in which he entirely concurred, in support of the
conclusion, that it was idle to attach importance to attempts
to establish a regular connection between barometrical variations and colliery explosions. Variations in dryness and
in temperature of the external atmosphere might, on the
other hand, in the present days of powerful ventilation, influence considerably the magnitude of explosions, in reference to the great influence of moisture upon the inflammability of coal-dust.

In referring to the increase of accidents due to falls of
coal and stone in mines, Mr. Bainbridge had pointed to
what certainly might be considered as one probable cause,

SIR FREDERICK ABEL.

namely, the gradual exhaustion of seams having the best roofs, and the consequent increase in the work done in seams with insecure roofs. Sir Warington Smyth had laid stress upon the importance of providing the miner with a good light; and the Author felt bound to state that, while he concurred with Mr. Henry Hall in his view that too much importance had been attached to the provision of a large amount of light by the lamps furnished to miners (especially as regarded miners' electric lamps), he must point out that he certainly had not advanced the obviously untenable view assigned to him by Mr. Hall, that falls of roof would be less frequent if the men had better light than was now provided. What he had maintained was, that casualties from falls would be diminished, if the men could apply sight in addition to ear in judging of the degree of imminence of danger threatened by a coming fall.

The information which he had brought before the Institution in his Paper respecting recent improvements in the construction of safety-lamps, and the progress made in the application of electricity to the illumination of mines, had been very usefully supplemented by the interesting exhibition of recent work in these directions.

Some points had been referred to in the discussion with respect to general details of construction in lamps of modern types, a few of which he would briefly notice. He concurred in Mr. Bainbridge's view, that a lamp which could be confidently depended upon as safe in a current velocity of 30 feet per second, was for all practical purposes a safe lamp in most mines, and that many designers of new lamps had fallen into the error of resorting to very complicated and costly arrangements, for enabling their lamps to withstand exceptionally severe tests. Such lamps presented the additional defect that they were heavy, and that their various parts were difficult to put together properly, so that reliance could not, especially in the absence of a gas-test, be placed upon their reaching the miners' hands in a safe condition. The most recent lamp of Mr. Bainbridge's construction certainly possessed the merit of simplicity; the readiness with

SIR FREDERICK ABEL.

which it could be cleaned and the arrangement for leaving the glass untouched, were very good points.

It would certainly not be found by Mr. Hall that the Author had especially recommended lamps with glasses; he had distinctly stated that, although such lamps were obviously superior in point of efficiency as illuminating agents, they were open to objection on the score of uncertainty of safety which the glass presented; and he had gone into considerable detail with respect to the various possible causes of the doubtful safety of such lamps, even when provided with double glasses. Sir Warington Smyth had referred to two unquestionable drawbacks presented by the hood or "bonnet," with which the majority of modern lamps, from the Marsaut to Mr. Bainbridge's latest lamp, were provided. The additional heating of the lamp, due to the retention of heat by the metal envelope surrounding the gauze, was no doubt a source of occasional inconvenience; but the more substantial objections were that the bonnet prevented the men from seeing what was going on inside the gauze, and also obstructed the distribution of light above a certain plane, so that the roof of a road or a working was even more imperfectly illuminated than by the old gauze lamps. The first of these objections was not difficult to remedy; by cutting two narrow slots opposite to each other, in the bonnets, and fitting these with mica plates, which could be easily done, small windows could be provided, through which all that took place inside the enclosed gauze cage could be readily seen, and the protection afforded by the bonnet would not in the least degree be diminished. He had fitted several bonneted lamps in this way, for the purpose of seeing how they behaved in powerful currents of explosive gas-mixtures, and the arrangement answered perfectly. The obstruction of light in the upward direction was inevitable, and this was undoubtedly a sacrifice in efficiency, which, however, was considered as more than compensated by the safety which the use of the bonnet secured. At any rate, the most experienced lamp-makers, such as Messrs. Bainbridge, Ashworth, and Marsaut, like other

SIR FREDERICK ABEL.

inventors of new forms of lamps, mostly adopted the hood or bonnet as an essential element of safety. Mr. Sawyer, one of H.M. Inspectors of Mines, had said that even Mueseler lamps should be fitted with bonnets, which should be easily movable, to facilitate the examination of the gauze by the fireman, and the Author believed that the bonneted Marsaut lamp had come into extensive use in some districts, with no inconvenient results, the superior illuminating power of the lamp compensating for the partial obstruction of the light in the upward direction.

Members of the Institution had an opportunity afforded them, by the interesting exhibition of lamps of various kinds in the building, of forming some judgment for themselves whether he had been too sanguine in predicting that the safe and thoroughly efficient application of the electric light to the purposes of the miner would speedily be accomplished. How far the cost and the weight of self-contained miners' electric lamps would be susceptible of sufficient reduction, to bring them thoroughly into competition with safety-lamps of the best modern types (for they would scarcely be likely to compete with the older forms of lamp in these respects), would probably be determined within a a brief period. Certainly the present original cost of the secondary battery in lamps was prohibitive, as pointed out by Mr. Tylden-Wright ; while their weight, although it had been already considerably reduced, was still very inconveniently great. On the other hand, the lightest of the improved forms of safety-lamps were at least double the weight given by Mr. Tylden-Wright as that with which the electric lamps had to compare. He could not agree with the view, taken by Mr. Sydney Walker, that the eventual method of applying electricity to the illumination of the face of the coal would be by supply-mains, or main-conductors. The objections to fixed lights, and to the attachment of lamps to main-conductors by branch wires, had been pointed out in the Paper. Those objections appeared to counterbalance the advantages to be secured, and they were not met by Mr. Walker. Moreover, the lamp which

SIR FREDERICK ABEL.

gave light to the miner for his work should also be available for lighting his path to and from work, the distances to be travelled rendering the illumination of the mine-roads throughout generally quite out of the question, from the point of view of cost alone. As to difficulties in the application of secondary-battery lamps, at collieries where electric-light installations already existed, consequent upon necessary complications of arrangement, he could assure Mr. Walker that practical experience had already given a satisfactory answer in the negative to this supposed objection. The chief advantages, at present possessed by such primary-battery lamps as had assumed a practically useful form, consisted in their comparative lightness and their lower cost. Mr. Tylden-Wright and Mr. J. A. Longden had pointed to two important objections to the general use of electric lamps to the exclusion of ordinary safety-lamps ; they afforded to the miner no means of warning him of the existence of foul air or choke-damp, nor could the air of the mine be tested for the presence of fire-damp by their means. There appeared at present no mode of meeting the first objection ; with respect to the second, he had pointed out that Mr. Swan had already applied an electric gas-detector as an adjunct to his miners' lamp ; it remained to be seen whether this would furnish a reliable and readily applicable substitute for the safety-lamp or other more sensitive gas-detectors now known.

It having long since been generally acknowledged that some more sensitive indicator of the presence of fire-damp than the Davy lamp, or such other forms of safety-lamp as were preferred by some for inspecting purposes, was much needed, he had felt some surprise that Mr. Lupton should have dismissed the subject of gas-indicators by a reference only to the earliest instruments of this class, the Ansell indicators, which had long been well known to possess radical defects, as pointed out in the Paper. Mr. George Seymour had also summarily dismissed the subject of gas-indicators generally with the statement that " experience " had demonstrated them to be of but little practical use ; but he had not even mentioned the kind of indicators of which he or others had acquired this unfavorable experience. He was glad to find, on the other hand, that Mr. Steavenson had spoken of the Liveing gas-indicator, from personal experience, as a very valuable instrument in the hands of a good overman. He felt convinced, from his own experience, that this instrument would not be at all difficult to use after very little practice ; and he could assure Mr. Hall that the handle, which actuated the arrangement for heating the little test-coils, did not require to be turned at a certain fixed speed in order to furnish uniform results. He felt confident that, for purposes of special inspection, at any rate, this gas-indicator would be a valuable acquisition ; and he believed that a form of eudiometrical gas-detector would also ere long be perfected as a reliable instrument. It could scarcely be denied that, while the skilful use of particular varieties of safety-lamp furnished the means of detecting small percentages of fire-damp in mine-air, it was desirable that overmen or firemen should be furnished with, and become accustomed to the use of, apparatus by which very small proportions of fire-damp could be detected, and their amount estimated with considerable accuracy. It had been thoroughly well established that a proportion of fire-damp in the air, which would altogether escape detection by means of a safety-lamp, might constitute an element of great danger in dry and dusty mines.

In referring to the subject of safety-lamps, Mr. Tylden-Wright had defended the alteration, made in the House of Lords, of the general rule relating to safety-lamps, which, as adopted by the House of Commons, excluded "unprotected" Davy, Stephenson, and Clanny lamps from the category of safety-lamps, and Sir Frederick Abel was surprised to find Sir Warington Smyth in agreement with Mr. Tylden-Wright on the subject, because when the former and the Author were Members of the Royal Commission together, Sir Warington's views regarding the dangerous character of the unprotected lamps in question, when used in any part of a mine where only a very moderate ventilat-

SIR FREDERICK ABEL

ing current was met with, were so strong, that he had no
hesitation in assisting in the preparation of a letter, addressed to the Home Secretary, on the 15th of December,
1880, which he signed as Chairman of the Commission, the
object of this letter being to recommend that it should be
made known as soon and as widely as possible, that "the
employment of the ordinary Davy lamp without a shield
of metal or glass, in an explosive mixture, when the current
exceeded 6 feet a second, is attended with risk of accident
almost amounting to certainty. The Clanny lamp, when
tested in a similar current, has proved to be scarcely, if
at all, less dangerous."[1]   Moreover, in the unanimous
final Report of the Commission, presented in March, 1886,
the following statements were made:[2]— "It results then,
from the improved ventilation of mines, that if the current becomes sufficiently charged with fire-damp, the
Davy and Clanny lamps" (which are frequently exposed
to current-velocities of from 20 to 25 feet per second
in the air-ways, and might occasionally be exposed to currents having velocities of from 30 to 35 feet per second)
"cease to be in any way safety-lamps, and the Stephenson (Geordie) lamp may often cause an explosion."   After
having stated that the "insecurity of these lamps" had
been conspicuously shown by the results of the Commission's experiments, and had previously been demonstrated by various Societies of Mining Engineers, the
Report proceeded:— "Under present conditions as to
ventilation, the danger of relying upon Davy and Clanny
lamps seemed to us so great that we felt it our duty, at an
early stage of our investigations, to address a letter to the
Secretary of State for the Home Department, calling his
special attention to the insecurity of these lamps."   He
could not comprehend on what grounds a simple reiteration,
though in less emphatic terms, of this condemnation of

---

[1] Accidents in Mines, Final Report of Her Majesty's Commission, 1886, p.
188.

[2] *Ibid.*, p. 67.

unprotected Davy and Clanny lamps, of which Sir Warington
Smyth was joint Author, was characterized by him as an
" onslaught " on these lamps.   Nor could he understand
what the exclusion of unprotected Davy, Clanny, and
Stephenson lamps from mines where it was necessary to use
safety-lamps, had to do with mines in "many districts in
the country where no gas had been perceptible from generation to generation," and where therefore, naked lights
would still, as hitherto, be used without any interference.
As regarded such mines, which, according to the late Chairman of the Commission " were scattered broadcast throughout the land, as in the Forest of Dean, South Staffordshire,
and other districts," where " gas was never noticed," the
retention of the House of Commons Clause, with respect to
unprotected lamps of the kind specified, would certainly not
have led to any dictation to the people working in them to
" take some new patent lamp capable of withstanding the
effect of a strong current," as there was certainly nothing in
that clause to enforce the use of lamps in place of naked
lights, where no gas had ever been noticed.   The Commons' Clause did not even prohibit the use of Davy and
Clanny lamps in any mine, but only insisted that they
should be protected ; and no one knew better than Sir
Warington Smyth, from the large number of experiments
in which he had taken part, as well as from the practical
trials he had witnessed, that these lamps, which he had considered it his duty to condemn as unsafe, could be protected
by very simple and inexpensive adjuncts, and had been so
altered in very large numbers by mine-owners, so as to render them as safe in the highest current-velocities ordinarily
met with in mines at the present time, as they were in the
first days of their invention, when only currents of very low
velocity existed underground, and thus preventing their
exclusion by the terms of the general rule, either as it now
stood or as it was approved of by the House of Commons.
Mr. Sawyer had pointed out that, in the district in which
he was Inspector, unprotected lamps were rapidly disappearing in all fiery mines; but there might be districts in

which such action, being purely at the option of the mine-owners, managers, or men, might be neglected, or very difficult to enforce, in consequence of the ambiguous wording of the general rule as it now existed, and of the ardent advocacy of the lamps in their original state by such influential gentlemen as Mr. Tylden-Wright.

That gentleman had said that nothing could be more definite than the present clause in the Act relating to safety-lamps, as amended by the House of Lords; but he went on to show that intelligent men (under which head the Author ventured to couple himself with Mr. Tylden-Wright), might put two very different constructions upon it, and thus to demonstrate the obvious ambiguity, as pointed out by him, of that passage in the rule which spoke of "that part of the mine in which the lamps are for the time being in use." Sir Warington Smyth well knew that currents of exceptionally high velocity might occasionally be encountered by men carrying unprotected Davy or Clanny lamps in mines in which "the current ordinarily prevailing" would not involve danger, and Mr. Sawyer had directed attention to the important fact that the safety of an unprotected gauze lamp, "when it was carried against an inflammable current of the smallest velocity, depended entirely on the rate at which the person who was carrying it was travelling," and that "this varied much and could not be regulated." A stronger argument in favor of the wisdom of the course which the House of Commons had agreed to adopt could not well be imagined, and Mr. Sawyer had aptly illustrated it by reference to a recent accident, which was ascribed to a Davy lamp, carried by a collier, who was hastening at the time in a direction contrary to an inflammable current which had, at the place and time of the explosion, a velocity of only 2 feet per second. He would commend to the notice of Mr. Bainbridge this accident, as being only one of several due to lamps which, in his comparatively brief experience, he had heard of.

As a man of science and a chemist, he could not yield to Mr. Tylden-Wright in his admiration of Davy, and of his beautiful researches which led to the construction of his safety-lamp, but could not admit that his great name would come under any " obloquy " because the Davy lamp, in its simple original form, was no longer the safe lamp which it undoubtedly was for many years after its first introduction, until other important advances in applied science had altered the conditions which presented themselves to Davy as those to be met by a safety-lamp. But it appeared that, after all, Mr. Tylden-Wright was mainly desirous of retaining the unprotected Davy lamp in use, not for the general purposes of the miner, but because it was looked upon in South Staffordshire as the most delicate and best practical appara- tus for testing for gas in mines. Mr. Tylden-Wright was, perhaps, not aware that a protected Davy lamp could be most easily taken out of its case, when the fireman arrived at a place in a mine which had to be examined for gas ; but even this was unnecessary, for Sir Warington Smyth had stated upon the high authority of Mr. Lindsay Wood, that the protected, or cased Davy, which stood very well in point of safety in the Commission's experiments, and was, indeed, thoroughly safe for all ordinary conditions, could be as readily and effectively used for testing purposes as the unprotected lamp. He was glad that reference had also been made, by Sir Warington Smyth, to the fact that com- petent practical authorities were by no means in accord in accepting the Davy lamp as the most sensitive lamp for pur- poses of inspection. Mr. Sawyer's published experiments, which were very complete, had established the superiority of the Mueseler lamp, which had been confirmed by Messrs. Mallard and Le Chatelier; while Kreischer and Winkler had been led by long experience to give the preference to lamps of the Clanny and Boty types. Mr. Sawyer had also stated, and no one was more competent to know than he, that men who had become used to the Mueseler lamp were now as wedded to it as they had been to the " Old Davy," and that no difficulty was experienced, after its use for a short time, in carrying it even in steep mines without fear of its being extinguished. Too much importance must,

15

SIR FREDERICK ABEL.

therefore, not be attached to Mr. Tylden-Wright's local experience, as to the unprotected Davy being indispensable; no doubt it was so considered by those who had always been accustomed to use it, but in several collieries the men who had been wedded to it were now equally attached to the cased Davy. He therefore maintained, against Mr. Tylden-Wright, and even against so high an authority as Sir Warington Smyth (whose own words, however, had strongly supported his contention), that the prohibition of the dangerous " unprotected " lamps, which was all that was contemplated by the House of Commons general rule, would neither have dimmed in the least the lustre of Davy's name in connection with his safety-lamp, nor have resulted in any hardship to those who had hitherto used the unprotected lamps.

He would assure Mr. Tylden-Wright that he was quite aware of the fact that hundreds of collieries in the United Kingdom were at a long distance from gas-mains; but he could also assure him that, if a gas-test for lamps had been established by law, there would have been no difficulty in providing, at little outlay and trouble, for the maintenance of the small gas-supply necessary for the systematic application of the test to the lamps in regular use. The bearing of Mr. Lupton's observations, with reference to the value of a gas-test for lamps, was difficult to fathom; he would only state that the value of such a method of testing, and the feasibility of applying a reliable and searching gas-test were beyond question, and he felt confident that Mr. Lupton would have no difficulty in himself arranging such a gas-test, as would furnish that check "upon the eye and skill of the lamp-man," which even the most implicit trust in that official rendered highly desirable.

There could be no doubt, as pointed out by Sir Warington Smyth, that blown-out shots, which had been a fruitful source of accident, and the starting-point of many serious explosions, were far more frequent than they should be in coal-mines, if more knowledge, skill, and care were brought to bear in the selection of the spot for the charge of explosive, the placing of the hole, the process of charging, and the adoption of simple measures for facilitating the operation of the charge. The neglect to hole and cut the coal at the fast-places before shot-firing, and the bad selection of places for the shot, had also been pointed out by Mr. Sawyer as constantly conducing to the occurrence of blown-out shots, and of consequent accidents. So long as knowledge and intelligence were not brought to bear on these important points, there was little hope of a general realization of Mr. Bainbridge's picture of the present freedom from risk of serious accident in well-regulated mines, from the occurrence of blown-out shots. Mr. Bainbridge had expressed his belief that the use of certain explosives of recent invention, such as roburite and carbonite, would have the effect of putting an end to the dangers arising from blown-out shots, and based his favorable opinion of the first of those materials upon the personal observation of a single "blown-out shot" underground, from which he saw no sparks produced. Sir Frederick Abel had repeatedly seen the same result with other explosives, which were not, however, invariably confirmed in repetitions of the trials; and that the same was the case with roburite had been demonstrated by experiments in this country, which had been noticed in the public prints, and by experiments in Germany. Thus, in some official trials at Neunkirchen, two charges of about 8 oz. of roburite had been fired, as blown-out shots, into atmospheres containing 6 per cent. and 8 per cent. of fire-damp. No explosion occurred in either case, but in two repetitions of the trial in the fire-damp- and air-mixture, a violent gas explosion was produced in each case by the blown-out shot. He had given reasons in the Paper (p. 59) why the explosive carbonite, to which Mr. Bainbridge had also referred, could not be expected to secure immunity from the dangers due to blown-out shots, and there was no reason to believe that securite, nor any other high explosive, applied *per se* in a shot-hole, could be relied upon to secure freedom from the projection of matter sufficiently highly heated to ignite an explosive gas-mixture, when a blown-out shot was produced.

SIR FREDERICK ABEL.

That the principle of cooling down the incandescent, or highly-heated matters projected by a shot, by means of water applied in one way or another, was now receiving beneficial application in connection with shot-firing, was a source of great gratification to him. He had, as Sir Warington Smyth kindly pointed out, labored quite disinterestedly to bring to bear, as a safe and efficient method of working in coal, the system of distributing the explosive force exerted by a detonated charge through the agency of water, by which it was completely surrounded, which he had elaborated fifteen years ago. He felt sure that if Mr. Tylden-Wright would pursue experiments a little further, he would find that certain nitro-glycerine preparations, such as gelatine-dynamite, would, through the agency of water, do work in coal quite equal to that performed by powder used in the ordinary way. He should add, in reference to a suggestion of Mr. Tylden-Wright's, that it would be labor thrown away to endeavor to ensure safety in the use of powder through the agency of water. This matter had been thoroughly dealt with in the report of the Commission. The only objection to the water-cartridge which had been raised was that mentioned by Mr. Hall and by Mr. A. L. Steavenson, namely, the weakness of the water-bag or envelope; this certainly did not exist in any form of cartridge which he had used and was easily guarded against. Mr. Sawyer had wisely pointed out that care and intelligence were necessary to ensure success, with the use of the arrangements for blasting in conjunction with water, as in any other operation needing attention to simple precautions. He was glad that Mr. Forster Brown had successfully employed, and had acquired confidence in, the comparatively simple method of using water in conjunction with a porous body, such as moss, of the efficiency of which, in conjunction with high explosives, the Commission had been led by experiment to entertain a high opinion.

Proposals, which had been repeatedly made, to apply as tamping materials, substances which contained water or carbonic acid or both, in considerable quantities, and which

SIR FREDERICK ABEL.

parted with those constituents more or less readily when exposed to heat, had been commented upon by the Author as possessing no value from the point of view of promoting safety in coal-blasting, because the extremely brief period during which portions of such tamping would be exposed to heat, upon the firing of the charge of explosive in rear of them, would be altogether insufficient to expel a quantity of either aqueous vapor or carbonic acid from them, adequate to exert any effect in extinguishing, or materially reducing the temperature of, the highly heated products of explosion or of projected flame and sparks.   He had much desired to test the correctness of his views by the results of actual experiment, and since the reading of the Paper he had succeeded in doing so.   A large cast-iron shell had been compactly filled with powder soda crystals, a cavity being afterwards made in the centre, for the reception of a charge of gunpowder.   The shell was closed with a metal screw-plug having a perforation through which a fuze was inserted into the charge.   Upon exploding the latter, the shell was not burst, but the products of explosion gradually escaped through the perforation in the shell-plug. The crystallized carbonate of soda was therefore exposed to the heat, developed by the explosion, for a much longer period than it would have been had it been employed as tamping in a shot-hole and at once projected, by the rush of escaping gases, if the shot had blown out.   A portion of the contents of the shell which was nearest to the gunpowder charge was found to contain 62·04 per cent. of water ; a sample of the soda crystals with which the shell was charged was found to contain 63·25 per cent.   The exposure of the salt to the heat of exploding gunpowder, under more severe conditions than those which obtained in the case of a blown-out shot, did not, therefore, expel a proportion of water sufficient to produce any practically useful effect in cooling down the products of explosion.

It was not improbable that a very different result would be obtained if a substance, containing large proportions of volatile constituents, such as soda crystals, alum, or an

Sir Frederick Abel.

ammonium-salt, were intimately mixed with an explosive
agent, in such proportions as not to interfere too greatly
with the transmission of explosion or detonation through a
charge of the diluted material; as in that case portions of
finely divided crystallized salt, or volatile substance, would
be individually exposed on all sides to the heat developed at
the instant of the explosion, and the cooling effect, due to
the conversion into vapor, and expansion, of the water or
other readily volatilizable constituents, would be brought
to bear upon the products of explosion almost instantaneously upon their generation. Experiments, which had been
quite recently made in this direction in Germany, appeared
to have furnished very promising results. Preliminary
trials, conducted by the Rhenish dynamite company, with
charges ranging from 8 to 18 oz. of a mixture of Nobel's
No. 1 dynamite with finely-powdered soda crystals, by firing them as blown-out shot in a gallery containing an explosive gas-mixture with much fine coal-dust suspended in it,
showed that only in one case, when the proportion of the salt
that had been mixed with the dynamite was very small,
was an explosion of the gas and dust-mixture produced.
The experiments were then taken up by Mr. Hilt, President
of the late Prussian Fire-damp Commission, and carried on
in the large experimental gallery at Neunkirchen, with comparatively heavy charges of the soda-dynamite, it having
been observed by Mr. Hilt, in the course of experiments
with roburite, securite, and carbonite, that explosive gas-
mixtures were seldom ignited by small charges, while they
were generally exploded when heavier charges were used.
Mr. Hilt stated that, so far as the experiments with this
modified dynamite had been carried, the effect of dilution
with the soda crystals was to modify the violent action of
the original explosive, so as to assimilate the results which
it furnished in coal-getting to those obtained with gunpowder. The experiments were still being pursued in Germany, and Mr. Max Georgi even went so far as to assert
that the perfect safety of soda-dynamite (*Wetterdynamit*)
had been quite established. At any rate, the results

obtained appeared to the Author so important, in reference to the provision of an efficient blasting agent for use in coal-mines, which would not require any adjunct, or the adoption of any other than the ordinary method of charging holes, to ensure perfect safety, that he was taking steps to carry on searching experiments with it, the results of which he hoped ere long to communicate to the mining public.

The conflicting nature of the observations made in the course of the discussion, and in the correspondence, with regard to the merits of wedging, and of lime-cartridges, when employed as substitutes for gunpowder in coal-getting seemed to show that the important and really obvious fact was frequently lost sight of, that neither of the two systems was calculated to do the same character of work in different varieties of coal, and that neither the inventors of particular forms of wedges, nor the elaborators of the compressed lime-cartridge, maintained that the explosive agent could be replaced by either in working all descriptions of coal. The somewhat extreme views of Mr. Stokes with regard to inconveniences and supposed dangers, attending the use of lime-cartridges, were evidently not shared by Mr. A. R. Sawyer, whose observations on this subject, also based upon personal knowledge, had, on several important points, confirmed the conclusions arrived at by the late Royal Commission.

In answering the various questions raised in the course of the discussion, he had endeavored to deal separately with each important subject on which it appeared necessary for him to comment and reply, and in order to do this thoroughly he had included in those replies the consideration of some of the communications of correspondents. Mr. Forster Brown had supplied interesting information on some other matters included in the Paper. With regard to his remarks on the subject of goaves, they appeared after all to admit that extensive accumulations of gas might occur in these. Mr. Coxon's account of the experiments with dust, which he had witnessed at Neunkirchen, con-

SIR FREDERICK ABEL.

firmed the statements made in the final report of the Royal Commission respecting the experiments of the Prussian Commission. With regard to his description of an explosion, which he ascribed purely to dust, the assumption that this was so was open to the objection that he assumed the absence of gas in the drift where the explosion occurred, simply upon the results furnished by inspection with a Davy lamp and a naked candle. This subject had, however, been thoroughly discussed in the Paper.

Mr. J. Ashworth was well known for the labor which he had devoted to effecting improvements in safety-lamps, and those described by him would doubtless, like that of Mr. Brainbridge, receive the attention of mine managers. Mr. Forster Brown was one of the few practical men who could already speak from somewhat considerable experience of the value of the electric light in mines, and it was satisfactory to find that he looked forward with confidence to the speedy provision of thoroughly efficient self-contained lamps. As regarded fixed lamps, he did not appear to comtemplate the future extension of their use beyond the main haulage roads, while Mr. Arthur Sopwith shared the view advanced by Mr. Sydney Walker, that the future would see the electric light applied to the face of the coal through the agency of main conductors, rather than by means of self-contained portable lamps. Mr. Sopwith made light of the objections which the Author had raised against the attachment of lamps, required at the working places, to main conductors by branch wires; but he did not suggest how these necessarily very light leads were to be protected from the liability to injury by falls of coal or stone and rough usage, to which Mr. Longden and Mr. Sennett had referred. The whole question of the application of the electric light underground had, however, only passed through the first stage of its development, and there was no doubt that practical electricians would, with proper encouragement from the owners of mines, and by wholesome competition with each other, achieve successes which were at present only foreshadowed. The importance of bringing the cost of

SIR FREDERICK ABEL.

electric lamps within such limits as to allow of their com-
peting, from an economical point of view, with safety-lamps
of the ordinary and improved types, if any such really
extensive trial was to be made of the new system of illumination as could alone lead to its thoroughly successful
development, gave force to the observations made by Mr.
Story-Maskelyne, which he would venture to commend to
the consideration of those who, at present, controlled the
supply to the public of the only form of electric light which
was susceptible of safe application in coal-mines.

In conclusion, the Author would only say that he cor-
dially agreed with Sir Warington Smyth in the observations
he had made, and which were in harmony with those of
several other highly competent speakers, that the safe
working of collieries must always be in a far greater degree
dependent upon the experience, judgment, constant vigilance and care, of those entrusted with their management,
and upon the intelligence and ceaseless watchfulness of the
subordinate officials, than upon inspection by Government
officials, however much it might be increased and elaborated.

LIST OF SAFETY APPLIANCES, ETC.,

IN CONNECTION WITH MINING,

EXHIBITED IN ILLUSTRATION OF SIR FREDERICK ABEL'S PAPER.

NOVEMBER, 1887.

DETACHMENT OF MINERAL FROM ITS BED.

	Contributors.
Bickford, Smith and Co.'s patent safety-fuze	BICKFORD, SMITH and Co.
Colliery lighters and coil	" "
Settle's patent gelatine water-cartridge	NOBEL'S EXPLOSIVES Co.
Glass cartridge and three tin cartridge-cases	J. ROUTLEDGE.
Gelatinous compound for safety blasting	D. MUNRO.
Improved electric battery for shot firing in mines	M. SETTLE.
Shot-firer for lighting fuze for blasting purposes	"
Safety water-cartridge	"
Gelatine water-cartridge	"
Magneto-exploder	JOHN DAVIS and SON.
" " (for water-cartridge)	SIEMENS BROS. and Co.
Fire-extinguishing compound	G. TRENCH.
Model of tonite-cartridge surrounded by ditto	"
Displaced cartridge in tube of gelatine	"
Safety-lamp for lighting fuze	D. MUNRO.
Compressed lime-cartridges (Sebastian Smith and Moore's)	THE COMPRESSED LIME-CARTRIDGE Co.
Draw-wedge (Bell and Ramsay's)	W. RAMSAY.
Model of the Haswell Mechanical Coal-getter	T. BELL.
" " " "	W. F. HALL.
Coal-getter	E. MOULD.

CARRIAGE OF MINERAL TO THE SURFACE.

Detaching hooks and safety-cages (King and Humble's)	S. HUMBLE.
Automatic gearing for preventing overwinding (model).	T. KIRKLAND.
Automatic arrangement for preventing overwinding (model)	M. SETTLE.
Nicholls' safety-hook and hoist (model)	T. CLARKSON, Stud. Inst. C. E.

Contributors.

Walker's detaching hook to prevent overwinding..... T. BELL.
Clip-pulleys (two models)......................... G. J. LAMPEN and Co.
West's simplex safety-link....................... " "
Mining bells and tappers (two).................... COX-WALKER and Co.
Dome bells (two)................................. " "
Double semaphore and signalling-bell.............. " "
Single semaphore................................. " "
Signal bell...................................... G. J. LAMPEN and Co.
Electric signal-bells and keys................... { S. F. WALKER (Assoc. M. Inst. C. E.) and OLLIVER.

DIFFICULTIES ATTENDANT ON THE PRESENCE OF GASES, EXPLOSIVE OR OTHERWISE, AND OF COAL-DUST.

Barton's respirator.............................. G. J. LAMPEN and Co.
Respirator....................................... " "
Fleuss apparatus for working in noxious gases........ { SIEBE, GORMAN and Co.
Loeb's (J.) respirators, several sets.................. { THE MARITIME AND GENERAL IMPROVEMENT Co.
Apparatus for testing the presence of carbonic acid in mines... { C. LE NEVE FOSTER.
Garforth's fire-damp detector...................... { J. D. THOMAS, Assoc. M. Inst. C.E.
Ashworth, Hepplewhite-Gray, and other lamps for testing fire-damp (stand of six)...................... { J. ASHWORTH.
Self-turning and other Biram anemometers (ten)...... JOHN DAVIS and SON.
Biram anemometers (two)......................... { J. DAGLISH, M. Inst. C.E.
Dickenson anemometer............................. "
Self-recording aneroid barometer.................. "

DIFFICULTIES ATTENDANT ON THE NECESSITY OF ARTIFICIAL LIGHT.

Safety-Lamps, oil and spirit.

Safety-lamp...................................... C. F. CLARK.
Marsaut (Mill's)................................. W. CLIFFORD.
Smethurst's...................................... "
Mercier's.. "
Davis's.. "
Bonneted Clanny.................................. "
W. Morgan's new.................................. "
Jack lamp.. "
Evan Thomas's No. 7.............................. "
Barrow-Hematite Mueseler......................... "
Aldwarke Mueseler................................ "
Davy lamp, 1813.................................. { S. B. COXON, M. Inst. C.E.

Contributors.

Bonneted Clanny (two)..........................	JOHN DAVIS and SON.
Mueseler (three).................................	" "
Marsaut (four)...................................	" "
Davis-Ashworth Mueseler (two)...................	" "
Deputies' and fire-triers' lamp....................	" "
Marsaut dialling lamp with Stokes' shut-off..........	" "
Douglas' self-extinguishing.......................	J. DOUGLAS.
Evans' self-extinguishing (two)...................	E. EVANS.
Davy, manufactured about seventy years ago.........	W. F. HALL.
Davy encased (three).............................	"
Hann's, lighted by the aid of electricity without un-locking..	E. M. HANN, M. Inst. C.E.
Bonneted Davy...................................	J. LAIDLER.
Safety...	G. J. LAMPEN and Co.
Mueseler...	" "
Safety Porch lamp...............................	" "
Morgan..	W. MAUER.
Marsaut...	JOHN MILLS and SONS.
Donald..	"
Pittuck..	F. W. PITTUCK.
Routledge and Johnson combined double safety (two).	J. ROUTLEDGE.
Davy, protected, newest pattern, Haswell Colliery (two)..	Sir WARINGTON W. SMYTH.
Miner's..	EVAN THOMAS and WILLIAMS.
Firemen's..	" "

Safety-Lamps, electric.

Edison-Swan (six) portable........................	EDISON-SWAN UNITED ELECTRIC LIGHT Co.
Pitkin (two) "	J. PITKIN.
Rees "	J. P. REES.
Schanschieff (six) "	A. SCHANSCHIEFF.
Thomson "	W. B. THOMSON.
Urquhart "	D. URQUHART.
Walker and Olliver (two)	S. F. WALKER (Assoc. M. Inst. C.E.) and OLLIVER.
Sennett, fixed	A. R. SENNETT, Assoc. M. Inst. C.E.
Settle (six) "	M. SETTLE.
Incandescent lamp-holders......................	COX-WALKER and Co.

MISCELLANEOUS.

Accidents from falls of roofs and sides (two series of illustrations)...................................	A. R. SAWYER.
Coked coal-dust from the Walker Colliery after an explosion..	J. B. ATKINSON.

Contributors.

Coal-dust from the Arley Seam, Wigan............. H. HALL.

Corf and corf greaser (model)....................... G. J. LAMPEN and Co.

Horn's tachometer................................ .... S. HUMBLE.

Improved indicating oil cistern.................... .... G. J. LAMPEN and Co-

Machine for plugging lead lock lamps............... JOHN DAVIS and SON.

Machine for moulding lead rivets................. ....   "   "

Ochwadt pressure-gauge for regulating atmospheric { THE MARITIME and currents in mines................................ (GENERAL IMPROVE-MENT Co.

Photographs of flame from dynamite cartridges incor- { E. SPON, Assoc. M. porated with materials of Schönweg's patent........ } Inst. C.E.

Screen wire..................................... .... G. J. LAMPEN and Co.

Telescope dial with Hoffmann head................. JOHN DAVIS and SON.

Water-gauge........................... .... { J. DAGLISH, M. Inst-C.E.

Working of mines (16 series of photographic views)... { A. SOPWITH, M. Inst. C.E.

MINING LAWS OF COLORADO.*

AN ACT TO AMEND CHAPTER SIXTEEN OF THE GENERAL STATUTES OF THE STATE OF COLORADO, ENTITLED "COAL MINES." APPROVED FEBRUARY 24, 1883.

SECTION 1. That chapter XVI. be amended so as to read as follows: SECTION 1. That the owner or agent of each coal mine or colliery in this State, employing ten or more men, shall make, or cause to be made, within six months after the passage of this act, an accurate map or plan of the workings of such coal mine or colliery, on a scale not exceeding one hundred feet to the inch, showing the bearings and distances of the workings, with the general inclinations of the stratum, and any material deflections in such workings, and the boundary lines of such coal mine or colliery, which shall be kept for the use of the Inspector, at the office of the said mine in the county where such mine or colliery is located, and which shall be kept up every three months; and shall also deposit a true copy of such map or plan with the Inspector of Coal Mines, and with the recorder of the county in which said coal mine or colliery is situated, to be filed in their respective offices; and said owner or agent shall cause, on or before the tenth day of January every year, a statement of the workings of such coal mine during the year past, from the last report to the end of the December month just preceding, to be marked on the original map or plan of said coal mine or colliery: *Provided*, If the owner or agent of any coal mine shall neglect, or refuse, or for any cause, fail' for the period of one month after the time prescribed, to furnish said map or plan as hereby required, or if the Inspector shall find or have reason to believe said map or plan is inaccurate in any material part, he is hereby authorized to cause a correct map or plan of the actual workings of such coal mine or colliery to be made at the expense of the owner thereof, the cost of which shall be recoverable from said owner by an action, as in cases of other debts, and shall cause a copy of the same to be filed in the office of the recorder of the county in which said coal mine or colliery is situated.

SEC. 2. It shall not be lawful, after six months from the passage of this act, for the owner or agent of any coal mine, wherein over fifteen thousand square yards have been excavated, to employ or permit more than fifteen persons to work therein, except in opening shafts or outlets, unless there are to every seam of coal worked in each mine, at least two separate outlets, separated by natural strata of not less than one hundred feet in breadth, by which shafts or outlets distinct means of ingress or egress are always available to the persons employed in the mine, and air shafts, in which are constructed and maintained ladder ways, shall be deemed and held to be an escape shaft within the provisions of this act, and no escape shaft be required; but it is not necessary for the two outlets to belong to the same mine; the second outlet need not be made until fifteen thousand square yards have been excavated in such mine, and to all other coal mines, whether opened and worked by shafts, slopes or drifts to such openings or outlets, must be provided within twelve months after fifteen thousand square yards have been excavated therein; and in case such outlets are not provided as herein stipulated, it shall not be lawful for the owner or agent of

* For amended Colorado Mine Inspection Law, approved April 1, 1889, see page 404.

such mine to permit more than fifteen persons to work therein during each twenty-four hours. In case a coal mine has but one shaft, slope or drift for the ingress or egress of the men working therein, and the owner thereof does not own suitable surface ground for another opening, he may select and approximate any adjoining land for that purpose, and for approach thereto, and shall be governed in his proceedings in appropriating such land by the provisions of law in force providing for the appropriation of private property by corporations, and such appropriation may be made whether he is a corporator or not; but no land shall be appropriated under the provisions of this act until the court is satisfied that suitable premises cannot be obtained by contract upon reasonable terms. Escapement shafts or other communication with a contiguous mine, as aforesaid, shall be constructed in connection with every vein or stratum of coal worked in such coal mine or colliery, as provided herein.

SEC. 3. In all cases where the human voice cannot be distinctly heard, the owner or agent shall provide and maintain a metal tube from top to the bottom of the slope or shaft, or a telephone connection suitably adapted to the free passage of sound, through which conversation may be held between persons at the bottom and at the top of the shaft or slope; also, the ordinary means of signaling to and from the top and bottom of the shaft or slope; and in the top of every shaft shall keep an approved safety gate and an approved safety catch, and sufficient cover overhead on every carriage used for lowering and hoisting persons: and the said owner or agent shall see that sufficient flanges or horns are attached to the sides of the drum of every machine that is used for lowering and hoisting persons in and out of the mine, and also, that adequate brakes are attached thereto; the main link attached to the swivel of the wire rope, shall be made of the best quality of iron, and shall be tested by weights satisfactory to the Inspector of Mines of the State; and bridle chains shall be attached to the main link from the cross-pieces of the carriage; and no single link chain shall be used for lowering or raising persons into or out of said mine; and not more than five persons for each ton capacity of the hoisting machinery used at any coal mine shall be lowered or hoisted by the machine at any one time.

SEC. 4. The owner or agent of every coal mine or colliery, whether shaft, slope or drift, shall provide and maintain for every such mine an amount of ventilation not less than one hundred cubic feet, and such additional number of cubic feet as may be ordered by said mine inspector, per minute, per person employed in such mine, and also an amount of ventilation of not less than five hundred cubic feet per minute for each mule or horse used in said mine, which shall be circulated and distributed throughout the mine in such a manner as to dilute and render harmless and repel the poisonous and noxious gases from each and every working place in the mine; and break-throughs or air-ways shall be driven as often as the Inspector of Mines may order, at the different mines inspected by him, and all break-throughs or air-ways, except those last made near the working faces of the mines, shall be closed up and made air-tight, by brattice, trap-doors or otherwise, so that the current of air in circulation in the mine may sweep to the interior of the mine, where the persons employed in such mine are at work; and all mines governed by this statute shall be provided with artificial means of producing ventilation, when necessary to provide a sufficient quantity of air, such as fanning, or suction fans, exhaust steam furnaces, or other contrivances of such capacity and power as to produce and maintain an abundant supply of air; but in case a furnace shall be used for ventilating purposes, it shall be built in such a manner as to prevent the communication of fire to any part of the works, by lining the upcast with an incombustible material for a sufficient distance up from the said furnace. All mines generating fire-damp shall be kept free from standing gas, and every working place shall be carefully examined every morning with a safety-lamp, by a competent person or persons, before any of the workmen are allowed to enter the mine; and the person making such examination shall mark on the face of the workings the day of the month; and in all mines, whether they generate fire-damp or not, the doors used in assisting or directing the ventilation of the mine shall be so hung and adjusted that they will shut up of their own accord and cannot stand open; and the owner or agent shall employ a practical and competent inside overseer, to be called a "mining boss," who shall keep a careful watch over the ventilating apparatus, and the air-ways, traveling ways, pumps, timbers and drainage; also, shall see that, as the miners advance their excavations, that all loose coal, slate and rock overhead are carefully secured against falling in or upon the traveling ways, and that sufficient timber, of suitable lengths and sizes, is furnished for the places where they are to be used, and placed in the working places of the mines; and he shall measure the ventilation at least once a week, at the inlet and outlet, and also at or near the face of all the entries; and the measurement of air so made shall be noted on blanks furnished by the Mine Inspector: and on the first week day of each month the "mining boss" of each mine shall sign one of such blanks, properly filled, and forward the same by mail to said Mine Inspector, a copy of which shall be filed at the office of the coal company, subject to inspection by miners.

SEC. 5. No person shall knowingly be employed as an engineer or mining boss, or take charge of any machinery or appliance whereby men are lowered into or hoisted out of any mine, but an experienced, competent and sober person; and no person shall ride upon a loaded wagon or cage used for hoisting purposes in any shaft or slope. No young person under twelve years of age, or woman or girl of any age, shall be permitted to enter any coal mine to work therein, nor any person under the age of sixteen years, unless he can read and write.

SEC. 6. All safety lamps used for examining or working coal mines, shall be the property of the owner of the mine, and shall be under the charge of the agent thereof. The term "owner" in this act shall mean the immediate proprietor, lessee, or occupier of any coal mine, or colliery, or any part thereof; and the term "agent" shall mean any person having, on behalf of the owner as aforesaid, the care and management of any coal mine, or colliery, or any part thereof.

SEC. 7. All boilers used in generating steam in and about coal mines and collieries, shall be kept in good order, and the owner or agent, as aforesaid, shall have said boilers examined and inspected, by a competent boiler-maker, or other well qualified person, as often as once every six months, and the result of such examination shall be certified, in writing, to the Mining Inspector; and every steam boiler shall be provided with a proper steam gauge, water gauge, and safety valve; and all underground, self-acting, or engine planes, or gauge-ways, on which coal cars are drawn and persons travel, shall be provided with some proper means of signaling between the stopping places and the ends of said planes or gaugeways; and sufficient places of refuge, at the sides of said planes or gaugeways, shall be provided, at intervals of not more than fifty feet apart; and there shall be cut, in the side of every hoisting shaft, at the bottom thereof, a traveling way, sufficiently high and wide to enable persons to pass the shaft, in going from one side of the mine to the other, without passing over or under the cage or hoisting apparatus.

SEC. 8. Whenever loss of life, or serious personal injury, shall occur by reason of any explosion, or of any accident whatsoever, in or about any coal mine or colliery, it shall be the duty of the owner or agent thereof to give notice to the Mine Inspector, and if any person is killed thereby, to the coroner of the county also, and the Inspector shall immediately go to the scene of said accident and render such assistance as he may deem necessary for the safety of the men, and shall ascertain, by the testimony before the coroner, or by taking other evidence, the cause of such explosion or accident, and file record thereof in his office.

SEC. 9. In all coal mines in the State, the miners employed and working therein, the owners of the land, or other person interested in the rental or royalty of any such mine, shall at all proper times have full right of access to, and examinations of, all scales, machinery, or apparatus used in or about such mine; to determine the quality of the coal mined, for the purpose of testing the accuracy of all such scales, machinery or apparatus; and such land owners or other persons may designate or appoint a competent person to act for them, who shall at all proper times have full right of access to, and examination of such scales, machinery or apparatus, and seeing all weights and measures of coal mined, and the accounts kept of the same; but not more than one person, on behalf of the land owners, or other person interested in the rental or royalty, jointly, shall have such right of access, examination and inspection of scales, weights, measures and accounts at the same time, and that such person shall make no unnecessary interference with the use of such scales, machinery or apparatus, and the miners employed in any mine may, from time to time, appoint two of their number to act as a committee to inspect, not oftener than once in every month, the mine and the machinery connected therewith, and to measure the ventilating current, and if the owner, agent, or manager so desires, he may accompany said miners, by himself, or two or more persons whom he may appoint for that purpose. The owner, agent, or manager shall afford every necessary facility for making such inspection and measurement; but the said miners shall not in any way interrupt or impede the work going on in the mine at the time of such inspection and measurement.

SEC. 10. Any miners, workmen, or rather persons, who shall intentionally injure any shaft, lamp, instrument, air-course or brattice, or obstruct or throw open air-ways, or open a door and not close it again, or carry lighted pipes or matches into places that are worked by safety lamps, or handle or disturb any part of the machinery, or enter any place of the mine against caution; or who wilfully neglects or refuses to securely prop the roof of any working place under his control, or disobey any order given in carrying out the provisions of this act, or do any other act whereby the lives or the health of persons, or the security of the mines or machinery is endangered, shall be deemed guilty of a misdemeanor, and upon conviction may be punished by a fine of not less than twenty-five dollars, nor more than two hundred dollars, or may be imprisoned

16

in the county jail not less than thirty days, nor more than one year, or may be punished by both such fine and imprisonment, at the discretion of the court.

SEC. 11. In case any owner or agent disregards the requirements of this act, any court of competent jurisdiction may, on application of the Inspector, by civil action in the name of the State, enjoin or restrain the owner or agent from working or operating such mine with more than twelve miners underground during each twenty-four hours, until it is made to conform with the provisions of this act. And such remedy shall be cumulative, and shall not take the place or affect any other proceedings against such owner or agent, authorized by law for the matter complained of in such action.

SEC. 12. For any injury to person or property occasioned by any violation of this act, or any wilful failure to comply with its provisions by any owner, or lessee or operator, of any coal mine or opening, a right of action against the party at fault shall accrue to the party injured for the direct damages sustained thereby ; and in any case of loss of life by reason of such violation or failure, a right of action against the owners and operators of such coal mine or colliery shall accrue to the widow and lineal heirs of the person whose life shall be lost, for like recovery of damages for the injury they shall have sustained.

SEC. 13. The provisions of this act shall not apply to or affect any coal mine in which not more than ten men are employed underground during each twenty-four hours, but on the application of the proprietor, or of the miners in any such mine, or when the Mine Inspector may deem it necessary, said Mine Inspector shall make, or cause to be made, an inspection of such mine, and shall direct and enforce any regulations in accordance with the provisions of this act, that he deems necessary for the safety and health of miners.

SEC. 14. That the board of examiners, heretofore appointed under the provisions of this act concerning coal mines, approved February 24, 1883, and amended by this act, shall hold their office for and during the time for which they were appointed, to wit: until January 1, A.D. 1887. And it shall be the duty of the board of examiners to meet at such times, and at such places within this State, as may be directed by the Governor of this State, and examine such persons as may present themselves for examination, touching their qualifications, for the office of Mine Inspector, as provided in this act, and shall inquire into their character and qualifications, and shall certify the names of such persons as they shall find to be competent to fill such office of Mine Inspector, to the Governor, which list of names, so certified, shall be placed on file in the office of the Secretary of State. Members of such board of examiners shall, before entering upon their duties, take and subscribe the following oath, viz.: We, the undersigned, do solemnly swear (or affirm), that we will perform the duties of examiners of applicants for appointment of Inspector of Coal Mines, to the best of our abilities, and that in recommending or rejecting said applicants, we will be governed by the evidence of qualifications to fill the position under the law creating the same, and not by any consideration of political or personal favors ; that we will certify to all whom we may find qualified, according to the true intent and meaning of the act, and none others, to the best of our judgment. The qualifications of candidates for said office of Inspector of Mines, to be inquired into and certified by said examiners, shall be as follows, namely: They shall be citizens of the United States, of temperate habits, of good repute as men of personal integrity, shall have obtained the age of thirty years, and shall have had at least one year's experience in the working of coal mines of Colorado, and five years of practical experience in the working of coal mines in the United States, and have a practical knowledge of mining engineering, and of the different systems of working and ventilating coal mines, and of the nature and properties of the noxious and poisonous gases of mines, particularly fire-damp. The board of examiners shall receive six dollars per day, and same mileage as is allowed to members of the legislature, to be paid out of the State treasury, upon the filing of the certificates of the examining board in the office of the Secretary of State, as hereinbefore provided. As often as vacancies in said office of Inspector of Mines shall occur, by death, resignation, or malfeasance in office, which shall be determined in the same manner as in the case of any other officer of the State government, the Governor shall fill the same, by appointment, for the unexpired term, from the names on file in the office of the Secretary of State, as hereinbefore mentioned as having passed examination. On January 1, A.D. 1887, and every four years thereafter, the Governor shall appoint one reputable mining engineer, of known ability, and shall notify the judges of four of the judicial districts of the State, within which coal mines are being operated, to each appoint one reputable coal miner, of known experience and practice, from their respective districts, and the five so appointed shall constitute a new board of examiners, whose duties, term of service and compensation, shall be the same as those provided for by this section; and from the names that may be certified by them, the Governor shall appoint the Inspector of Mines provided for in this act. Nothing in this act shall be construed to prevent the re-appointment of any Inspector of Coal Mines. The Inspector of Coal Mines shall receive for his services an annual salary of two thousand dollars, and ten cents per mile mileage for all distances travelled in the discharge of his official duties, to be paid monthly by State Treasurer; and said Inspector shall reside in the State, and shall keep an office at the capitol, or other building, in which the offices of the State are located, Each Inspector is hereby authorized to procure such instruments, and chemical tests, and stationery, from time to time, as may be necessary to the proper discharge of his duties under this act, at the expense of the State, which shall be paid by the State Treasurer, upon accounts duly certified by him and audited by the proper department of the State. All instruments, plans, books, memoranda, notes, etc., pertaining to the office, shall be the property of the State and shall be delivered to their successors in office.

SEC. 15. The Inspector of Coal Mines shall, before entering upon the discharge of his duties, give bond in the sum of five thousand dollars, with sureties, to be approved by the Judge of the District Court in which he resides, conditioned for the faithful discharge of his duty, and take an oath (or affirmation) to discharge his duties impartially and with fidelity, to the best of his knowledge and ability.

SEC. 16. No person acting as a manager or agent of any coal mine, or as a mining engineer for any coal mining company, or to be interested in operating, any coal mine, shall at the same time act as an Inspector of Coal Mines under this act.

SEC. 17. The Inspector of Coal Mines shall devote the whole of his time to the duties of his office. It shall be his duty to enter into and thoroughly examine all coal mines in this State, in which more than ten men are employed, at least once each quarter, to see that all the provisions of this act are observed and strictly carried out; and the Inspector may enter, inspect and examine any coal mine in the State, and the works and machinery belonging thereto, at all reasonable times, by night or day, but so as not to unnecessarily obstruct or impede the working of the mine; and the owner or agent of such mine is hereby required to furnish the means necessary for such entry and inspection, of which inspection the Inspector shall make a record, to be filed in his office, and which shall show the number of mines, and development on the same, during the past year, and of persons employed in and about each mine, and the extent to which the law is obeyed, the progress made in the improvements sought to be secured by the passage of this act, the number of accidents and deaths resulting from injuries received in coal mines, as also statistics showing output of coal and development made annually at each mine, with all facts concerning the production and transportation of coal to market, and other facts of public interest, coming under the provisions of this act, which record shall, on or before the first Monday in November preceding the biennial sessions of the Legislature, be filed in the office of the Secretary of State, to be by him included in the biennial report of his department.

SEC. 18. That the owner or agent of each coal mine or colliery in the State, employing ten or more men, shall, when working in close proximity to an abandoned mine, or part of a mine, containing inflammable gas or fire-damp, cause bore-holes to be kept at least twelve feet in advance of the coal-face of all working places in such mine or colliery; and when directed to do so by said Mine Inspector, shall cause bore-holes to be driven in a like manner on both sides of said workings; and said owner or agent shall cause all abandoned shafts, airshafts, slopes or cave-holes to be securely and safely fenced off, for the protection of persons working in said mine.

SEC. 19. The mining boss, or other competent person, shall make daily inspection of ropes, chains, cages and other hoisting appliances, guides and shaft timbers, and make a record of such daily inspection in a book, kept at the office of the mine, for that purpose, and the fire boss shall keep a daily record of any defects in the ventilating appliances, and any standing gas that may be found in said mine, designating the entry and room in which said gas is found. Each of the records herein required to be kept, shall be open at all times to the Mine Inspector's and miners' committee's inspection, and a copy thereof shall be filed in the office of the said Mine Inspector on the first Monday of December of each year.

SEC. 20. The neglect or refusal to perform the duties required to be performed by any section of this act or the violation of any of the provisions hereof, shall be deemed a misdemeanor, and any person so neglecting or refusing to perform such duties, or violating such provisions, shall, upon conviction, be punished by a fine of not less than one hundred dollars, nor exceeding five hundred dollars, at the discretion of the court, and all penalties recovered under this act shall be paid into the treasury of the State.

SEC. 21. All acts or parts of acts, inconsistent with the provisions of this act, are hereby repealed.

SEC. 22. An emergency exists; therefore, this act shall take effect and be in force from and after its passage.

Approved April 8, 1885.

MINING LAWS OF ILLINOIS.

AN ACT providing for the health and safety of persons employed in coal mines, Approved May 28, 1879, in force July 1, 1879; as amended by acts approved June 18, 1883, and June 21, 1883; in force July 1, 1883; as amended by an act approved June 30, 1885, in force July 1, 1885; and as amended by an act approved June 16, 1887, in force July 1, 1887.

(The amendments of 1887 appear in brackets.)

1. SURVEYS AND MAPS TO BE MADE.—SECTION 1. Be it enacted by the People of the State of Illinois, represented in the General Assembly: That the owner, or agent, or operator of each and every coal mine in this State shall make or cause to be made, at the discretion of the inspector, or person acting in that capacity, an accurate map or plan of the workings of such coal mine, and of each and every vein thereof, showing the general inclination of the strata, together with any material deflections in the said workings, and the boundary lines of said coal mines, and deposit a true copy of said map or plan with the inspector of coal mines, to be filed in his office, and another true copy, of said map or plan with the recorder of the county in which said coal mine is situated, to be filed in his office, both of which said copies shall be deposited as aforesaid within three (3) months from the day when this act shall go into effect; and the original, or a copy of such map or plan, shall also be kept for inspection at the office of such coal mine; and during the month of January, of each and every year after this act shall go into effect, the said owner, agent or operator, shall furnish the inspector and recorder, as aforesaid, with a statement and further map or plan of the progress of the workings of such coal mine, continued from the last report to the end of the December month just preceding; and the inspector shall correct his map or plan, of said workings, in accordance with the statement and map or plan thus furnished; and when any coal mine is worked out or abandoned, that fact shall be reported to the inspector, and the map or plan of such coal mine, in the office of said inspector, shall be carefully corrected and verified. The several coal mine inspectors in this State, shall furnish copies of all maps or plans of mines to be filed with the Bureau of Labor Statistics. (*As amended by an act approved June* 18, 1883, *in force July* 1, 1883.)

2. INSPECTOR MAY PROCURE MAPS AT OWNER'S COST.—§ 2. Whenever the owner, agent or operator of any coal mine shall neglect or refuse to furnish the said inspector and recorder, as aforesaid, with the statement, the map or plan, or addition thereto, as provided in the first section of this act, at the times and in the manner therein provided, the said inspector is hereby authorized to cause an accurate map or plan of the workings of such coal mine to be made at the expense of said owner, agent or operator, and the cost thereof may be recovered by law from said owner, agent or operator, in the same manner as other debts, by suit in the name of the inspector and for his use.

3. ESCAPEMENT SHAFTS AND PLACES OF EXIT—THEIR CHARACTER.—LOCATION AND CONSTRUCTION.—§ 3. *a* In all coal mines that are, or have been, in operation prior to the first day of July, 1870, and which are worked by or through a shaft, slope or drift, if there is not already an escapement shaft to

each and every said coal mine or a communication between every such coal mine and some other contiguous mine, then there shall be an escapement shaft or such other communication as shall be approved by the mine inspector, making at least two distinct means of ingress and egress for all persons employed or permitted to work in such coal mine. Such escapement shaft or communication with a contiguous mine, as aforesaid, shall be constructed in connection with every vein or stratum of coal worked in such mine [and all passage ways communicating with the escapement shafts or places of exit, from main hauling ways to the escapement shaft shall be at least five feet wide and five feet high].

b. [In all cases where the working face of one mine has by the agreement of adjacent owners been driven into the workings of another mine, the respective owner of such mine while operating the same, shall keep open a roadway at least five feet wide and five feet high, thereby forming a communication as contemplated in this act, and in no case hereafter shall the workings of any mine be driven closer than ten feet to the line of land of any adjacent owner, without the written consent of such owner. And in all cases where the shaft of one mine has been used or may be hereafter used as an air or escapement shaft for another mine, neither owner or operator shall close or obstruct his shaft or workings so as to prevent the use of the same as an escapement or air shaft without first giving one year's notice in writing to the other operator or owner of his intention to aban.on his mine. But the operator continuing the working of his mine shall be at the expense of keeping abandoned workings in repair.]

c Every escapement shaft shall be separated from the main shaft by such extent of natural strata as shall secure safety to the men employed in such mines [and before any escapement shaft shall be located, or the excavations for it be begun, the district inspector of mines shall be duly notified to appear and determine what shall be a suitable distance for the same; the distance from main shaft for such escapement shaft shall not be less than 300 feet without the consent of the mine inspector, nor more than 300 feet without the consent of the operator. Such escapement shafts shall be equipped after the passage of this act, shall be supplied with stairways, partitioned off from the main airway, and having substantial handrails and platforms, and such stairways shall be built at an angle not greater than forty-five degrees : Provided, that in lieu of stairways such hoisting apparatus may be substituted as will insure the safe and speedy removal of persons employed in such mines in case of danger. No accumulations of ice shall be permitted in any escapement shaft, nor any obstructions to travel upon any stairways or ladders.

d [The time to be allowed for sinking such escapement shafts as are now required by law, shall be one year for sinking any shaft two hundred feet or less in depth, and one additional year, or pro rata portion thereof, for every additional two hundred feet or fraction thereof. Time shall be reckoned from the date on which coal is first hoisted from the original shaft for sale or use; and it shall be the duty of the inspectors of mines to see that all escapement shafts are begun in time to secure their completion within the period here specified : And provided further], that nothing in this section shall be construed to extend the time heretofore allowed by law for constructing escape. ment shafts. (*As amended by act approved June* 16, 1887, *in force July* 1, 1887.)

4. VENTILATION—THE VOLUME AND DISTRIBUTION OF AIR CURRENT.—§ 4.
a The owner, agent or operator of every coal mine, whether operated by shaft, slope or drift, shall provide and maintain for every such mine a good and sufficient amount of ventilation for such men and animals as may be employed therein, the amount of air in circulation to be in no case less than one hundred cubic feet for each man, and six hundred cubic feet for each animal, per minute, measured at the foot of the downcast, and the same to be increased at the discretion of the inspector according to the character and extent of the workings, or to the amount of powder used in blasting; and said volume of air shall be forced and circulated to the face of every working place throughout the mine, so that such mine shall be free from standing powder smoke and gases of every kind. Whenever the inspector shall find men working without sufficient air, or under any unsafe conditions [he shall first give the operator a reasonable notice to rectify the same, and upon his refusal so to do may himself order them out until said portions of said mine shall be put in proper condition].

b [All mines in which men are employed shall be examined every morning by a duly authorized agent of the proprietor, to determine whether there are any dangerous accumulations of gas, or lack of proper ventilation, or obstructions to roadways, or any other dangerous conditions, and no person shall be allowed to enter the mine until such examiner shall have reported all the conditions safe for beginning work. Such examiner shall make a daily record of the condition of the mine in a book kept for that purpose, which shall be open at all times to the examination of the inspector.]

c [The currents of air in mines shall be split so as to give a separate current to at least every one hundred men at work, and inspectors shall have discretion to order a separate current for a smaller number of men if special conditions render it necessary.] The ventilation required by this section may be produced by any suitable appliances, but in case a furnace shall be used for ventilating purposes, it shall be built in such a manner as to prevent the communication of fire to any part of the works, by lining the upcast with incombustible material for a sufficient distance up from said furnace : [Provided], it shall not be lawful to use a furnace for ventilating purposes, or for any other purpose, that shall emit smoke into any compartment constructed in, or adjoining any hoisting shaft or slope where the hoisting shaft or slope is the only means provided for the ingress or egress of persons employed in said coal mines.

d That it shall be unlawful, where there is but one means of ingress and egress provided at a coal' shaft or slope, to construct and use a ventilating furnace that shall emit smoke into a shaft, as an upcast, where the shaft or slope used as a means of ingress or egress by persons employed in said coal mines is the only means provided for furnishing air to persons employed therein. (*As amended by an act approved June* 30, 1885, *in force July* 1, 1885, *and as amended by an act approved June* 10, 1887, *in force July* 1, 1887.)

5. BORE-HOLES.—§ 5. The owner, agent or operator shall provide that bore-holes shall be kept twenty feet in advance of the face of each and every working place, and if necessary, on both sides, when driving towards an abandoned mine or part of a mine suspected to contain inflammable gases, or to be inundated with water.

6. CAGES—COVERS—SAFETY CATCHES AND BRAKES; WOMEN AND CHILDREN —WATCHMEN—LIGHTS AND SIGNALS.—§ 6. *a.* The owner, agent, or operator of every coal mine operated by shaft shall provide safe means of hoisting and lowering persons in a cage covered with boiler iron, so as to keep safe, so far as possible, persons descending into and ascending out of such shaft; and such cage shall be furnished with guides to conduct it on slides through such shaft, with a sufficient brake on every drum to prevent accident in case of the giving out or breaking of the machinery; and such cage shall be furnished with safety catches intended and provided as far as possible, to prevent the consequences of cable breaking or the loosening or disconnecting of machinery.

b No person under the age of fourteen years nor females of any age, shall be permitted to enter any mine to work therein [and before any boy shall be permitted to work in any mine he shall be required to produce an affidavit from his parent or guardian, sworn and subscribed to before a justice of the peace or notary public, that said boy is fourteen years of age. Such affidavits of all the boys employed in any mine shall be produced upon the demand of the inspector.

c The owner, agent or operator of every coal mine operated by shaft and by steam-power shall place competent persons at the top and bottom of such shaft for the purpose of attending to the signals while men are being lowered into or hoisted out of the mine; they shall be at their post of duty at least thirty minutes before the hoisting of coal is commenced in the morning, and remain at least thirty minutes after the hoisting of coal has ceased at night. It shall also be their duty to see that the men do not carry any tools, timber or material with them on the cage, and that only the proper number of men are allowed upon the cage at one time. A sufficient light shall be furnished at the top and bottom of the shaft to insure as far as possible the safety of persons getting on or off the cage.

d The following code of signals between the top-man, bottom-man and engineer are prescribed for use at all mines operated by shaft and by steam-power:

From the Bottom to the Top.

One bell shall signify to hoist coal or empty cage, and also to stop either when in motion.

Two bells shall signify to lower cage.

Three bells shall signify that men are coming up. When return signal is received from the engineer, men will get on the cage and ring one bell to start.

Four bells shall signify to hoist slowly, implying danger.

From the Top to the Bottom.

One bell shall signify all ready, get on the cage.

Two bells shall signify send away empty cage.

Provided, that the manager of any mine may add to this code of signals in his discretion for the purpose of promoting their efficiency, or the safety of the men, but any code which may be established shall be conspicuously posted at the top and bottom of the shaft and in the engine room.]

e Any person neglecting or refusing to perform the duties required to be performed by sections three, four, five, six, seven and eight of this act shall be deemed guilty of a misdemeanor and punished by a fine in the discretion of the court trying the same, subject, however, to the limitations as provided by section ten of this act. (*As amended by an act approved June* 18, 1883, *in force July* 1, 1883; *and as amended by act approved June* 16, 1887, *in force July* 1, 1887.)

7. ENGINEERS AND FIREMEN—NUMBER OF PERSONS PERMITTED ON CAGES. —§ 7. *a* No owner, agent or operator of any coal mine operated by shaft or slope shall place in charge of any engine whereby men are lowered into or hoisted from the mine, any [other than] competent experienced and sober [engineers and firemen, and they shall not be less than eighteen years of age.] No person shall ride upon a loaded cage [or car] used for hoisting purposes in any shaft or slope, and in no case shall more than twelve persons ride on any cage or car at one time, nor shall any coal be hoisted out of any coal mine while persons are descending into such mine.

b The number of persons permitted to ascend out of or descend into any coal mine [at one time] shall be determined by the inspector [and they shall not be] lowered or hoisted more rapidly than six hundred feet per minute. [Whenever a cage load of persons shall come to the bottom to be hoisted out, who have finished their day's work or otherwise been prevented from working, an empty cage shall be given them to ascend, except in mines having slopes or provided with stairways in escapement shafts.] (*As amended by an act approved June* 16, 1887, *in force July* 1, 1887.)

8. INSPECTION OF BOILERS—THE PROTECTION OF SHAFT OPENINGS—PLACES OF REFUGE—PASSAGE-WAYS AT THE BOTTOM—SUMPS.—§ 8. *a* All boilers used in generating steam in and about coal mines shall be kept in good order, and the agent, owner or operator, as aforesaid, shall have said boilers examined and inspected by a competent boiler maker or other qualified person as often as once every six months, and oftener if the inspector shall deem it necessary, and the result of every such examination shall be certified in writing to the mine inspector.

b The top of each and every shaft, and the entrance to each and every intermediate working vein shall be securely fenced by gates, properly protecting such shaft and entrance thereto; and the entrance to every abandoned slope, air or other shaft shall be securely fenced off; and every steam boiler shall be provided with a proper steam gauge, water guage and safety valve.

c All underground, self-acting or engine planes, or gangways, on which coal cars are drawn and persons travel, shall be provided with some proper means of signaling between the stopping places and the ends of said planes or gangways, and sufficient places of refuge at the sides of such planes or gangways shall be provided at intervals of not more than [twenty yards, and they shall be not less than six feet wide and six feet in depth, and shall be whitewashed or otherwise distinguished from the surrounding walls.

d The bottom of every shaft shall be supplied with a traveling-way to enable men to pass from one side of the shaft to the other without passing under or over the cages. All sumps shall be securely planked over so as to prevent accidents to men.] (*As amended by an act approved June* 16, 1887, *in force July* 1, 1887.)

9. ACCIDENTS IN MINES—DUTY OF INSPECTOR—FAILURE TO REPORT—PENALTY.—§ 9. *a* Whenever loss of life, or serious personal injury shall occur by reason of any explosion, or of any accident whatsoever, in or about any coal mine, it shall be the duty of the person having charge of such coal mine to report the facts thereof, without delay, to the mine inspector of the district in which said coal mine is situated; and if any person is killed thereby, to notify the coroner of the county also, or, in his absence or inability to act, any justice of the peace of said county; and the said inspector shall if he deem it necessary from the facts reported, immediately go to the scene of said accident and make such suggestions and render such assistance as he may deem necessary for the safety of the men.

b The inspector shall investigate and ascertain the cause of such explosion or accident, and make a report thereof, which he shall preserve with the other records of his office; and to enable him to make such investigations he shall have the power to compel the attendance of witnesses, and administer oaths or affirmations to them, and the cost of such investigations shall be paid by the county in which such accident has occurred, in the same manner as costs of coroners' inquests are now paid. And the failure of the person in charge of the coal mine in which any such accident may have occurred, to give notice to the inspector or coroner, as provided for in this section, shall subject such person to a fine of not less than twenty-five dollars ($25), nor more than one hundred dollars ($100) to be recovered in the name of the People of the State of Illinois, before any justice of the peace of such county, and such fine, when collected, shall be paid into the county treasury for the use of the county in which any such accident may have occurred. (*As amended by an act approved June* 18, 1883, *in force July* 1, 1883.)

10. FINES AND PENALTIES.—§ 10. In all cases in which punishment is provided by fine under this act for a breach of any of its provisions, the fine for a first offence shall not be less than fifty dollars ($50), and not more than two hundred dollars ($200), and for the second offence not less than one hundred dollars ($100), or more than five hundred dollars ($500), in the discretion of the court, except as specially provided for in section nine of this act.

11. INSPECTION DISTRICTS—DISTRICT INSPECTORS AND COUNTY INSPECTORS.—§ 11. *a* This State shall be divided into five inspection districts, as follows: The first district shall be composed of the counties of Boone, McHenry, Lake, DeKalb, Kane, DuPage, Cook, LaSalle, Kendall, Grundy, Will, Livingston, Kankakee and Iroquis. The second district, the counties of JoDaviess, Stephenson, Winnebago, Carroll, Ogle, Whiteside, Lee, Rock Island, Henry, Bureau, Mercer, Stark, Putnam, Marshall, Henderson, Warren, Knox, Hancock, McDonough, Schuyler, Adams and Brown. The third district, the counties of Fulton, Peoria, Woodford, Tazewell, McLean, Ford, Mason, Cass, Menard, Logan, DeWitt, Piatt, Champaign and Vermilion. The fourth district, the counties of Pike, Scott, Morgan, Sangamon, Calhoun, Greene, Jersey, Madison, Bond, Macoupin, Montgomery, Christian, Fayette, Macon, Moultrie, Shelby, Effingham, Douglas, Coles, Cumberland, Jasper, Edgar, Clark, Crawford, Clay, Richland and Lawrence. The fifth district, the counties of St. Clair, Clinton, Washington, Marion, Jefferson, Wayne, Edwards, Wabash, Hamilton, White, Monroe, Randolph, Perry, Jackson,

Franklin, Williamson, Saline, Gallatin, Union, Johnson, Pope, Hardin, Alexander, Pulaski and Massac.

b The Governor shall, upon the recommendation of a board of examiners selected for that purpose, composed of two practical coal miners, two coal operators, and one mining engineer, to be appointed by the Bureau of Labor Statistics of this State, all of whom shall be sworn to a faithful discharge of their duties, appoint five properly qualified persons to fill the offices of inspectors of coal mines of this State, (being one inspector for each district provided for in this act) whose commissions shall be for the term of two years, but they shall at all times be subject to removal from office for neglect of duty, or malfeasance in the discharge of duty, as hereinafter provided for.

c The inspectors so appointed shall have attained the age of thirty years, be citizens of this State, and have a knowledge of mining engineering sufficient to conduct the development of coal mines, and a practical knowledge of the methods of conducting mining for coal in the presence of explosive gases, and of the proper ventilation of coal mines. They shall have had a practical mining experience of ten years, and shall not be interested as owner, operator, stockholder, superintendent or mining engineer of any coal mine during their term of office, and shall be of good moral character and temperate habits, and shall not be guilty of any act tending to the injury of miners or operators of mines during their term of office. They shall be provided by the State with the most approved modern instruments for carrying out the intention of this act. The inspectors, before assuming the duties of their several offices, shall take an oath of office, as provided for by the constitution, and shall be required to enter into a bond to the State in the sum of five thousand dollars ($5,000), with sureties to be approved by the Governor, conditioned upon the faithful performance of their duties in every particular, as required by this act; said bond, with the approval of the Governor endorsed thereon, together with the oath of office, shall be deposited with the Secretary of State. The salaries of the inspectors provided for by this act shall be eighteen hundred dollars ($1,800) per annum each, and the Auditor of Public Accounts is hereby authorized to draw his warrant on the treasury in their favor, quarterly, for the amount specified in this section for the salary of each inspector.

d Provided, that the county board of any county may appoint an assistant inspector for such county, who shall act under the directions of the district inspector in the performance of his duties, and shall receive not less than three dollars ($3), nor more than five dollars ($5) per day, for the time actually employed, to be paid out of the county treasury; and he may be removed by such county board at any time. (*As amended by an act approved June* 18, 1883, *and an act approved June* 30, 1885, *in force July* 1, 1885.)

12. INSPECTORS—THEIR DUTIES AND REMOVAL—BOARD OF EXAMINERS—RIGHT OF WAY UNDERGROUND BETWEEN MINES.—§ 12. *a* The inspectors provided for by this act shall devote their whole time and attention to the duties of their office, and make personal examination of every mine within their respective districts, and shall see that every necessary precaution is taken to insure the health and safety of the workmen employed in such mines, and that the provisions and requirements of the mining laws of this State are faithfully observed and obeyed and the penalties of the same enforced. They shall also make annual reports to the Bureau of Labor Statistics of their acts during the year in

the discharge of their duties, with their recommendations as to legislation necessary on the subject of mining, and shall collect and tabulate upon blanks furnished by said Bureau all desired statistics of the mines and miners within their districts, to accompany said annual report; they shall also furnish such information as they may have obtained on this subject, when called for, to the State Geologist.

b Upon a petition signed by not less than three reputable coal operators, or ten coal miners, setting forth that any inspector of coal mines neglects his duties, or that he is incompetent, or that he is guilty of malfeasance in office, or guilty of any act tending to the injury of miners or operators of mines, it may be lawful for the Bureau of Labor Statistics of this State, to issue a citation to the said inspector to appear, at not less than fifteen days' notice on a day fixed, before them, when the said Bureau shall proceed to inquire into and investigate the allegations of the petitioners; and if the said Bureau find that the said inspector is neglectful of his duty, or that he is by reason of causes that existed before his appointment, or that have arisen since his appointment incompetent to perform the duties of said office, or that he is guilty of malfeasance in office, or guilty of any act tending to the injury of miners or operators of mines the said Bureau shall declare the office of inspector of the said district vacant, and a properly qualified person shall be appointed to fill the office in compliance with the provisions of this act; and the cost of said investigation by the said Bureau shall be borne by the removed inspector; but if the allegations of the petitioners are not sustained by the final decision of the said Bureau, the costs shall be paid by the petitioners.

c The board of examiners provided for in section eleven of this act shall be appointed by the Bureau of Labor Statistics, and shall hold their offices for two years. They shall meet biennially at the State capital on the second Monday in September, and special meetings may be called at any time by the Bureau of Labor Statistics when the office of coal mine inspector becomes from any cause vacant. They shall receive as compensation the sum of three dollars ($3) per day, each, for time actually employed in the duties of there office, and actual travelling expenses, to be verified by affidavit: *Provided*, that in no case shall the per diem received by any member of said board exceed the sum of thirty dollars ($30) per annum. The Auditor of Public Accounts is hereby authorized to draw his warrant in favor of each member of the board of examiners at the close of their annual session, for the full amount due them for attending annual and special sessions, and expenses, upon vouchers sworn to by them and approved by the Secretary of the Bureau of Labor Statistics, and the Governor.

d And provided further, that when two or more coal mines are so located as to allow the said mines to be connected by permanent entries between, and the land or mining rights lying between such mines is owned by any person or persons with whom the owner or owners of said mine or mines are unable to agree for the purchase of the right of way for the connecting entry or entries between such mines, and the right to maintain and use such entry as a connecting entry, such owner or owners of any such coal mine or mines, or either of them, may acquire such right or title in the manner that may be now or hereafter provided for by any law of eminent domain. (*As amended by an act approved June* 18, 1883, *and by an act approved June* 30, 1885, *and in force July* 1, 1885.)

13. AUTHORITY OF INSPECTOR AND MODE OF PROCEDURE.]—§ 13. *a* It shall be lawful for the inspector, provided for in this act, to enter, examine and inspect any and all coal mines and machinery belonging thereto, at all reasonable times, by day or by night, but so as not to obstruct or hinder the necessary workings of such coal mine, and the owner, agent or operator of every such coal mine is hereby required to furnish all necessary facilities for entering for such examination and inspection, and if the said owner, agent or operator aforesaid shall refuse to permit such inspection or to furnish the necessary facilities for such entry, examination and inspection, the inspector shall file his affidavit setting forth such refusal with the Judge of the Circuit Court in said county in which said mine is situated, either in term time or vacation, or, in the absence of said judge, with the Master in Chancery in said county in which said mine is situated, and obtain an order on such owner, agent or operator so re fusing as aforesaid, commanding him to permit and furnish such necessary facilities for the inspection of such coal mine, or to be adjudged to stand in contempt of court and punished accordingly.

b If the said inspector shall, after examination of any coal mine and the works and machinery pertaining thereto, find the same to be worked contrary to the provisions of this act, or unsafe for the workmen therein employed, said inspector shall, through the State's attorney of his county, or any attorney, in case of his refusal to act, acting in the name and on behalf of the State, proceed against the owner, agent or operator of such coal mine by injunction without bond, after giving at least two days' notice to such owner, agent or operator, and said owner, agent or operator shall have the right to appear before the Judge or Master to whom the application is made, who shall hear the same on affidavits, and such other testimony as may be offered in support as well as in opposition thereto ; and if sufficient cause appear, the court, or judge in vacation by order, shall prohibit the further working of any such coal mine in which persons may be unsafely employed contrary to the provisions of this act until the same shall have been made safe and the requirements of this act shall have been complied with, and the court shall award such costs in the matter of the said injunction as may be just ; but any such proceedings so commenced shall be without prejudice to any other remedy permitted by law for enforcing the provisions of this act.

14. INJURIES—RIGHT OF ACTION—DAMAGES.—§ 14. For any injury to person or property, occasioned by any wilful failure to comply with any of its provisions, a right of action shall accrue to the party injured for any direct damages sustained thereby; and in case of loss of life by reason of such wilful violation or wilful failure, as aforesaid, a right of action shall accrue to the widow of the person so killed, his lineal heirs or adopted children, or to any other person or persons, who were before such loss of life, dependent for support on the person or persons so killed, for a like recovery of damages for the injuries sustained by reason of such loss of life or lives; [not to exceed the sum of five thousand dollars.] (*As amended by an act approved June* 16, 1887, *in force July* 1, 1887.)

15. TAMPERING WITH MACHINERY—CARELESSNESS—DISOBEYING RULES. —§ 15. Any miner, workman or other person who shall knowingly injure any water-gauge, barometer, air-course or bratice, or shall obstruct, or throw open any air-ways, or carry any lighted lamps or matches into places that are worked by the light of safety lamps, or shall handle or disturb any part of the machinery of the hoisting engine, or open a door in the mine and not have the same closed again, whereby danger is produced either to the mine or those at work therein; or who shall enter into any part of the mine against caution; or who shall disobey any order given in pursuance of this act; or who shall do any wilful act whereby the lives and health of persons working in the mine, or the security of the mine, or mines, or the machinery thereof, is endangered, shall be deemed guilty of a misdemeanor, and, upon conviction, shall be punished by fine or imprisonment, at the discretion of the court.

16. PROPS AND CAP-PIECES.—§ 16. The owner, agent or operator of every coal mine shall keep a supply of timber [constantly on hand, of sufficient length and dimensions to be used as props and cap-pieces, and shall deliver the same as required, with the miner's empty car], so that the workmen may at all times be able to properly secure said workings [for their own safety]. (*As amended by an act approved June* 16, 1887, *in force July* 1, 1887.)

17. REPEALING CLAUSE.—§ 17. All acts or parts of acts inconsistent with the provisions of this act are and the same are hereby repealed.

18. MINES WITHOUT ESCAPEMENTS—BUILDINGS TO BE MADE FIRE-PROOF —COUNTY INSPECTORS.—§ 18. That all mines hoisting coal by steam power from shaft or slope, having no other means of ingress or egress afforded to persons employed therein than by said shaft or slope, shall, within ninety days after July 1st, A.D. 1883, have all engine and boiler-houses roofed and sided with fire-proof materials, and they shall be situated not less than fifty feet from the mouth of the said shaft or slope; that the hoisting derricks erected over said hoisting shaft or near said slope, if enclosed, and all the coal chutes, buildings and constructions within a radius of fifty feet of the mouth of said hoisting shaft or slope, shall be covered and sided with fire-proof materials, and the person in charge, the owners or operators thereof, shall provide a steam pump and have the same conveniently situated, and a sufficient supply of water and hose always ready for use in any part of the buildings, chutes or constructions within a radius of fifty feet of said coal hoisting shaft or slope; and if the person in charge of any such coal shaft or slope shall refuse or neglect to comply with the provisions of this act, then the inspector of coal mines for the county in which the said shafts or slopes are situated, shall proceed, through the State's attorney of his county, or any attorney, in case of his refusal to act, acting in the name and on the behalf of the State, against the owner, agent or operator of said shaft or slope, by information without bond, after giving at least two days' notice to such owner, agent or operator; and the said owner, agent or operator shall have the right to appear before the judge or master to whom the application is made, who shall hear the same on affidavits, and such other testimony as may be offered in support as well as in opposition thereto; and if it be found that the owner, agent or operator of said shaft or slope has refused or neglected to comply with the provisions of this act, the court, or judge in vacation, by order, shall prohibit the further working of any such coal shaft or slope until the owner, agent or operator shall have complied with the terms of this act. (*An act approved June* 21, 1883, *in force July* 1, 1883.)

19. COPPER TOOLS.—§ 19. That all miners and employés engaged in mining coal shall use copper needles in preparing blasts in coal, and not less than five

(5) inches of copper on the end of all iron bars used for tamping blasts of powder in coal, and the use of iron needles and iron tamping bars not tipped with five inches of copper is hereby declared to be unlawful. Any failure on the part of a coal miner or an employé in any coal mine to conform to the terms and requirements of this act shall subject such miner or employé to a fine of not less than five dollars, nor more than twenty-five dollars, with costs of prosecution for each offence, to be recovered by civil suit, before any justice of the peace; said fines, when collected, to be paid into the treasury of the county where the offence was committed, to the credit of the fund provided for the payment of the county inspector of mines. (*An act approved June* 21, 1883, *in force July* 1, 1883.)

THE WEIGHING LAW.

AN ACT to Provide for the Weighing of Coal at the Mines, and to Repeal a
Certain Act therein Named.

1. SCALES TO BE PROVIDED.—SECTION 1. *Be it enacted by the People of the State of Illinois, represented in the General Assembly:* That the owner, agent or operator of every coal mine in this State, at which the miners are paid by weight, shall provide at such mines suitable and accurate scales of standard manufacture for the weighing of all coal which shall be hoisted or delivered from such mines.

2. WEIGHING OF COAL—RECORD OF WEIGHTS—WEIGHMAN.—§ 2. *a* All coal so delivered from such mines shall be carefully weighed upon the scales as above provided, and a correct record shall be kept of the weight of each miner's car, which record shall be kept open at all reasonable hours for the inspection of all miners or others pecuniarily interested in the product of such mine.

b The person designated and authorized to weigh the coal and keep such record shall, before entering upon his duties, make and subscribe to an oath before some magistrate or other officer authorized to administer oaths, that he will accurately weigh and carefully keep a true record of all coal delivered from such mine, and such oath shall be kept conspicuously posted at the place of weighing.

3. CHECK-WEIGHMAN MAY BE EMPLOYED BY MINERS—HIS DUTIES— QUALIFICATIONS—OATH.—§ 3. *a* It shall be lawful for the miners employed in any coal mine in this State to furnish a check-weighman at their own expense, whose duty it shall be to balance the scales and see that the coal is properly weighed, and that a correct account of the same is kept, and for this purpose he shall have access at all times to the beam box of said scale, and be afforded facilities for the discharge of his duties while the weighing is being performed.

b The agent employed by the miners as aforesaid to act as check-weighman shall be an employé of the person or persons operating the mine, a citizen of the State and county wherein the mine is situated, and shall, before entering upon his duties, make and subscribe to an oath before some officer duly authorized to administer oaths, that he is duly qualified, and will faithfully discharge the duties of check-weighman; such oath shall be kept conspicuously posted at the place of weighing.

4. FRAUDULENT WEIGHING OR RECORDING—PENALTIES.—§ 4. Any person, company or firm having or using any scale or scales for the purpose of weighing the output of coal at mines, so arranged or constructed that fraudulent weighing may be done thereby, or who shall knowingly resort to or employ any means whatsoever by reason of which such coal is not correctly weighed or reported in accordance with the provisions of this act; or any weighman or check-weighman who shall fraudulently weigh or record the weights of such coal, or connive at or consent to such fraudulent weighing and recording, shall be deemed guilty of a misdemeanor, and shall upon conviction, for each offence, be punished by a fine of not less than two hundred dollars ($200) nor more than five hundred dollars ($500), or by imprisonment in the county jail for a period not to exceed sixty (60) days, or by both such fine and imprisonment, proceedings to be instituted in any court of competent jurisdiction.

5. NON-COMPLIANCE WITH LAW OR OBSTRUCTIUG REQUIREMENTS—PENALTIES—EXCEPTIONS.—§ 5. Any person, owner or agent operating a coal mine in this State who shall fail to comply with the provisions of this act, or who shall obstruct or hinder the carrying out of its requirements, shall be fined for the first offence not less than fifty dollars ($50); for the second offence not less than two hundred dollars ($200) or more than five hundred dollars ($500), and for a third offence not less than five hundred dollars ($500), or be imprisoned in the county jail not less than six months nor more than one year: *Provided*, that the provisions of this act shall apply only to coal mines whose product is shipped by rail or water.

6. REPEALING CLAUSE.—§ 6. That an act entitled " An act to provide for the weighing of coal at the mines," approved June 14, 1883, in force July 1, 1883, as amended and approved June 29, 1885, in force July 1, 1885, be and the same is hereby repealed. (*Approved June* 16, 1887, *in force July* 1, 1887.)

MINING LAWS OF INDIANA.

5458. " Mine " defined. 1. The term "mine," as used in this Act, includes every shaft, slope, or drift, which is used, or has been used, in the mining and removing of coal from and below the surface of the ground.

5459. Number of employés—Outlets. 2. Six months from and after the taking effect of this Act, it shall not be lawful for the owner or agent of any coal mine now operated, or which may be hereafter opened, worked by shaft, slope, or drift, wherein over fifteen thousand square yards have been excavated, to employ more than ten persons to work in such mine, unless there are, to every seam or stratum of coal worked in such mine, at least two separate outlets, separated by natural strata of not less than one hundred feet in breadth, by which shafts or outlets, distinct means of ingress or egress are always available to the persons employed in the mine; but it shall not be neccessary for the two outlets to belong to the same mine. In every mine opened after the passage of this Act, and after fifteen thousand square yards shall have been mined out, it shall be unlawful for the owner or agent to employ more than ten persons to work in said mine, in every twenty-four hours, unless there are two distinct outlets; and in all slopes, drifts, and main entries, a sufficient number of refuge holes shall be established.

1. As to the duties of the lessee of a mine to leave sufficient supports for the ground overhead, see Yandes v. Wright, 66 Ind. 319.

2. Mining leases are construed in McDowell v. Hendrix, 67, Ind. 513; Watson Coal and Mining Co. v. Casteel, 73 id. 206.

(1881, p. 8. In force March 5, 1881.)

5460. Maps. 3. At the request of the owner of any coal mine, the owner of the land, the miners working therein, or other person interested in the working of such mine, the Mine Inspector shall cause to be made an accurate map or plan of the workings of such mine on a scale of not less than one inch to the one hundred feet, showing the area mined or excavated, and the location and connection of the lines of all adjoining lands with such excavation of the mine, and the name of the owners of such lands, so far as known, marked on each tract of land. Such map shall show the complete working of the mine; which map, when complete, shall be sworn to by the Mine Inspector to be a correct map of the working of such mine, and shall be kept on file in the office of the Mine Inspector, for inspection at all times. The Mine Inspector shall be allowed a reasonable fee for making such survey, provided that he employs a surveyor to make the same, but he shall not be allowed anything for making the map of same. All expenses shall be paid by the party causing such survey and map to be made.

(1879, p. 19. In force May 1, 1879.)

5461. Copy of map, when furnished. 5. Upon payment of the fees, the Mine Inspector shall make, within a reasonable time, and deliver to the party, so demanding the same, an accurate copy of any map or plan of the working of such mine that may be on file in his office.

5462. Map or copy, evidence. 6. The original map or plan of any coal mine, or the copy filed with the Inspector, or a certified copy issued under the hand and seal of such inspector, shall be evidence in any Court of justice in this State.

5463. "Owner" and "Agent" defined. 7. The term "owner," as used in this Act, is hereby defined to mean the immediate proprietor, lessee or occupier of any coal mine or any part thereof; and the term "agent," is hereby defined to mean any person, other than the owner thereof, having the care and management of any coal mine, or any part thereof, and in case the mine is owned or occupied by a corporation, then any of its officers shall be deemed its agent.

5464. Ventilation. 8. The owner or agent of every coal mine shall within six months from the time this Act takes effect, provide and establish a circulation of sufficient amount of pure air to dilute and expel therefrom the noxious and poisonous gases, to such an extent that the entire mine shall be in a fit state, at all times, for the men to work therein, and be free from danger to their health and lives from said gases and impure air—said ventilation to be produced by any suitable appliance that will produce and insure a constant supply of pure air throughout the entire mine. But in no case shall a furnace be used at the bottom of the shaft in the mine for the purpose of producing a hot up-cast of air where the hoisting apparatus and buildings are built directly over the top of the shaft. Every such mine shall have ventilation affording one hundred cubic feet per minute for each and every person employed in such mine, which shall be circulated through the main headings and cross-

17

headings, to an extent that will dilute and render harmless the noxious gases generated therein.

5465. Precautions as to gas and water. 9. When a place is likely to contain a dangerous accumulation of water or gases, the working, approaching such place, shall not exceed eight feet in width, and there shall be constantly kept, at a sufficient distance (not less than three yards in advance), one bore-hole near the centre of the working, and sufficient flank bore-holes on each side; and when two veins are worked in the same shaft, the upper shall be so protected that no danger will occur to the miners working in the lower vein.

5466. Management of engines and cages. 10. No owner or agent of any coal mine shall place in charge of any engine used for conveying into or hoisting out of such mine, any but experienced, competent, and sober engineers. No engineer, in charge of such engine shall allow any person, except such as may be deputed for that purpose by the owner or agent, to interfere with it or any part of the machinery; and no person shall interfere or in any way intimidate the engineer in the discharge of his duties. In no case shall more than six men ride in any cage or car at one time; and no person shall ride upon a loaded cage or car when the same is being hoisted out of or being conveyed into the mine.

5467. Cover for cages—Safety gate—Safety spring—Brake—Indicator. 11. The owner or agent of every coal mine operated by shaft or slope, shall provide a sufficient cover overhead, on all carriages or cages used for lowering and hoisting persons into and out of the mine, and, on the top of every shaft, an approved safety gate; also, an approved safety spring on the top of every slope. An adequate brake shall be attached to every drum or machine used for lowering or raising persons into or out of all shafts or slopes; and also a proper indicator, in addition to any mark on the rope, which shall show to the person who works the machine the position of the cage or load in the shaft. And there shall be cut in the side of every hoisting shaft, at the bottom thereof, a travelling-way sufficiently high and wide to enable persons to pass the shaft in going from one side to the other, without passing over or under the cage or other hoisting apparatus.

5468. Fencing shafts. 12. The owner or agent of every coal mine shaft or slope, at the end of six months from the time this Act takes effect, shall keep the top of every such shaft or slope, and the entrance thereof, securely fenced off by vertical or flat gates, covering and protecting the mouth of such shaft or slope. The entrance of an abandoned shaft or slope shall be securely fenced off, so that no injury can arise therefrom. The owner or agent, or either of them, violating the provisions of this section shall be fined in any sum not exceeding one hundred dollars for each day or part of a day the same is violated.

5469. Injuring appliances. 13. Any miner, workman, or other person, who shall, knowingly, injure or interfere with any safety-lamp, air-course, or with any brattice, or obstruct or throw open doors, or disturb any part of the machinery, or ride upon a loaded car or wagon in any shaft or slope, or do any act whereby the lives or the health of the persons, or the security of the mines and machinery are endangered, shall be deemed guilty of a misdemeanor, and, upon conviction, shall be fined any sum not exceeding ten dollars.

5470. Examination of machinery and books. 14. The Mine Inspector, miners employed and working in and about the mine, the owner of the land, or other persons interested in the royalty or rental of such mine, shall, at all proper times, have full right of access and examination of all scales, machinery, or apparatus used in or about said mine, including the bank book in which the weight of coal is kept, to determine the amount of coal mined, for the purpose of attesting the accuracy thereof.

5471. Liens, how acquired—Wages. 15. In all coal mines in this State the miners and other persons employed and working in and about the mines, and the owners of the land and others interested in the rental or royalty on the coal mined therein, shall have a lien on said mine and all machinery and fixtures connected therewith, including scales, coal-bank cars, and everything used in and about the mine, for work and labor performed within two months, and the owner of the land, for royalty on coal taken out from under his land, for any length of time not exceeding two months; and such liens shall be paramount to and have priority over all other liens, except the lien of the State for taxes; and such liens shall have priority, as against each other, in the order in which they accrued and for labor over that for royalty on coal. Any person, to acquire such lien, shall file in the Recorder's office of the county where the coal mine is situate, within sixty days from the time the payment became due, a notice of his intention to hold a lien upon such property for the amount of his claim, stating in such notice the amount of his claim, and the name of the coal-works, if known, or any other designating, describing the location of said mine; and the Recorder shall record the said notice, when presented, in a book used for recording mechanics' liens, for which the Recorder shall receive a fee of twenty-five cents. Suits brought to enforce any lien herein created shall be brought within one year from the date of filing said lien in the Recorder's office; and all judgments rendered on the foreclosure of such liens shall include the amount of the claim found to be due, with the interest on the same from the time due, and with a reasonable attorney's fee, the judgment to be collected without relief from valuation, appraisement or stay laws. All wages of miners and other persons working in and about the mine shall be due and payable on the second Saturday of the month after the month in which the work was done, and all payments shall be made in bankable funds of the State of Indiana.

5472. Daily examinations. 16. The rope used for hoisting and lowering in every coal mine shall be examined, by some competent person, every morning, before the men descend into the shaft. When gas is known to exist there shall be a competent fire-boss, whose duty it shall be to examine each and every place in the mine before the men are permitted to enter and work; and the said fire-boss shall be at the mouth or bottom of the mine each day, to inform every man as to the state of his room or entry. Said works shall be carefully examined every morning with a safety lamp, by a competent person, before workmen are allowed to enter.

(1881, p. 8. In force March 5, 1881.)

5473. Mine Inspector—Appointment—Oath—Bond. 17. Within thirty days after this Act shall take effect, the Governor, with the advice and consent of the Senate, shall appoint a Mine Inspector, who shall hold his office for two years and until his successor shall be appointed and qualified. Such Inspector shall be a resident of the State of Indiana, and a practical miner in said State; and no person shall be eligible to hold the office of Mine Inspector who is or may be pecuniarily interested in any coal mine within this State, directly or indirectly. Said Mine Inspector, before entering upon the duties of his office, shall execute a bond, with sufficient surety, payable to the State of Indiana, in the sum of one thousand dollars, for the faithful discharge of the duties of his office; which bond shall be approved by and filed with the Secretary of State. He shall take an oath of office which shall be indorsed on the back of his bond.

5474. Office—Salary. 18. The Mine Inspector shall hold his office in some central part of the mining district; and, for his services, he shall receive the annual compensation of fifteen hundred dollars, to be paid quarterly on the first days of January, April, July, and October of each year, out of any moneys in the State Treasury not otherwise appropriated.

(1879, p. 19. In force May 1, 1879.)

5475. Inspector's and mine-owner's duty. 19. It shall be the duty of the Mine Inspector appointed under this Act to enter, examine, and inspect any and all coal mines, and the works and the machinery belonging thereto, at any reasonable time, by day or by night, but so as not to hinder or obstruct the working of any coal mine more than is reasonably necessary, in the discharge of his duties; and the agent or the owner of such coal mine is hereby required to furnish the necessary facilities for such entry, examination and inspection. Should the owner or agent fail or refuse to permit such inspection or furnish such facilities, the owner or agent so failing shall be deemed to have committed a misdemeanor. And it is hereby made the duty of such Inspector to charge such owner or agent with such violation, under oath, in any court having jurisdiction; and, upon conviction, the owner or agent, or either or both, shall be fined in any sum not exceeding one hundred dollars for each offence.

5476. Inspector's duties—Report. 20. The Inspector appointed under this Act shall devote his entire time and attention to the duties of his office. He shall make personal inspection, at least twice a year, of all coal mines in this State, and shall see that every precaution is taken to insure the health and safety of the workmen therein employed, that the provisions and requirements of this Act are faithfully carried out, and that the penalties of the law are enforced against all who wilfully disobey its requirements. He shall also collect and tabulate the following facts: The number and thickness of each vein or stratum of coal, and their respective depths below the surface, which are now worked or may be hereafter worked; the kind or quality of coal; how the same is mined, whether by shaft, slope, or drift; the number of mines in operation in each county; the owners thereof; the number of men employed in each mine; and the aggregate yearly production of tons from each mine; estimate the amount of capital employed at each mine; and give any other information relative to coal and mining that he may deem necessary; all of which facts, so tabulated, together with a statement of the condition of mines as to safety and ventilation, he shall freely set forth in an annual report to the Governor, together with his recommendation as to such other legislation on the subject of mining as he may think proper.

5477. No boys under fourteen employed. 21. No boy under fourteen years of age shall be employed to work in any of the mines of this State.

5478. Violating Act, a misdemeanor. 22. Any person violating any of the provisions of this Act shall be deemed guilty of a misdemeanor, and, upon conviction thereof, shall be fined in any sum not exceeding five hundred dollars for each offence.

(1881, p. 8. In force March 5, 1881.)

5479. To what mines Act does not apply. 3. Nothing in this Act, or the Act, which this Act amends, shall apply to any coal mine when there is less than ten men used in and about such mine.

5480. Inspection of scales—Notice—Penalty. 4. It shall be the duty of the Mine Inspector, in addition to his other duties, to examine all scales used at any coal mine in the State for the purpose of weighing coal taken out of said mine; and on inspection, if found incorrect, he shall notify the owner or agent of any such mine that the same is incorrect; and after such notice it shall be unlawful for any owner or agent to use or suffer the same to be used, until the same is so fixed that the same will give the true and correct weight. Any person violating the provisions of this section shall, upon conviction, be fined in any sum not less than ten dollars nor more than one hundred dollars for each day or part of a day the same is so used.

MINING LAWS OF IOWA.

An Act to Regulate Mines and Mining, and to Repeal Chapter 202, of the Acts of the Eighteenth General Assembly. Approved March 18, 1884.

Section 7. The agent or owner of every coal mine shall make or cause to be made, an accurate map or plan of the working of such mine on a scale of not less than one hundred feet to the inch, showing the area mined or excavated. Said map or plan shall be kept at the office of such mine. The agent or owner shall on or before the first day of September of each year, cause to be made a statement and plan of the progress of the workings of such mine up to said date, which statement and plan shall be marked on the map or plan herein required to be made. In case of refusal on the part of said owner or agent for two months after the time designated to make the map or plan, or addition thereto, the inspector is authorized to cause an accurate map or plan of the whole of said mine to be made at the expense of the owner thereof, the cost of which shall be recoverable against the owner in the name of the person or persons making said map or plan. And the owner or agent of all coal mines hereafter wrought out and abandoned, shall deliver a correct map of said mine to the inspector, to be filed in his office.

Sec. 8. It shall be unlawful for the owner or agent of any coal mine worked by a shaft, to employ or permit any person to work therein unless there are to every seam of coal worked in such mine, at least two separate outlets, separated by natural strata of not less than one hundred feet in breadth, by which shafts or outlets distinct means of ingress and egress are always available to the persons employed in the mine, but in no case shall a furnace shaft be used as an escape shaft; and if the mine is a slope or drift opening, the escape shall be separated from the other openings by not less than fifty feet of natural strata; and shall be provided with safe and available travelling ways, and the travelling ways to the escapes in all coal mines shall be kept free from water and falls of roof; and all escape shafts shall be fitted with safe and convenient stairs at an angle of not more than sixty degrees descent, and with landings at easy and convenient distances, so as to furnish easy escape from such mine, and all air shafts used as escapes where fans are employed for ventilation, shall be provided with suitable appliances for hoisting the underground workmen; said appliances to be always kept at the mine ready for immediate use, and in no case shall any combustible material be, allowed between any escape shaft and hoisting shaft, except such as is absolutely necessary for the operation of the mine; *provided*, that where a furnace shaft is large enough to admit of being divided into an escape shaft and a furnace shaft, there may be a partition placed in said shaft, properly constructed so as to exclude the heated air and smoke from the side of the shaft used as an escape shaft, such partitions to be built of incombustible material for a distance of not less than fifteen feet up from the bottom thereof; and *provided*, that where two or more mines are connected underground, each owner may make joint provisions with the other owner for the use of the other's hoisting shaft or slope as an escape, and in that event the owners thereof shall be deemed to have complied with the requirements of this section. And *provided further*, that in any case where the escape shaft is now situated less than one hundred feet from the hoisting shaft, there may be provided a properly constructed underground travelling way from the top of the escape shaft, so as to furnish the proper protection from fire for a distance of one hundred feet from the hoisting shaft; and in that event the owner or agent of any such mine shall be deemed to have complied with the requirements of this section; and *provided further*, that this act shall not apply to mines operated by slopes or drifts openings where not more than five persons are employed therein.

SEC. 9. In all mines there shall be allowed one year to make outlets as provided in section eight when such mine is under two hundred feet in depth, and two years when such mine is over two hundred feet in depth; but not more than twenty men shall be employed in such mine at one time until the provisions of section eight are complied with, and after the expiration of the period above mentioned should said mines, not have the outlets aforesaid, they shall not be operated until made to conform to the provisions of section eight.

SEC. 10. The owner or agent of every coal mine, whether it be operated by shaft, slope, or drift, shall provide and maintain for every such mine an amount of ventilation of not less than one hundred cubic feet of air per minute for each person employed in such mine, and not less than five hundred cubic feet of air per minute for each mule or horse employed in the same, which shall be distributed and circulated throughout the mine in such manner as to dilute, render harmless and expel the poisonous and noxious gases from each and every working place in the mine. And all mines governed by the provisions of this act shall be provided with artificial means for producing ventilation, such as exhaust or forcing fans, furnaces, or exhaust steam, or other contrivances of such capacity and power as to produce and maintain an abundant supply of air for all the requirements of the persons employed in the mine; but in case a furnace is used for ventilating purposes it shall be built in such manner as to prevent the communication of fire to any part of the works by lining the upcast with incombustible material for a sufficient distance up from said furnace to insure safety.

SEC. 11. The owner or agent of every coal mine operated by a shaft or slope, in all cases where the human voice cannot be distinctly heard, shall forthwith provide and maintain a metal tube, or other suitable means for communication from the top to the bottom of said shaft or slope, suitably calculated for the free passage of sound therein, so that communication can be held between persons at the bottom and top of the shaft or slope. And there shall be provided a safety catch of approved pattern and a sufficient cover overhead on all carriages used for lowering and hoisting persons, and on the top of every shaft an approved safety gate and also an approved safety spring on the top of every slope, and an adequate brake shall be attached to every drum or machine used for raising or lowering persons in all shafts or slopes, and a trail shall be attached to every train used on the slope, all of said appliances to be subject to the approval of the inspector.

SEC. 12. No owner or agent of any coal mine operated by shaft or slope shall knowingly place in charge of any engine used for lowering into or hoisting out of such mine persons employed therein, any but experienced, competent, and sober engineers, and no engineer in charge of such engine shall allow any person except such as may be deputed for that purpose by the owner or agent, to interfere with it, or any part of the machinery; and no person shall interfere or in any way intimidate the engineer in his discharge of his duties; and the maximum number of persons to ascend out of or descend into any coal mine on one cage shall be determined by the inspector, but in no case shall such number exceed ten, and no person shall ride upon or against any loaded cage or car in any shaft or slope except the conductor in charge of the train.

SEC. 13. No boy under twelve years of age shall be permitted to work in any mine; and parents or guardians of boys shall be required to furnish an affidavit as to the ages of their boys when there is any doubt in regard to their age, and in all cases of minors applying for work the agent or owner of the mines shall see that the provisions of this section are not violated.

SEC. 14. In case any coal mine does not, in its appliances for the safety of the persons working therein, conform to the provisions of this act, or the owner or agent disregards the requirements of this act for twenty days after being notified by the inspector, any court of competent jurisdiction, while in session or the judges in vacation, may, on application of the inspector, by civil action in the name of the State, enjoin or restrain by writ of injunction, the said agent or owner from working or operating such mines with more than ten persons at once, except as provided in sections eight and nine, until it is made to conform with the provisions of this act, and such remedies shall be cumulative, and shall not take the place of, or affect any other proceedings against such owner or agent authorized by law, for the matter complained of in such action; and for any wilful failure or neglect to comply with the provisions of this law by any owner, lessee, or operator of any coal mine or opening whereby anyone is injured, a right of action shall accrue to the party so injured for any damage he may have sustained thereby, and in case of loss of life by reason of such wilful neglect or failure aforesaid, a right of action shall accrue to the widow, if living, and if not living, to the children of the person whose life shall be lost, for like recovery of damages for the injury they shall have sustained.

SEC. 15. Any miner, workman or other person who shall knowingly injure or interfere with any air-course or brattice, or obstruct, or throw open doors, or disturb any part of the machinery, or disobey any order given in carrying out the provisions of this act, or ride upon a loaded car or wagon in a shaft or slope except as provided in section twelve, or do any act whereby the lives and health of the persons, or the security of the mines and machinery is endangered; or if any miner or person employed in any mine governed by the provisions of this act, shall neglect or refuse to securely prop or support the roof and entries under his control, or neglect or refuse to obey any order given by the superintendent in relation to the security of the mine in the part of the mine under his charge or control, every such person shall be deemed guilty of a misdemeanor, and upon conviction thereof shall be punished by a fine not exceeding one hundred dollars, or imprisonment in the county jail not exceeding thirty days.

SEC. 16. Whenever written charges of gross neglect or duty or malfeasance in office against any inspector shall be made and filed with the Governor, signed by not less than fifteen miners, or one or more operators of mines, together with a bond in the sum of five hundred dollars, payable to the State, and signed by two or more responsible freeholders, and conditioned for the payment of all costs and expenses arising from the investigation of such charges, it shall be the duty of the Governor to convene a board of examiners, to consist of two practical miners, one mining engineer and two operators, at such time and place as he may deem best, giving ten days' notice to the inspector against whom charges may be made, and also the person whose name appears first in the charges; and said board when so convened, and having first been duly sworn or affirmed, truly to try and decide the charges made, shall summon any witness desired by either party and examine them on oath or affirmation, which may be administered by any member of the board, and depositions may be read on such examination as in other cases, and report the result of their investigation to the Governor, and if their report shows that said inspector has grossly neglected his duties, or is incompetent, or has been guilty of malfeasance in office, it shall be the duty of the Governor forthwith to remove said inspector and appoint a successor, and said board shall award the costs and expenses of such investigation against the inspector or person signing said bond.

SEC. 17. In all coal mines in this State the miners employed and working therein shall at all proper times have right of access and examination of all scales, machinery or apparatus used in or about said mine to determine the quantity of coal mined for the purpose of testing the accuracy and correctness of all such scales, machinery or apparatus, and such miners may designate or appoint a competent person to act for them, who shall at all proper times have full right of access and examination of such scales, machinery or apparatus, and seeing all weights and measures of coal mined, and the accounts kept of the same, provided not more than one person on behalf of the miners collectively shall have such right of access, examination and inspection of scales, weights, measures and accounts at the same time, and that such person shall make no unnecessary interference with the use of such scales, machinery or apparatus.

SEC. 18. The owner, agent or operator of any coal mine shall keep a sufficient supply of timber to be used as props, so that the workmen may at all times be able to properly secure the workings from caving in, and it shall be the duty of the owner, agent or operator to send down all such props when required.

Sec. 19. Any person wilfully neglecting or refusing to comply with the provisions of this act when notified by the mine inspector to comply with such provisions, shall be deemed guilty of a misdemeanor, and upon conviction thereof shall be punished by a fine not exceeding five hundred dollars, or imprisonment in the county jail not exceeding six months, except when different penalties are herein provided.

Sec. 20. Chapter 202 of the acts of the Eighteenth General Assembly is hereby repealed.

Sec. 21. This act being deemed of immediate importance, shall be in force on and after its publication in the Iowa State *Register* and Iowa State *Leader*, newspapers published in Des Moines, Iowa.

An Act to repeal sections 1, 2, 3, 4, 5 and 6 of chapter 21, Acts of the Twentieth General Assembly, and enact substitutes therefor, providing for mine inspectors, their manner of appointment, compensation and defining their duties and terms of office. Approved April 10, 1886.

Section 1. That there shall be appointed by the Governor with the advice and consent of the Senate, three inspectors of mines who shall hold their offices for two years. The said inspectors subject, however, to be removed by he Governor for neglect of duty or malfeasance in office. Said term of office shall commence on the first day of April of each even numbered year. Said inspectors shall have a theoretical and practical knowledge of the different systems of working and ventilating coal mines and of the nature and properties of the noxious and poisonous gases of mines and of mining engineering; and said inspectors before entering upon the discharge of their duties shall take an oath or affirmation to discharge the same faithfully and impartially, which oaths or affirmations shall be endorsed upon their commissions, and their commissions so endorsed shall be forthwith recorded in the office of the Secretary of State, and such inspectors shall each give bonds in the sum of two thousand (2,000) dollars, with sureties to the approval of the Governor, conditioned for the faithful discharge of their duties. The Governor shall divide the State into inspection districts and shall assign the inspectors to duty in such place or district as he shall deem proper.

Sec. 2. Said inspectors shall give their whole time and attention to the duties of their offices respectively and shall examine all the mines in this State as often as their duties will permit, to see that the provisions of this act are obeyed, and it shall be lawful for such inspectors to enter, inspect and examine any mine in this State, and the works and machinery belonging thereto, at all reasonable times by night or by day, but so as not to unnecessarily obstruct or impede the working of the mines, and to make inquiry and examination into the state and condition of the mine as to ventilation and general security as required by the provisions of this act. The inspectors shall make a record of all examinations of mines inspected by them, showing the date when made, the condition in which the mines are found, the extent to which the laws relating to mines and mining are observed or violated, the progress made in the improvement and security of life and health sought to be secured by the provisions of this chapter, number of accidents, injuries or deaths in or about the mines; the number of mines visited, the number of persons employed in or about the mines, together with all such facts and information of public interest concerning the condition of mines as they may think useful and proper, or so much thereof as may be of public interest to be included in their biennial report. The owner and agents of all coal mines are hereby required to furnish the means necessary for such inspection, and it shall be the duty of the person having charge of any mine, whenever any loss of life shall occur by accident connected with the workings of such mine to give notice forthwith by mail or otherwise to the inspector of mines of his district and to the coroner of the county in which such mine is situated, and the coroner shall hold an inquest on the body of the person or persons whose death has been caused, and inquire carefully into the cause thereof and shall return a copy of the verdict and all testimony to the said inspector. No person having a personal interest in or employed in the mine where a fatal accident occurs shall be qualified to serve on the jury empaneled on the inquest, and the owner or agent of all coal mines shall report to the inspector all accidents to miners in and around the mines, giving cause of same, such report to be made in writing and within ten days from the time any accident occur.

SEC. 3. Said inspectors while in office shall not act as agents or managers or mining engineers, or be interested in operating any mine, and the inspector shall biennially, or before the fifteenth day of August preceding the regular session of the General Assembly make a report to the Governor of their proceedings and the condition and operation of the mines in this State, enumerating all accidents in or about the same, and giving all such information as they may think useful and proper, and making such suggestion as they may deem important as to future legislation on the subject of mining.

SEC. 4. The inspectors provided for in this act shall each receive a salary of twelve hundred dollars ($1,200) per annum, payable monthly, and shall be furnished with necessary stationery, and actual traveling expenses not to exceed five hundred dollars ($500), per annum; [provided] that each inspector shall file at the end of each quarter of his official year with the Auditor of State a sworn statement of his actual traveling expenses incurred in the performance of his official duty for such quarter. The said salary and expenses to be paid by the State as the salaries and expenses of other State officers are provided for. They shall have and keep an office in the Capitol at Des Moines, in which shall be kept all records, correspondence, papers, apparatus and property pertaining to their duties belonging to the State, and which shall be handed over to their successors in office.

SEC. 5. Any vacancy occurring in the office of inspector when the Senate is not in session, either by death or resignation, removal by the Governor or otherwise, shall be filled by appointment by the Governor, which appointment shall hold good until his successor is appointed and qualified.

SEC. 6. There shall be provided for such inspectors all instruments necessary for the discharge of their duties under this act, which shall be paid for by the State on the certificate of the inspectors, and shall be the property of the State.

SEC. 7. That sections 1, 2, 3, 4, 5 and 6 of chapter 21, acts of the Twentieth General Assembly, be and the same are hereby repealed.

AN ACT to amend Section 4, Chapter 140 of the Laws of the Twenty-first General Assembly and to amend Chapter 21 of the Laws of the Twentieth General Assembly relative to State Mine Inspectors, their duties and manner of appointment. Approved April 12, 1888.

SECTION 1. That section 4, chapter 140, of the acts of the twenty-first General Assembly be and the same is hereby amended by adding thereto the following words: And each of said Mine inspectors shall during his term of office have and keep a residence in the district to which he is assigned without expense to the State. Also have and keep an office at a place designated by the Governor, accessible to railroad and telegraph in their respective districts where at all reasonable times and when not actually engaged elsewhere such inspectors shall be found.

SEC. 2. That Chapter 21 laws of the Twentieth General Assembly be and the same is hereby amended by enacting the following supplementary sections.

SECTION 22. The executive Council shall appoint a board of examiners composed of two practical miners—two mine operators and one mining engineer who shall have at least five years experience in his profession. The members of said board shall be of good moral character, and citizens of the United States and State of Iowa, and they shall before entering upon their duties take the following oath (or affirmation) I——— do solemnly swear (or affirm) that "I will perform the duties of examiner of candidates for the office of mine inspector to the best of my ability and that in recommending any candidate I will be governed by the evidence of qualification to fill the position under the law creating the same, and not by any consideration of political or personal favors; that I will grant certificates to candidates according to their qualifications and the requirements of the law." They shall hold their office for two years.

SECTION 23. Said board shall meet biennially on the first Monday in April of each even numbered year except that for the year 1888 said board shall meet on the second Monday in the office of the State Mine inspector in the Capitol, and they shall publish in at least one newspaper published in each mining district of the State the date fixed by them for the examination of candidates. They shall be furnished with the necessary stationery and other necessary material for said examination in the same manner as other State officers are now provided. They shall receive as compensation the sum of $5.00 per day for time actually employed in the duties of their office and actual traveling expenses. The said compensation and expenses shall be paid in the same manner as the salaries and expenses of other State officers are now paid; provided that in no case shall the per diem received by any member exceed $50.00 for each biennial session.

SECTION 24. Certificates of competency shall be granted only to citizens of the United States and State of Iowa of good moral character, not less than twenty-five years of age, who shall have at least five years experience in the mines and who shall not have been acting as agent or superintendent of any mine for at least six months prior to their appearance for examination.

SECTION 25. The examination of candidates for the office of mine inspector shall consist of oral and written questions in theoretical and practical mining and mine engineering, on the nature and properties of noxious and poisonous gases found in mines and on the different systems of working and ventilating of coal mines. The candidates shall not be allowed to have in their possession at the time of their examination, any books, memoranda or notes to be used as aids in said examination. The board of examiners shall give to all persons examined who in their judgment possess the requisite qualifications, certificates of such qualification, and from the persons holding such certificates the governor shall appoint the State Mine inspectors.

AN ACT to Amend Chapter 21 of the Acts of the 20th General Assembly, Providing for the Weighing of Coal at Mines. Approved April 6, 1888.

SECTION 1. That the owner or agent of each coal mine within this State, at which the miners are paid by weight shall provide at such mine suitable scales of standard make for the weighing of all coal mined.

SEC. 2. The owner or agent of such mine shall require the person authorized to weigh the coal delivered from said mine to be sworn before some person having authority to administer an oath, to keep the scales correctly balanced, to accurately weigh, and to record a correct account of the amount weighed of each miner's car of coal delivered from such mine, and such oath shall be kept conspicuously posted at the place of weighing. The record of the coal mined by each miner shall be kept separate and shall be open to his inspection at all reasonable hours and also for the inspection of all other persons pecuniarily interested in such mine.

SEC. 3. In all coal mines in this State the miners employed and working therein may furnish a competent check-weighman, who shall at all proper times have full right of access and examination of such scales, machinery or apparatus and seeing all measures and weights of coal mined and accounts kept of the same, provided that not more than one person on behalf of the miners collectively shall have such right of access, examination and inspection of scales, measures and accounts at the same time and that such persons shall make no unnecessary interference with the use of such scales, machinery or apparatus. The agent of the miners, as aforesaid shall, before entering upon his duties, make and subscribe to an oath before some officer duly authorized to administer oaths, that he is duly qualified and will faithfully discharge the duties of check-weighman. Such oath shall be kept conspicuously posted at the place of weighing.

SEC. 4. Any person, company or firm having or using any scale or scales for the purpose of weighing the output of coal at mines so arranged or constructed that fraudulent weighing may be done thereby, or who shall knowingly resort to or employ any means whatsoever by reason of which such coal is not correctly weighed or reported in accordance with the provisions of this act; or any weighman or check-weighman who shall fraudulently weigh or record the weights of such coal, or connive at or consent to such fraudulent weighing, shall be deemed guilty of a misdemeanor and shall, upon conviction for each such offence be punished by a fine of not less than two hundred dollars [$200] nor more than five hundred dollars [$500], or by imprisonment in the county jail for a period not to exceed sixty days, or by both such fine and imprison ment; proceedings to be instituted in any court of competent jurisdiction.

SEC. 5. Any person, owner or agent, operating a coal mine in this State who shall fail to comply with the provisions of this act, or who shall obstruct or hinder the carrying out of its requirements, shall be fined for the first offence not less than fifty dollars ($50) nor more than two hundred dollars ($200); for the second offense not less than two hundred dollars ($200) nor more than five hundred dollars ($500); and for a third offense not less than five hundred dollars ($500); provided, that the provisions of this act shall apply only to coal mines whose product is shipped by rail or water.

SEC. 6. That section 17 of chapter 21 of the laws of 1884 is hereby repealed. Approved April 12, 1888.

AN ACT to Establish a Uniform System of Weighing Coal at the Mines of this State, and to Punish certain Irregularities connected therewith.

SECTION 1. That all coal mined in this State under contract for payment by the ton or other quantity shall be weighed before being screened unless otherwise agreed upon in writing, and the full weight thereof shall be credited to the miner of such coal; and eighty pounds of coal as mined shall constitute a bushel, and two thousand pounds of coal, as mined, shall constitute a ton. Provided that nothing in this act shall be so construed as to compel payment for sulphur rock slate black jack or other impurities including slack and dirt which may be loaded with or amongst such coal.

SEC. 2. Each State Mine inspector shall procure from the State Superintend- ent of weights and measures at the expense of the State a full and complete set of standards, balances and other means of adjustment such as are necessary in the comparison and adjustment of the scales, beams and other apparatus used in weighing coal at the mines to the State Standards of weight; and it shall be the duty of said inspectors to examine, test and adjust as often as occasion demands all scales, beams and other apparatus used in weighing coal at the mines.

SEC. 3. Any person damaged by reason of coal mined not having been weighed and credited to him in accordance with the provisions of this act may recover his damages in a civil action against the employer, but such action must be begun within two years after the right thereto accrued; but his right to recover in such action shall not be barred by reason of his having knowl- edge of the violation of this act at the time.

AN ACT to Provide for the Payment of Wages of Workmen Employed in Mines, in the State of Iowa, in Lawful Money of the United States, and to Protect said Workmen in the Management and Control of their own Earn- ings. Approved April 6, 1888.

SECTION 1. It shall be unlawful for any person, firm, company or corpora- tion, owning or operating coal mines in the State of Iowa, to sell, give, deliver or in any manner issue, directly or indirectly, to any person employed by him or it, in payment for wages due for labor, or as advances on wages of labor not due, any scrip, check, draft, order or evidence of indebtedness, payable or redeemable otherwise than in their face value in money; any such person, firm, company or corporation who shall violate any of the provisions of this section, shall be deemed guilty of a misdemeanor and upon conviction thereof shall be punished by a fine not exceeding three hundred [300] dollars nor less than twenty-five dollars, and the amount of any scrip, token, check, draft, order or other evidence of indebtedness, sold, given, delivered or in any manner issued in violation of the provisions of this act, shall recover in money at the suit of any holder thereof, against the person, firm, company or corporations selling, giving, delivering, or in any manner issuing the same : provided that this act shall not apply to any person, firm, company or corporation employing less than ten [10] persons.

SEC. 2. Whoever compels, or in any manner seeks to compel or coerce an employe of any person, firm, company or corporation, to purchase goods or supplies from any particular person, firm, company or corporation, shall be deemed guilty of a misdemeanor, and upon conviction thereof, shall be punished by a fine not exceeding five hundred [500] dollars or imprisonment in the county jail, not exceeding sixty days, or both, at the discretion of the court.

SEC. 3. The county attorney of any organized county, upon complaint being made to him of the violation of any of the provisions of this act within his county, shall cause such complaint to be investigated before the grand jury of the county where such wrong has been complained of, at its next session following the time such complaint is made.

AN ACT to Amend Sections 8, 9, 10 and 14 Chapter 21 Acts of the 20th General Assembly of the State of Iowa.   Approved April 9, 1888.

That Sections 8, 9, 10 and 14 Chapter 21 Acts of the 20th General Assembly be and the same are hereby amended as follows :

SECTION 1. That section 8 be amended by adding thereto the following And Provided further, that any escapement shaft that is hereafter sunk and equipped before said escapement shaft shall be located or the excavation for it be begun the District Inspector of Mines shall be duly notified to appear and determine what shall be a suitable distance for the same.   The distance from main shaft shall not be less than three hundred feet without the consent of the Inspector and no buildings shall be put nearer the escape shaft than one hundred feet, except the house necessary to cover the fan.

SEC. 2. That section 9 be amended by adding thereto the following : and Provided further, that this act shall not apply to mines where the escape way is lost or destroyed by reason of the drawing of pillars preparatory to the abandonment of the mine ; Provided, that not more than twenty persons shall be employed in said mine at any one time.

SEC. 3. That section 10 be amended by inserting after the words "every working place in the Mine" the following : "And whenever the Inspector shall find men working without sufficient air or under any unsafe conditions he shall first give the Operator or his agent a reasonable notice to rectify the same and upon a refusal or neglect so to do the Inspector may himself order them out until said portion of said Mine shall be put in proper condition.

SEC. 4. That section 14 be amended by striking out the words "with more than ten persons at once" where they occur in said Sections and insert the following: "With more persons at once than are necessary to make the improvements needed."

Approved April 9, 1888.

AN ACT for the Protection of Discharged Employés and to prevent Black Listing. Approved April 16, 1888.

SECTION 1. That if any person, agent, company or corporation, after having discharged any employé from his or its service shall prevent or attempt to prevent by word or writing of any kind such discharged employé from obtaining employment with any other person, company, or corporation, except by furnishing in writing on request a truthful statement as to the cause of his discharge, such person, agent or corporation, shall be guilty of a misdemeanor and shall be punished by a fine not exceeding five hundred dollars nor less than one hundred dollars, and such person, agent, company or corporation shall be liable in penal damages to such discharged person to be recovered by civil action; but this section shall not be construed as prohibiting any person or agent of any company or corporation from informing in writing any other person, company or corporation setting forth a truthful statement of the reasons for such discharge.

SEC. 2. If any railway company, any other company or partnership or corporation in this State shall authorize or allow any of its or their agents to blacklist any discharged employés or attempt by word or writing of any other means whatever to prevent such discharged employé or any employé who may have voluntarily left said company's service from obtaining employment with any other person or company except as provided for in section 1 hereof, such company or co-partnership shall be liable in treble damages to such employé so prevented from obtaining employment, to be recovered by him by civil action.

MINING LAWS OF KENTUCKY.

AN ACT to provide for and regulate the ventilation of coal mines in this State and for the better protection of miners. Enacted by the General Assembly of 1883–'84 (approved May 10, 1884) and amended by the General Assembly of 1887–'88 (amendments approved April 6, 1888).

§ 1. That there shall be appointed by the Governor, with the advice and consent of the Senate, an Inspector of Mines, who shall hold his office for four years, but shall be liable to be removed by the Governor for wilful neglect of duty or malfeasance in office. Said Inspector shall have a practical knowledge of chemistry, geology, and mineralogy, and shall also possess a practical knowledge of the different systems of working and ventilating coal mines, and of the nature and properties of the noxious and poisonous gases of the mines, especially fire-damp, and he shall also have a practical knowledge of mining and engineering; and said Inspector shall, before he enters upon the discharge of his official duties, be sworn to discharge them faithfully and impartially, which

oath shall be subscribed on his commission and certified by the officer admin-
istering it; and his commission, so indorsed, shall be filed with the Secretary of
State in his office, and said Inspector shall give bond in the penal sum of five
thousand dollars, with surety, to be approved by the Governor, for the faithful
discharge of his official duties.

§ 2. Said Inspector shall give his entire time and attention to the discharge
of the duties of his office, and it shall be a part of his duty to visit and inspect,
as often as may be necessary, all the coal mines in actual operation in Kentucky,
and to see that the provisions of this act are complied with by the owners,
agents, and superintendents of all the mines in this State.

§ 3. Said Inspector shall have power to visit and inspect any mine to which
this act applies. He shall examine into the condition of such mine with respect
to ventilation, drainage, timbering and general security; and if, upon inspection,
he finds that such ventilation, drainage or timbering as the health or safety of
the persons employed in the mine would require has not been provided, or
should he find the mine insecure in any part, or should he find that sufficient
and safe means of ingress and egress have not been provided, said Inspector
shall at once notify the agent, superintendent or owner of the mine as to the
unsafe or unwholesome condition of such mine, and require him to put the
mine in a safe and wholesome condition, and such mine shall forthwith be rendered safe and healthful. For a failure to comply with the directions of the
Inspector to render such mine safe, and to provide such ventilation as is sought
to be secured by this act, and to provide safe and suitable means of ingress and
egress within sixty (60) days from the date of the inspection. the agent or
superintendent and owner so delinquent shall be liable to a fine of fifty ($50)
dollars a day for every day that such mine shall be suffered to remain in such
unsafe or unhealthful condition, after the expiration of the sixty (60) days above
provided in which the required improvements should be made, which fine may
be collected by indictment by the grand jury of the county in which such fine is
situate. But in cases in which the Inspector is satisfied, from personal investigation, that, even due diligence is observed, the required improvements cannot
be completed within the sixty (60) days above provided, he shall have authority
to extend the time for not more than sixty (60) days longer; but when the time
is thus extended, the agent, superintendent or owner who is delinquent after the
expiration of the additional time shall be subject to indictment and fine as above
provided.

§ 4. The Inspector of Mines shall keep an office in the State House at Frank-
fort, and shall keep a record of all the inspections made by him, and shall furnish
a certified copy of his report of the inspection of any mine inspected by him to
the Commonwealth's Attorney of the district in which the mine is situate on
application therefor, which copy shall be admissible in evidence in any court in
this Commonwealth, and shall be *prima facie* evidence of the truth of recitals
therein contained.

§ 5. [Acts 1884.] Such Inspector, while in office, shall not act as agent or as
a manager or mining engineer, or be interested in operating any mine, and he
shall annually, on or before the tenth day of October, make report to the
Governor of his proceedings, and of the condition and operation of the coal
mines in this State, enumerating all accidents which shall have occurred in or
about the same, and giving such other information as he may deem useful and

making such suggestions as he may deem important as to further legislation on the subject of mining.

[Acts 1888. The Inspector shall also report the number of persons employed in and about the mines, and the amount of coal mined; and for the purpose of enabling him to make such report as is required by this section, the owner, lessee, agent or superintendent of every mine to which this act applies is hereby required to give accurate information, on blanks to be furnished by the Inspector, as to all accidents occurring in and about the mines, the number of persons employed, and the amount of coal mined; and the owner, lessee, agent or superintendent refusing to furnish the Inspector such information, shall be liable to a fine of fifty dollars, to be collected by indictment by the grand jury of the county in which the mine concerning which such information is refused is situate. The Inspector is authorized to extend his observations so as to be prepared to report upon the mining possibilities and mineral resources of the counties to which he is called in the prosecution of his duties as Inspector. One thousand copies of the Inspector's annual report shall be printed for general distribution.]

§ 6. The Inspector shall receive an annual salary of eighteen hundred dollars, payable monthly, and shall likewise be allowed and paid his necessary travelling expenses when absent from his office on business connected with his department; and he shall make out and keep on file in his office maps and plans of all coal mines in operation in this State, which maps, plans, and all the books, records, and apparatus of his office he shall carefully keep, and turn over the same with all official correspondence pertaining to his office, to his successor.

§ 7. Any vacancy in the office of Inspector which may occur when the Senate is not in session, shall be filled by appointment of the Governor till the close of the next session of the Senate.

§ 8. There shall be provided for said Inspector all instruments and chemical tests necessary for the discharge of his duties under this act, which shall be paid for on the order of the Inspector, and which shall belong to the State.

§ 9. [Acts 1884.] The owner, agent, or superintendent of every coal mine in this State shall make or cause to be made, an accurate map or plan of the working of such mine, on a scale of not less than one hundred feet to the inch, showing the area mined or excavated, and the location and connection with such excavation of the mine of the lines of all adjoining lands, and the name or names of each owner or owners, so far as known, marked on each tract, a true copy of which map the said owner or agent shall deposit with the Inspector within twelve months after the passage of this act, and another copy of which shall be kept at the office of such mine; and the owner, agent, or superintendent shall, on or before the first day of December, eighteen hundred and eighty-four, and every six months thereafter, file with said Inspector a statement and plan of the progress of the workings of said mine up to said date, which statement or plan shall be so prepared as to enable the Inspector to mark the same on the original map or plan herein required to be made. In event of the failure or refusal of such owner, agent, or superintendent, for two months after the time designated, to make the plan or map, or the addition thereto, the Inspector is authorized to cause accurate map or plan of such mine to be made at the expense of the owner of such mine, the cost of which shall be recoverable against

18

the owner by the person making said map or plan in any court of competent jurisdiction.

[Acts 1888.] In case of refusal of the owner, agent, or superintendent to make or cause to be made such map and additions thereto, for sixty days after notice from the Inspector, said owner, agent, or superintendent so refusing shall be liable to a fine of five dollars a day for each day elapsing until such map is made, said fine to be collected by indictment by the grand jury of the county in which the mine to be mapped is situate.

§ 10. Twelve months from and after the passage of this act it shall not be lawful for the owner, agent, or superintendent of any coal mine, worked by a shaft wherein over fifteen thousand square yards have been excavated, to employ any person to work therein, or to permit any person to work in such mine. unless there are to every seam of coal worked in each mine at least two separate outlets, separated by natural strata of not less than one hundred feet in breadth, by which shafts or outlets, distinct means of ingress and egress, are always available to the persons employed in such mine; but it shall not be necessary for the two outlets to belong to the same mine ; and every shaft opened after the passage of this act shall have two such separate outlets, after fifteen thousand square yards shall have been excavated; and to all other mines, whether slopes or drifts, two such openings or outlets shall be provided within twelve months after the passage of this act, provided fifteen thousand square yards have been excavated at or before the passage of this act ; or if not, then within twelve months after that extent has been excavated. In case such outlets are not provided as herein stipulated, it shall not be lawful for the owner, agent, or superintendent of such mine to permit more than ten persons to work therein at one time. In case any coal mine has but one shaft, slope or drift for the ingress or egress of the men working therein, and the owner thereof does not own suitable ground for another opening, such owner may select appropriate adjacent surface ground for that purpose, and have the same condemned, and appropriate the same by proceedings in the county court of the county where the mine is situate, similar to proceedings now allowed by law for securing a private passway.

§ 11. The owner, agent, or lessee of every coal mine, whether slope, shaft, or drift, to which this act applies, shall provide and maintain for every such mine an amount of ventilation of not less than one hundred cubic feet of air per minute per person employed in such mine, which shall be circulated and distributed throughout the mine in such a manner as to dilute, render harmless, and expel the poisonous and noxious gases from each and every working place in the mine, and no working place shall be driven more than sixty feet in advance of a break-through or air-way ; and all break-throughs or air-ways, except those last made near the working-face of the mine, shall be closed up and made air tight by brattice. trap doors, or otherwise, so that the currents of air in circulation in the mine may sweep to the interior of the excavations where the persons employed in the mine are at work ; and all mines governed by this statute shall be provided with artificial means of producing ventilation, such as suction or forcing fans, exhaust steam, furnaces, or other contrivances, of such capacity and power as to produce and maintain an abundant supply of air. All mines generating fire-damp shall be kept free from standing gas, and every working place shall be carefully examined every morning with a safety-lamp by a competent person or persons, before any of the workmen are allowed to enter the mine.   And at every mine operated by a shaft there shall be provided an approved safety-catch, and a sufficient cover overhead, on all cages used for lowering and hoisting persons, and at the top of every shaft a safety gate shall be provided, and an adequate brake shall be attached to every drum or machine used in lowering or raising persons in all shafts and slopes.

§ 12. Coal mines in which not more than five persons are employed at one time, shall be exempt from the provisions of this act.

[Section 5 of amendments approved April 6, 1888: Any person employed in any mine governed by this statute who intentionally and wilfully neglects or refuses to securely prop the roof of any working place under his control, or neglects or refuses to obey any order given by the superintendent of the mine in relation to the security of that part of the bank where he is at work, and whoever knowingly and wilfully does any act endangering the lives or health of the persons employed in a mine, or the security of the mine or machinery shall be liable to a fine of not less than ten dollars nor more than fifty dollars, to be collected by indictment by the grand jury of the county in which the mine is situate.]

[Section 6 of amendments approved April 6, 1888 : All acts and parts of acts in conflict with this act are hereby repealed.]

§ 13. This act shall be in force from its passage. [The same provision is contained in section 7 of amendments approved April 6, 1888.]

MINING LAWS OF MISSOURI.

The Thirty-fourth General Assembly passed an act, approved March 30, 1887, which radically changed the existing manner of inspecting mines, by creating the office of State Mine Inspector, and requiring the inspection of all mines.   Heretofore this inspection was confined to coal mines, and was done by County Mine Inspectors appointed by the county courts.   Under this system, salaries being inconsequential, many counties neglected to make appointments or frequently appointed incompetent or neglectful inspectors, and, as a consequence, the coal mines were but partially inspected, while lead and zinc mines, possibly the greatest of our mining industries, were not inspected and reported upon at all.   It was to remedy this omission and imperfection that the following law was enacted :

SECTION 1. The act providing for the health and safety of persons employed in coal mines, and providing for the inspection of same, approved March 23, 1881 ; also, the act entitled " an act to amend section one (1) of the act of 1881, entitled ' an act providing for the health and safety of persons employed in coal mines, and providing for the inspection of same,' " approved March 20, 1885, are hereby repealed.

SEC. 2. The owner, agent or operator of each and every mine in this State, employing ten or more men, shall make, or cause to be made, at the discretion of the inspector or other person acting in that capacity, an accurate map or plan of the workings of such mine, and of each and every vein or deposit thereof, showing the general inclination of the strata, together with any material deflections in the said workings, and the boundary lines of said mine, and deposit a true copy of said maps or plan with the clerk of the county court of each county wherein may be located the said mine; which said map or plan shall be so filed or deposited within three months after the time when this act shall take effect; and a copy of such map or plan shall also be kept for inspection at the office of the said mine, and during the month of January, of each and every year, after this act shall have taken effect, the said owner, agent or operator shall furnish the inspector and clerk of the county court as aforesaid, with a sworn statement, and a further map or plan of the progress of the workings of such mine, continued from last report to the end of the month of December next preceding, and the inspector shall correct his map or plan of said workings in accordance with the statement and map or plan thus furnished, and when any mine is worked out or abandoned, that fact shall be reported to the inspector, and the map or plan of such mine in the office of the clerk of the county court shall be carefully corrected and verified.

SEC. 3. Whenever the owner, agent or operator of any mine shall neglect, fail or refuse to furnish the said inspector and clerk as aforesaid with a statement, the map or plan or addition thereto, as provided in the second section of this act, at the time and in the manner therein provided, the said inspector is hereby authorized to cause an accurate map or plan of the workings of such mine to be made at the expense of the said owner, agent or operator, and the cost thereof may be recovered by law from said owner, agent or operator, in the same manner as other debts, by suit in the name of the inspector and for his use.

SEC. 4. In all mines that are or have been in operation prior to the first day of January, 1887, and which are worked by or through a shaft, slope or drift, if there is not already an escapement shaft to each and every said mine, or communications between each and every mine, and some other contiguous mine, then there shall be an escapement shaft or other communication, such as shall be approved by the mine inspector, making at least two distinct means of ingress and egress for all persons employed or permitted to work in such coal mine. Such escapement shaft or other communication with a contiguous mine aforesaid, shall be constructed in connection with every vein or stratum of coal or mineral worked in such a mine, and the time to be allowed for such construction shall be one year when such mine is under one hundred (100) feet in depth; two years when such mine is over one hundred (100) feet and under three hundred (300) feet, and three years when it is over three hundred (300) and under four hunded (400) feet, and four years when it is over four hundred (400) feet in depth, and five years for all mines over five hundred (500) feet, from the time this act goes into effect; and in all cases where the working force of one mine has been driven up to or into the workings of another mine, the respective owners of such mine while operating the same shall keep open a roadway at least two and one-half feet high and four feet wide, thereby forming a communication as contemplated in this act, and for a failure to do so shall be subject to the penalty provided for in section 11 of this act, for each and every day such roadway is unnecessarily closed; each and every such escapement shaft shall be separated from the main shaft by such extent of natural strata as shall secure safety to the men employed in such mines; such distances to be left to the discretion and judgment of the mine inspector or person acting in that capacity, and in all coal mines that shall go into operation for the first time after the first day of January, 1888, such an escapement or other communication with a contiguous mine, as aforesaid, shall be constructed within one year after such mine shall have been put into operation. And it shall not be lawful for the owner, agent or operator of any such mine as aforesaid, to employ any person to work therein, or permit any person to go therein for the purpose of working, except such persons as may be necessary to construct such an escapement shaft, unless the requirements of this section shall have first been complied with; and the term "owner" used in this act shall mean the immediate proprietor, lessee, or occupant of any mine or any part thereof, and the term "agent" shall mean any person having, on behalf of the owner, the care or management of any mine or any part thereof: provided, nothing in this section shall be construed to extend the time allowed by law for constructing escapement shafts.

SEC. 5. The owner, agent or operator of every mine, whether operated by shaft, slope or drift, shall provide and maintain for every such mine a sufficient amount of ventilation, to be determined by the inspector, at the rate of one hundred cubic feet of air per man per minute, measured at the foot of the downcast, which shall be forced and circulated to the face of every working place throughout the mine, so that said mine shall be free from standing gas of whatsoever kind, and in all mines where fire-damp is generated, every working place where such fire-damp is known to exist shall be examined every morning with a safety lamp by a competent person before any other persons are allowed to enter. The ventilation required by this section may be produced by any suitable appliances, but in case a furnace shall be used for ventilating purposes, it shall be built in such a manner as to prevent the communication of fire to any part of the works, by lining the upcast with incombustible material for sufficient distance up from said furnace.

SEC. 6. The owner, agent or operator shall provide that bore-holes shall be kept twenty feet in advance of the face of each and every working place, and, if necessary, on both sides when driving towards an abandoned mine or part of a mine, suspected to contain inflammable gases, or to be inundated with water.

SEC. 7. The owner, agent or operator of every mine operated by shaft shall provide suitable means of signaling between the bottom and the top thereof and shall also provide safe means of hoisting and lowering persons in a cage covered with boiler iron, so as to keep safe, as far as possible persons descending into and ascending out of said shaft; and such cage shall be furnished with guides to conduct it on slides through such a shaft, with a sufficient brake on every drum to prevent accident in case of the giving out or breaking of machinery; and such cage shall be furnished with spring-catches, intended and provided so far as possible, to prevent the consequences of cable breaking or the loosening or disconnecting of the machinery; and no props or rails shall be lowered in a cage while men are descending into or ascending out of said mine : provided, that the provisions of this section in relation to covering cages with boiler iron, shall not apply to mines less than one hundred (100) feet in depth where the coal or other mineral is raised by horse-power. No male person under the age of twelve (12) years, or female of any age shall be permitted to enter any mine to work therein; nor shall any boy under the age of fourteen years, unless he can read and write, be allowed to work in any mine. Any party or person neglecting or refusing to perform the duties required to be performed by sections 5, 6, 7, 8 and 9, shall be deemed guilty of a misdemeanor, and punished by fine in the discretion of the court trying the same; subject, however, to the limitations as provided by section 11 of this act.

SEC. 8. No owner, agent or operator of any mine operated by shaft or slope shall place in charge of any engine whereby men are lowered into or hoisted out of the mines, any but an experienced, competent and sober person not under eighteen years of age; and no person shall be permitted to ride upon a loaded cage or wagon used for hoisting purposes in any shaft or slope; and in no case shall more than twelve persons ride on any cage or car at one time, nor shall any mineral be hoisted out of any mine while persons are descending into such mine; and the number of persons to ascend out of or descend into any mine on one cage, shall be determined by the inspector; the maximum number so fixed, shall not be less than four nor more than twelve, nor shall be lowered or hoisted more rapidly than five hundred (500) feet to the minute.

SEC. 9. All boilers used in generating steam in and about mines, shall be kept in good order, and the owner, agent or operator as aforesaid shall have the said boilers examined and inspected by hydrostatic pressure and warm water by a competent boiler maker or other qualified person as often as once every six months and the result of every such examination shall be certified in writing to the mine inspector; and each and every landing on a level and above the surface of the ground, and the entrance to each and every intermediate working vein, shall be securely fenced by a gate and a "bonnet," so prepared to cover and protect such shaft and entrances thereto; and the entrance to every abandoned slope, air or other shaft shall be securely fenced off; and every steam boiler shall be provided with a proper steam gauge, water gauge and safety valve, and all under ground self-acting or engine planes or gangways on which cars are drawn and persons travel, shall be provided with some proper means of signaling between the stopping place and the end of said planes or gangways, and sufficient places of refuge at the side of such planes or gangways shall be provided at intervals of not more than twenty feet apart.

SEC. 10. Whenever loss of life or serious personal injury shall occur by reasons of any explosion or of any accident whatsoever in or about any mine, it shall be the duty of the person having charge of such mine to report the facts thereof, without delay to the mine inspector, and if any person is killed thereby to notify the coroner of the county, also, or in his absence or inability to act, to any justice of the peace of said county and the said inspector shall, if he deem it necessary from the facts reported, immediately go to the scene of said accident and make suggestions and render such assistance as he may deem necessary for the safety of the men: and the inspector shall investigate and ascertain the cause of such explosion or accident, and make a report thereof, which he shall preserve with the other records of his office; and to enable him to make such investigation, he shall have the power to take depositions, compel the attendance of witnesses and administer oaths or affirmations to them, and the cost of such investigation shall be paid by the county court of the county in which such accident shall have occurred, in the same manner as costs of coroners' inquests are now paid, and a failure on the part of the person having charge of any mine in which any such accident may have occurred to give notice to the inspector or coroner, as provided for in this section, shall subject such person to a fine of not less than one hundred nor more than three hundred dollars, to be recovered of him in the name of the State of Missouri, before any justice of the peace of such county wherein the mine is situated and the accident occurred, and such a fine, when collected, shall be paid into the county treasury for the use and benefit of the said county.

Sec. 11. In all cases in which punishment is not provided for by fine under this act for a breach of any of its provisions, the fine for the first offence shall not be less than fifty nor more than two hundred dollars, and for the second offence not less than two hundred nor more than five hundred dollars, to be recovered in any court of the State having competent jurisdiction.

Sec. 12. Upon the recommendation of a board of examiners, to be appointed by the Commissioner of Labor Statistics and Inspection, to consist of two practical miners, two operators and one mining engineer, the Governor shall appoint an inspector of mines, who shall serve for two years, and shall have a practicable mining experience, but not be interested in any mine, and shall receive a salary of $1,800 per annum. He shall have his office in the office of the Commissioner of Labor Statistics, and when not inspecting mines act as a clerk in said office, giving his whole time to the State; said inspector shall visit and inspect personally all mines in the State at least twice within each and every year, and shall receive his actual expenses while so engaged, to be approved by the Commissioner of Labor and audited as other contingent expenses are.

Sec. 13. The inspector provided for in this act shall see that every necessary precaution is taken to insure the health and safety of the workmen employed in any of the mines in the State; that the provisions and requirements provided for in this act be faithfully observed and obeyed, and the penalties of the law enforced. He shall also collect and tabulate in his report, to be made to the Bureau of Labor Statistics, on the 15th day of October of each year, the extent of workable mining lands in this State, by counties; also, the manner of mining, whether by shaft, slope or drift. the number of mines in operation, the number of men employed therein, the amount of capital invested and the amount of mineral, coal, etc., produced.

Sec. 14. There is hereby appropriated, out of the money not otherwise appropriated, for the execution of the duties provided for in this act, the sum of $4,000.

Sec. 15. It shall be lawful for the inspector provided for in this act to enter, examine and inspect any and all mines and machinery belonging thereto, at all reasonable times, by day or by night, but so as not to obstruct or hinder the necessary workings of such mine, and the owner, agent or operator of every such mine is hereby required to furnish all necessary facilities for entering such examination and inspection; and if the said owner, agent or operator aforesaid, shall refuse to permit such inspection, or to furnish the necessary facilities for such entry, examination and inspection, the inspector shall file his affidavit, setting forth such refusal before the judge of circuit court in said county in which said mine is situated, either during the term of the court or

during vacation, and obtain an order on such owner, agent or operator so refusing as aforesaid, commanding him to permit and furnish such facilities for the
inspection of such mine, or to be adjudged to stand in contempt of court, and
punished accordingly; and if the said inspector shall, after examination of any
mine and the works and machinery pertaining thereto, find the same to be
worked contrary to the provisions of this act, or unsafe for the workmen therein
employed, said inspector shall, through the circuit attorney of his county, or
any attorney in case of his refusal to act, acting in the name and on behalf of
the State, proceed against the owner, agent or operator of such mine, either
separately or collectively, by injunction, without bond, after giving at least two
days' notice to such owner, agent or operator ; and said owner, agent or operator shall have the right to appear before the judge, to whom application is
made, who shall hear the same on affidavits, and such other testimony as may
be offered in support, as well as in opposition thereto ; and if sufficient cause
appear, the court, or judge in vacation, by order, shall prohibit the further
working of any such mine in which persons may be unsafely employed, contrary to the provisions of this act, until the same shall have been made safe,
and the requirements of this act shall have been complied with ; and the court
shall award such costs, in the matter of said injunction, as may be just, but any
such proceedings, so commenced, shall be without prejudice to any other
remedy permitted by law for enforcing the provisions of this act.

SEC. 16. For any injury to persons or property occasioned by any wilful
violations of this act, or wilful failure to comply with any of its provisions, a
right of action shall accrue to the party injured for any direct damages sustained thereby; and in case of loss of life, by reason of such wilful violation or
wilful failure as aforesaid, a right of action shall accrue to the widow of the
person so killed, his lineal heirs or adopted children, or to any person or persons who were, before such loss of life, dependent for support on the person or
persons so killed, for a like recovery of damages sustained by reason of such
loss of life or lives.

SEC. 17. Any miner, workman or other person who shall knowingly injure
any water gauge, barometer, air-course or brattice, or shall obstruct or throw
open any air-ways, or carry any lighted lamps, or matches into places that are
worked by the light of safety-lamps, or shall handle or disturb any part of the
machinery of the hoisting engine, or open a door to a mine and not have the
same closed again, whereby danger is produced, either to the mine or those at
work therein, or who shall enter into any part of the mine against caution, or
who shall disobey any order given in pursuance of this act, or who shall do any
wilful act whereby the lives and health of persons working in the mine, or the
security of the mine or miners, or the machinery thereof is endangered, shall
be deemed guilty of a misdemeanor, and upon conviction thereof shall be punished by fine or imprisonment at the discretion of the court.

SEC. 18. The owner, agent or operator of any mine shall keep a sufficient supply of timber, when required, to be used as props, so that the workmen may, at
all times, be able to properly secure the said workings from caving in ; and it
shall be the duty of the owner, agent or operator to send down all such props
when required.

[SEC. 19. All acts or parts of acts inconsistent with this act are and the same
are hereby repealed.]

SEC. 20. The necessity for securing to the people of this State the benefits of this act at as early date as practicable, creates an emergency in the meaning of the Constitution of the State; therefore, this act shall take effect and be in force from and after its passage.

Approved March 30, 1887.

MINING LAWS OF OHIO.

SECTION 290. For the purpose of facilitating an efficient and thorough inspection of mines in Ohio, and to provide an adequate inspecting force therefor, the governor shall appoint, by and with the consent of the Senate one chief inspector, who, with the approval of the governor, shall appoint five district inspectors of mines; the chief inspector shall hold his office for the term of four years, and the district inspectors shall hold their office for the term of three years from the date of their appointment, and until their successors are appointed and qualified; the first appointments hereunder shall be made within thirty days from the date when this act shall take effect; and in case of the resignation, removal or death of the chief inspector, or any district inspector, the vacancy shall be filled in the manner above provided for original appointments for the unexpired term only, of the position so made vacant. No person shall be appointed chief inspector of mines unless he is possessed of a competent knowledge of chemistry, the geology of Ohio, and mineralogy, in so far as those sciences relate to mining, and has a practical knowledge of mining, engineering, and the different systems of working and ventilating mines, and the nature and properties of the noxious and poisonous gases of mines, particularly fire-damp, and of the best means of preventing and removing the same; and no person shall be appointed district inspector of mines unless he be a practical miner of at least five years' experience, and a resident of the district for which he is appointed, for at least two years, and is possessed of a practical knowledge of the best mode of working and ventilating mines, of the means of detecting the presence of bad or foul air, noxious and poisonous gases, and of the best means of preventing and removing the same.

SEC. 291. Before entering upon the discharge of the duties of their respective offices, the chief inspector and district inspectors shall give bond to the State, the former in the sum of five thousand dollars, and the latter in the sum of two thousand dollars each, to be approved by the governor, conditioned for the faithful performance of their duties, respectively; said bonds, with an oath of office on each, and approval of the governor indorsed thereon, shall be forthwith deposited with the secretary of state; the inspectors, while in office, shall not act as agent, manager, or mining engineer for any operator, or in any way be interested in operating any mine.

SEC. 292. The chief inspector and district inspectors shall give their whole time and attention to the duties of their offices, respectively; it shall be the duty of the district inspectors to examine all the mines in their respective districts as often as possible, to see that all the provisions and requirements of this chapter are strictly observed and carried out; they shall particularly examine the works and machinery belonging to any mine, examine into the state and condition of the mines as to ventilation, circulation and condition of air, drainage and general security; they shall make a record of all examinations of mines in their respective districts, showing the date when made, the condition in which the mines are found, the extent to which the laws relating to mines and mining are observed or violated, the progress made in the improvement and security of life and health sought to be secured by the provisions of this chapter, number of accidents, injuries received, or deaths in or about the mines, the number of mines in their respective districts, the number of persons employed in or about each mine, together with all such other facts and information of public interest concerning the condition of mines, development and progress of mining in their respective districts, as they may think useful and proper; which record shall, on or before the first Monday of every month, be filed in the office of the chief inspector, to be by him recorded and so much thereof as may be of public interest, to be included in his annual report; in case of any controversy or disagreement between a district inspector and the owner and [or?] operator of any mine, or the persons working therein, or in case of conditions of emergencies requiring counsel, the district inspector may call on the chief inspector for such assistance and counsel as may be necessary; should the district inspector find any of the provisions of this chapter violated, or not complied with, by any owner, lessee, or agent in charge of any mine, he shall immediately notify such owner, lessee, or agent in charge, of such neglect or violation, and unless the same is, within a reasonable time, rectified, and the provisions of this chapter fully complied with, he shall institute a prosecution under the provisions of section six thousand eight hundred and seventy-one (6871) of the Revised Statutes. The inspectors shall exercise a sound discretion in the enforcement of the provisions of this act, and if in any respect (which is not provided against by, or may result from a rigid enforcement of any express provisions of this chapter), the inspector find any matter, thing or practice in or connected with any such mine, to be dangerous or defective, so as in his opinion to threaten or tend to the bodily injury of any person, the inspector may give notice in writing thereof to the owner, agent or manager of the mine, and shall state in such notice the particulars in which he considers such mine, or any part thereof, or any matter, thing of [or?] practice to be dangerous or defective, and require the same to be remedied. For the purpose of making the inspection and examinations provided for in this section, the chief inspector and the district inspectors shall have the right to enter any mine at all reasonable times, by night or by day, but in such manner as shall not unnecessarily obstruct the working of the mine; and the owner or agent of such mine is hereby required to furnish the means necessary for such entry and inspection; the inspection and examination herein provided for shall extend to fire-clay, iron ore, and other mines, as well as coal mines.

SEC. 293. The chief inspector shall designate the counties or portions thereof in the State which shall compose the different districts, and may at any time change the same, when in his judgment the best interests of the service may require, and shall issue such instructions, make such rules and regulations for the government of the district inspectors, not inconsistent with the powers and duties vested in them by law, as shall secure uniformity of action and proceedings throughout the different districts; and he may order one district inspector to the assistance of any other district inspector, or make temporary transfers of district inspectors, when, in his judgment, the efficiency or necessity of the service demands or permits; and he may, with the consent of the governor, remove any district inspector at pleasure; the district inspectors are hereby invested with all the powers and authority of county auditors, as sealers of weights and measures in the different counties of this State, and for any service performed as such sealers they shall receive the same compensation as now provided by section ten hundred and sixty-two [1062] of the Revised Statutes; but said inspectors shall exercise said authority in connection with weights and measures only at mines in their respective districts; the chief inspector shall render such personal assistance to the district inspectors as they, from time to time, may require, and shall make such personal inspection of the mines as he may deem necessary and his other duties will permit; he shall keep in his office and carefully preserve all maps, surveys and other reports and papers required by law to be filed with him, and so arrange and preserve the same as shall make them a permanent record of ready, convenient and connected reference; he shall compile and consolidate the reports of district inspectors, and annually make report to the governor of all his proceedings, as well as those of the district inspectors, the condition and operation of the different mines of the State, and the number of mines and the number of persons employed in or about such mines, the amount of coal, iron ore, limestone, fire-clay, or other mineral mined in this State; and for the purpose of enabling him to make such report, the owner, lessee or agent in charge of such mine, who is engaged in mining, and the owner, lessee or agent of any firm, company or corporation in charge of any fire-clay, or iron ore mined [mine?] or any limestone, or quarry, or who is engaged in mining or producing any mineral whatsoever in this State, shall, on or before the 31st day of January in every year, send to the office of the chief inspector of mines, upon blanks furnished by him, a correct return specifying with respect to the year ending on the preceding 31st day of December, the quantity of coal, iron ore, fire-clay, limestone, or other mineral product in such mine, or quarry, and the number of persons ordinarily employed in or about such mine, or quarry, below and above ground, distinguishing the persons and labor below ground and above ground. Every owner, lessee or agent of a mine or quarry who fails to comply with this section, or makes any return which to his knowledge is false in any particular, shall be deemed guilty of an offence against this section, and shall be fined one hundred dollars, to be recovered at the suit of the chief inspector in the name of the State of Ohio; he shall also include in such report such facts relative to the mineral resources of the State and the development of the same, as shall, in his judgment, be of public interest; he shall enumerate all accidents, and the manner in which they occurred, in or about the mines, and give all such other information as he thinks useful and proper, and make such suggestions as he deems important relative to mines and mining, and any other legislation that may be necessary on the subject for the better preservation of the life and health of those engaged in such industry.

SEC. 204. The chief inspector shall have an office in the state house, in which shall be carefully kept the maps and plans of all mines in the State, and all records, correspondence, papers, and apparatus and property pertaining to his duties, belonging to the State, and shall be handed over to his successor in office; the district inspectors shall keep their offices in such place in their respective districts as will be most central and convenient to the mining region of their respective districts, and shall keep and preserve in their offices all maps, plans, surveys, and other papers belonging to their offices, in such manner as shall be of easy access and convenient reference to persons entitled to examine them. The district inspectors shall receive an annual salary of twelve hundred dollars ($1,200) per annum, and the chief inspector shall receive the same salary as is now provided for inspector of mines under section twelve hundred and eight-four of the revised statutes.

SEC. 295. There shall be provided for the inspectors weights and measures and all instruments and chemical tests necessary for the discharge of their respective duties under this chapter, which shall be paid for on the certificate of the chief inspector, from his contingent fund, and shall belong to the State.

SEC. 296. The owner or agent of any mine having an excavation of not less than fifteen thousand cubic yards, shall make, or cause to be made, an accurate map or plan of the working of such mine on a scale of not less than two hundred feet to the inch, showing the area mined or excavated, and the location and connection with such excavation of the mine of the lines of all adjoining lands, and the name or names of each owner or owners, so far as known, marked on each tract, and the owner or agent shall annually thereafter make, or cause to be made, an addition to said map, showing the progress and plan of the working of such mine during the previous year up to the date of survey; provided, that said additions shall be made semi-annually whenever the mine inspector deems it necessary and so directs. The map shall be kept at the office of such mine, and open to the inspection of the mine inspector, or his assistants, at all reasonable times, and at the request of the inspector the owner or agent shall file a correct copy of such map with said mine inspector at Columbus, and in case of refusal on the part of the owner or agent to make and file such map, the inspector is authorized and required hereby to cause such map or maps to be made in duplicate, at the expense of said owner or agent, the cost of which shall be recoverable against the owner or agent in the name of the state mine inspector; and in case of refusal by said owner or agent to make, or cause such map and the additions thereto to be made, for sixty days after notice by the mine inspector, said agent or owner shall be liable to a fine of five dollars for each and every day until said map is made, which shall be collected in the name of the State of Ohio, at the suit of the state mine inspector, and the amount so recovered shall be paid into the township school fund of the township when collected. And when any mine is exhausted or abandoned, and before the pillars are drawn in any portion of the mine, the owner or agent thereof shall cause to be made a correct map of such mine, showing the area and working of the same to the day of abandoning, or of drawing pillars for the purpose of abandoning, and file such map within ninety days thereafter at the office of the county recorder in the county where such mine is located; said map shall have attached thereto the sworn certificate of the mining engineer making the map, and of the mine boss in charge of the underground workings of said mine; such map shall be properly labeled and filed by the recorder, and be preserved as a part of the records of the land on which such mines are located, and the recorder shall receive for said filing from said owner or agent a fee of fifty cents.

SEC. 297. It is unlawful for the owner or agent of any coal mine, worked by shaft, to employ or permit any person to work therein, unless there are, to every seam of coal worked in each mine, at least two separate outlets, separated by natural strata of not less than one hundred feet in breadth, by which shafts or outlets distinct means of ingress and egress are always available to the persons employed in the mine ; but it is not necessary for the two outlets to belong to the same mine if the persons employed therein have safe, ready and available means of ingress and egress by not less than two openings. This section shall not apply to opening a new mine while being worked for the purpose of making communication between said two outlets so long as not more than twenty persons are employed at any one time in such mine, neither shall it apply to any mine or part of a mine in which the second outlet has been rendered unavailable by reason of the final robbing of pillars previous to abandonment, so long as not more than twenty persons are employed therein at any one time. The cage or cages, and other means of egress shall at all times be available for the persons employed, where there is no second outlet. The escapement shafts shall be fitted with safe and available appliances, by which the persons employed in the mine may readily escape in case an accident occurs deranging the hoisting machinery at the main outlets, and such means or appliances for escape shall always be kept in a safe condition ; and in no case shall an air shaft, with a ventilating furnace at the bottom, be construed to be an escapement shaft, within the meaning of this section. To all other coal mines, whether slopes or drifts, two such openings or outlets must be provided within twelve months after shipments of coal have commenced from such mine ; and in case such outlets are not provided as herein stipulated, it shall not be lawful for the agent or owner of such slope or drift to permit more than ten persons to work therein at any one time. In case a coal mine has but one shaft, slope or drift, for the ingress or egress of the men working therein, and the owner thereof does not own suitable surface ground for another opening, he may select and appropriate any adjoining land for that purpose, and may make an additional shaft or outlet under, through or upon any intervening land, or landing adjoining, and shall be governed in his proceeding in appropriating such land by the provisions of law in force, providing for the appropriation of private property by corporations, and such appropriation may be made, whether he is a corporator or not ; but no land shall be appropriated under the provisions of this chapter until the court is satisfied that suitable premises cannot be obtained upon reasonable terms.

SEC. 298. The owner or agent of every coal mine, whether shaft, slope or drift, shall provide and maintain for every such mine an amount of ventilation of not less than 100 cubic feet, per minute, per person employed in such mine, which shall be circulated and distributed throughout the mine in such a manner as to dilute, render harmless and expel the poisonous and noxious gases from each and every working place in the mine, and no working place shall be driven more than sixty feet in advance of a break-through, or air-way ; and all break-throughs, or air-ways, except those last made near the working-faces of the mine shall be closed up and made air-tight, by brattice, trap doors or otherwise, so that the currents of air in circulation in the mine may sweep to the interior of the mine, where the persons employed in such mine are at work, and all mines governed by the statute shall be provided with artificial means of producing ventilation, such as forcing, or suction fans, exhaust steam, furnaces or other contrivances, of such capacity and power as to produce and maintain an abundant supply of air, and all mines generating fire-damp shall be kept free from standing gas, and every working place shall be carefully examined every morning with a safety lamp, by a competent person or persons, before any of the workmen are allowed to enter the mine. All underground entrances to any places not in actual course of working or extension shall be properly fenced across the whole width of such entrances so as to prevent persons from inadvertently entering the same.

SEC. 299. The owner or agent of every coal mine operated by shaft, in all cases where the human voice cannot be distinctly heard, shall forthwith provide and maintain a metal tube from the top to the bottom of such shaft, suitably calculated for the free passage of sound therein, so that conversation may be held between persons at the bottom and top of the shaft; there shall also be provided an approved safety catch, and a sufficient cover overhead, on all carriages used for lowering and hoisting persons, and in the top of every shaft an approved safety gate, and an adequate brake shall be attached to every drum or machine used for lowering or raising persons in all shafts or slopes; and there shall also be provided in every shaft a travelling or passage way from one side of a shaft bottom to the other, so that persons working therein may not have to pass under descending cages; and all slopes or engine planes, used as travelling ways by persons in any mine, shall be made of sufficient width to permit persons to pass moving cars with safety; but if found impracticable to make any slope or engine plane of sufficient width, then safety holes of ample dimensions, and not more than sixty feet apart, shall be made on one side of said slope or engine plane. Such safety holes shall always be kept free from obstructions, and the roof and sides shall be made secure. The boilers used for generating steam, and the buildings containing the boilers shall not be nearer than sixty feet to any shaft or slope, or to any building or inflammable structure connecting with or surrounding said shaft or slope; but this section shall not apply to any shaft or slope until the work of development and shipment of coal has commenced.

SEC. 300. No owner or agent of any coal mine operated by a shaft or slope shall place in charge of any engine used for lowering into or hoisting out of such mine persons employed therein, any but experienced, competent and sober engineers; and no engineer in charge of such engine shall allow any person, except such as may be deputed for that purpose, by the owner or agent, to interfere with it or any part of the machinery, and no person shall interfere or in any way intimidate the engineer in the discharge of his duties; and in no case shall more than ten men ride on any cage or car at one time, and no person shall ride upon a loaded cage or car in any shaft or slope.

SEC. 301. All safety-lamps used for examining coal mines, or which are used in any coal mine, shall be the property of the owner of the mine, and shall be under the charge of the agent thereof, and in all mines, whether they generate fire-damp or not, the doors use[d] in assisting or directing ventilation of the mine, shall be so hung or adjusted that they will shut of their own accord and cannot stand open; and all main doors shall have an attendant, whose constant duty shall be to open them for transportation and travel, and prevent them from standing open longer than is necessary for persons or cars to pass through; and the mining boss shall keep a careful watch over the ventilating apparatus and the airway, and he shall measure the ventilation at least once a week, at the inlet and outlet, and also at or near the face of all the entries, and the measurements of air so made shall be noted on blanks, furnished by the chief inspector; and on the first day of each month the mining boss of each mine shall sign one of such blanks, properly filled with the said actual measurements, and forward the same to the chief inspector, and any mining boss making false returns of such air measurements shall be deemed guilty of an offence against this section. Every person having charge of any mine, whenever loss of life occurs by accident, connected with the working of such mine, or by explosion, shall give notice thereof forthwith, by mail or otherwise, to the inspector of mines, and to the coroner of the county in which such mine is situated, and the coroner shall hold an inquest upon the body of the person or persons whose death has been caused, and inquire carefully into the cause thereof, and shall return a copy of the findings and all the testimony to the chief inspector. The owner, agent, or manager of every mine shall, within twenty-four hours next after any accident or explosion, whereby loss of life or personal injury may have been occasioned, send notice in writing to the chief inspector, and shall specify in such notice the character and cause of the accident, and the name or names of the persons killed and injured, with the extent and nature of the injuries sustained. When any personal injury, of which notice is required to be sent under this section, results in the death of the person injured, notice in writing shall be sent to the chief inspector within twenty-four hours after such death comes to the knowledge of the owner, agent or manager; and when loss of life occurs in any mine by explosion, or accident, the owner, agent, or manager of such mine shall notify the chief inspector, or the district inspector, forthwith, of the fact, and it shall be the duty of the chief inspector to go himself, or require one of the district inspectors to go, at once to the mine in which said death occurred, and inquire into the cause of the same, and to make a written report, fully setting forth the condition of the part of the mine where such death occurred, and the cause which led to the same; which report shall be filed by the chief inspector in his office as a matter or [of?] record, and for future reference.

For any injury to persons or property, occasioned by any violation of this act, or any wilful failure to comply with its provisions by any owner, agent or manager of any mine, a right of action shall accrue to the party injured, for any direct damage he may have sustained thereby; and, in any case of loss of life, by reason of such wilful neglect or failure, aforesaid, a right of action shall accrue to the widow and lineal heirs of the person whose life shall be lost, for like recovery of damages for the injury they have sustained.

The owner, agent, or manager of any mine shall also give notice to the chief inspector of mines in any or all of the following cases.

1. Where any change occurs in the name of any mine, or in the name of any owner, agent, or manager of any mine, or in the officers of any incorporated company which owns or operates a mine.

2. Where any working is commenced for the purpose of opening a new shaft, slope or mine, to which this act applies.

3. Where any mine is abandoned or the working thereof discontinued.

4. Where the working of any mine is re-commenced after any abandonment or discontinuance for a period exceeding three months.

5. Where the pillars of a mine are about to be removed or robbed.

6. Where a squeeze or crush, or any other cause or change may seem to
affect the safety of persons employed in any mine, or where fire occurs, or a
dangerous body of gas is found in any mine.

SEC. 302. No boy under twelve years of age shall be allowed to work in
any mine, nor any minor between the ages of twelve and sixteen years unless
he can read and write; and in all cases of minors applying for work the
agent of such mine shall see that the provisions of this section are not
violated; and the mine inspector may, where doubt exists as to the age of
any minors found working in any mine, qualify the said minor or his parents
as to his age.

SEC. 303. In case any coal mine does not, in appliances for the safety of the
persons working therein, conform to the provisions of this chapter, or the
owner or agent disregards the requirements of this chapter, any court of
competent jurisdiction may, on application of the inspector, by civil action in
the name of the State, enjoin or restrain the owner or agent from working or
operating such mine until it is made to conform to the provisions of this
chapter; and such remedy shall be cumulative, and shall not take the place of
or affect any other proceedings against such owner or agent authorized by law
for the matter complained of in such action.

SEC. 304. When written charges of gross neglect of duty or malfeasance in
office against any inspector is made and filed with the governor, signed by not
less than fifteen coal miners, or one or more operator, of mines, together with
a bond in the sum of five hundred dollars, payable to the State, and signed by
two or more responsible freeholders, and conditioned for the payment of all
costs and expenses arising from the investigation of such charges, the governor
shall convene a board of examiners, to consist of two practical coal miners, one
chemist, one mining engineer and one operator, at such time and place as he
deems best, giving ten days' notice to the inspector against whom the charges
are made, and also the person whose name appears first in the charges; and the
board, when so convened, and having been first duly sworn, truly to try and
decide the charges made, shall summon any witnesses so desired by either
party, and examine them on oath, which may be administered by any member
of the board, and depositions may be read on such examination, as in other
cases; and the board shall examine fully into the truth of such charges, and
report the result of their investigation to the governor; and the board shall
award the costs and expenses of such investigation against the inspector or the
persons signing the bond according to their finding, against said inspector or in
his favor, which costs and expenses shall include the compensation of such
board, of five dollars per day for each member, for the time occupied in the
trial and in travelling from and to their homes; and the attorney general shall
forthwith proceed to collect such costs and expenses, and pay the same into
the state treasury, being in the first instance paid out of the state treasury on
the certificate of the president of such board.

SEC. 305. In all coal mines in the state the miners employed and working

therein, the owners of the land or other persons interested in the rental or
royalty of any such mine, shall at all proper times have full right of access and
examination of all scales, machinery or apparatus used in or about such mine
to determine the quantity of coal mined, for the purpose of testing the accuracy
and correctness of all such scales, machinery or apparatus; and such miners,
landowners or other persons may designate or appoint a competent person to
act for them, who shall at all proper times have full right of access and examination of such scales, machinery, or apparatus, and seeing all weights and
measures of coal mined, and the accounts kept of the same; but not more than
one person on behalf of the miners collectively, or one person on behalf of the
landowners or other persons interested in the rental or royalty jointly, shall
have such right of access, examination and inspection of scales, weights, measures and accounts at the same time, and that such persons shall make no
unnecessary interference with the use of such scales, machinery or apparatus;
and the miners employed in any mine may, from time to time, appoint two of
their number to act as a committee to inspect, not oftener than once in every
month, the mine and the machinery connected therewith, and to measure the
ventilating current, and if the owner, agent or manager so desires, he may
accompany said committee by himself or two or more persons, which he may
appoint for that purpose; the owner, agent or manager shall afford every
necessary facility for making such inspection and measurement, but the committee shall not in any way interrupt or impede the work going on in the mine
at the time of such inspection and measurement, and said committee shall,
within ten days after such inspection and measurement, make a correct report
thereof to the inspector of mines, on blanks to be furnished by said inspector
for that purpose; and if such committee make to the inspector a false or
untrue report of the mines, such act shall constitute a violation of this section.

SEC. 300. The provisions of this chapter shall not apply to or affect any coal
mine in which not more than ten men are employed at the same time; but the
inspector shall at all times have free ingress to such mines for the purpose of
examination and inspection, and shall direct and inforce any regulations in
accordance with provisions of this chapter that he may deem necessary for the
safety of the health and lives of the miners employed therein.

SEC. 6871. Whoever knowingly violates any of the provisions of sections
two hundred and ninety-seven, two hundred and ninety-eight, two hundred and
ninety-nine, three hundred, three hundred and one, three hundred and two, and
three hundred and five, or does any act whereby the lives or health of the persons, or the security of any mine and machinery are endangered; or any miner
or other persons employed in any mine governed by the statute, who intentionally and wilfully neglects or refuses to securely prop the roof of any working place under his control; or neglects or refuses to obey any order given by
the superintendent of a mine in relation to the security of the mine in the part
thereof where he is at work, and for fifteen feet back from the face of his working place; or any miner, workman, or other person who shall knowingly
injure any water guage, barometer, air course or brattice, or shall obstruct or
throw open any air ways, or shall handle or disturb any part of the machinery
of the hoisting engine, or open a door of the mine and not have the same closed
again, whereby danger is produced either to the mine or those that work
therein; or who shall enter any part of the mine against caution; or who shall

10

disobey any order given in pursuance of this act; or who shall do any wilful act, whereby the lives and health of persons working in the mine, or the security of the mine, or the machinery thereof, is endangered; or any person having charge of a mine, whenever loss of life occurs by accident connected with the working of such mine, or by explosion, who neglects or refuses to give notice thereof forthwith, by mail or otherwise, to the chief inspector of mines, and to the coroner of the county in which such mine is situate; or any such coroner who neglects or refuses to hold an inquest upon the body of the person whose death has been thus caused, and return a copy of his findings and all the testimony to the inspector, shall be fined not less than fifty dollars, or imprisoned in the county jail not more than thirty days, or both.

MINING LAWS OF PENNSYLVANIA.

An Act to provide for the health and safety of persons employed in and about the anthracite coal mines of Pennsylvania, and for the protection and preservation of property connected therewith. Approved June 30, 1885.

ARTICLE I.

Section 1. This act shall apply to every anthracite coal mine or colliery in the Commonwealth, provided the said mine or colliery employs more than ten (10) persons.

ARTICLE II.

INSPECTORS AND INSPECTION DISTRICTS.

Section 1. The counties of Sullivan, Susquehanna, Wayne, Luzerne, Lackawanna, Carbon, Schuylkill, Northumberland, Columbia, Lebanon and Dauphin, or so much of them as may be included under the provisions of this act shall be divided into seven inspection districts, as follows:

First. That portion of the Wyoming coal field included in the counties of Lackawanna, Wayne and Susquehanna.

Second. The county of Sullivan, and that portion of the Wyoming coal field situated in Luzerne county, east of and including Plains and Kingston townships.

Third. The remaining portion of the Wyoming coal field west of Plains and Kingston townships, including the city of Wilkes-Barre and the boroughs of Kingston and Edwardsville.

Fourth. That part of Luzerne county lying south of the Wyoming coal field, together with Carbon county.

Fifth. That part of the Schuylkill coal field in Schuylkill county, lying north of the Broad mountain and east of a meridian line through the centre of the borough of Girardville.

Sixth. That part of the Schuylkill coal field in Schuylkill county, lying north of the Broad mountain and west of a meridian line through the centre of the borough of Girardville, together with Columbia, Northumberland and Dauphin counties.

Seventh. All, that part of the Schuylkill coal field in Schuylkill county lying south of the Mahanoy valley, and the county of Lebanon.

SEC. 2. In order to fill any vacancy that may occur in the office of inspector of mines by reason of expiration of term, resignation, removal for cause, or from any other reason whatever the judges of the court of common pleas of the county of Luzerne shall appoint an examining board for the counties of Sullivan, Susquehanna, Wayne, Luzerne, Lackawanna and Carbon, and the judges of the court of common pleas of the county of Schuylkill shall appoint an examining board for the counties of Schuylkill, Northumberland, Columbia Lebanon and Dauphin.

SEC. 3. The said board of examiners shall be composed of three reputable coal miners in actual practice, and two reputable mining engineers, all of whom shall be appointed at the first term of court in each year to hold their places during the year. Any vacancies that may occur in the board of examiners shall be filled by the court as they occur.

SEC. 4. Whenever candidates for the office of inspector are to be examined, the said examiners shall give public notice of the fact, in not less than two papers published in the county, and at least two weeks before the meeting, specifying the time and place where such meetings shall be held. The said examiners shall be sworn to a faithful discharge of their duties, and four of them shall agree in their recommendation of candidates to the Governor, and shall recommend only such applicants as they find qualified for the office.

Should the board of examiners not be able to agree in their selection and recommendation of a candidate, the judges of the court of common pleas shall dissolve the said board, and appoint a new board of like qualifications and powers. The said board of examiners shall be permitted to engage the services of a clerk, and they, together with the clerk, shall each receive the sum of five dollars per day, for every day they are actually engaged in the discharge of their duties under this appointment, and mileage, at the rate of six cents per mile, from their home to the place of meeting and return by the nearest practicable railway route.

Upon the recommendation of the board of examiners as aforesaid, the Governor shall appoint such person to fill the office of inspector of mines, under this act, and shall issue to him a commission for the term of five years, subject, however, to removal for neglect of duty or malfeasance in office, as hereinafter provided for.

SEC. 5. The person so appointed must be a citizen of Pennsylvania, and shall have attained the age of thirty years. He must have a knowledge of the different systems of working coal mines, and have been practically connected with the anthracite coal mines of Pennsylvania for a period of not less than five years, and he must also have had experience in the working and ventilation of coal mines where noxious and explosive gases are evolved. Before entering upon the duties of his office, he shall take an oath, or affirmation, before an officer properly qualified to administer the same, that he will perform his duties with fidelity and impartiality, which oath or affirmation shall be filed in the office of the prothonotary of the county.

He shall also provide himself with the most modern instruments and appliances for carrying out the intentions of this act.

SEC. 6. The salary of each of the said inspectors shall be three thousand dollars per annum, which salary, together with the expenses incurred in carrying into effect the provisions of this act, shall be paid by the State Treasurer, out of the treasury of the Commonwealth upon the warrant of the Auditor General.

SEC. 7. Each of the said inspectors shall reside in the district for which he is appointed, and shall give his whole time and attention to the duties of the office. He shall examine all the collieries in his district as often as his duties will permit, not less than four times a year, or oftener if the exigencies of the case or the condition of the mines require it, see that every necessary precaution is taken to secure the safety of the workmen and that the provisions of this act are observed and obeyed, attend every inquest held by the coroner or his deputy, upon the bodies of persons killed in or about the collieries, in his district, visit the scene of the accident for the purpose of making an examination into the particulars of the same whenever loss of life or serious personal injury occurs, as elsewhere herein provided for, and make an annual report of his proceedings to the Secretary of Internal Affairs of the Commonwealth at the close of every year, enumerating all the accidents in and about the collieries of his district, marking in tabular form those accidents causing death or serious personal injury, the condition of the workings of the said mines with regard to the safety of the workmen therein, and the ventilation thereof, and the result of his labors generally shall be fully set forth.

SEC. 8. The board of examiners, as hereinbefore provided for, in order to divide more equitably among the several mine inspectors the labor to be performed and the territory to be covered by them in the performance of the duties of the office, may, at any time, when they shall deem it desirable or necessary, readjust the several districts by the creation of new boundary lines, thereby adding to or taking from, as the case may be, the districts as at present bounded and described, if the court approve the same.

SEC. 9. The mine inspector shall have the right, and it is hereby made his duty, to enter, inspect and examine any mine or colliery in his district, and the workings and machinery belonging thereto, at all reasonable times, either by day or night, but not so as to impede or obstruct the working of the colliery, and shall have the power to take one or more of his fellow inspectors into or around any mine or colliery in the district for which he is appointed, for the purpose of consultation or examination.

He shall also have the right, and it is hereby made his duty, to make inquiry into the condition of such mine or colliery, workings, machinery, ventilation, drainage, method of lighting or using lights, and into all matters and things connected with or relating to as well as to make suggestions providing for the health and safety of persons employed in or about the same, and especially to make inquiry whether the provisions of this act have been complied with.

The owner, operator or superintendent of such mine or colliery is hereby required to furnish the means necessary for such entry, inspection, examination, inquiry and exit.

The inspector shall make a record of the visit, noting the time and the material circumstances of the inspection.

SEC. 10. No person who shall act or practice as a land agent, or as the manager or agent of any coal mine or colliery, or as a mining engineer, or who is pecuniarily interested in operating any coal mine or colliery, in his district, shall at the same time hold the office of inspector of mines under this act.

Sec. 11. Whenever a petition, signed by fifteen or more reputable coal operators, or miners, or both, setting forth that any inspector of mines neglects his duties, or is incompetent, or is guilty of malfeasance in office, it shall be the duty of the court of common pleas of the proper county to issue a citation in the name of the Commonwealth to the said inspector to appear, at not less than fifteen days notice, on a day fixed, before said court, and the court shall then proceed to inquire into and investigate the allegations of the petitioners If the court find that the said inspector is neglectful of his duties, or that he is incompetent to perform the duties of the office for any cause that existed previous to his appointment, or that has arisen since his appointment, or that he is guilty of malfeasance in office, the court shall certify the same to the Governor of the Commonwealth, who shall declare the office of inspector for the district vacant, and proceed, in compliance with the provisions of this act, to appoint a properly qualified person to fill the office.

The cost of said investigation shall be borne by the removed inspector, but, if the allegations in the petition are not sustained, the costs shall be paid by the petitioners.

Sec. 12. The maps and plans of the mines and the records thereof, together with all the papers relating thereto shall be kept by the inspector, properly arranged and preserved in a convenient place in the district, for which each inspector has been appointed, and shall be transferred by him, with any other property of the Commonwealth that may be in his possession, to his successor in office.

Sec. 13. The persons who, at the time this act goes into effect, are acting as inspectors of mines under the acts hereby repealed, shall continue to act in the same manner, as if they had been appointed under this act, and until the term for which they were appointed has expired.

ARTICLE III.

SURVEYS, MAPS AND PLANS.

Section 1. The owner, operator or superintendent of every coal mine or colliery shall make, or cause to be made, an accurate map or plan of the workings or excavations of such coal mine or colliery, on a scale of one hundred feet to the inch. which map or plan shall exhibit the workings or excavations in each and every seam of coal, and the tunnels and passages connecting with such workings or excavations. It shall state, in degrees, the general inclination of the strata, with any material deflection therein, in said workings or excavations, and shall also state the tidal elevations of the bottom of each and every shaft, slope tunnel and gangway, and of any other point in the mine or on the surface, where such elevation shall be deemed necessary by the inspector. The map or plan shall show the number of the last survey, station and date of each survey, on the gangways or the most advanced workings. It shall also accurately show the boundary lines of the lands of the said coal mine or colliery, and the proximity of the workings thereto ; a true copy of which map or plan, the said owner, operator or superintendent shall deposit with the inspector of mines for the district in which the said coal mine or colliery is situated, showing the workings of each seam, if so desired by the inspector, on a separate sheet of tracing muslin. One copy of the said map or plan shall be kept at the colliery.

SEC. 2. The said owner, operator or superintendent, shall, as often as once in every six months, place or cause to be placed, on the said inspector's map or plan of said coal mine or colliery, the plan of the extensions made in such coal mine or colliery during the preceding six months. The said extensions shall be placed on the inspector's map and the map returned to the inspector within two months from the date of the last survey.

SEC. 3. When any coal mine or colliery is worked out preparatory to being abandoned, or when any lift thereof is about to be abandoned, the owner, operator or superintendent of such coal mine or colliery shall have the maps or plans thereof extended to include all excavations as far as practicable, and such portions thereof as the case may require, shall be carefully verified.

SEC. 4. Whenever the owner, operator or superintendent of any coal mine or colliery shall neglect or refuse, or from any cause not satisfactory to the inspector, shall fail, for a period of three months, to furnish to the inspector the map or plan of said colliery, or of the extensions thereto, as provided for in this act, the inspector is hereby authorized to cause an accurate map or plan of such coal mine or colliery to be made at the expense of the owner thereof, which cost shall be recoverable from said owner as other debts are by law recoverable.

SEC. 5. If the inspector finds, or has reason to believe that any map or plan of any coal mine or colliery, furnished under the provisions of this act, is materially inaccurate, it shall be his duty to make application to the court of common pleas of the county in which such colliery is situate for an order to have an accurate map or plan of said colliery prepared, and if such survey shall prove that the map furnished was materially inaccurate or imperfect, such owner, operator or superintendent shall be liable for the expense incurred in making the same.

SEC. 6. If it shall be found that the map or plan furnished by the owner, operator or superintendent, was not materially inaccurate or imperfect, the Commonwealth shall be held liable for the expense incurred in making said test survey.

SEC. 7. If it shall be shown that the said owner, operator or superintendent, has knowingly or designedly caused or allowed such map or plan when furnished to be incorrect or false, such owner, operator or superintendent thus offending, shall be guilty of a misdemeanor, and, upon conviction thereof, shall be punished by a fine not exceeding five hundred dollars, or imprisonment not exceeding three months at the discretion of the court.

SEC. 8. The maps or plans of the several coal mines or collieries in each district, and which are placed in the custody of the inspector shall be the property of the Commonwealth, and shall remain in the care of the inspector of the district in which the said collieries are situated, to be transferred by him to his successor in office, and in no case shall a copy of the same be made without the consent of the owner, operator or superintendent.

SEC. 9. The inspector's map or plan of any particular colliery shall be open to the inspection (in the presence of the inspector,) of any miner of that colliery whenever said miner shall have cause to fear that his working place is becoming dangerous by reason of its proximity to other workings, which may be supposed to contain water or dangerous gases, but only to the miner working in such supposed dangerous place.

ARTICLE IV.

SHAFTS, SLOPES, OPENINGS AND OUTLETS.

SECTION 1. It shall not be lawful for the owner, operator or superintendent of any mine to employ any person or persons in such mine, or permit any person or persons to be in such mine for the purpose of working therein, unless they are in connection with every seam or stratum of coal, and from every lift thereof worked in such mine, not less than two openings or outlets, separated by a strata of not less than sixty (60) feet in breadth under ground, and one hundred and fifty (150) feet in breadth at the surface, at which openings or outlets safe and distinct means of ingress and egress are at all times available for the person or persons employed in the said mine ; but it shall not be necessary for the said two openings to belong to the same mine, if the persons employed therein have safe, ready and available means of ingress and egress by not less than two openings. This section shall not apply to opening a new mine, or to opening any new lift of a mine while being worked for the purpose of making communication between said two outlets, so long as not more than twenty persons are employed at any one time in such mine or new lift of a mine, neither shall it apply to any mine or part of a mine in which the second outlet has been rendered unavailable by reason of the final robbing of pillars previous to abandonment, so long as not more than twenty persons are employed therein at any one time. The cage or cages and other means of egress shall at all times be available for the persons employed where there is no second outlet.

SEC. 2. The owner, operator or superintendent of any mine, to which there is only one shaft, slope or outlet, may petition the court of common pleas in and for the county in which such mine is situated, which said court is hereby empowered to act in the premises, setting forth that in consequence of intervening lands between the working of his mine and the most practicable point, or the only practicable point, as the case may be, at which to make or bring to the surface from the working of his mine, he is unable to make an additional shaft, slope or outlet, in accordance with the requirements of this act ; whereupon the court may make an order of reference, and appoint three disinterested persons, residents of the county, viewers, one or more of whom shall be a practical mining engineer, all of whom after being sworn to a faithful discharge of their duties, shall view and examine the premises, and determine as to whether the owner should have the privilege of making an additional outlet through or upon any intervening lands as the case may require, and report in writing to the court, which report shall be entered and filed of record. If the finding of the viewers, or any two of them, is in favor of the owner of such coal mine or colliery, he may make an additional shaft, slope or outlet under, through or upon intervening lands, as may be determined upon and provided for by the award. If the finding of the viewers is against the owner, or if no award be made by reason of any default or neglect on the part of the owner, he shall be bound to comply with the provisions of this act in the same manner as if this section had not been enacted. In case the said owner, operator or superintendent desires to, and claims that he ought to make an additional opening under, through or upon any adjoining or intervening lands, to meet the requirements of this act, for the ingress and egress of the men employed in his or their mine, he or they shall make a statement of the facts in the petition, with a survey setting forth the point of commencement and the point of termination of the proposed outlet which he or they, their engineers, agents or employés, may enter upon said intervening lands and survey and mark, as he or they shall find it proper to adopt, for such additional outlet, doing as little damage as possible to the property explored; and the viewers shall state in their report what damage will be sustained by the owner or owners of the intervening lands by the opening, constructing and using of the outlet; and if the report is not appealed from, it shall be confirmed or rejected by said court, as to right and justice shall appertain; and any further and all proceedings in relation thereto shall be in conformity with like proceedings, as in the case of a lateral railroad across or under intervening lands, under the act in relation to lateral railroads, approved the fifth day of May, Anno Domini one thousand eight hundred and thirty-two, and the supplements thereto, so far as the provisions of the same are applicable hereto; and the notices, to the owner of intervening lands, of the intention to apply for the privilege of making an outlet, and meeting of the viewers, shall be given, and the costs of the case shall be paid, as provided in the said act of fifth day of May, Anno Domini one thousand eight hundred and thirty-two, and the supplements thereto.

SEC. 3. The escapements, shafts or slopes shall be fitted with safe and available appliances, by which the persons employed in the mine may readily escape, in case an accident occurs deranging the hoisting machinery at the main outlets.

SEC. 4. In slopes, where the angle of inclination is fifteen degrees (15°) or less, there must be provided a separate travelling way, which shall be maintained in a safe condition for travel and kept free from steam and dangerous gases.

SEC. 5. From and after the passage of this act no inflammable structure, other than a frame to sustain pulleys or sheaves, shall be erected over the entrance of any opening connecting the surface with the underground workings of any mine, and no "breaker," or other inflammable structure for the preparation or storage of coal, shall be erected nearer than two hundred (200) feet to any such opening, but this act shall not be construed to prohibit the erection of a fan drift for the purpose of ventilation, or of a trestle for the transportation of cars from any slope to such breaker, or structure, neither shall it apply to any shaft or slope until the same has been driven to its proposed limit, or until the work of development and shipment of coal has commenced : *Provided*, That this section shall not apply to breakers that are now erected or that are in course of erection.

SEC. 6. The top of each shaft and also of each slope, if dangerous, or any intermediate lift thereof, shall be securely fenced off by railing or by vertical or flat gates.

SEC. 7. Every abandoned slope, shaft, air hole and drift shall be properly fenced around or across its entrance.

SEC. 8. All underground entrances to any places not in actual course of work'

ing or extension shall be properly fenced across the whole width of such entrances, so as to prevent persons from inadvertently entering the same.

SEC. 9. The owner, operator or superintendent of any coal mine or colliery, which is worked by shaft or slope, shall provide and maintain a suitable appliance by or through which conversation can be held by and between persons at the bottom and at the top of the shaft or slope, and also an efficient means of signaling from the bottom of such shaft or slope to the engineer in charge of the hoisting engine.

SEC. 10. Hand rails and efficient safety catches shall be attached to, and a sufficient cover overhead shall be provided on, every cage used for lowering or hoisting persons in any shaft.

SEC. 11. Wherever practicable, every cage or gunboat, used for lowering or hoisting persons in any slope, shall be provided with a proper protector, so constructed, that persons while on such cage or gunboat, shall not be struck by anything which may fall or roll down said slope.

SEC. 12. The main link of the chain, connecting the rope to the cage, gunboat or car in any shaft or slope, shall be made of the best quality of iron. Bridle chains, made of the same quality of iron, shall be attached to the main link rope or rope socket from the cross-head of the cage or gunboat, when persons are being lowered or hoisted thereon.

SEC. 13. The ropes, safety catches, links and chains shall be carefully examined every day they are used, by a competent person delegated for that purpose, and any defects therein found, by which life or limb may be endangered, shall be immediately remedied.

SEC. 14. An efficient brake shall be attached to every drum that is used for lowering or raising persons or material in any mine.

SEC. 15. Flanges or horns, of sufficient dimensions to prevent the rope from slipping off the said drum, shall be provided and properly attached to the drum, and all machines used for lowering or hoisting persons in mines shall be provided with an indicator to show the position of the cage, car or gunboat in the shaft or slope.

SEC. 16. Over all shafts, which are being sunk or shall hereafter be sunk, a safe and substantial structure shall be erected to sustain the sheaves or pulleys, at a height of not less than twenty (20) feet above the tipping place, and the top of such shaft shall be arranged in such manner that no material can fall into the shaft while the bucket is being emptied.

SEC. 17. The said structure shall be erected as soon as a substantial foundation is obtained, and in no case shall a shaft be sunk to a depth of more than fifty (50) feet without such structure.

SEC. 18. If provision is made to land the bucket upon a truck, the said truck shall be constructed in such manner that material cannot fall into the shaft.

SEC. 19. All rock and coal from shafts as they are being sunk shall not be raised, except in a bucket or on a cage, and such bucket or cage must be connected to the rope or chain by a safety hook, clevis or other safe attachment.

SEC. 20. Such shafts shall be provided with guides and guide attachments, applied in such a manner as to prevent the bucket from swinging while descending or ascending therein, and such guides and guide attachments shall be maintained at a distance of not more than seventy-five (75) feet from the bottom of such shaft, until its sinking shall have been completed, but this sec·tion shall not apply to shafts one hundred (100) feet or less in depth.

SEC. 21. Where the strata are not safe, every shaft shall be securely cased, lined or otherwise made secure.

SEC. 22. The following rules shall be observed, as far as practicable, in every shaft to which this act applies :

First. After each and every blast, the chargeman must see that all loose material is swept down from the timbers, before the workmen descend to their work.

Second. After a suspension of work, and also after firing a blast in a shaft where explosive gases are evolved, the person in charge must have the said shaft examined and tested with a safety lamp, before the workmen are allowed to descend.

Third. Not more than four persons shall be lowered or hoisted in any shaft on a bucket at the same time, and no person shall ride on a loaded bucket.

Fourth. Whenever persons are employed on platforms in shafts the person in charge must see that the said platforms are properly and safely constructed.

Fifth. While shafts are being sunk all blasts therein must be exploded by an electric battery.

Sixth. Every person, who fails to comply with, or who violates the provi-sions of this article, shall be guilty of an offence against this act.

ARTICLE V.

BOILERS AND CONNECTIONS, MACHINERY, ETC.

SECTION. 1. All boilers used for generating steam in and about mines and collieries shall be kept in good order, and the owner, operator or superintend-ent shall have them examined and inspected by a competent boiler maker, or other well qualified person, as often as once in six months, and oftener if needed. The result of such examination, under oath, shall be certified in writ-ing to the inspector for the district, within thirty (30) days thereafter.

SEC. 2. From and after the passage of this act, it shall not be lawful to place any boiler or boilers for the purpose of generating steam under, nor nearer than one hundred (100) feet to, any coal breaker or other structure, in which persons are employed in the preparation of coal : *Provided*, That this section shall not apply to breakers already erected or that are in course of erection.

SEC. 3. Each nest of boilers shall be provided with a safety valve, of sufficient area for the steam to escape and with weights or springs properly adjusted.

SEC. 4. Every boiler house shall be provided with a steam gauge, properly connected with the boilers, to indicate the steam pressure, and another steam gauge shall be attached to the steam pipe in the engine house, and placed in such position, that the engineer or fireman can readily examine them and see what pressure is carried. Such steam gauges shall be kept in good order, tested and adjusted as often as once in every six months, and their condition reported to the inspector in the same manner as the report of boiler inspection.

Sec. 5. All machinery used in or around the mines and collieries, and especially in breakers, such as engines, rollers, wheels, screens, shafting and belting shall be protected by covering or railing, so as to prevent persons from inadvertently walking against or falling upon the same. The sides of stairs, trestles and dangerous plank walks, in and around the collieries, shall be provided with hand and guard railing to prevent persons from falling over their sides. This section shall not forbid the temporary removal of a fence, guard rail or covering for the purpose of repairs or other operations, if proper ·precautions are used, and the fence, guard rail or covering is replaced immediately thereafter.

Sec. 6. A sober and competent person, not under eighteen (18) years of age, shall be engaged to run the breaker engine, and he shall attend to said engine while the machinery is in motion.

Sec. 7. A signal apparatus shall be established at important points in every breaker, so that in case of an accident, the engineer can be promptly notified to stop the machinery.

Sec. 8. No person under under fifteen (15) years of age shall be appointed to oil the machinery, and no person shall oil dangerous parts of such machinery while it is in motion.

Sec. 9. No person shall play with, loiter ,around or interfere with any machinery in or about any mine or colliery.

Sec. 10. Failure to comply with the provisions of this article shall be deemed an offence against this act.

ARTICLE VI.

WASH HOUSES.

Section 1. It shall be the duty of the owner, operator or superintendent of each mine or colliery, at the request, in writing, of the inspector of mines, to provide a suitable building, not an engine or boiler house, which shall be convenient to the principal entrance of such mine, for the use of the persons employed therein, for the purpose of washing themselves and changing their clothes, when entering the mine and returning therefrom. The said building shall be maintained in good order, be properly lighted and heated, and supplied with pure cold and warm water, and shall be provided with facilities for persons to wash. If any person or persons shall neglect or fail to comply with the provisions of this article, or maliciously injure or destroy, or cause to be injured or destroyed, the said building, or any part thereof, or any of the appliances or fittings used for supplying light, heat and water therein, or doing any act tending to the injury or destruction thereof, he or they shall be deemed guilty of an offence against this act.

ARTICLE VII.

AMBULANCES AND STRETCHERS.

Section 1. The owner, operator, or superintendent of every mine or colliery except as hereinafter provided, shall provide and keep, at such mine or colliery, an ambulance, and also at least two (2) stretchers, for the purpose of conveying to their places of abode any person or persons, who may be injured while in the discharge of his or their work, at such mine or colliery.

SEC. 2. The said ambulance shall be constructed upon good, substantial, and easy springs. It shall be covered and closed, and shall have windows on the sides or ends. It shall be of sufficient size to convey at least two injured persons, with two attendants, at one time, and shall be provided with spring mattresses, or other comfortable bedding, to be placed on roller frames, together with sufficient covering for the comfort and protection, and convenient moving of the injured. It shall also be provided with seats for the attendants. The stretchers shall be constructed of such material, and in such manner, as to afford the greatest ease and comfort in the carriage of the injured person.

SEC. 3. Whenever any person or persons employed in or about a mine or colliery shall receive such injury, by accident or otherwise, while so employed, as would render him, or them, unable to walk to his, or their, place of abode, the owner, operator, or superintendent of such mine or colliery shall immediately cause such person or persons to be removed to his, or their, place of abode, or to an hospital, as the case may require.

SEC. 4. It is provided, however, that the owner, operator, or superintendent of any mine or colliery shall be excepted from the requirement of an ambulance as aforesaid, if the places of abode of all the workmen at such mine or colliery be within a radius of a half mile from the principal entrance to such mine.

SEC. 5. It is provided further that where two or more mines or collieries are located within one mile of each other, or the ambulance is located within one mile of each colliery, but one ambulance, as aforesaid, shall be required, if the said mines or collieries have ready and quick means of communication, one with the other, by telegraph or telephone.

SEC. 6. An ambulance, as aforesaid, shall not be required at any mine or colliery at which less than twenty (20) persons are employed.

SEC. 7. In case the distance from any mine or colliery, to the place of abode of the person injured, is such as to permit his conveyance to his home, or to an hospital, more quickly and conveniently by railway, such mode of conveyance shall be permitted, but in such case the conveyance must be under cover and the comfort of the injured person must be provided for.

ARTICLE VIII.

CERTIFIED MINE FOREMAN.

SECTION 1. From and after the first day of July, one thousand eight hundred and eighty-six, no person shall be permitted to act as mine foreman, unless he is registered as a holder of a certificate under this act.

SEC. 2. Certificates of qualification to mine foremen shall be granted by the Secretary of Internal Affairs, to every applicant, who may be reported by the examiners, as hereinafter provided, as having passed a satisfactory examination, and as having given satisfactory evidence of at least five years practical experience and of good conduct, capability and sobriety.

The certificate shall be in manner and form as shall be prescribed by the

Secretary of Internal Affairs, and a record of all certificates issued shall be kept in his department.

SEC. 3. For the purpose of examination of candidates, or such certificates, a board of examiners shall be appointed in each of the inspection districts provided for by this act. The said board shall consist of the district inspector of mines, a practical miner, and one owner, operator or superintendent of a mine. The said inspector shall act *ex-officio*, and the said engineer and owner, operator or superintendent shall be appointed in like manner, and at the same time, as the boards of examiners for candidates for mine inspectorship under this act are now appointed. The said board shall act as such for the period of one year from the date of their appointment. Meetings of the board may be held at any time, and they may make such rules and conduct such examinations as in their judgment may seem proper for the purpose of such examinations. The said board shall report their action to the Secretary of Internal Affairs, and at least two of the members thereof shall certify to the qualification of each candidate, who has passed such examination. The travelling expenses of the members of such board to and from their place of meeting, together with the sum of five dollars per day each to the said practical miner and owner, operator or superintendent, members of each board, for each day they are actually engaged therein, not exceeding ten (10) days, in all during the year shall be paid by the Commonwealth, on an order of the Auditor General, drawn on the State Treasurer upon the certificate of the mine inspector, member of such board.

SEC. 4. Certificates of service which shall have the same effect for the purposes of this act as certificates of qualification, shall be granted by the Secretary of Internal Affairs, on the report of the examining board, to each person who for at least one year prior to the first day of July, one thousand eight hundred and eighty-six, has acted at any mine under this act as mine foreman. Certificates of qualification and certificates of service shall contain the full name, age and place of birth of the applicant, as also the length and nature of his previous service in or about mines.

SEC. 5. Before certificates as aforesaid shall be granted, applicants for same shall pay to the Secretary of Internal Affairs the following fees, namely: For examination one dollar, for registration of certificate one dollar, for certificate one dollar. All fees so received shall be covered into the treasury of the Commonwealth.

SEC. 6. No mine shall be operated for a longer period than thirty (30) days without the supervision of a mine foreman: *Provided, however,* That any mine employing ordinarily less than ten (10) persons underground, or one whose daily output is less than fifty (50) tons of coal, shall be exempt from the operations of this section.

SEC. 7. In case any mine, except as hereinafter excepted, is worked a longer period than thirty (30) days without such certificated mine foreman, the owner, operator or superintendent thereof shall be subject to a penalty of twenty dollars per day, for each day over the said thirty (30) days during which the said mine is worked, unless it shall be clearly shown that the said owner, operator or superintendent has used all reasonable means for the enforcement of this article, and to prevent the mine from being worked contrary to this act: *And provided further*, That in case no suitable or satisfactory certificated mine foreman may at the time be obtained, some suitable person may be appointed to act as mine foreman for the space of three months, or until such person can obtain the proper certificate under this act.

SEC. 8. In case of the loss or destruction of a certificate, the Secretary of Internal Affairs may supply a copy thereof to the person losing the same, upon the payment of the sum of fifty cents: *Provided*, It shall be shown to the satisfaction of the Secretary that the loss has actually occurred.

SEC. 9. If any person or persons shall forge or counterfeit a certificate, or knowingly make, or cause to be made, any false statement in any certificate under this act, or in any official copy of same, or shall urge others to do so, or shall utter or use any such forged or false certificate or unofficial copy thereof, or shall make, give, utter, produce or make use of any false declaration, repre. sentation or statement in any such certificate, or copy thereof, or any document containing the same, he or they shall be guilty of a misdemeanor, and upon conviction thereof shall be fined two hundred dollars, or imprisoned for a term not exceeding one year or both, at the discretion of the court trying the case.

ARTICLE IX.

EMPLOYMENT OF BOYS AND FEMALES.

SECTION 1. No boy under the age of fourteen years and no woman or girl of any age, shall be employed or permitted to be in any mine for the purpose of employment therein. Nor shall a boy under the age of twelve years, or a woman or girl of any age be employed or permitted to be in or about the outside structures or workings of a colliery for the purpose of employment, but it is provided however, that this prohibition shall not affect the employment of a boy or female of suitable age in an office, or in the performance of clerical work at a colliery.

SEC. 2. When an employer is in doubt as to the age of any boy or youth applying for employment in or about a mine or colliery, he shall demand and receive proof of the said lawful employment age of such boy or youth by certificate from the parent or guardian, before said boy or youth shall be employed.

SEC. 3. If any person or persons contravene, or fail to comply with the provisions of this act in respect to the employment of boys, young male persons, or females, or if he or they shall connive with, or permit others to contravene or fail to comply with said provisions, or if a parent or guardian of a boy or young male person make or give a false certificate of the age of such boy or young male person. or knowingly do or perform any other act for the purpose of securing employment for a boy or young male person under the lawful employment age, and in contravention of the provisions of this act, he or they shall be guilty of an offence against this act.

ARTICLE X.

VENTILATION.

SECTION 1. The owner, operator or superintendent of every mine shall provide and maintain an adequate supply of pure air for the same, as hereinafter provided.

SEC. 2. At the expiration of one year from and after the passage of this act, it shall not be lawful to use a furnace for the purpose of ventilating any mine wherein explosive gases are generated.

SEC. 3. The minimum quantity of air thus produced shall not be less than two hundred (200) cubic feet per minute, for each and every person employed in any mine, and as much more as the circumstances may require.

SEC. 4. The ventilating currents shall be conducted and circulated to and along the face of each and every working place throughout the entire mine, in sufficient quantities to dilute, render harmless, and sweep away smoke and noxious and dangerous gases, to such an extent that all working places and travelling roads shall be in a safe and fit state to work and travel therein.

SEC. 5. All worked out or abandoned parts of a mine, so far as practicable, shall be kept free of dangerous bodies of gases.

SEC. 6. One year after the passage of this act, every mine employing more than seventy-five (75) persons must be divided into two or more districts. Each district shall be provided with a separate split of pure air and the ventilation shall be so arranged that not more than seventy-five (75) persons shall be employed at the same time in any one current or split of air.

The inlet and return air passages for any particular district must be separated by a pillar of coal or stone, if the thickness and dip of the vein will permit, except where it is necessary to cut through said dividing pillar for the purposes of ventilation, traffic or drainage.

SEC. 7. All air passages shall be of a sufficient area to allow the free passage of not less than two hundred (200) cubic feet of air per minute for every person working therein, and in no case, in mines generating explosive gases, shall the velocity exceed four hundred and fifty (450) lineal feet per minute in any opening through which the air currents pass, if gauze safety-lamps are used, except in the main inlet or outlet airways.

SEC.. 8. All cross cuts, connecting the main inlet and outlet air passages of every district, when it becomes necessary to close them permanently, shall be substantially closed with brick or other suitable building material laid in mortar, or cement whenever practicable, but in no case shall said air-stoppings be constructed of plank, except for temporary purposes or as above provided.

SEC. 9. All doors used in assisting or in any way affecting the ventilation shall be so hung and adjusted, that they will close of their own accord and cannot stand open.

SEC. 10. All main doors shall have an attendant, whose constant duty it shall be to open them for transportation and travel, and prevent them from standing open longer than is necessary for persons or cars to pass through.

SEC. 11. All main doors shall be so placed that when one door is open, another which has the same effect upon the same current, shall be and remain closed, and thus prevent any temporary stoppage of the air current.

SEC. 12. An extra main door shall be so placed and kept standing open so as to be out of reach of accident, and so fixed that it can be at once closed in the event of an accident to the doors in use.

SEC. 13. The frame work of such main doors shall be substantially secured in stone or brick, laid in mortar or cement, unless otherwise permitted in writing by the inspector.

SEC. 14. All permanent air bridges shall be substantially built of such material, and of such strength as the circumstances may require.

SEC. 15. The quantities of air in circulation shall be ascertained with an anemometer, or other efficient instrument. Such measurements shall be made by the inside foreman, or his assistant, once every week at the inlet and outlet airways, also at or near the face of each gangway, and shall be entered in the colliery report book.

SEC. 16. A copy of these air measurements shall be sent to the inspector before the twelfth (12th) day of each month for the preceding month, together with a statement of the number of persons employed in each district.

SEC. 17. All ventilators, used at mines generating explosive gases, shall be provided with recording instruments, by which the number of revolutions of the fan shall be registered for each hour, and such data shall be taken and reported in the colliery report book.

SEC. 18. Any person or persons who shall neglect or fail to comply with the provisions of this article, or who shall knowingly make any false report in regard to air measurements, shall be guilty of an offence against this act.

ARTICLE XI.

PROPS AND TIMBERS.

SECTION 1. It shall be the duty of the owner, operator, superintendent or mine foreman or every mine, to furnish to the miners, at their request, all props and timbers necessary for the safe mining of coal and for the protection of the lives of the workmen. Such props and timbers shall be suitably prepared, and shall be delivered to the workmen, as near to their working places as they can be conveyed in ordinary mine cars, free of charge.

SEC. 2. Every workman in want of props or timbers shall notify the mine foreman, or his assistant, of the fact, at least one day in advance, giving the length of the props or timber required, and in case of danger from loose roof or sides, he shall not continue to cut or load coal, until the said props and timber have been properly furnished, and the place made secure.

SEC. 3. A failure to comply with the provisions of this article shall be deemed an offence against this act, and shall be taken to be negligence *per se* on the part of the owner, operator, superintendent or mine foreman, as the case may be, of such mine, in action for the recovery of damages for accidents resulting from the insufficient propping of such mine through failure to furnish the necessary props or timbers.

ARTICLE XII.

GENERAL RULES.

The following general rules shall be observed in every mine to which this act applies.

Rule 1. The owner, operator or superintendent of a mine or colliery shall place the underground workings thereof, and all that is related to the same under the charge, and daily supervision of a competent person who shall be called " mine foreman."

Rule 2. Whenever a mine foreman cannot personally carry out the provisions of this act so far as they pertain to him, the owner, operator or superintendent shall authorize him to employ a sufficient number of competent persons to act as his assistants who shall be subject to his orders.

Rule 3. The mine foreman shall have charge of all matters pertaining to ventilation, and the speed of the ventilators shall be particularly under his charge and direction.

Rule 4. All accessible parts of an abandoned portion of a mine, in which explosive gases have been found, shall be carefully examined by the mine foreman or his assistants at least once a week, and all danger found existing therein, shall be immediately removed. A report of said examination shall be recorded in a book kept at the colliery for that purpose and signed by the person making the same.

Rule 5. In mines, generating explosive gases, the mine foreman or his assistants shall make a careful examination every morning of all working places and travelling roads, before the workmen shall enter the mine, and such examination shall be made with a safety lamp within three hours at most before time for commencing work, and a workman shall not enter the mine or his working place until the said mine or part thereof and working place are reported to be safe. Every report shall be recorded without delay in a book, which shall be kept at the colliery for the purpose, and shall be signed by the person making the examination.

Rule 6. The person who makes said examination shall establish proof of the same by marking plainly the date thereof, at the face of each working place.

Rule 7. A station or stations shall be established at the entrance to each mine, or different parts of each mine, as the case may require, and a workman shall not pass beyond any such station until the mine or part of the mine beyond the same has been inspected and reported to be safe.

Rule 8. If at any time it is found by the person for the time being in charge of the mine or any part thereof, that by reason of noxious gases, prevailing in such mine or such part thereof, or of any cause whatever the mine or the said part is dangerous, every workman, except such persons as may be required to remove the danger, shall be withdrawn from the mine, or such part thereof as is so found dangerous until the said mine or said part thereof, is examined by a competent person, and reported by him to be safe.

Rule 9. In every working, approaching any place where there is likely to be an accumulation of explosive gases, or in any working in which danger is imminent from explosive gases, no light or fire, other than a locked safety lamp, shall be allowed or used. Whenever safety-lamps are required in any mine, they shall be the property of the owner of said mine, and a competent person who shall be appointed for the purpose, shall examine every safety-lamp immediately before it is taken into the workings for use and ascertain it to be clean, safe and securely locked; and safety-lamps shall not be used until they have been so examined and found safe, clean and securely locked, unless permission be first given by the mine foreman to have the lamps used unlocked.

Rule 10. No one, except a duly authorized person, shall have in his possession, a key, or any other contrivance, for the purpose of unlocking any safety-

20

lamp in any mine where locked lamps are used. No lucifer matches or any
other apparatus for striking light shall be taken into said mine or parts
thereof.

Rule 11. No blast shall be fired in any mine where locked safety-lamps are
used, except by permission of the mine foreman or his assistant, and, before a
blast is fired, the person in charge must examine the place and adjoining places
and satisfy himself that it is safe to fire such blast before such permission is
given.

Rule 12. The mine foreman, or his assistant, shall visit and examine every
working place in the mine, at least, once every alternate day, while the men of
such place are, or should be at work, and shall direct that each and every working place is properly secured by props or timber, and that safety in all respects
is assured by directing that all loose coal or rock shall be pulled down or secured, and that no person shall be permitted to work in an unsafe place, unless
it be for the purpose of making it secure.

Rule 13. The mine foreman, or some other competent person or persons to
be designated by him, shall examine, at least once every day, all slopes, shafts,
main roads, travelling ways, signal apparatus, pulleys and timbering and see that
they are in safe and efficent working condition.

Rule 14. Any person having charge of a working-place in any mine shall
keep the roof and sides thereof properly secured by timber or otherwise, so as
to prevent such roof and sides from falling, and he shall not do any work, or
permit any work to be done, under loose or dangerous material except for the
purpose of securing the same.

Rule 15. Whenever a place is likely to contain a dangerous accumulation of
water, the working approaching such place shall not exceed twelve (12) feet in
width, and there shall be constantly kept at a distance of not less than twenty
(20) feet in advance at least one bore hole near the centre of the working and
sufficient flank bore holes on each side.

Rule 16. No person shall ride upon or against any loaded car, cage or gunboat in any shaft, slope or plane, in or about a mine or colliery.

Rule 17. Not more than ten (10) persons shall be hoisted or lowered at any
one time in any shaft or slope ; and whenever ten persons shall arrive at the
bottom of any shaft or slope in which persons are regularly hoisted or lowered,
they shall be furnished with an empty car or cage and be hoisted, except, however, in mines where there is provided a travelling way having an average pitch
of fifteen degrees (15°) or less, and not more than one thousand feet in length.

Rule 18. An engineer placed in charge of an engine whereby persons are
hoisted or lowered in any mine shall be a sober and competent person, of not
less than twenty-one (21) years of age.

Rule 19. Every engineer shall work his engine slowly and with great care
when any person is being lowered or hoisted in a shaft or slope, and no one
shall interfere with or intimidate him while in the discharge of his duties.

Rule 20. An engineer who has charge of the hoisting machinery by which
persons are lowered or hoisted in a mine shall be in constant attendance for
that purpose during the whole time any person or persons are below ground,
and he shall not allow any person or persons except such as may be deputed
by the owner, operator or superintendent to handle or meddle with the engine
under his charge or any part of its machinery.

Rule 21. When any person is about to descend or ascend a shaft or slope the headman or footman, as the case may be, shall inform the engineer by signal or otherwise of the fact, and the engineer shall return a signal before moving or starting the engine. In the absence of a headman or footman, the person or persons about to descend or ascend shall give and receive the signals in the same manner.

Rule 22. The owner, operator or superintendent of a colliery shall place a competent person, to be called outside foreman, in charge of the breaker and the outside work of such colliery, and who shall direct, and, as far as practicable, see that the provisions of this act are complied with in respect to the breaker, outside machinery, ropes, cages, and all other things pertaining to the outside work, unless otherwise provided for in this act.

Rule 23. In all coal breakers where the coal dust is so dense as to be injurious to the health of persons employed therein, the owner, operator or superintendent of said breaker shall, upon the request of the inspector, immediately adopt measures for the removal of the dust as far as practicable.

Rule 24. Any miner or other workmen who shall discover anything wrong with the ventilating current or with the condition of the roof, side, timber or roadway or with any other part of the mine in general such as would lead him to suspect danger to himself or to his fellow-workmen or to the property of his employer shall immediately report the same to the mine foreman or other person for the time being in charge of that portion of the mine.

Rule 25. Any person or persons who shall knowingly or wilfully damage or without proper authority remove or render useless any fencing, means of signaling, apparatus, instrument or machine, or shall throw open or obstruct any airway, or open a ventilating door, and not have the same closed, or enter a place in or about a mine against caution, or carry fire, open lights or matches in places where safety-lamps are used or handled without authority, or disturb any machinery or cars, or do any other act or thing whereby the lives or health of persons or the security of the property in or about a mine or colliery are endangered, shall be guilty of an offence against this act.

Rule 26. Gunpowder or any other explosive shall not be stored in a mine, and a watchman shall not have at any one time, in any one place more than one keg or box containing twenty-five (25) pounds, unless more is necessary for a person to accomplish one day's work.

Rule 27. Every person who has gunpowder or other explosive in a mine shall keep it in a wooden or metallic box, securely locked, and such box shall be kept at least ten feet from the tracks, in all cases where room at such distance is available.

Rule 28. Whenever a workman shall open a box containing explosive, or while in any manner handling the same, he shall first place his lamp not less than five feet from such explosive, and in such a position that the air current cannot convey sparks to it, and a workman shall not approach nearer than five feet to an open box containing powder with a lamp, lighted pipe or any other thing containing fire.

Rule 29. When high explosives other than gunpowder are used in any mine, the manner of storing, keeping, moving, charging and firing, or in any manner using such explosives shall be in accordance with special rules as furnished by the manufacturers of the same. The said rules shall be endorsed with his or their official signature and shall be approved by the owner, operator or superintendent of the mine in which such explosives are used.

Rule 30. In charging holes for blasting in slate or rock in any mine, no iron or steel-pointed needle shall be used, and a tight cartridge shall not be rammed into a hole in coal, slate or rock with an iron or steel tamping bar unless the end of the tamping bar is tipped with at least six (6) inches of copper or other soft metal.

Rule 31. A charge of powder or any other explosive in slate or rock which has missed fire shall not be withdrawn or the hole re-opened.

Rule 32. A miner or other person who is about to explode a blast by the use of patent or other squibs or matches shall not shorten the match, nor saturate it with mineral oil, nor turn it down when placed in the hole, nor ignite it except at its extreme end, nor do anything tending to shorten the time the match will burn.

Rule 33. When a workman is about to fire a blast, he shall be careful to notify all persons who may be in danger therefrom, and shall give sufficient alarm, so that any person or persons who may be approaching shall be warned of the danger.

Rule 34. Before commencing work, and also after the firing of every blast, the miner working a breast or any other place in a mine shall enter such breast or place to examine and ascertain its condition, and his laborer or assistant shall not go to the face of such breast or place until the miner has examined the same and found it to be safe.

Rule 35. No person shall be employed to blast coal or rock unless the mine foreman is satisfied that such person is qualified by experience and judgment to perform the work with ordinary safety.

Rule 36. A person who is not a practical miner shall not charge or fire a blast in the absence of an experienced miner unless he has given satisfactory evidence of his ability to do so with safety and has obtained permission from the mine foreman or person in charge.

Rule 37. An accumulation of gas in mines shall not be removed by brushing where it is practicable to remove it by brattice.

Rule 38. When gas is ignited by blast or otherwise the person igniting the same shall immediately extinguish it if possible and notify the mine foreman or his assistant of the fact, and workmen must see that no gas-blowers are left burning upon leaving their working-places.

Rule 39. Every fireman in charge of a boiler or boilers for the generation of steam shall keep a constant watch of the same. He shall see that the steam pressure does not at any time exceed the limit allowed by the outside foreman or superintendent. He shall frequently try the safety-valve and shall not increase the weight on the same. He shall maintain a proper depth of water in each boiler, and if anything should happen to prevent this, he shall report the same without delay to the foreman for the time being in charge and take such other action as may, under the particular circumstances, be necessary for the protection of life and preservation of property.

Rule 40. At every shaft or slope in which provision is made in this act for lowering and hoisting persons, a headman and footman shall be designated by the superintendent or foreman, to be at their proper places from the time that persons begin to descend until all the persons who may be at the bottom of said shaft or slope when quitting work shall be hoisted. Such headman and footman shall personally attend to the signals and see that the provisions of this act in respect to lowering and hoisting persons in shafts or slopes shall be complied with.

Rule 41. No person except the man giving the signal shall jump on a car, cage or gunboat after the signal to start has been given, and if any person should enter a car, cage or gunboat in excess of the lawful number the headman or footman shall notify him of the fact and request him to get off, which request must be immediately complied with. Any violation of this rule must be reported promptly to the mine foreman.

Rule 42. Every passage-way used by persons in any mine, and also used for transportation of coal or other material, shall be made of sufficient width to permit persons to pass moving cars with safety, but if found impracticable to make any passage-way of sufficient width, then safety-holes of ample dimensions and not more than one hundred and fifty feet apart shall be made on one side of said passage-way. The said passage-way and safety-holes shall be kept free from obstructions and shall be well drained; the roof and sides of the same shall be made secure.

Rule 43. When locomotives are used in any mine their speed shall not exceed six miles per hour, and an efficient alarm shall be provided and attached to the front end of every train of cars pushed by a locomotive in any mine or part of a mine.

Rule 44. Locomotives propelled by steam, if using fire, shall not be used in any passage-way which is also used as an in-take air-way to any mine or part of a mine where persons are employed unless there be a sufficient quantity of air circulating therein to maintain a healthy atmosphere.

Rule 45. No person except the driver and helper shall couple or uncouple loaded or empty cars while the same are in motion.

Rule 46. When cars are run on gravity roads by brakes or sprags, the runner shall only ride on the rear end of the last car, and when said cars are run by sprags, a space of not less than two feet from the body of the car shall be made on one or both sides of the track wherever it may be necessary for the runner to pass along the side of the moving car or cars, and said space or passage-way shall always be kept free from obstructions.

Rule 47. No person shall run cars on gravity roads or act as a driver or runner, or sprag any mine car after it has been started from the face of a chamber unless he is authorized to do so by the mine foreman or his assistant, and all runners engaged in any mine or part of a mine must have attained the age of fifteen (15) years.

Rule 48. When deemed necessary by the mine inspector and upon his request in writing to the owner, operator or superintendent, safety-holes shall be made at the bottom of all slopes and planes, and be kept free from obstruction to enable the footman to escape readily in case of danger.

Rule 49. Safety-blocks, or some other device for the purpose of preventing cars from falling into a shaft or running away on a slope or plane, shall be placed at or near the head of every shaft, slope or plane, and said safety-blocks or other device must be maintained in good working order.

Rule 50. No person shall travel on any gravity plane while cars are being hoisted or lowered thereon. Whenever ten persons arrive at the bottom or top of any plane on which it is necessary for men to travel, traffic thereon shall be suspended for a period of time long enough to permit them to reach the top or bottom of said plane.

Rule 51. From and after the passage of this act no mine car shall be built or constructed for use in any mine unless the bumpers are of sufficient length and width to keep the bodies of said cars separated by not less than twelve (12) inches when the cars stand on a straight, level road, and the bumpers touch each other, and five years after the passage of this act, no mine car shall be used in any mine unless it complies with the above conditions.

Rule 52. Every person who wilfully or negligently acts in contravention of, or fails to comply with, any of the foregoing rules, or any of the provisions of this article, shall be guilty of an offence against this act.

ARTICLE XIII.

PROVISION FOR SPECIAL RULES.

SECTION 1. There shall be established in every mine or colliery to which this act applies such rules for the conduct and guidance of the person acting in the management of such mine or colliery, or employed in or about the same, as under the particular state and circumstances of such mine or colliery may appear best calculated to prevent dangerous accidents, and to provide for the safety and proper discipline of the persons employed in and about the mine or colliery, and such special rules, when established, shall be signed by the inspector, who is the inspector of the district at the time such rules are established, and shall also be approved by the court of the county in which the mine or colliery is located, and after having been so signed and approved, the said special rules shall be observed in and about every such mine or colliery in the same manner as if they were enacted in this act.

SEC. 2. If any person who is bound to observe the special rules established for any mine or colliery acts in contravention of, or fails to comply with, any of such special rules, he shall be guilty of an offence against this act, and the owner, operator or superintendent of such mine shall also be guilty of an offence against this act unless he proves that he had taken all reasonable means by publishing, and to the best of his power, enforcing the said rules as regulations for the working of the mine or colliery so as to prevent such contravention or non-compliance.

SEC. 3. The owner, operator or superintendent of every mine or colliery to which this act applies shall forward to the inspector of his district, for his approval, a copy of the proposed special rules for such mine or colliery, within three months after the commencement of this act, or within three months after the commencement of any work for the purpose of opening a new mine, or renewing the work of an old mine. The proposed special rules, together with a printed notice specifying that any objection to such rules, on the ground of anything contained therein, or omitted therefrom, may be sent by any of the persons employed in the mine to the inspector of the district at his address stated in such notice, shall, during not less than two weeks before such rules are transmitted to the inspector, be posted up in like manner as is provided in this act respecting the publication of special rules for the information of persons employed in the mine, and a certificate that such rules and notice lave been so posted up shall be sent to the inspector, with the rules signed by he person sending the same.

If the rules are not objected to by the inspector or by the court within thirty 30) days after their receipt by him, they shall be established.

If the inspector is of the opinion that the proposed special rules, or any of .hem, do not sufficiently provide for the prevention of dangerous accidents in :he mine or colliery, or for the safety of the persons employed in or about the mine or colliery, or are unreasonable, he may, within thirty (30) days after the receipt of rules, object to them and propose to the owner, operator or superintendent, in writing, any modifications in the rules by way of omission, alteration, substitution or addition.

If the owner, operator or superintendent does not, within twenty days after the receipt of the proposed modifications, object to them in writing, the proposed special rules, with such modification, shall be established.

If the owner, operator or superintendent sends his objections in writing within the said twenty days, the matter shall be referred to arbitration, and the rules shall be established as settled by an award or arbitration.

SEC. 4. After special rules have been established under this act, in any mine or colliery, the owner, operator or suprintendent of such mine or colliery may from time to time propose in writing to the inspector, or the inspector may from time to time propose in writing to the owner, operator or superintendent of the mine or colliery, any new special rules or any amendment to the special rules, and the provisions of this act with respect to the original special rules shall apply to all such amendments and new rules in like manner as near as may be, as they apply to the original rules.

SEC. 5. For the purpose of making known the special rules and the provisions of this act to all persons employed in or about such mine or colliery, to which this act applies, an abstract of the act, together with the special rules, shall be posted up in legible characters in some conspicuous place or places at or near the mine or colliery, where they may be conveniently read by the persons employed, and so often as the same becomes obliterated or destroyed, the owner, operator or superintendent shall cause them to be renewed with all reasonable dispatch.

Every person who pulls down, injures or defaces any abstract or special rules when posted up in pursuance to the provisions of this act shall be guilty of an offence against this act.

ARTICLE XIV.

INQUESTS.

SECTION 1. Whenever loss of life to a miner or other employé occurs in or about a mine or colliery, notice thereof shall be given promptly to the inspector of mines for the district in which the accident occurred by the mine foreman or outside foreman, or other person having immediate charge of the work at the time of the accident; and when death results from personal injury, such notice shall be given promptly after the knowledge of the death comes to the said foreman or person in charge.

SEC. 2. Whenever loss of life occurs or whenever the lives of persons employed in a mine or at a colliery are in danger from any accident, the inspector of mines shall visit the scene of the accident as soon as possible thereafter, and offer such suggestions as in his judgment shall be necessary to protect the lives and secure the safety of the persons employed. In case of death from such accident, and after examination, he finds it necessary that a coroner's inquest shall be held, he shall notify the coroner to hold such inquest without delay, and if no such inquest be held by the coroner within twenty-four (24) hours after such notice, the inspector shall institute a further and fuller examination of such accident, and for this purpose he shall have power to compel the attendance of witnesses at such examination and to administer oaths and affirmations to persons testifying thereat. The inspector shall make a record of all such investigations and accidents, which record shall be preserved in his office. The costs of such investigations shall be paid by the county in which the accident occurred in like manner as costs of inquests held by coroners or justices of the peace are now paid.

SEC. 3. An inquest held by the coroner upon the body of a person killed by explosion or other accident shall be adjourned by the coroner if the inspector of mines be not present to watch the proceedings, and the coroner in such case shall notify the inspector in writing of such adjourned inquest, and the time and place of holding the same at least three days previous thereto.

SEC. 4. Due notice of an intended inquest to be held by the coroner shall be given by the coroner to the inspector, and at any such inquest the inspector shall have the right to examine witnesses.

SEC. 5. If at any inquest held over the body or bodies of persons whose death was caused by an accident in or about a mine or colliery, the inspector be not present, and it is shown by the evidence given at the inquest that the accident was caused by neglect or by any defect in or about the mine or colliery, which in the judgment of the jury requires a remedy, the coroner shall send notice in writing to said inspector of such neglect or default.

SEC. 6. No person who is interested personally, nor a person employed in the mine or at a colliery in or at which loss of life has occurred by accident, shall be qualified to serve on a jury empaneled on the inquest, and a constable or other officer shall not summon such a person so disqualified as juror, but the coroner shall empanel a majority of the jury from persons who are qualified to judge of the nature of the accident. Every person who fails to comply with the provisions of this article shall be guilty of an offence against this act.

ARTICLE XV.

RETURNS, NOTICES, ETC.

SECTION 1. Notices of deaths or serious injuries, resulting from accidents in or about mines or collieries shall be made to the inspector of mines in writing, and shall specify the name, age, and occupation of the person killed or injured, and also the nature and character of the accident, and of the injury caused thereby.

SEC. 5. The owner, operator or superintendent of a mine or colliery shall within two weeks. give notice to the inspector of the district in which said mine or colliery is situated, in any or all of the following cases :

First. Where any working is commenced for the purpose of opening a new slope or mine to which this act applies.

Second. Where any mine is abandoned or the working thereof discontinued.

Third. Where the working of any mine is recommenced after any abandonment or discontinuance for a period exceeding three months.

Fourth. Where any new coal breaker is completed and work commenced therein for the purpose of preparing coal for market.

Fifth. Where the pillars of a mine are to be removed or robbed.

Sixth. Where a squeeze or crush, or any other cause or change may seem to affect the safety of persons employed in any mine, or where fire occurs or a dangerous body of gas is found in any mine.

SEC. 3. On or before the first day of February in each year, the owner, operator or superintendent of every mine or colliery shall send to the inspector of the district a correct report, specifying with respect to the year ending December thirty-first (31st) previously, the name of the operator and officials of the mine, the quantity of coal mined, the amount of powder consumed, the number of persons employed above and below ground, in or about such colliery, classifying the persons so employed. The report shall be in such form as may be from time to time prescribed by the inspector of the district. Blank forms for said reports shall be furnished by the Commonwealth.

ARTICLE XVI.

INJUNCTIONS.

SECTION 1. Upon application of the inspector of mines of the proper district, acting in behalf of the Commonwealth, any of the courts of law or equity having jurisdiction where the mine or colliery proceeded against is situated, whether any proceedings have or have not been taken, shall prohibit, by injunction or otherwise, the working of any mine or colliery in which any person is employed or is permitted to be for the purpose of working in contravention of the provisions of this act, and may award such costs in the matter of the injunction or other proceedings as the court may think just, but this section shall be without prejudice to any other remedy permitted by law for enforcing the provisions of this act. Written notice of the intention to apply for such injunction in respect to any mine or colliery shall be made to the owner, operator or superintendent of such mine or colliery not less than five (5) days before the application is made.

ARTICLE XVII.

ARBITRATION.

SECTION 1. Whenever an inspector finds any mine or colliery or part thereof, or any matter, thing or practice connected with such mine, which, in any respect thereof, is not covered by or provided against by any provision of this act or by any special rule, to be dangerous or defective, or in his judgment tends to bodily injury to a person, he shall give notice thereof in writing to the owner, operator or superintendent of such mine or colliery, stating in such notice the particular matter or defect requiring remedy, and may demand that the same be remedied, but the owner, operator or superintendent of said mine

or colliery shall have the right to refer the demand of the inspector to a board
of arbitration, and the matter shall then be arbitrated within forty-eight (48)
hours of the time such complaint or demand be made.   The said board of
arbitration shall be composed of three persons, one of whom shall be chosen by
the inspector, one by the said owner, operator or superintendent, and the third
by the two thus selected, and the decision of a majority of such board shall be
final and binding in the matter.

ARTICLE XVIII.

PENALTIES.

SECTION 1. Any judge of the court of quarter sessions of the peace of the
county in which the mine or colliery at which the offence, act or omission as
hereinafter stated has occurred is situated, is hereby authorized and required
upon the presentation to him of the affidavit of the mine inspector of the district, setting forth that the owner, operator or superintendent or any other
person employed in or about such mine or colliery had been wilfully or negligently guilty of an offence against the provisions of this act, whereby a dangerous accident had resulted or might have resulted to any person or persons
employed in such mine or colliery, to issue a warrant to the sheriff of said
county, directing him to cause such person or persons to be arrested and
brought before said judge, who shall hear and determine the guilt or innocence
of the person or persons so charged, and, if convicted, he or they shall be sentenced to pay a fine not exceeding fifty dollars, in all cases not otherwise provided for in this act, or an imprisonment in the county jail, for a period not
exceeding three months, or both, at the discretion of the court : *Provided*, That
any defendant may waive a trial before a judge as herein provided, and at any
time, at or before the time of such trial, demand a trial by a jury in the court of
quarter sessions, in which case he may enter into a recognizance before said
judge, with such surety or sureties, and in such sum as said judge may approve,
condition for his appearance at the next court of quarter sessions, to answer
the charge against him, and abide the orders of the court in the premises,
meanwhile to be of good behavior and keep the peace, or in default of such
recognizance to be committed to the county jail to await such trial.

SEC. 2. If any person shall feel himself aggrieved by such conviction and
sentence before a judge as aforesaid, he may appeal therefrom, subject to the
following conditions, namely :   The appellant shall, within seven days after
the decree has been made, give notice to the prosecutor of his intention to
appeal, and within the same time enter into a recognizance with such surety or
sureties, and in such sum as shall be approved by said judge, conditioned to
appear and try such appeal before the next court of quarter sessions of the
peace, and to abide the judgment of the court thereon, and to pay all such
costs and penalties as may be there awarded, and upon the compliance with
such conditions the judge shall release the appellant from custody pending the
appeal.

SEC. 3. Nothing in this act shall prevent any person from being indicted, or
liable, under any other act, to any higher penalty or punishment than is herein
provided, and if the court before whom any such proceedings is had shall be
of the opinion that proceedings ought to be taken against such persons under

any other act, or otherwise, he may adjourn the case to enable such proceedings to be taken.

SEC. 4. All offences under this act are declared to be misdemeanors, and in default of payment of any penalty or costs by the party or parties sentenced to pay the same, he or they may be imprisoned for a period not exceeding three months and not less than thirty days.

SEC. 5. If any mine inspector shall be notified in writing of any violation of this act, as above provided, with the names of witnesses who can prove the fact and with the name of the person giving the information subscribed thereto, and he shall wilfully and corruptly neglect or refuse to make complaint to the judge as herein provided, shall be guilty of a misdemeanor, and, upon conviction, shall pay a fine not exceeding five hundred dollars and be removed and discharged from his said office by the sentence of the court, such neglect or refusal in the absence of any just or reasonable cause or ground thereof shall be deemed corrupt.

SEC. 6. All fines imposed under this act shall be paid into the county treasury, and shall, if the judge trying the cause so order, be payable to the person or persons injured by an accident resulting from the commission of the offences for which such fines were imposed, or to their families in case of death : *Provided*, That the same shall not be payable to the person or persons who caused or contributed to such accident. If the judge before whom the cause is tried shall find the person or persons against whom the complaint is made not guilty of any offence, he shall decree that the county shall pay the costs, unless he shall be of the opinion that the complaint was wantonly or maliciously brought or made, in which case the costs shall be imposed upon the inspector or informer or both, at the discretion of the court.

SEC. 7. No conviction or acquittal under this act in any complaint shall be received in evidence upon the trial of any action for damages arising from the negligence of any owner, operator or superintendent or employé in any mine or colliery.

SEC. 8. That for any injury to persons or property occasioned by any violation of this act, or any wilful failure to comply with its provisions by any owner, operator or superintendent of any coal mine or colliery, or any other person, a right of action shall accrue to the party injured for any direct damages he may have sustained thereby, and in case of loss of life by reason of such wilful neglect or failure aforesaid, a right of action shall accrue to the widow and lineal heirs of the person whose life shall be lost for like recovery of damages for the injury they shall have sustained.

ARTICLE XIX.

DEFINITION OF TERMS.

In this act, unless the context otherwise requires the term, "coal mine or colliery" includes every operation and work, both under ground and above ground used or to be used for the purpose of mining and preparing coal.

The term "workings" includes all the excavated parts of a mine, those abandoned as well as the places actually at work.

The term "mine" includes all underground workings and excavations and shafts, tunnels and other ways and openings ; also, all such shafts, slopes, tunnels and other openings in course of being sunk or driven, together with all roads, appliances, machinery and materials connected with the same below the surface.

The term "shaft" means a vertical opening through the strata and which is or may be used for the purpose of ventilation or drainage, or for hoisting men or material in connection with the mining of coal.

The term "slope" means any inclined way or opening used for the same purpose as a shaft.

The term "breaker" means the structure containing the machinery used for the preparation of coal.

The term "owners" and "operators" means any person or body corporate who is the immediate proprietor or lessee or occupier of any coal mine or colliery, or any part thereof. The term "owner" does not include a person or body corporate who merely receives a royalty, rent or fine from a coal mine or colliery, or part thereof, or is merely the proprietor of the mine, subject to any lease, grant or license for the working or operating thereof, or is merely the owner of the soil, and not interested in the minerals of the mine or any part thereof. But any "contractor" for the working of a mine or colliery, or of any part or district thereof, shall be subject to this act as an operator or owner in like manner as if he was the owner.

The term "superintendent" means the person who shall have, on behalf of the owner, general supervision of one or more mines or collieries.

ARTICLE XX.

All laws or parts of laws inconsistent or in conflict with the provisions of this act are hereby repealed.

AN ACT to provide for securing the health and safety of persons employed in and about the bituminous coal mines of Pennsylvania. Approved June 30, 1885.

SECTION 1. Be it enacted by the Senate and House of Representatives of the Commonwealth of Pennsylvania in General Assembly met, and it is hereby enacted by the authority of the same, That the owner, operator or superintendent of every bituminous coal mine, shall make or cause to be made, an accurate map or plan of such coal mine on a scale not exceeding one hundred feet to the inch, which map or plan shall exhibit all the openings or excavations, the shafts, tunnels, slopes, planes, gangways, entries, cross-headings, rooms, et cetera, and shall show the direction of the air currents therein, and shall accurately delineate the boundary lines between said coal mine and adjoining mines operated by other parties, and show the relation and proximity of the workings thereto. The maps shall also show the changes of level of the lowest entry in use for drainage connecting with each independent opening. The said map or plan, or a true copy thereof, together with a record of all the surveys of said boundary lines, and openings and excavations aforesaid, shall be kept at such mine by the said owner, operator or superintendent for the use of the mine inspector, and for the inspection of any miner working in said mine, whenever said miner shall have cause to fear that the working place where he is working is becoming dangerous by reason of its proximity to other workings, which may be supposed to contain water or dangerous gas. The said owner, operator or superintendent, shall as often as once in every six months, accurately place or cause to be placed on the map or plan of said coal mine, a plan of the excavations made of all the working places or other parts of such coal mine during the preceding six months, and whenever the workings or excavations of said coal mine or any part of the same have been driven to within ten feet of the boundary line, or when said coal mine or any part of the same is abandoned, the owner, operator or superintendent thereof, shall furnish the mine inspector within three months after the proximity to the boundary line as aforesaid, or after abandonment of the said mine or any part of the same, with a correct copy on tracing muslin of the map or plan of said mine, which shall accurately show all excavations and workings of such mine to date, exhibiting clearly the part or parts abandoned, and the part or parts in proximity to the boundary line aforesaid. The maps or plans of the several coal mines in each district, which are furnished to mine inspector as last aforesaid shall be the property of the Commonwealth, and shall remain in the care of the inspector of the district in which the said mines are situated, to be transferred by him to his successor in office, and in no case shall any copy of the same be made without the consent of the owner, operator or his agent. If the mine inspector shall find or have good reason to believe, that any map or plan of any coal mine made or furnished in pursuance of the provision of this act is materially inaccurate or imperfect, he is hereby authorized to cause a correct map or plan of said coal mine to be made at the expense of the owner or operator thereof, the cost of which shall be recoverable from said owner or operator as other debts are recoverable by law. Provided, however, That if the map or plan which is claimed to be inaccurate shall prove to have been correct then the Commonwealth shall be held liable for the expense incurred in making said test survey, and the same shall be paid by the State Treasurer upon warrants of the Auditor General, who shall require proper vouchers and satisfactory proof of the same.

SEC. 2. It shall not be lawful for the owner, operator, contractor, lessee or agent of any bituminous coal mine or for any firm, company, corporation or association, their clerks, servants, agents or employés, to employ any person at work within said coal mine or permit any person to be in said coal mine for the purpose of working therein, unless they are in communication with at least two openings, if the mine be worked by shaft or slope, which two shafts or slopes shall be separated by natural strata at all points by a distance of not less than one hundred and fifty feet except in mines already opened ; such distance may be less if in the judgment of the mine inspector one hundred and fifty feet is impracticable, and if the mine be worked by drift two openings exclusive of the air shaft and not less than twenty-four feet apart shall be required except in drift mines heretofore opened where the mine inspector of the district shall deem it impracticable. Provided, however, That an aggregate number not exceeding twenty persons may be employed in the mine at any one time until the second opening shall be reached and made available, which said second opening the mine inspector shall cause to be made without unnecessary delay, and in case of furnace ventilation being used before the second opening is reached, the furnace shall not be placed within forty feet of the foot of the shaft, slope or drift, and shall be well secured from danger from fire by brick or stone walls of sufficient thickness while being driven for making and perfecting the second opening.

SEC. 3. When the second opening or outlet is made which does not exceed 75 feet in vertical depth from the surface to the seam or stratum of coal that is being mined, it shall be set apart exclusively for the purpose of ingress or egress to or from the mine by any person or persons employed therein, and it shall not be clogged or obstructed with ice, machinery, pumps or currents of heated air or steam, and if the opening is a shaft it shall be fitted with safe and convenient stairs not less than two feet wide, and to not exceed an angle of sixty degrees descent, and landings of not less than eighteen inches wide and four feet long at easy and convenient distances, and all water coming from the surface or out of the strata in the shaft shall be conducted by rings, casing or otherwise, and be prevented from so falling down the shaft as to wet persons who are ascending or descending the stairway of the shaft ; if the second opening is a slope for a travelling way it shall not have a greater angle of descent than twenty degrees and may be any depth, but when the seam or stratum of coal at main outlet or escapement shaft, in connection with any mine exceeds 75 feet in vertical depth from the surface, the miners or other employes in the mine shall be lowered into or raised from said mine by machinery, and when the employés are lowered into or raised from said mine at the main outlet, the escapement shaft shall be fitted with safe and available machinery or safe and convenient stairs by which persons employed in the mine may readily escape in case of accident. The hoisting machinery and stairs used for lowering or raising the employés into or out of the mine shall be kept in a safe condition and inspected once each 24 hours by a competent person employed in whole or in part for that purpose. And such machinery and the method of its inspection shall be approved by the mining inspector of the district where the mine is situated; provided, that when miners are not at work in the mine, the said second shaft or slope may be used for the purpose of lowering material; provided further, that the requirements of this section shall not be applicable to stairways now in use when in the judgment of the inspector they are sufficient. The owner, operator, lessee or agent shall provide and maintain a metal tube from the top to the bottom of the shaft, suitably adapted to the free passage of sound through which conversation may be held between persons at the bottom and at the top of the shaft ; also, the ordinary means of signalling to and from the top and bottom of the shaft and an approved safety catch and sufficient cover overhead on every carriage, used for lowering and hoisting persons; and the said owner, operator, lessee or superintendent shall see that sufficient flanges are attached to the sides of the drum of every machine that is used for lowering and hoisting persons in and out of the mine, and also that adequate brakes are attached to the drum ; the main coupling chain attached to the socket of the wire rope shall be made of the best quality of iron and shall be tested by weights or otherwise to the satisfaction of the inspector of the district, and bridle chains shall be attached to the main socket from the cross pieces of the carriage, so that no single chain shall be used for lowering or raising persons into or out of the mine, and no greater number of persons shall be lowered or hoisted at any one time than may be permitted by the inspector of the district, and notice of the number so allowed to be lowered or hoisted at any one time shall be kept posted up by the owner, operator or superintendent in a conspicuous place at the opening of the shaft.

SEC. 4. The owner or agent of every bituminous coal mine, whether shaft or slope or drift, shall provide and hereafter maintain for every such mine simple means of ventilation, affording not less than one hundred cubic feet per minute for each and every person employed in said mine, and as much more as the circumstances may require, which shall be circulated around the main headings and cross headings and working places to an extent that will dilute, carry off and render harmless the noxious or dangerous gases generated therein, and all mines generating fire-damp shall be kept free of standing gas in the worked-out or abandoned parts of the same, as far as practicable and the entrance thereto shall be properly closed and cautionary notice shall be posted to warn persons of danger, and every working place and all other places where gas is known to exist or supposed to exist shall be carefully examined by the fire boss immediately before each shift with a safety-lamp, and in making said examina-tion it shall be the duty of the fire boss at each examination to leave at the face of every place so examined evidence of his presence, and it shall not be lawful for any miner to enter any mine or part of a mine generating fire-damp until it has been examined by the fire boss as aforesaid and reported by him to be safe.

SEC. 5. In order to better secure the proper ventilation of every coal mine and promote the health and safety of the persons employed therein, the owner or agent shall employ a competent and practical inside overseer to be called mining boss, who shall be a citizen and an experienced coal miner, and shall keep a careful watch over the ventilating apparatus and the airways, travelling ways, pumps and pump timbers and drainage and shall see that as the miners advance their excavations all loose coal, slate and rock overhead are carefully secured against falling therein or on the travelling ways, and that sufficient props, caps and timbers are furnished of suitable size and cut square at both ends, and as near as practicable to a proper length for the places where they are to be used, and such props, caps or timbers shall be delivered and placed in the working places of the miners, and every workman in want of props or timber and cap pieces shall notify the mining boss or his assistant of the fact at least one day in advance, giving the length and number of props or timbers and cap pieces required, but in cases of emergency the timbers may be ordered immediately upon the discovery of any danger; the place and manner of leaving the orders for the timber shall be designated and specified in the rules of the mine, and said working place shall be vacated until supplied with the timber needed; and shall see that all water be drained or hauled out of all working places before the miner enters, and as far as practicable kept dry while the miner is at work. And it shall be the duty of the mining boss to see that proper cut-throughs are made in the room pillars of the miners' places at such distances apart as in the judgment of the inspector may be deemed requi-site, not more than thirty-five, and not less than sixteen yards each for the pur-pose of ventilation. And in all travelling ways or road holes for shelter shall be made at least every thirty yards and be kept whitewashed; a space two feet six inches between the wagon and the rib shall be deemed sufficient for shelter. And the mining boss shall measure the air current at least once a week at the inlet and outlet, and at or near the face of the headings; he shall keep a record of such measurements, which shall be placed by him in a book kept for that purpose, the said book to be open for the examination of the inspector of the district. He shall also, on or about the 15th day of each month, mail to the inspector of his district a true copy of the air measurements given, stating also the number of persons employed in or about said mine, the number of mules and horses used and the number of days worked in each month. Blanks for such purpose shall be furnished him by the inspector of the district.

It shall be the further duty of the mining boss to immediately notify the agent or owner of the mine in writing of his inability to comply with the provisions of this section. It shall then become the duty of said superintendent operator, lessee or owner at once to attend to the matter complained of by the mining boss to comply with the provisions hereof. The safety lamps used for examining m nes or which may be used in working therein shall be furnished by and be the property of the owner of said mines and shall be in charge of the agent of such mine, and in all mines the doors used in assisting or directing the ventilation of the mine shall be so hung and adjusted that they will close themselves or be supplied with springs or pulleys so that they cannot be left standing open, and bore holes shall be kept not less than twelve feet in advance of the face and, when necessary, on the sides of working places which are being driven towards and in dangerous proximity to an abandoned mine or part of a mine suspected of containing inflammable gases or which is inundated with water. The mining boss, his assistant or assistants, shall visit and examine every working place in the mine at least once every alternate day while the miners of such place are or should be at work, and shall direct that each and every working place be properly secured by props or timber so that safety in all respects be assured and that no person shall be directed to work in an unsafe place unless it be for the purpose of making it safe. All owners or operators of bituminous coal mines shall keep posted in a conspicuous place about their mines printed rules submitted to and approved by the district mining inspector, defining the duties of all persons employed in or about said mines or collieries, which said notices shall be printed in the language or languages used by any ten miners working therein.

SEC. 6. Any miners, workmen or other person who shall intentionally injure any shaft, lamp, instrument, air course or brattice, or obstruct or throw open airways or carry lighted pipes or matches into places that are worked by safety-lamps, or handle or disturb any part of the machinery or open a door and not close it again, or enter any place of the mine against caution, or disobey any order given in carrying out the provisions of this act, or do any other act whereby the lives or the health of persons or the security of the mines or the machinery is endangered, shall be deemed guilty of a misdemeanor, and may be punished in a manner provided in the twenty-first section of this act ; all machinery about mines shall be properly fenced off and there shall be cut in the side of every hoisting shaft at the bottom thereof a travelling way sufficiently high and wide to enable persons to pass the shaft in going from one side of the mine to the other without passing over or under the cage or other hoisting apparatus.

SEC 7. If any person, firm or corporation is or shall hereafter be seized in his or their own right of coal lands, and it shall not be practicable to comply with the requirements of this act in regard to drainage and ventilation by means of opening on his or their own land and the same can be done by means of openings on adjacent lands, he or they may apply by petition to the court of quarter sessions of the proper county after ten days' notice to the owner or owners, their agent or attorney, setting forth the facts under oath or affirmation particularly describing the place or places where such opening or openings can be made, and that he or they cannot agree with the owner or owners of the land as to the amount to be paid for the privilege of making such opening or openings, whereupon the said court shall appoint three disinterested and competent citizens of the county to view the grounds designated and lay out from the point or points mentioned in such petition a passage or passages for air and water not more than sixteen feet in diameter by the shortest and most convenient route to the coal of such person, firm or corporation, preferring in all cases an opening through the coal strata where the same is practicable.

The said viewers shall at the same time assess the damages to be paid by the petitioner or petitioners to the owner or owners of such lands, which damages shall be fully paid before such opening is made. It shall be the duty of the petitioner or the viewers to give notice by at least three written or printed handbills posted on the premises at or near the place where such opening is proposed to be made at least five days prior to the time of meeting to attend to the duties of their appointment setting forth distinctly the time, place and object of their meeting and also to give personal notice to the owners, their agents or attorneys if residing in the same county, and the said viewers shall within thirty days after their appointment make report of their proceedings to the said court, stating the amount of damages awarded, accompanied by a map or plan of the proposed openings, and if no exceptions be filed to the said report within ten days after notice to the opposite party, his agent or attorney, of the filing of said report, it shall be marked, confirmed by the clerk, and the petitioner or petitioners may proceed to make said opening or openings and shall have the right to use the same for the purpose of ventilation and drainage as aforesaid and as a passage-way. The proceedings shall be recorded in the road docket of the proper county and the pay of viewers shall be the same as in road cases. If exceptions be filed they shall be disposed of by the said court as speedily as possible, and both parties to have the right to take depositions as in road cases. If, however, the petitioner desires to make such opening before the final disposition of such exceptions he shall have the right to do so by giving bond to be approved by the court, securing the damages as provided by law in the case of lateral railroads.

SEC. 8. In the year one thousand eight hundred and eighty-nine and every four years thereafter the Governor shall as hereinafter provided during the month of February appoint two mining engineers of good repute and of known experience and practice at the time. He also shall as hereinafter provided during the same month and every four years thereafter notify three president judges of the courts of common pleas of the judicial districts of the State containing bituminous coal mines, whose duty it shall be, each of them, to appoint one reputable miner of at least five years' practical experience in the mining region of Pennsylvania, in practice at least three months prior to his appointment, and a citizen of the Commonwealth not less than five years: Provided, That any person having been employed five months prior to the meeting of the examining board as superintendent, State or county officer,

21

shall not serve on examining board.   The two engineers and the three miners so appointed shall constitute a board of examiners whose duty it shall be to inquire into the character and qualifications of candidates for the office of inspector of mines under the provisions of this act.   The examining board so constituted shall meet in the city of Pittsburg on the first Monday of April, and when called together by the Governor for extra occasions at such time and place as he may designate, and after being duly organized, and having taken and subscribed before any officer authorized to administer the same, the follow-ing oath, namely: We the undersigned do solemnly swear or affirm that we will perform the duties of examiners of applicants for appointment as inspec-tor of bituminous coal mines to the best of our abilities and that in recom-mending or rejecting said applicants we will be governed by the evidence of the qualifications to fill the position under the law creating the same, and not by any consideration of political or other personal favor; that we will certify all whom we may find qualified according to the true intent and meaning of the act and none others; shall proceed to the examination which shall be in writing, of those who may represent themselves as candidates for said office, and they shall certify to the Governor the names of all such applicants as they shall find competent to fill the office under the provisions of this act, which names with the certificates and their percentage and the oath of the examiner shall be mailed to the Secretary of the Commonwealth and be filed in his office; Provided, That no person shall be returned as competent whose percent-age shall be less than ninety per cent., and such certificate shall be valid only when recommended by four of the examining board.   The qualification of candidates for said office of inspecters of mines to be inquired into and certi-fied by said examiners shall be as follows, namely: They shall be citizens of Pennsylvania, of temperate habits, of good repute, as men of personal integ-rity, shall have attained the age of thirty years, and shall have had at least five years practical experience in the workings of the coal mines of Pennsylvania, and upon the examination they shall give evidence of such theoretical as well as practical knowledge and general intelligence regarding mines and mining and the working thereof, and all noxious gases, as will satisfy the examiners of their capability and fitness for the duties imposed upon inspectors of mines by the provisions of this act.   The board of examiners shall also at their meeting or when at any time called by the Governor together for an extra meeting divide the bituminous coal counties of the State into eight inspection districts as nearly equal to the labor to be performed as is possible, and at any subsequent calling of the board of examiners, this division may be revised as experience may prove to be advisable, and they shall immediately after the examination, furnish each person who came before said examination board to be examined all questions which were given at the examination, on printed slips of paper and to be marked, solved right or wrong, as the case may be. The board of examiners shall each receive five dollars per day and all neces-sary expenses, to be paid out of the State Treasury.

Upon the filing of the certificates of the examining board in the office of the Secretary of the Commonwealth, the Governor shall from the names so certi-fied, commission one person to be inspector of mines for each district, as fixed by the examiners in pursuance of the act, whose commission shall be for a full term of four years, to be computed from the fifteenth day of May, one thousand eight hundred and eighty-five. Always provided, however, the highest candidate or candidates in percentage shall have priority to be commissioned for a full term or unexpired term, before those candidates of a lower percentage, and in case of a tie in percentage, the oldest candidate shall be commissioned. As often as vacancies occur in said offices of inspectors of mines, the Governor shall commission for the unexpired term from the names on file the highest in percentage above ninety per centum, in the office of the Secretary of the Commonwealth, until the number shall be exhausted, and whenever this may occur, the Governor shall cause the aforesaid board of examiners to meet, who shall examine persons who may present themselves for the vacant office of inspector in the same manner as herein provided, and the board of examiners shall certify to the Governor one person highest in percentage to be commissioned by him for the office of inspector for the unexpired term, and any vacancies that may occur in the examining board shall be filled by those or their successors in whose jurisdiction the vacancy occurred.

Each inspector of mines shall receive for his services an annual salary of two thousand dollars and actual travelling expenses, to be paid quarterly by the State Treasurer upon warrant of the Auditor General, and all mine inspectors hereafter appointed shall make their residence and keep an office in the district for which they are commissioned. Each inspector is hereby authorized to procure such instruments and chemical tests, stationery, and to incur such expense of communication from time to time as may be necessary to the proper discharge of his duties under this act at the cost of the State, which shall be paid by the State Treasurer upon accounts duly certified by him and audited by the proper department of the State. All instruments, plans, books, memoranda, notes, et cetera, pertaining to the office shall be the property of the State and shall be delivered to their successors in office. That in addition to the expenses now allowed by law to the mine inspector in enforcing the several provisions of this act to which this is supplementary, they shall be allowed all necessary expenses by them incurred in enforcing the several provisions of said laws in the respective courts of the Commonwealth, the same to be paid by the State Treasurer on warrants drawn by the Auditor General after auditing the same. All such accounts presented by the mine inspector to the Auditor General shall be itemized and first approved by the court before which the proceedings were instituted.

SEC. 9. Each inspector of bituminous coal mines shall, before entering upon the discharge of his duties, give bond in the sum of five thousand dollars, with sureties to be approved by the president judge of the district in which he resides, conditioned for the faithful discharge of his duty, and take an oath (or affirmation) to discharge his duties impartially and with fidelity to the best of his knowledge and ability.

But no person who shall act as a manager or agent of any coal mine or as a mining engineer, or to be interested in operating any coal mine, shall at the same time act as an inspector of coal mines under this act.

SEC. 10. The inspector of bituminous coal mines shall each devote the whole of his time to the duties of his office. It shall be his duty to examine the mines in his district as often as possible, which shall not be less than once in three months, and report how often he has visited each mine in the year to see that all the provisions of this act are observed and strictly carried out, and he shall make record of all examinations of mines, showing the condition in which he finds them, especially in reference to ventilation and drainage, the number of mines in his district, the number of persons employed in each mine, the extent to which the law is obeyed, the progress made in the improvement sought to be secured by the passage of this act, the number of accidents and deaths resulting from injuries received in or about the mine, with cause of such accident or death, which record completed to the 31st day of December of each and every year, shall, on or before the first day of February following, be filed in the office of the Secretary of Internal Affairs, to be by him recorded and included in the annual report of his department.

SEC. 11. That the inspectors may be enabled to perform the duties herein imposed upon them, they shall have the right at all times to enter any bituminous coal mine to make examination or obtain information. They shall notify the owners, operators, lessees, superintendent or mining bosses in writing and keep a copy thereof immediately of the discovery of any violation of this act and of the penalty imposed thereby for such violation, and in case of such notice being disregarded for the space of five days, they shall institute proceedings against the owner, operator, lessee, superintendent or mining boss of the mine under the provisions of section twenty-one of this act. In case, however, where in the judgment of the inspector of any district, delay may jeopardize life or limb, he shall at once notify one of the inspectors of the other districts, whereupon they shall at once proceed to the mine where the danger exists and examine into the matter, and if after full investigations thereof they shall be agreed in the opinion that there is immediate danger they shall apply, in the name of the Commonwealth, to the court of common pleas of the county, or in case the court should not be in session, to the judge of the said court in chambers in which the mine may be located for an injunction to suspend all work in and about such mine, whereupon said court or judge shall at once proceed to hear and determine speedily the same, and if the cause appears to be sufficient after hearing the parties and their evidence as in like cases shall issue their writ to restrain the working of said mine, until all cause of danger is removed, and the cost of said proceedings, including the charges of attorney prosecuting the same, shall be borne by the owner, lessee or agent of the mine ; provided, that no fee exceeding the sum of twenty-five dollars shall be taxed in any one case for the attorney prosecuting such case ; provided further, that if said court shall find the cause not sufficient, then the case shall be dismissed and the costs shall be borne by the county.

SEC. 12. Whenever by reason of any explosion or other accident in any bituminous coal mine, or the machinery connected therewith, loss of life or serious personal injury shall occur, it shall be the duty of the person having charge of such mine or colliery to give notice thereof forthwith to the inspector of the district, and if any person is killed thereby, to the coroner of the county, who shall give due notice of the inquest to be held. If the coroner shall determine to hold an inquest the mine inspector shall be allowed to testify and offer such testimony as he may deem necessary to thoroughly inform the said inquest of the causes of the death. And the said inspector shall have authority at any time to appear before such coroner and jury and question or cross-question any witness, and in choosing a jury for the purpose of holding such inquest it shall be the duty of the coroner to impanel a jury, no one of whom shall be directly or indirectly interested. It shall be the duty of the inspector upon being notified as herein provided to immediately repair to the scene of the accident and make such suggestions as may appear necessary to secure the future safety of the men, and if the results of the explosion or accident do not require an investigation by the coroner he shall proceed to investigate and ascertain the cause of the explosion or accident and make a record thereof, which he shall file as provided for, and to enable him to make the investigation he shall have power to compel the attendance of persons to testify and to administer oaths or affirmations. The cost of such investigation shall be paid by the county in which the accident occurred in the same manner as costs of inquests held by the coroners or justices of the peace are paid.

SEC. 13. The court of common pleas of any county in the proper district, upon a petition signed by not less than fifteen reputable citizens, who shall be miners, owners or lessees of mines, and with the affidavit or one or more of said petitioners attached setting forth that any inspector of mines neglects his duty or is incompetent, or that he is guilty of a malfeasance in office, shall issue a citation in the name of the Commonwealth to 'the said inspector to appear on not less than fifteen days notice, upon a day fixed before said court, at which time the court shall proceed to inquire into and investigate the allegations of the petitioners. . If the court find that said inspector is neglectful of his duties or is incompetent to perform the duties of his office or that he is guilty of malfeasance in office, the court shall certify the same to the Governor, who shall declare the office of said inspector vacant and proceed in compliance with the provisions of this act to supply the vacancy. The costs of said investigation shall, if the charges are sustained, be imposed upon the inspector, but if the charges are not sustained, they shall be imposed upon the petitioners.

SEC. 14. The inspector shall exercise a sound discretion in the enforcement of the provisions of this act, and if the operator, owner or miners shall not be satisfied with any decision the inspector may arrive at in the discharge of his duties under this act, which said decision shall be in writing, signed by the mine inspector, the said owner, operator, miner or miners shall forthwith appeal from such decision to the Court of Quarter Sessions of the county wherein the mine is located, and said court shall speedily determine the question involved in said decision, and appeal which said decision shall be binding and conclusive. The court in its discretion may appoint three practicable, reputable, competent and disinterested persons whose duty it shall be, under instructions from the said court, to forthwith examine such mine, and make report under oath of the facts as they exist, or may have been together with their opinions thereon. The report of said Board shall become absolute, unless exceptions thereto shall be filed within ten days after notice of the filing thereof to the owner, operator, miner or miners or inspector, and if exceptions are filed the court shall at once hear and determine the same, and the decision shall be final and conclusive. If the court shall finally sustain the decision of the inspector then the appellant shall pay all costs of such proceedings. And if the court shall not sustain the decision of the inspector, then such costs shall be paid by the county, or by the appellant and county in such proportion as the court shall determine. That no appeal from any decision made by any mine inspector shall work as a supersedeas to such decision during the pendency of such appeal but all such decisions shall be in full force until reversed or modified by the proper court.

SEC. 15. On the petition of the mine inspector of any district, the courts of common pleas in any county in said district, shall at the first term after the passage of this act, appoint an Examining Board consisting of a mine inspector, an operator and a miner, who are citizens of the United States, and shall have at least five years experience in the bituminous mines of the State, who shall examine any person applying thereto as to his competency and qualifications to discharge the duties of mining boss. The said Board of Examiners shall meet at the call of the inspector, and they shall grant certificates to all persons whose examination shall disclose their fitness for the duties of mining boss ; and such certificates shall be sufficient evidence of the holder's competency and qualifications for the duties of the said office : Provided, That any person who shall have been employed as a miner at least five years in the bituminous mines of Pennsylvania, and as mining boss continuously by the same person or firm for the period of one year next preceding the passage of this act, shall be entitled to a certificate without undergoing said examination, but he shall not be employed by any other person or firm without having undergone such examination. The Examining Board shall hold their office for the period of four years from the date of their appointment, and shall receive five dollars per day for each day necessarily employed, and mileage at the rate of three cents per mile for each mile necessarily travelled, to be paid by the Conmonwealth. For each certificate granted the Board shall receive the sum of one dollar, which shall be for the use of the Commonwealth.

No person shall act as a fire boss in any bituminous mine unless granted a certificate of competency by any of the mine inspectors of the bituminous region of Pennsylvania, and it shall be unlawful for any owner, operator, contractor, superintendent or agent to employ any person as fire boss who has not obtained such certificate.

After January first, one thousand eight hundred and eighty-six, no owner, operator, contractor, lessee, superintendent or agent shall employ any mining boss or fire boss who does not have the certificate of competency or service required by this section.

And if any accident shall occur in any mine in which a mining boss or fire boss shall be employed who has no certificate of competency or service as required by this section by which any miner shall be killed or injured, he or his heirs shall have right of action against such operator, owner, superintendent, contractor, lessee or agent, and shall recover the full value of the damages sustained.

SEC. 16. No boy under the age of twelve years, and no woman or girl of any age shall be employed or permitted to be in any bituminous coal mine for the purpose of employment therein, nor shall any boy under the age of ten years or any woman or girl of any age be employed or permitted to be in or about the outside structure or workings of any bituminous mine or colliery for the purpose of employment : Provided, however, that this provision shall not effect the employment of a boy or a female of suitable age in an office or in the performance of clerical work at such mine or colliery.

SEC. 17. For any injury to person or property occasioned by any violation of this act or any wilful failure to comply with its provisions a right of action against the party at fault shall accrue to the party injured for the direct damage sustained thereby, and in any case of loss of life by reason of such violation or wilful failure a right of action against the party at fault, shall accrue to the widow and lineal heirs of the person whose life shall be lost for like recovery of damages for the injury they shall have sustained.

SEC. 18. It shall be the duty of owners, operators, contractors superintendents, lessees or agents to keep at the mouth of the drift, shaft or slope, or at such other places as shall be designated by the mine inspectors, stretchers, properly constructed, for the purpose of carrying away any miner or employo working in or about such mine who may in any way be injured in and about his employment.

SEC. 19. It shall be the duty of the mine inspector on each visit to any mine to make out a written or partly written and partly printed report of the condition in which he finds such mine and post the same in the office of the mine. The said report shall give the date of the visit, the number of visits during the year, the total number of mines in the district, the number of feet of air in circulation and where measured and such other information as he shall deem necessary. And the said report shall remain posted in the office for one year and said report may be examined by any miner or person employed in and about such mine.

SEC. 20. On or before the fifteenth day of January in each year, the owner, operator or superintendent of every mine or colliery shall send to the inspector of the district a correct report specifying with respect to the year ending the thirty-first of December, preceding such report, the name of the owner or operator and officers of the mine and the quantity of coal mined. The report shall be in such form and give such information as may be from time to time required and prescribed by the mine inspector of the district. Blank forms for such reports shall be furnished by the Commonwealth.

SEC. 21. The neglect or refusal to perform the duties required to be performed by any section of this act by the parties therein required to perform them or the violation of any of the provisions or requirements hereof shall be deemed a misdemeanor, and shall upon conviction be punished by a fine of not less than two hundred dollars and not exceeding five hundred dollars, at the discretion of the court. And in default of payment of such fine and costs for the space of ten days the defendant shall be sentenced to imprisonment in the county jail for a period not exceeding six months.

SEC. 22. The provisions of this act shall not apply to any mine employing less than ten persons in any one period of twenty-four hours.

SEC. 23. All acts or parts of acts supplied or·inconsistent herewith are hereby repealed.

MINING LAWS OF WASHINGTON TERRITORY.

AN ACT in relation to coal mines, approved Feb. 2, 1888.

SECTION 1. That the owner or agent, operator, of each and every coal mine in this Territory, shall make, or cause to be made, at the discretion of the inspector, or person acting in that capacity, an accurate map or plan of the workings of such coal mine, and of each and every vein thereof, showing the general inclination of the strata, together with any material deflections in said workings, and the boundary lines of said coal mines, and deposit a true copy of said map or plan with the inspector of coal mines, to be filed in his office, said map or plan, with the recorder of the county in which said coal mine is situated, to be filed in his office, both of which said copy shall be deposited as aforesaid within three months from the day when this act shall go into effect; and the original or a copy of such map or plan, shall also be kept for inspection at the office of said coal mine; and during the month of January of each and every year, after this act shall go into effect, the said owner, agent or operator, snall furnish the inspector as aforesaid, with a statement and further map or plan, of the progress of the workings of such coal mine, continued from the last report to the end of the December month just preceding, and the inspector shall correct his map or plan of said workings in accordance with the statement and map or plan thus furnished; and when any coal mine is worked out or abandoned, that fact shall be reported to the inspector, and the map or plan of such coal mine in the office of said inspector shall be carefully corrected and verified.

SEC. 2. Whenever the owner, agent or operator of any coal mine shall neglect or refuse to furnish the said inspector as aforesaid, with the statement, the map or plan, or addition thereto, as provided in the first section of this act, at the times and in the manner therein provided, the said inspector is hereby authorized to cause an accurate map or plan of the workings of such coal mine to be made at the expense of said owner, agent or operator, and the cost thereof may be recovered by law from said owner, agent or operator, in the same manner as other debts, by suit in the name of the inspector and for his use.

SEC. 3. In all coal mines that are, or have been in operation prior to the first day of January, in the year of our Lord, one thousand eight hundred and eighty-eight, and which are worked by or through a shaft, slope or drift, if there is not already an escapement shaft to each and every said coal mine, or communication between each and every coal mine, and some other contiguous mine, then there shall be an escapement shaft or other communication, such as shall be approved by the mine inspector, making at least two distinct means of ingress and egress for all persons employed or permitted to work in such coal mine; such escapement shaft should be a downcast and an upcast, and located three hundred yards from the engine house. Such escapement shaft or other communication with a contiguous mine as aforesaid, shall be constructed in connection with every vein or stratum of coal worked in such coal mine, which shall be at least three and one-half feet high, and at least five feet wide, and in no instance shall the height of said roadway be less than the thickness of the vein or stratum of coal through which it is driven ; and the time to be allowed for such construction shall be one year, when such mine is under five hundred feet in depth ; two years for all mines over five hundred (500) feet in depth from the first day of July, A. D. 1888; and in all cases where the working force of one mine has been driven up to or into the workings of another mine, the respective owners of such mines, while operating the same, shall keep open a roadway, at least five feet high and five feet wide, thereby forming a communication as contemplated in this act ; and for a failure to do so, shall be subject to the penalty provided for in section ten of this act, for each and every day such roadway is unnecessarily closed; each and every such escapement shaft shall be separated from the main shaft by such extent of natural strata as shall secure safety to the men employed in such mines, such distance to be left to the discretion of the mine inspector or person acting in that capacity, and shall be equipped with stairways or ladders, having landing places or platforms at least every twenty feet from the bottom to the top, or in lieu thereof such hoisting apparatus as will enable the employés in the mine to make safe and speedy exit in case of danger. In all coal mines that shall go into operation for the first time after the first day of January A. D., eighteen hundred and eighty-eight, and in all cases where such mine or mines shall hereafter be put in operation in this Territory, the owner thereof, or the lessee or occupant of the same shall construct an escapement shaft as is required by this act to be constructed in coal mines in this Territory, at the rate of five hundred feet per annum until such escapement shaft shall have been fully completed ; and provided further, that nothing in this section shall be construed to extend the time heretofore allowed by law for constructing escapement shafts in mines going into operation for the first time before said first day of January, A. D., eighteen hundred and eighty-eight.

SEC. 4. The owner, agent or operator of every coal mine, whether operated by shaft, slope or drift, shall provide and maintain in every such mine a good and sufficient amount of ventilation for such men and animals as may be employed therein, the amount of air in circulation to be in no case less than one hundred cubic feet for each man per minute and six hundred cubic feet for each animal per minute, measured at the foot of the downcast, and the same to be increased at the discretion of the inspector, according to the character and extent of the workings, or the amount of powder used in blasting ; and said volume of air shall be forced and circulated to the face of every working place throughout the mine, so that said mine shall be free from standing powder smoke and gases of every kind. In all mines where fire-damp is generated, every working place, where the same is known or thought to exist, shall be examined every morning with a safety-lamp, by a competent person, before any other persons are allowed to enter, and whenever the inspector shall find men working without sufficient air, or under any unsafe condition, he may remove the same to other parts of the mine or from the mine altogether. The inspector shall visit and inspect breasts and working faces of the mines and leave a mark as to safety. The ventilation required by this section may be produced by any suitable appliances, but in case a furnace shall be used for ventilating purposes, it shall be built in such a manner as to prevent the communication of fire to any part of the works, by lining the upcast with incombustible material for a sufficient distance up from said furnace; *provided*, it shall not be lawful to use a furnace for ventilating purposes, or for any other purposes, that shall emit smoke into any compartment constructed in, or adjoining any coal hoisting shaft or slope, where the hoisting shaft or slope is the only means provided for the ingress or egress of persons employed in said coal mines.   That it shall be unlawful where there is but one means of ingress or egress provided at a coal shaft or slope, to construct and use a ventilating furnace that shall emit smoke into a shaft as an upcast, where the shaft or slope used as a means of ingress or egress by persons employed in said coal mines is the only means provided for furnishing air to persons employed therein.

SEC. 5. The owner, agent or operator shall provide that bore holes shall be kept twenty feet in advance of the face of each and every working place, and if necessary, on both sides, when driving towards an abandoned mine or part of a mine suspected to contain inflammable gases, or to be inundated with water.

SEC. 6. The owner, agent or operator of every coal mine operated by shaft shall provide suitable means of signalling between the bottom and top thereof, and shall also provide safe means of hoisting and lowering persons in a cage covered with boiler iron, so as to keep safe, as far as possible, persons descend-ing into and ascending out of such shaft, and such cage shall be furnished with guides to conduct it on slides through such shaft, with a sufficient brake on every drum to prevent accident in case of the giving out or breaking of the machinery; and such cage shall be furnished with spring catches intended and provided, as far as possible, to prevent the consequences of cable breaking or the loosening or disconnecting of the machinery; and no props or rails shall be lowered in a cage while men are descending into or ascending out of said mine.   The hoisting ropes shall be inspected by the manager of the mine or his agent with respect to safety each morning; *provided*, that the provisons of this section, relating to covering cages with boiler iron, shall not apply to coal mines less than one hundred feet in depth, where the coal is raised by horse power.   No person under the age of fifteen years, or females of any age, shall be permitted to enter any mine to work therein.   Any party or person neglecting or refusing to perform the duties required to be performed by sections three, four, five, six, seven and eight shall be deemed guilty of a mis-demeanor and punished by fine in the discretion of the court trying the same, subject, however, to the limitations as provided by section ten of this act.

SEC. 7. No owner, agent or operator of any coal mine, operated by shaft or slope, shall place in charge of any engine, whereby men are lowered into or hoisted out of the mines, any but an experienced, competent and sober person not under the age of eighteen years; and no person shall ride upon a loaded cage or wagon used for hoisting purposes in any shaft or slope, and in no case shall more than twelve persons ride on any cage or car at one time, nor shall any coal be hoisted out of any coal mine while persons are descending into such coal mine; and the number of persons to ascend out of or descend into any coal mine, on one cage, shall be determined by the inspector; the maximum number so fixed shall not be less than four nor more than twelve, nor shall be lowered or hoisted, nor no man shall handle the bell rope, except the man in charge at the bottom of the shaft.

SEC. 8. All boilers used in generating steam in and about coal mines shall be kept in good order, and the agent, owner or operator, as aforesaid, shall have said boilers examined and inspected by a competent boiler maker, or other qualified person, as often as once every six months, and oftener if the inspector shall deem it necessary, and the result of every such examination shall be certified, in writing, to the mine inspector; and the top of each and every shaft, and the entrance to each and every intermediate working vein shall be securely fenced by gates properly covering and protecting such shaft, and entrance thereto ; and the entrance to every abandoned slope, air or other shaft shall be securely fenced off; and every steam boiler shall be provided with a proper steam gauge, water gauge and safety valve ; and all underground, self-acting or engine planes, or gangways, on which coal cars are drawn and persons travel, shall be provided with some proper means of regulating between the stopping places and the end of said planes or gangways, and sufficient places of refuge at the sides of such planes or gangways shall be provided at intervals of not more than twenty feet apart.

SEC. 9. Whenever loss of life, or serious personal injury shall occur by reason of any explosion, or of any accident whatsoever, in or about any coal mine, it shall be the duty of the person having charge of such coal mine to report the facts thereof, without delay, to the mine inspector of the district in which said coal mine is situated; and if any person is killed thereby, to notify the coroner of the county also, or in his absence or inability to act, any justice of the peace of said county ; and the said inspector shall, if he deem it necessary from the facts reported, immediately go to the scene of said accident, and make such suggestion and render such assistance as he may deem necessary for the safety of men.   And the inspector shall investigate and ascertain the cause of such explosion or accident, and make a report thereof, which he shall preserve with the other records of his office ; and to enable him to make such investigations, he shall have power to compel the attendance of witnesses, and administer oaths or affirmations to them, and the cost of such investigation shall be paid by the county in which such accident has occurred, in the same manner as costs of coroner's inquests are now paid.   And the failure of the person in charge of the coal mine in which any such accident may have occurred, to give notice to the inspector or coroner, as provided for in this section, shall subject such person to a fine of not less than twenty-five dollars nor more than one hundred dollars, to be recovered in the name of the people of the Territory of Washington, before any justice of the peace of such county, and such fine, when collected, shall be paid into the county treasury for the use of the county in which any such accident may have occurred.

SEC. 10. In all other cases in which punishment is provided by fine under this act for a breach of any of its provisions, the fine for a first offence shall not be less than five hundred dollars and not more than one thousand dollars, and for the second offence not less than one thousand dollars nor more than two thousand dollars, in the discretion of the court, except as specially provided for in section nine of this act.

SEC. 11. The first and second judicial districts shall constitute the first inspection district, the third and fourth judicial districts shall constitute the same inspection district ; an inspector of coal mines for each of said districts shall be appointed by the governor, by and with the advice and consent of the Territorial council.   Each inspector shall hold his office for the term of two years, except as provided for in section twelve of this act, from and after the first Monday in February, A. D. 1888, and until his successor is appointed and qualified. Each inspector shall be a qualified elector and have a knowledge of mining engineering sufficient to conduct the development of coal mines, and a practical knowledge of the methods of conducting mining for coal in the presence of explosive gases, and of the proper ventilation of coal mines. He shall have had a practical mining experience of ten years, two of which shall have been in this Territory, and shall not be interested as owner, operator, stockholder, superintendent or mining engineer of any coal mine during his term of office, and shall be of good moral character and temperate habits, and shall not be guilty of any act tending to the injury of miners or operators of mines during his term of office. The inspectors shall be provided by the Territory with the most approved modern instruments for carrying out the intention of this act. The inspectors, before assuming the duties of their several offices, shall take an oath of office, as provided for by the statutes of the Territory as in case of other Territorial officers. The salary of the district inspectors shall be fifteen hundred dollars ($1500) per annum each, and the auditor of the Territory is hereby authorized to draw his warrant on the treasury in their favor, quarterly, for the amount specified in this section for the salary of each inspector out of any moneys not otherwise appropriated; *provided*, that the county board of any county may appoint an assistant inspector for such county, who shall act under the direction of the district inspector in the performance of his duties, and shall receive not less than three dollars ($3.00) and not more than five dollars ($5.00) per day for the time actually employed, to be paid out of the county treasury, and he may be removed by such county board at any time.

SEC. 12. The inspectors provided for by this act shall devote their whole time and attention to the duties of their office, and make personal examination of every mine within their respective districts, and shall see that every necessary precaution is taken to insure the health and safety of the workmen employed in such mines, and that the provisions and requirements of the mining laws of this Territory are faithfully observed and obeyed and the penalties of the same enforced. Upon a petition signed by not less than three reputable coal operators, or ten coal miners, setting forth that any inspector of coal mines neglects his duties, or that he is incompetent, or that he is guilty of malfeasance in office, or guilty of any act tending to the injury of miners or operators of mines, it may be lawful for the governor to issue a citation to the said inspector to appear, at no less than fifteen days notice on a day fixed, before him, when he shall proceed to inquire into and investigate the allegations of the petitioners, and if he find that the said inspector is neglectful of his duty, or that he is, by reason of causes that existed before his appointment, or that have arisen since his appointment, incompetent to perform the duties of said office, or that he is guilty of malfeasance in office, or guilty of any act tending to the injury of miners or operators of mines, he shall declare the office of inspector of said district vacant, and shall appoint a properly qualified person to fill the office, in compliance with the provisions of this act; and the cost of said investigation shall be borne by the removed inspector; but [if] the allegations of the petitioners are not sustained by the decision of the governor, the costs shall be paid by the petitioner.

SEC. 13. That when two or more coal mines are so located as to allow the said mines to be connected by permanent entries between and the land or mining rights lying between such mines is owned by any person or persons with whom the owner or owners of said mine or mines are unable to agree for the purchase of the right of way for the connecting entry or entries between such mines, and the right to maintain and use such entry as a connecting entry is claimed, such owner or owners of any such coal mine or mines, or either of them, may acquire such right or title in the manner that may be now or hereafter provided by any law of eminent domain.

SEC. 14. It shall be lawful for the inspector, provided for in this act, to enter, examine and inspect any and all coal mines and machinery belonging thereto, at all reasonable times, by day or by night, but so as not to obstruct or hinder the necessary workings of such coal mines, and the owner, agent or operator of every such coal mine is hereby required to furnish all necessary facilities for entering and making such examination and inspection, and if the said owner, agent or operator aforesaid shall refuse to permit such inspection, the inspector shall file affidavit setting forth such refusal with the judge of the district court in said county in which said mine is situated and obtain an order on such owner, agent or operator so refusing as aforesaid, commanding him to permit and furnish such necessary facilities for the inspection of such coal mine, or to be adjudged to stand in contempt of court and punished accordingly, and if the said inspector shall after examination of any coal mine and the works and machinery pertaining thereto, find the same to be worked contrary to the provisions of this act, or unsafe for the workmen therein employed, said inspector shall, through the prosecuting attorney of his county, or any attorney, in case of his refusal to act, acting in the name and on behalf of the Territory, proceed against the owner, agent or operator of such coal mine by injunction without bond, after giving at least two days' notice to such owner, agent or operator; and said owner, agent or operator shall have the right to appear before the judge to whom the application is made who shall hear the same on affidavits and such other testimony as may be offered in support as well as in opposition thereto, and if sufficient cause appear, the court or judge in vacation by order shall prohibit the further working of any such coal mine in which persons may be unsafely employed contrary to the provisions of this act, until the same shall have been made safe and the requirements of this act shall have been complied with, and the court shall award such costs in the matter of said injunction as may be just; but any such proceedings so commenced shall be without prejudice to any other remedy permitted by law for enforcing the provisions of this act.

SEC. 15. For any injury to person or property, occasioned by any wilful violations of this act or wilful failure to comply with any of its provisions, a right of action shall accrue to the party injured for any direct damages sustained thereby; and in case of loss of life by reason of such wilful violation or wilful failure as aforesaid, a right of action shall accrue to the widow of the person so killed, his lineal heirs or adopted children or to any other person or persons who were before such loss of life dependent for support on the person or persons so killed for a like recovery of damages for the injuries sustained by reason of such loss of life or lives; *provided*, that the occurrence of any accident in such mine or mines which shall result in injury or death to any person employed therein, shall be *prima facie* evidence of neglect upon the part of the person or corporation operating such mine. And *provided further,* that no employé or his legal representative shall be debarred recovery in such action where the injury was occasioned by the negligence of a co-employé, unless such employé was selected and employed by such person.

SEC. 16. Any miner, workman or other person who shall knowingly injure any water-gauge, barometer, air-course or brattice, or shall obstruct, or throw open any air-ways, or carry any lighted lamps or matches into places that are worked by the light of safety-lamps, or shall handle or disturb any part of the machinery of the hoisting engine, or open a door in the mine and not have the same closed again, whereby danger is produced, either to the mine or those at work therein ; or who shall enter into any part of the mine against caution ; or who shall disobey any order given in pursuance of this act ; or who shall do any wilful act whereby the lives and health of persons working in the mine, or the security of the mine or mines or the machinery thereof is endangered, shall be deemed guilty of a misdemeanor, and, upon conviction, shall be punished by fine or imprisonment, at the discretion of the court ; *provided,* that where such wilful violation of the provisions of this act shall result in death, that the owner, operator, manager or managing officer of the corporation or other person so violating the provisions of this act shall be deemed guilty of murder.

SEC. 17. The owner, agent or operator of any coal mine shall keep a sufficient supply of timber, where required to be used as props, so that the workmen may at all times be able to properly secure the said workings from caving in ; and it shall be the duty of the owner, agent or operator to send down all such props when required, and the same to be delivered at the entrance to the working face.

SEC. 18. That all mines hoisting coal by steam power, from shaft or slope, having no other means of ingress or egress than that afforded to persons employed therein and [than] by said shaft or slope, shall within ninety days after the first day of July, A. D. 1888, have all engine and boiler houses roofed and sided with fire-proof materials, and they shall be situated not less than fifty feet from the mouth of the said shaft or slope ; that the hoisting derricks erected over said hoisting shaft or near said slope, if enclosed, and all the coal chutes, buildings and constructions, within a radius of fifty feet of the mouth of the said hoisting shaft or slope, shall be covered and sided with fire-proof materials : and the person in charge, the owners or operators thereof, shall provide a steam pump and have the same conveniently situated, and a sufficient supply of water and hose always ready for use in any part of the buildings, chutes or constructions within a radius of fifty feet of said coal hoistings, shaft or slope ; and if the person in charge of any such coal shaft or slope shall refuse or neglect to comply with the provisions of this act, then the inspector of coal mines for the county in which the said shafts or slope is situated, shall proceed, through the prosecuting attorney of his country, or any attorney, in case of his refusal to act, acting in the name and on behalf of the Territory, against the owner, agent or operator of said shaft or slope, by injunction, without bond, after giving at least two days' notice to such owner, agent or operator ; and the said owner, agent or operator shall have the right to appear before the judge to whom the application is made, who shall hear the same on affidavits, and such other testimony as may be offered, in support as well as in opposition thereto ; and if it be found that the owner, agent or operator of said shaft or slope has refused or neglected to comply with the provisions of this act, the court, or judge in vacation, by order, shall prohibit the further workings of any such coal shaft or slope until the owner, agent or operator shall have complied with the terms of this act.

SEC. 19. The use of iron needles and iron tamping bars, not tipped with five inches of copper, is hereby declared unlawful. Any failure on the part of a coal miner, or an employé in any coal mine, to conform to the terms and requirements of this act, shall subject such miner or employé to a fine of not less than five dollars nor more than twenty-five dollars, with costs of prosecution for each offence, to be recovered by civil suit before any justice of the peace ; said fines, when collected, to be paid into the treasury of the county where the offence was committed, to the credit of the fund provided for the payment of the county inspector of mines.

SEC. 20. It shall be the duty of the grand jury of each county or at least once a year or oftener, if so directed by the judge of the district court, to inspect all coal mines in operation and worked in such county, and certify their condition to the court, as in the case of the inspection of jails and other public institutions. It shall also be the duty of the coroner of the county when death results from accident in the operation and working of any coal mine, to hold an inquest as to the cause of death, as in case of death from an unknown cause, and reduce to writing the testimony of witnesses taken before the coroner's jury or have the same reduced to writing under his direction, and he shall forthwith file the written testimony with the clerk of such court ; and if death results from any wilful act in violation of the provisions of this act, he shall also recognize such witnesses to appear and testify at the next term of the district court of the county.

SEC. 21. That all contracts for the mining of coal, in which the weighing of coal as provided for in this act, shall be dispensed with, shall be null and void.

SEC. 22. All acts and parts of acts in conflict herewith are hereby repealed.

SEC. 24. This act to take effect and be in force from and after its approval.

MINING LAWS OF WEST VIRGINIA.

AN ACT to regulate the working, ventilation and drainage of coal mines in the State of West Virginia, to provide for the appointment of mine inspectors, and to repeal chapter seventy, of the acts of one thousand eight hundred and eighty-three. Approved February 26, 1887.

1. For the purpose of adopting an efficient system of mine inspection, the State of West Virginia is hereby divided into two mining districts, as follows :

The counties of Barbour, Berkeley, Brooke, Calhoun, Doddridge, Gilmer, Grant, Hampshire, Hancock, Hardy, Harrison, Jackson, Jefferson, Lewis, Marion, Marshall, Mason, Mineral, Monongalia, Morgan, Ohio, Pendleton, Pleasants, Preston, Putnam, Randolph, Ritchie, Roane, Taylor, Tucker, Tyler, Upshur, Wetzel, Wirt and Wood shall compose the first district.

The counties of Boone, Braxton, Cabell, Clay, Fayette, Greenbrier, Kanawha, Lincoln, Logan, McDowell, Mercer, Monroe, Nicholas, Pocahontas, Raleigh, Summers, Wayne, Webster and Wyoming shall compose the second district.

2. The governor shall, on or before the first day of July, one thousand eight hundred and eighty-seven, and in every four years thereafter, appoint one inspector of mines for each of the districts created by the next preceding section, who shall, unless he be sooner removed, as hereinafter provided, continue in office until his successor is appointed and qualified.

Every person so appointed must be a citizen of West Virginia, of temperate habits, and of good repute as a man of personal integrity, and must possess a competent, practical and theoretical knowledge of mining and mine engineering, and properly ventilating and draining mines, and of the nature and constituent parts of the noxious gases and impure air of mines, and of the best methods of preventing and removing the same ; and he shall not, while in office, be interested as owner, operator, agent, stockholder, superintendent or mining engineer of any coal mine.

An inspector of mines may be removed from office by the governor for incompetency, neglect of duty, drunkenness, malfeasance in office, or for other good cause. Vacancies in office of inspector shall be filled by appointment by the governor for the unexpired term.

3. Every person appointed inspector of mines shall, before entering on the discharge of the duties of his office, take an oath before some person authorized by law to administer oaths, that he will support the constitution of the United States and the constitution of the State of West Virginia ; and that he will faithfully and impartially, and to the best of his ability, discharge the duties of his office, and file a certificate of his having done so in the office of the secretary of state ; and he shall give a bond in the penalty of three thousand dollars with sureties, to be approved by the governor, conditioned that he will faithfully and impartially discharge the duties of his office. The salary of each inspector shall be one thousand dollars per annum, and his travelling expenses, which shall not exceed seven hundred dollars per annum ; such salary

and expenses shall be paid quarterly out of the State treasury. *Provided,* That before payment of travelling expenses shall be made to the inspector he shall file an account of such expenses, and make oath that they were incurred in the discharge of his official duties.

4. Each inspector shall examine the mines of his district as often as practicable, to see that all the provisions of this act are observed and strictly carried out. He shall particularly examine into the condition of the mines as to ventilation, drainage and general safety, and shall make a record of all such examinations. He shall also for each year, ending with the thirtieth day of June, make a report to the governor, of his proceedings as such inspector, stating therein the number of mines in his district, the number of persons employed in each mine, the condition in which the mines were found, the extent to which this act is obeyed or violated, the number of accidents and deaths resulting from injuries received in or about the mines, with the cause of each of such accidents and deaths, and such other information in relation to mines and mining as he may deem of public interest. He shall also suggest or recommend such legislation on the subject of mining as he may think necessary. Such report shall be filed with the governor on or before the thirteenth day of December next succeeding the year for which it is made.

5. The operator or agent of every coal mine shall, within six months after the passage of this act, make or cause to be made, an accurate map or plan of such mine, on a scale to be stated thereon, not exceeding one hundred feet to the inch. Such map or plan shall show the openings or excavations, the shafts, slopes, entries, air-ways, headings, rooms, pillars, etc., the general inclination of the coal strata, and so much of the property lines and of the outcrop of the coal seam of the tract of land on which said mine is located, as may be within one thousand feet of any part of the workings of such mine.

A true copy of such map or plan, shall, within the six months aforesaid, be delivered by such operator, to the inspector of his district, to be preserved among the records of his office and turned over to his successor in office; and the original map, or a true copy thereof, shall be kept by such operator, at the office of the mine, and open at all reasonable times for the examination and use of the inspector; and such operator shall twice within every twelve months, and not more than seven months apart while the mine is in operation, cause such mine to be surveyed and the map thereof extended so as to accurately show the progress of the workings, the property lines and outcrop as above provided; and he shall immediately thereafter deliver, to the inspector of his district, a map or plan and statement of the progress of the workings and extensions aforesaid, so as to enable the inspector to trace the same on the map or plan furnished him as above required.

Before any mine or part of a mine is abandoned, or the pillars drawn therein, it shall be accurately surveyed, and the maps thereof extended as aforesaid, and within one month after any mine is abandoned, the person who was the last operator thereof, shall file with the clerk of the county court of the county, in which the mine is located, a correct map, showing all the excavations of such mine, to be preserved as a part of the records of the county.

If any operator fail to comply with any provision of this section, the inspector is hereby authorized to have the survey and maps made or extended, as may be necessary in such case, at the expense of such operator, and the rea-

sonable fees an expensesd may be recovered in any court of competent jurisdiction, by the person performing the work.

6. After six months, from and after the passage of this act, it shall be unlawful for the operator or agent of any coal mine, to employ any persons at work
in said mine, or permit any persons to be in said mine for the purpose of working therein, unless they are in communication with at least two openings or
outlets, separated by natural strata, of not less than one hundred feet in
breadth, if the mine be worked by shaft, and of not less than fifty feet in breadth,
if worked by slope or drift. To each of said outlets there shall be provided,
from the interior of the mine, a safe and available roadway, which shall at all
times while the mine is in operation, be kept free from all obstructions that
might prevent travel thereon in case of an emergency, and if either of said outlets be by shaft, it shall be fitted with safe and available appliances, such as
ladders stairs, or hoisting machinery, which shall at all times, when the mine,
is in operation, be kept in order and ready for immediate use, whereby persons
employed in the mine may readily escape in case of an accident.

This section shall not apply to any mine while work is being prosecuted with
reasonable diligence in making communication between said outlets, so long
as not more than twenty persons are employed at any one time in said mine;
neither shall it apply to any mine, or part of a mine, in which the second outlet has been rendered unavailable by reason of the final robbing of pillars preparatory to abandonment, so long as not more than twenty persons are employed therein at any one time.

7. In case a coal mine has but one opening, and the owner thereof does not
own suitable surface ground for another opening, as required by the next preceding section, he may select and appropriate any adjoining land for that
purpose and for approach thereto, and he shall be governed in his proceeding
in appropriating such land, by the laws in force providing for the appropriation of private property by corporations, and such appropriation may be made
whether he is a corporator or not; but no lands shall be appropriated under
the provisions of this act until the court is satisfied that suitable premises cannot be obtained on reasonable terms.

8. The operator or agent of every coal mine worked by shaft shall forthwith
provide, and hereafter maintain, a metal tube from the top to the bottom of
such shaft, suitably adapted to the free passage of sound, through which conversation may be held between persons at the top and at the bottom of the
shaft, also the ordinary means of signalling, and an approved safety catch and
a sufficient cover overhead on every carriage used for lowering or hoisting persons, and at the top of the shaft an approved safety gate, and adequate brakes
on the drum of every machine used to lower or hoist persons in such shaft;
and the said operator or agent shall have the machinery used for lowering or
hoisting persons into or out of the mine, kept in safe condition and inspected
once in each twenty-four hours by some competent person.

9. No operator or agent of any coal mine, worked by shaft or slope, shall
place in charge of any engine, used for lowering into or hoisting out of said
mine persons employed therein, any but competent and sober engineers; and
no engineer in charge of such machinery shall allow any person except such as
may be deputed for that purpose, by the operator or agent to interfere with any
part of the machinery; and no person shall interfere with or intimidate the

engineer in the discharge of his duties; and in no case shall more than ten persons ride on any cage or car at one time, and no person shall ride on a loaded cage or car in any shaft or slope.

All slopes or engine-planes, used as travelling-ways by persons in any mine, shall be made of sufficient width to permit persons to pass moving cars with safety, or refuge holes of ample dimensions, and not more than sixty feet apart, shall be made on one side of said slope or engine plane. Such refuge holes shall be kept free from obstructions, and the roof and sides thereof shall be made secure.

10. The operator or agent of every coal mine, whether worked by shaft, slope or drift, shall provide and hereafter maintain for every such mine, ample means of ventilation, affording not less than one hundred cubic feet of air per minute for each and every person employed in such mine, and as much more as the circumstances may require, which shall be circulated around the main headings and cross headings and working places, to an extent that will dilute, render harmless and carry off the noxious and dangerous gases generated therein; and as the working places shall advance, break-throughs for air shall be made in the pillars, or brattices shall be used, so as to keep such working places well and properly ventilated.

All mines generating fire-damp shall be kept free of standing gas in the worked out or abandoned parts of the same as far as practicable, and the entrances thereto shall be properly closed and cautionary notices posted to warn persons of danger, and the doors used therein for directing the ventilation shall be so hung as to close themselves, and every working place and all other places where gas is known to exist or is liable to exist, shall be carefully examined by some competent person appointed for that purpose, to be known as "fire-boss," immediately before each shift, with a safety-lamp, and in making such examinations it shall be the duty of the fire-boss at each examination, to leave at the face of every place so examined, evidence of his presence, and no workman shall enter or be permitted to enter, any mine or part of a mine, generating fire-damp, until it has been examined by the fire-boss as aforesaid and reported by him to be safe. In all mines generating fire-damp accumulations of fine, dry, coal dust shall, as far as practicable, be prevented, and such dust shall, whenever necessary, be kept properly watered down. The safety-lamps used for examining any mine, or which may be used for working therein, shall be furnished by, and be the property of the operator of the mine, and shall be in charge of an agent thereof, and at least one safety-lamp shall be kept at every coal mine, whether such mine generates fire-damp or not.

11. In order to better secure the proper ventilation of every coal mine and promote the health and safety of persons employed therein, the operator or agent shall employ a competent and practical inside overseer, to be called "mining-boss," who shall be a citizen and an experienced coal miner, or any person having two years' experience in a coal mine, and shall keep a careful watch over the ventilating apparatus and the air-ways, travelling ways, pumps and drainage; and shall see that as the miners advance their excavations, proper break-throughs are made as provided in section ten of this act, and that all loose coal, slate and rock overhead in the working places, and along the haulways, be removed or carefully secured so as to prevent danger to persons employed in such mine; and that sufficient props, caps and timbers are fur-

nished of suitable size and cut square at both ends, and as near as practicable, to the proper lengths for the places where they are to be used; and such props, caps and timbers shall be delivered and placed in the working places of the miners, and every workman in want of props or timbers and cap pieces, shall notify the mining-boss or his assistant of the fact at least one day in advance, giving the length and number of props or timbers and cap pieces required; but in case of an emergency the timbers may be ordered immediately upon the discovery of any danger; and the place and manner of leaving the orders for timbers shall be designated in the rules of the mine; and shall have all water drained or hauled out of the working places before the miners enter, and the working places kept dry, as far as practicable, while the miners are at work. On all haulways, space not less than ten feet long and two feet six inches wide between the wagon and the rib, shall be kept open at distances not exceeding one hundred feet apart, in which shelter from passing wagons may be secured. It shall further be the duty of the mining-boss to have bore holes kept not less than twelve feet in advance of the face, and, when necessary, on the sides, of the working places that are being driven towards and in dangerous proximity to an abandoned mine or part of a mine suspected of containing inflammable gases or which is filled with water.

The mining-boss or his assistant shall visit and examine every working place in the mine at least once in every three days, and oftener when necessary, while the miners of such places are at work and shall direct that each and every working place shall be secured by props or timbers wherever necessary, so that safety in all respects be assured, and no person shall be directed to work in an unsafe place, unless it be for the purpose of making it safe. The mining-boss shall notify the operator or agent of the mine of his inability to comply with any requirements of this section; it shall then become the duty of such operator or agent at once to attend to the matter complained of by the mining-boss, to comply with the provisions hereof.

12. The operator or agent of every coal mine shall furnish the inspector proper facilities for entering such mines, and making examinations or obtaining information; and if any inspector shall discover that any mine does not in its appliances, for the safety of the persons employed therein, conform to the provisions of this act, or that by reason of any defect or practice in or at such mine, the lives or health of persons employed therein, are endangered, he shall immediately, in writing, notify such operator or agent thereof, stating in such notice the particulars in which he considers such mine to be defective or dangerous, and if he deem it necessary for the protection of the lives or health of the persons employed in such mine, he shall, after giving notice to the said operator or agent, of his intention so to do, apply without bond, to the circuit court of the county in which said mine is located, or to the judge thereof in vacation, for an injunction to restrain the operating of said mine until said danger be removed; and such court or judge, when so applied to, shall at once proceed to hear the case and determine the same, and if the cause appear to be sufficient, and such danger appear to exist, after hearing the parties and their evidence, he shall issue an injunction restraining the operating of said mine until the cause of such danger be removed, and the cost of the proceedings, including the charges of the attorney prosecuting the same, shall be borne by the operator of the mine, but no fee exceeding twenty-five dollars shall be taxed

in any one case for the attorney prosecuting such case; but if said court or judge shall find the cause not sufficient, then the case shall be dismissed and the costs shall be paid by the county in which the mine is located.

13. No boy under twelve years of age, nor female person of any age, shall be permitted to work in any coal mine, and in all cases of doubt the ,parents or guardians of such boys shall furnish affidavits of their ages.

14. No miner, workman nor other person, shall knowingly injure any shaft, lamp, instrument, air-course or brattice, or obstruct or throw open air-ways, or carry matches or open lights into places worked by safety-lamps, or disturb any part of the machinery, or open a door used for directing the ventilation and not close it again, or enter any part of the mine against caution, or disobey any order given in carrying out the provisions of this act, or do any other act whereby the life or health of any person employed in the mine, or the security of the mine, is endangered. Nor shall any person or persons or combination of persons, by force, threats, menace or intimidation of any kind, prevent or attempt to prevent from working in or about any mine, any person or persons who have the lawful right to work in or about the same and who desire so to work.

15. Whenever by reason of any explosion or other accidents in any coal mine or the machinery connected therewith, loss of life or serious personal injury shall occur, it shall be the duty of the superintendent of the colliery, and in his absence the mining-boss in charge of the mine, to give notice thereof forthwith, by mail or otherwise, to the inspector of the district, stating the particulars of such accident. And if any one is killed thereby, to the coroner of the county also, or in his absence or inability to act, to any justice of the peace; and the said inspector shall, if he deem it necessary from the facts reported, immediately go to the scene of such accident and make such suggestions and render such assistance as he may deem necessary for the future safety of the men; and investigate the cause of such explosion or accident, and make a record thereof, which he shall preserve with the other records of his office; and to enable him to make such investigation, he shall have the power to compel the attendance of witnesses, and to administer oaths or affirmations; and the costs of such investigation shall be paid by the county in which such accident occurred, in the same manner as the costs of coroner's inquests are now paid. If the coroner or justice shall determine to hold an inquest upon the body of any person killed, as aforesaid. he shall impanel a jury, no one of whom shall be directly or indirectly interested, and the inspector of mines, if present at such inquests, shall have the right to appear and testify and to offer any testimony that may be relevant, and to question and cross-question any witness; and the coroner or justice shall deliver to the inspector a copy of the testimony and verdict of the jury.

16. The operator or agent of every coal mine shall annually, during the month of July, mail or deliver to the inspector of his district a report for the preceding twelve months, ending with the thirtieth day of June. Such report shall state the names of the operator and officers of the mine, the quantity of coal mined, and such other information, not of a private nature. as may from time to time be required by the inspector. Blank forms for such reports shall be furnished by the inspector.

17. The operator or agent of any coal mine who shall neglect or refuse to

perform the duties required of him by any section of this act, or who shall violate any of the provisions hereof, and any person who shall neglect or refuse to perform the duties required of him by sections nine, ten, eleven, thirteen and fourteen, or who shall violate any of the provisions thereof, or knowingly do any act whereby the health or life of any person employed in a mine, or the security of a mine, is endangered, shall be guilty of a misdemeanor, and upon conviction shall be punished by a fine of not less than ten nor more than one hundred dollars. In default of payment of such fine and costs, for the space of ten days, the defendant may, in the discretion of the court, be imprisoned in the county jail for a period not exceeding three months.

18. The provisions of this act shall apply only to coal mines in which ten or more persons are employed in a period of twenty-four hours.

19. Chapter seventy, of the acts of one thousand eight hundred and eighty-three, and all other acts and parts of acts inconsistent with this act, are hereby repealed.

MINING LAWS OF WYOMING.

AN ACT relating to coal mines, and providing for the lives, health, safety and welfare of those employed therein. Approved February 25, 1886.

SECTION 1. The owner, operator or superintendent of every coal mine shall make or cause to be made an accurate map or plan of such coal mine, on a scale not exceeding two hundred feet to the inch; which map or plan shall exhibit all the openings or excavations, the shafts, tunnels, slopes, planes, gangways, entries, crossheadings, rooms, etc., and shall show the direction of the air currents therein, and shall accurately delineate the boundary line between said coal mine and adjoining mines, and show its relation and proximity thereto. The said map or plan, or a true copy thereof, shall be kept at such mine by the said owner, operator or superintendent, for the use of the territorial inspector of coal mines, and for the inspection of any miner working in said mine, whenever said miner shall have cause to fear that the place where he is working is becoming dangerous by reason of its proximity to other workings, which may be supposed to contain water or dangerous gases. The said owner, operator or superintendent shall as often as once in every six months accurately place or cause to be placed on a map or plan of said coal mine, a plan of the excavations made of all the working places or other parts of such coal mine during the preceding six months, and whenever the workings or excavations of said coal mine, or any part of the same have been driven to within ten feet of the boundary line, or when said coal mine or any part of the same is abandoned, the owner, operator or superintendent thereof, shall furnish the territorial inspector of coal mines, within three months thereafter, the proximity to the boundary line as aforesaid, or after abandonment of the said mine, or any part of the same, with a correct copy on tracing muslin or blue print of the map or plan of said mine, which shall accurately show all excavations and workings of such mines to date, exhibiting clearly the part or parts abandoned, and the part or parts in proximity to the boundary line aforesaid. The several coal maps or plans of mines in the Territory which are furnished to the territorial inspector of coal mines, as last aforesaid, shall be the property of the Territory, and shall remain in the care of the said territorial inspector of coal mines, to be transferred by him to his successor in office, and in no case shall any copy of the same be made without the consent of the owner, operator or his agent. If the said territorial inspector of coal mines shall find or have good reason to believe that any map or plan of any coal mine made or furnished in pursuance of the provisions of this act is materially inaccurate or imperfect, he is hereby authorized to cause a correct plan or map of said coal mine to be made at the expense of the owner or operator thereof, the cost of which shall be recoverable from the said owner or operator, in the name of the Territory, as other debts are recoverable by law; *Provided, however,* That if the map or plan which is claimed to be inaccurate shall prove to have been correct, then the Territory shall be held liable for the expenses incurred in making such test survey, and the same shall be paid by territorial treasurer upon the warrant of the territorial auditor, who shall require proper vouchers and satisfactory proof of the same.

SEC. 2. It shall not be lawful for the owner, operator, contractor, lessee or agent of any coal mine, or for any firm, company, corporation or association, their clerks, servants, agents or employés, to employ any person at work within any coal mine, or permit any person to be in any coal mine for the purpose of working therein, unless such mine is in communication with at least two openings, if the mine be worked by shaft or slope, which two shafts or slopes shall be separated by natural strata at all points by a distance of not less than fifty feet, except in drift mines heretofore opened, where the mine inspector shall deem it impracticable; *Provided, however,* An aggregate number not exceeding twenty persons may be employed in the mine at any one time until the second opening shall be reached and made available, which said second opening the said inspector of coal mines shall cause to be made without unnecessary delay, and in case of furnace ventilation being used before the second opening is reached, the furnace shall not be placed within forty feet of the foot of the shaft, slope or drift, and shall be well secured from danger from fire, by brick or stone walls of sufficient thickness.

SEC. 3. When a second opening or outlet is made, which does not exceed seventy-five feet in vertical depth from the surface to the seam or strata of coal that is being mined, it shall be set apart exclusively for the purpose of ingress or egress to or from the mine by any person or persons employed therein, and it shall always be kept clear of any obstruction, and if the opening is a shaft it shall be so fitted with safe and convenient stairs not less than two feet wide, and not to exceed an angle of sixty degrees descent, and landings of not less than eighteen inches wide and four feet long, at easy and convenient distances, and all water coming from the surface or out of the strata in the shaft, shall be so conducted as to be prevented from falling down the shaft on the stairs, or on persons ascending or descending the stairway of the shaft. If the second opening is a slope for a travelling way, and has a greater angle of descent than twenty-five degrees, it shall be provided with suitable stairs not less than two feet wide, but when the seam or stratum of coal at main outlet or escapement shaft in connection with any mine exceeds seventy-five feet in vertical depth from the surface, the miners or other employés in the mine shall be lowered into or raised from said mine by machinery, and when the employés are lowered into or raised from the said mine at the main outlet, the escapement shall be fitted with safe and available machinery or safe and convenient stairs, by which persons employed in the mines may readily escape in case of accident. The hoisting machinery and stairs used for lowering or raising the employés into or out of the mine shall be kept in a safe condition and inspected once each twenty-four hours by a competent person employed in whole or in part for that purpose, and such machinery and the method of its inspection shall be approved by the territorial inspector of coal mines.

SEC. 4. The owner or agent of any coal mine, whether shaft, slope or drift, shall provide and maintain for every such mine, ample means of ventilation, affording not less than one hundred cubic feet per minute for each and every person employed in said mine, and as much more as the circumstances may require, which shall be circulated around the main headings and cross headings and working places to an extent that it will dilute, carry off and render harmless the noxious or dangerous gases generated therein, and all mines generating fire-damp shall be kept free of standing gas in the worked out or abandoned parts of the same, and the entrance thereto shall be properly closed, and cautionary notice shall be posted to warn persons of danger, and every working place and all other places where gas is known or supposed to exist, shall be carefully examined by the fire-boss, within three hours immediately before each shift, with a safety-lamp, and in making said examination it shall be the duty of the fire-boss, at each examination, to leave at the face of every place examined, evidence of his presence, and it shall not be lawful for any miner to enter any mine or part of a mine generating fire-damp until it has been examined by the fire-boss aforesaid, and by him reported to be safe.

SEC. 5. It shall be unlawful for any miner, fire-boss, employé in any mine, or other person, to brush fire-damp from any place in a coal mine by means of a coat, sack, sail cloth, or any like article or material; and any person so offending shall be deemed guilty of a misdemeanor, and upon conviction, shall be imprisoned for the term not exceeding six months, or fined in any sum not to exceed one hundred dollars, or punished by both such fine and imprisonment. And any owner or superintendent, mine boss or fire-boss, who shall knowingly employ any person to perform or engage in any such work prohibited by this section, or shall knowingly permit the same to be done, shall be deemed guilty of a misdemeanor, subject to the same penalties as hereinbefore prescribed.

SEC. 6. In order to better secure the proper ventilation of every coal mine and promote the health and safety of the persons employed therein, the owner or agent shall employ a competent and practical inside overseer, to be called mining-boss, who shall be an experienced coal miner, and who shall keep a careful watch over the ventilating apparatus and the air-ways, travelling ways, pumps and drainage, and shall see that as the miners advance their excavations all loose coal, slate and rock overhead are carefully secured against falling on the travelling ways, and that sufficient props, caps and timbers are furnished upon order of the miner, of suitable size and cut square at both ends, and as near as practicable to a proper length for the places where they are to be used, and such props, caps or timbers shall be delivered at the mouth of the rooms, and shall see that all water be drained or hauled out of all working places before the miner enters, and as far as practicable kept dry while the miner is at work; and it shall be the further duty of the mining-boss to see that the proper cut-throughs are made in the room pillars of the miners' places at intervals of not more than sixteen yards for the purpose of ventilation, and in all hauling roads, holes for shelter shall be made at least every thirty yards, and be kept whitewashed, when a space two feet and six inches between the wagon and the rib shall be deemed sufficient for shelter, and the mining-boss shall measure the air current at least once a week at the inlet and outlet and at or near the face of the headings. He shall keep a record of such measurements, which shall be placed by him in a book kept for that purpose, said book to be open for the examination of the said territorial inspector; he shall also, on or about the fifteenth day of each month, mail to the territorial inspector of coal mines a true copy of the air measurements given, stating also the number of persons employed in or about said mine, the number of mules and horses used, and the number of days worked in each month, for which purpose blanks shall be furnished by the said inspector. It shall be the further duty of the mining-boss to immediately notify the owner or agent of the mine of his inability to comply with the provisions of this section. It shall then become the duty of the said superintendent, operator, owner or agent, at once to attend to the matter complained of by the mining-boss, and to comply with the provisions hereof. The safety-lamps used for examining mines, or which may be used in working therein, shall be furnished by and be the property of the owner of said mine, and shall be in charge of the agent of such mine, and in all mines the doors used in assisting or directing the ventilation of the mine shall be so hung and adjusted that they will close themselves, or be supplied with springs or pulleys so that they cannot be left standing open, and bore holes shall be kept not less than twelve feet in advance of the face of every working place, and when necessary on the sides of the same when they are being driven towards and in dangerous proximity to an abandoned mine or part of a mine, suspected of containing inflammable gases, or which is inundated with water, The mining-boss or his assistant shall visit and examine every working place in the mine at least once every alternate day while the miners of such place are or should be at work, and shall direct that each and every working place is properly secured by props or timber, and that safety in all respects is assured, and that no person shall be permitted to work in an unsafe place, unless it be for the purpose of making it safe. All owners and operators of coal mines shall keep posted in a conspicuous place about their mine printed rules, submitted to and approved by the territorial inspector, defining the duties of all persons employed in or about said coal mines, which said notices shall be printed in the language or languages used by the miners working therein.

SEC. 7. Any miner, workman or other person who shall intentionally injure any shaft, lamp, instrument, air course or brattice, or obstruct or throw open air ways, or carry lighted pipes or matches into places that are worked by safety-lamps, or handle or disturb any part of the machinery, or open a door and not close it again, or enter any place of the mine against caution, or disobey any order given in carrying out the provisions of this act, or do any other act, whereby the lives or the health of persons or security of the mines or machinery is endangered, shall be deemed guilty of a misdemeanor, and may be punished in a manner provided in the twentieth section of this act. All machinery about mines shall be properly fenced off, and there shall be cut in the side of every hoisting shaft, at the bottom thereof, a travelling way sufficiently wide and high to enable persons to pass the shaft in going from one side of the mine to the other, without passing over or under the cage or other hoisting apparatus.

SEC. 8. The governor shall nominate, and by and with the consent of the council appoint, during the present session of the Legislative Assembly, and every two years thereafter, a territorial inspector of coal mines, who shall hold his office for two years, and until his successor is duly appointed and qualified, who shall be a man having a thorough knowledge of practical mining and mining engineering, and who shall not be an employé, owner or part owner in any coal mine in the Territory. He shall not be less than thirty years of age, a citizen of the United States, and if practicable, of this Territory, of good repute and temperate habits. The said territorial inspector of coal mines shall receive an annual salary of two thousand five hundred dollars, and actual travelling expenses while in the discharge of his duties, to be paid quarterly by the territorial treasurer, upon warrants of the auditor, and he shall make his residence and keep his office as near as practicable to the mines under his jurisdiction. Said inspector is hereby authorized to procure such instruments and chemical tests and stationery, and to incur such expense of communication from time to time as may be necessary to the discharge of his duties under this act, at the cost of the Territory, subject to the approval of the governor of the Territory, which shall be paid out of the territorial treasury, upon accounts duly certified by him and audited by the auditor. All instruments, plans, books, memoranda, notes and other property pertaining to the office hereby created shall be the property of the Territory, and shall be delivered by each inspector to his successor in office, and said inspector shall be allowed all expenses necessarily incurred in enforcing the provisions of this act in the courts of the territory, when such expenses are certified to be correct by the courts before which the proceedings were had.

SEC. 9. The territorial inspector of coal mines shall, before entering upon the discharge of his duties, give bond in the sum of ten thousand dollars to the Territory of Wyoming in the penal sum of ten thousand dollars, with sufficient sureties, to be approved by the chief justice of the supreme court of the Territory, said bond to be filed in the office of the territorial auditor, which bond shall be conditioned for the faithful discharge of his duties, and he shall take and subscribe an oath or affirmation to discharge his duties impartially and with fidelity to the best of his knowledge and ability. The said inspector shall devote the whole of his time to the duties of his office; it shall be his duty to examine the coal mines of the Territory as often as possible, which shall not be less than once in three months, and report the number of times he has visited each mine in a year, to see that all the provisions of this act are observed and strictly carried out; and he shall make records of all examinations of mines, showing the condition in which he finds them, especially in reference to ventilation and drainage, the number of mines in the Territory, the number of persons employed in each mine, the extent to which the laws are obeyed, the progress made in the improvement sought to be secured by the passage of this act, the number of accidents and deaths resulting from injuries received in or about the mine, with cause of such accident or death, said report to be made quarterly, and published in at least one paper in each county in which any coal mines are located, at least one time.

Sec. 10. That the territorial inspector of coal mines shall have the right at all times to enter any coal mine to make examinations or obtain information, and the owner or superintendent shall afford any assistance necessary to the said inspector in making such examination. The said inspector shall notify the owner, lessee, superintendent or mining-boss, immediately of the discovery of any violation of this act and of the penalty imposed thereby for such violation, and in case of such notice being disregarded for the space of five days, he shall institute proceedings against the owner, agent, lessee or mining-boss, under the provisions of section twenty of this act; in case, however, where, in the judgment of the said inspector, delay may jeopardize life or limb, he may at once enter proceedings (except the defects be remedied) to restrain working of the mine ; and the cost of said proceedings, including the charge of the attorney prosecuting the same, shall be borne by the owner, lessee or superintendent, against whom such proceedings are had; *Provided*, That no attorney fee exceeding the sum of fifty dollars shall be taxed in any one case for the prosecution of such case; and, *Provided, further*, That if the court shall find the case not sufficient, then the case shall be dismissed and the costs be borne by the Territory.

Sec. 11. Whenever by reason of any explosion or any other accident in any coal mine or the machinery connected therewith, loss of life or serious personal injury shall occur, it shall be the duty of the person having charge of such mine or colliery to give notice thereof forthwith to the said territorial inspector, and if any person is killed thereby to the coroner of the county, who shall give due notice of the inquest to be held. If the coroner shall determine to hold an inquest, the inspector shall be allowed to testify, and offer such testimony as he shall deem necessary to thoroughly inform the said inquest of the causes of the death, and the said inspector shall have authority at any time to appear before said coroner and jury and question or cross-question any witness, and in choosing a jury for the purpose of holding such inquest, it shall be the duty of the coroner to empanel at least three experienced miners on such jury. It shall be the duty of the said inspector, upon being notified as herein ·provided, to immediately repair to the scene of the accident and make such suggestions as may appear necessary to secure the future safety of the men, and if the results of the explosion or accident do not require an investigation by the coroner, he shall proceed to investigate and ascertain the cause of the explosion or accident and make a record thereof, which he shall file as provided for, and to enable him to make the investigation he shall have the power to compel the attendance of persons to testify, and to administer oaths or affirmations ; the cost of such investigations shall be paid by the county in which the accident occurred, in the same manner as costs of coroner's inquests are paid by law.

Sec. 12. The district court within the proper county, or judge thereof in vacation or recess, upon a petition signed by not less than fifteen reputable citizens, who shall be miners, owners or lessees of mines, and with the affidavit of one or more of said petitioners attached, setting forth that the territorial inspector of coal mines neglects his duty or is incompetent, or that he is guilty of malfeasance in office, shall issue a citation in the name of the Territory to the said inspector, to appear upon a day to be therein fixed and stated before said court, which notice shall be served at least fifteen days before the time fixed to appear, at which time the court or judge thereof in vacation or recess, shall proceed to inquire into and investigate the allegations of the petitioners, and if the court find that said inspector is neglectful of his duties, or is incompetent to perform the duties of his office, or if he is guilty of malfeasance therein, the court or judge shall certify the same to the governor, who shall thereupon declare the office of said inspector vacant, and proceed to supply said vacancy by appointment; and all vacancies in said office shall be filled by appointment by the governor; the cost of said investigations shall, if the charges are sustained, be taxed against the inspector, but if the charges be not sustained, they shall be taxed against the petitioners.

SEC. 13. The inspector shall exercise his sound discretion in the enforcement of the provisions of this act, and if the operator, owner or miners shall not be satisfied with any decision of the inspector rendered in the discharge of his duties under this act, which said decision shall be in writing, and signed by said inspector, the said owner, operator, miner or miners may, within fifteen days after such decision is rendered, appeal to the district court of the county in which the mine concerned is located, and said court shall speedily determine the point involved in said decision and appeal, which said decision shall be binding and conclusive, subject only to an appeal to the supreme court of the Territory. The court, in its discretion, may appoint three practical, competent and disinterested persons, whose duty it shall be, under instructions of the said court, to forthwith examine such mine and make report under oath of the facts as they exist or may have been, together with their opinion thereon, which report of said board shall become absolute, unless exceptions thereto shall be filed within ten days after the notice of the filing thereof, to the owner, operator, miner or miners, or inspector, and if exceptions be filed, the court shall at once hear and determine the same, and the decision shall be final and conclusive, subject only to appeal as aforesaid. If the court shall finally sustain the decision of the inspector, then the appellants shall pay all costs of such proceedings, and if the court shall not sustain the decision of the inspector, then such costs shall be paid by the county or by the appellants and county in such proportions as the court shall determine. That no appeal from any decision made by any inspector shall work as a supersedeas during the pendency of such appeal, but all such decision shall be in full force until reversed or modified by the court.

SEC. 14. On the petition of the mining inspector the district court in any county in this Territory shall, at the first term after the passage of this act, appoint an examining board for such county, consisting of the territorial inspector of coal mines, an operator of a coal mine and a coal miner, who shall be citizens of the United States, and the latter two of which board shall have at least five years of experience in the mines of the Territory, whose duty it shall be to examine any person applying thereto as to his competency and qualifications to discharge the duties of mining-boss. Said board of examiners shall meet at the call of the inspector, and they shall grant certificates to all persons whose examination shall disclose their fitness for the duties of mining-boss, and such certificate shall be sufficient evidence of the competency and qualification of the holders for the duties of said office; *Provided*, That any person who shall have been employed as a miner at least five years in the coal mines of Wyoming, and as mining-boss continuously by the same person or firm or corporation, for the period

of one year preceding the passage of this act, may be entitled, if in the judgment of the inspector he be qualified, to a certificate without undergoing
such examination; but he shall not be employed by any other person or firm
or corporation without having undergone such examination. The members of
the examining board, other than the inspector, shall hold their office for the
period of two years from the date of their appointment, and shall receive five
dollars per day for each day necessarily and actually employed, and mileage
at the rate of fifteen cents per mile for each mile necessarily travelled, to be paid
by the Territory. Vacancies in the membership of the board shall be filled
by the court of the proper county, except the vacancy in the office of inspector.
Sessions of the examining board shall not exceed three days in each quarter,
and for any certificate granted the board shall receive the sum of one dollar,
the same to be paid into the territorial treasury. No person shall act as fire-
boss unless granted a certificate of competency by the territorial inspector of
coal mines. After the passage of this act no owner, operator, contractor,
lessee or agent, shall employ any mining boss or fire-boss who does not have
the certificate of competency required. Said certificate shall be posted up in
the office of the mine, and if any accident shall occur in any mine in which a
mining boss or fire-boss shall be employed, who has no certificate of competency as required by this act, by which any miner shall be killed or injured, he
or his estate shall have a right of action against such operator, owner, lessee
or agent, and shall recover the full damages sustained; in case of death, such
action to be brought by the administrator of his estate, within three years from
the date of accident, the proceeds recovered to be divided among the heirs of
the deceased, according to law.

SEC. 15. No boy under the age of fourteen years, and no woman or girl of
any age, shall be employed or permitted to be in or about any coal mine for
the purpose of employment therein; *Provided however*, That this provision
shall not affect the employment of a boy or female of suitable age in an office,
or in the performance of clerical work at such mine or colliery.

SEC. 16. For any injury to person or property occasioned by any violation
of this act, or any wilful failure to comply with its provisions, a right of action
against the party at fault shall accrue to the party injured for the direct
damages sustained thereby, and in any case of loss of life, by reason of such
violation or wilful failure, a right of action against the party at fault shall
accrue to the administrator of the estate whose life shall be lost, for like
recovery of damages for the injuries they shall have sustained; *Provided*, That
nothing in this section shall be so construed as to prevent the recovery of any
lawful damages against the person or company operating mines if said company
should be found in fault or shall have contributed to any accident by means of
carelessness on their part; and, *Provided, further*, That in no case shall the
Territory of Wyoming be liable for damages under this act.

SEC. 17. It shall be the duty of owners, operators, lessees, superintendents
and agents of coal mines, to keep at the mouth of the drift, shaft or slope, or at
any such other place or places as shall be designated by the inspector, stretchers in such number as the inspector shall designate, properly constructed for
the purpose of carrying away any miner or employé working in and about such
mine, who may in any way be injured in and about his employment.

SEC. 18. It shall be the duty of the territorial inspector of coal mines on each visit to any mine, to make out a written or partly written and partly printed report of the condition in which he finds such mines, and post the same in the office at the mine; the said report shall give the date of visit, the number of visits during the year, the total number of mines in the Territory, the number of feet of air in circulation and where measured, and such other information as he shall deem necessary, and the report shall remain posted in the office for one year, and said report may be examined by any miner or person employed in and about such mine.

SEC. 19. On or before the thirty-first day of January in each year, the owner, operator or superintendent of every mine or colliery shall send to the territorial inspector a correct report, specifying with respect to the year, ending the thirty-first day of the preceding December, the name of the owner, operator and officers of the mine, and the quantity of coal mined, and the number of men employed; the report shall be in such form and give such information as may be from time to time required and prescribed by the inspector; blank forms for such report shall be furnished by the Territory.

SEC. 20. The neglect or refusal to perform the duties required to be performed by any section of this act by the parties therein required to perform them, or the violations of any of the provisions or requirements thereof, shall be deemed a misdemeanor, and shall upon conviction, except wherein otherwise provided, be punished by a fine of not less than two hundred dollars and not exceeding five hundred dollars, at the discretion of the court; *Provided*, That in case the neglect, or failure, or violation occurs in the case of the territorial inspector of coal mines, if such violation, failure or neglect is shown to have been wilful, such punishment shall be by a fine of not less than five hundred dollars nor more than one thousand dollars, or by imprisonment not less than six months nor more than one year, or by both such fine and imprisonment; and in default of payment of any fine imposed upon any person under this act, such person may be committed to jail until the same shall be paid.

SEC. 21. The provisions of this act shall not apply to any mine employing an average of less than ten persons during any one twenty-four hours.

SEC. 22. All acts and parts of acts inconsistent or in conflict herewith are hereby repealed.

SEC. 23. This act shall take effect and be in force from and after its passage.

MINING LAWS OF THE STATE OF MARYLAND.

CHAPTER CLVII.

AN ACT to repeal the act of January session, eighteen hundred and seventy-six, chapter one hundred and seventy-three, entitled " An act regulating the working and proper ventilation of coal mines in Alleghany and Garrett counties, and providing for the appointment of an inspector for said mines, and to re-enact the same with amendments."

SECTION 1. *Be it enacted by the General Assembly of Maryland*, That the act of January session, eighteen hundred and seventy-six, entitled, an act regulating the working and proper ventilation of coal mines in Alleghany and Garrett counties, and providing for the appointment of an inspector for said mines, be and the same is hereby repealed and re-enacted, so as to read as follows :

SEC. 2. *And be it enacted*, That the Governor shall, by and with the advice and consent of the Senate, appoint one mine inspector for the counties of Alleghany and Garrett, who shall hold his office for two years from the date of his appointment.

SEC. 3. *And be it enacted*, That no person shall be eligible to the office of mine inspector until he shall have attained the age of thirty-five years, and shall possess a competent knowledge of all the different systems of mining and working and properly ventilating coal mines, and the nature and constituent parts of noxious gases of mines, and of the various ways of expelling the same from said mine.

SEC. 4. *And be it enacted*, That before entering upon and discharging the duties of his office, said inspector of mines shall take an oath to faithfully discharge the duties hereinafter set forth, in an impartial manner; and for the faithful performance of his duties the said mine inspector shall receive a salary of fifteen hundred dollars per annum, which said salary shall be paid out of the State's money, by a warrant of the Comptroller upon the State Treasurer for the same.

SEC. 5. *And be it enacted*, That it shall be the duty of the said mine inspector to carefully examine all mines that may be in operation in the counties of Alleghany and Garrett, at least once in every month, and oftener, if necessary, to see that every precaution is taken to insure safety to all workmen that may be engaged in said mines, and to see that the provisions of this act are strictly observed ; and it shall further be the duty of the said inspector, after being notified by the magistrate or coroner of either of said counties of Alleghany or Garrett, to attend at every inquest that may be held on the bodies of any person or persons that may lose their lives while engaged at work in or about any of the coal mines of said counties, and he shall examine closely into the cause by which said person or persons lost their lives, and, if it shall be fully proven that the said person or persons lost their lives by any wilful violation of this act, or any wilful failure to comply with its provisions, the widow or lineal heirs of the person or persons whose life shall be so lost, may institute a suit against the owner, lessee or operator of said mine wherein the accident took place, and may recover such damages as the courts may determine, for the loss they have sustained by the death of the person or persons whose life or lives have been lost while engaged at work in said mines.

SEC. 6. *And be it enacted*, That the said mine inspector, while in office, shall not act as land agent, or as agent or superintendent and manager of any mine, and shall in no manner whatever be under the employ of any of the mining companies operating mines in said counties ; and it shall be the duty of said mine inspector, on or before the first day of January in every year, to make a report to the Governor of his proceedings as such mine inspector and the condition of each and every mine in said counties, stating therein all accidents that may have happened in or about the said mines, and to set forth in said reports all such information that may be proper and beneficial, and also to make such suggestions as he may deem important as to any further legislation on the subject of mining.

SEC. 7. *And it be enacted*, That the owner or owners or lessees of every coal mine that may be in operation in the said counties of Alleghany and Garrett shall make or cause to be made an accurate map or plan of the workings of such mine which shall be kept at the office of the company, lessee or individual so mining, and shall be at all times accessible to the said inspector for reference only.

SEC. 8. *And be it enacted*, That the owner, lessee or agent of every coal mine that may now or hereafter be in operation in the said counties of Alleghany or Garrett, whether worked by slope, shaft or draft, shall provide and establish within six months from the passage of this act, for every such mine a proper system of pure air ventilation by such modes as are now in use in the coal mines of Alleghany and Garrett counties, which said ventilation shall be maintained through every working heading throughout the entire mine, and to expel from said mines the noxious gases or impure air, so that the entire mine shall be in a healthful condition for the men working therein, and free from danger to their lives by keeping therefrom such impure air or gases.

SEC. 9. *And be it enacted*, That to secure and provide for the proper ventilation of every coal mine in the counties of Alleghany and Garrett, and to provide for the health and safety of the men employed therein, the owner, lessee or agent of each respective mine shall employ a competent and practical inside overseer, whose duty it shall be to keep a careful watch over all the ventilating apparatus that may be placed in said mine, as well as all the air-ways, all the travelling-ways, and all the timberings, and to see that all loose coal or rocks overhead be carefully secured against falling upon any of the miners engaged at work therein as they advance in their excavations; and it shall be the duty of the inside overseer so employed to take charge of and keep a careful watch over all things connected with and appertaining to the safety of the men at work in the mine, and to report to the owner, lessee or agent of said mine when and where anything under his charge is unfit for mining purposes; and it shall also be the duty of the inside overseer so employed to take charge of and pay strict attention to all the air doors used in the ventilation of said mines, and all air doors used in the ventilation of said mines shall be suspended in such a manner that they will close of their own accord.

SEC. 10. *And be it enacted*, That the owner, lessee or agent of every mine in operation in the said counties of Alleghany and Garrett shall furnish at their own expense all props and all the requisite timber that may be used in the working of said mines, and as the miners employed at work therein proceed with the working of their excavations, it shall be the duty of the owner, lessee or agent of said mines to furnish a sufficient quantity of timber at the place where the miner is at work, and whenever the said workmen engaged in the said excavation shall deem it safe and proper to have any of the props or timbers removed from said excavations, it shall be the duty of the person or persons so employed by the owner, lessee or agent to remove the said props or timbers to whatever point or place the workmen engaged therein may require, but no props or timber whatever shall be removed that might endanger the lives of any of the workmen engaged therein by such removal.

SEC. 11. *And be it enacted*, That whenever any gases or impure air is known to exist in any of the mines in the said counties of Alleghany and Garrett, and which is likely to endanger the lives of the miners employed therein, it shall be the duty of the mine inspector, upon the same being made known to him, to proceed at once to make a careful examination of the ventilating apparatus of the said mine, and if he shall find that the gases and impure air existing in said mine was the cause of the bad condition of the ventilating apparatus connected therewith, he shall immediately notify the owner, lessee or agent to expel from the said mine all noxious gases and impure air existing therein, and to properly ventilate the same.

SEC. 12. *And be it enacted*, That the mine inspector shall also be an inspector of weights, at all the mines, now or hereafter operated in said Alleghany and Garrett counties, and shall have power to weigh the coal mined therein, from time to time, on the scales at the different mines in said counties, and to test the accuracy of said scales, and to do any other act that he may deem necessary to ascertain, whether or not the miners are allowed full weight of coal in the mining cars, when placed upon the scales of the different mines, and it shall be the duty of every person acting as weighmaster, for the owner, lessee, or agent, of any of said mines before entering upon the performance of his duties, as said weighmaster, or before making any report as said weighmaster to said owner, lessee, or agent, to make oath before some justice of the peace of the said county in which such mine, or the opening thereof is situated, that he will perform, or has performed, the duties of weighmaster, at such mine, with honesty and fidelity, and will keep, or has kept, a true account of all the coal so weighed by him, or under his direction, and will credit and allow, or has credited, and allowed the full weight of coal in each mining car, to the party or parties who mined the same, at the rate of 2,240 pounds per ton, and it shall be the duty of every person, acting as weighmaster for the owners, lessee or agent of any of said mines, to keep a list of the number of cars and the weight of coal in each car, and place said list in some place where the miners interested may inspect it daily, and shall make a daily report to the owner, lessee or agent of said mines, and he shall deliver a copy of the affidavit required by this act, to the mine inspector under the hand and seal of said justice of the peace, and it shall be the duty of said weighmaster to perform the several acts and matters specified in said affidavit.

SEC. 13. *And be it enacted*, That it shall be the duty of every person or body corporate, operating a mine or mines in either of said counties, as owners, lessee or agent, to provide correct and accurate scales for weighing the coal mined

23

therein, before the same shall be taken from the mine cars, used by the miners therein.

SEC. 14. *Be it enacted*, That any owner, lessee, agent or operator of any coal mine in said counties of Alleghany or Garrett, or any other person therein, neglecting or refusing to comply with the provisions of this act, or violating in any manner any of its provisions, may be held and deemed guilty of a misdemeanor and upon indictment and conviction thereof may be fined for each and every said offence a sum not less than ten dollars nor more than five hundred dollars, in the discretion of the court.

SEC. 15. *And be it enacted*, That the Governor shall appoint a commission of three competent persons to examine the mines of Alleghany and Garrett counties and report before the next session of the General Assembly, with recommendations for such legislation as to said commission may appear just and necessary for the proper supervision and regulation of said mines.

SEC. 16. *And be it enacted*, That this act shall take effect from and after the date of its passage.

Approved March 27, 1878.

MINING LAWS OF GREAT BRITAIN.

1. This act may be cited as the Coal Mines Regulation Act, 1887.

2. This Act shall not come into operation until the first day of January one thousand eight hundred and eighty-eight, which date is in this Act referred to as the commencement of this Act.

3. This Act shall apply to mines of coal, mines of stratified ironstone, mines of shale, and mines of fire-clay; and in this Act, unless the context otherwise requires, the word "mine" means a mine to which this Act applies.

PART I.

EMPLOYMENT OF BOYS, GIRLS, AND WOMEN.

4. No boy under the age of twelve years, and no girl or woman of any age, shall be employed in or allowed to be for the purpose of employment in any mine below ground.

5. A boy of or above the age of twelve years shall not be employed in or allowed to be for the purpose of employment in any mine below ground for more than fifty-four hours in any one week, nor more than ten hours in any one day, nor otherwise than in accordance with the regulations hereinafter contained with respect to the employment of boys in a mine below ground.

6. With respect to the employment of boys in a mine below ground, the following regulations shall have effect; that is to say,

(1.) There shall be allowed an interval of not less than eight hours between the period of employment on Friday and the period of employment on the following Saturday, and in other cases of not less than twelve hours between each period of employment:

(2.) The period of each employment shall be deemed to begin at the time of leaving the surface, and to end at the time of returning to the surface:

(3.) A week shall be deemed to begin at midnight on Saturday night and to end at midnight on the succeeding Saturday night.

7. With respect to boys, girls, and women employed above ground, in connection with any mine, the following provisions shall have effect:

(1.) No boy or girl under the age of twelve years shall be so employed:

(2.) No boy or girl under the age of thirteen years shall be so employed—

a. for more than six days in any one week; or

b. if employed for more than three days in any one week, for more than six hours in any one day; or

c. in any other case for more than ten hours in any one day:

(3.) No boy or girl of or above the age of thirteen years and no woman shall be so employed for more than fifty-four hours in any one week or more than ten hours in any one day:

(4.) No boy, girl, or woman shall be so employed between the hours of nine at night and five on the following morning, nor on Sunday, nor after two o'clock on Saturday afternoon :

(5.) There shall be allowed an interval of not less than eight hours between the termination of employment on Friday and the commencement of employment on the following Saturday, and in other cases of not less than twelve hours between the termination of employment on one day, and the commencement of the next employment :

(6.) A week shall be deemed to begin at midnight on Saturday night and to end at midnight on the succeeding Saturday night:

(7.) No boy, girl, or woman shall be employed continuously for more than five hours, without an interval of at least half an hour for a meal, nor for more than eight hours on any one day, without an interval or intervals for meals amounting altogether to not less than one hour and a half :   —

(8.) No boy, girl, or woman shall be employed in moving railway wagons.

The provisions of this section as to the employment of boys, girls, and women after two o'clock on Saturday afternoon, shall not apply in the case of any mine in Ireland, so long as it is exempted by order of a Secretary of State.

8. (1.) The owner, agent or manager of every mine shall keep in the office at the mine a register, and shall cause to be entered in that register, in such form as the Secretary of State may from time to time prescribe or sanction, the name, age, residence, and date of first employment of all boys employed in the mine below ground, and of all boys, girls, and women employed above ground in connection with the mine ; and shall on request, produce the register to any inspector under this Act, and to any officer of a school board or school attendance committee in the district in which the mine is situate, at the mine at all reasonable times, and shall allow any such inspector or officer to inspect and copy the same.

(2.) The immediate employer of every boy, other than the owner, agent or manager of the mine, before he causes the boy to be below ground in any mine, shall report to the manager of the mine or to some person appointed by that manager, that he is about to employ the boy in the mine.

9. If any person contravenes or fails to comply with, or permits any person to contravene or fail to comply with, any provision of this Act with respect to the employment of boys, girls, or women, or to the register of boys, girls and women, or to reporting the intended employment of boys, he shall be guilty of an offence against this Act ; and in the event of any such contravention or non-compliance by any person whomsoever, the owner, agent and manager of the mine shall each be guilty of an offence against this Act, unless he proves that he had taken all reasonable means, by publishing and to the best of his power enforcing the provisions of this Act, to prevent the contravention or non-compliance.

10. (1.) After a request in writing by the principal teacher of a public elementary school which is attended by any boy or girl employed in or in connection with a mine, the person who pays the wages of the boy or girl shall as long as he employs the boy or girl pay to the principal teacher of that school, for every week that the boy or girl attends the school, the weekly sum specified in the application, not exceeding twopence per week, and not exceeding one-twelfth part of the wages of the boy or girl, and may deduct the sum so paid by him from the wages payable for the services of the boy or girl.

(2.) If any person after such application refuses to pay on demand any sum that becomes due as aforesaid, he shall be liable to a penalty not exceeding ten shillings.

WAGES.

11. (1.) No wages shall be paid to any person employed in or about any mine at or within any public house, beer shop, or place for the sale of any spirits beer, wine, cider or other spirituous or fermented liquor, or other house of entertainment, or any office, garden or place belonging or contiguous thereto, or occupied therewith.

(2.) Every person who contravenes or fails to comply with or permits any person to contravene or fail to comply with this section shall be guilty of an offence against this Act; and in the event of any such contravention or non-compliance by any person whomsoever, the owner, agent and manager of the mine shall each be guilty of an offence against this Act, unless he proves that he had taken all reasonable means by publishing and to the best of his power enforcing the provisionsof this section to prevent the contravention or non-compliance.

12. (1.) Where the amount of wages paid to any of the persons employed in a mine depends on the amount of mineral gotten by them, those persons shall be paid according to the actual weight gotten by them of the mineral contracted to be gotten, and the mineral gotten by them shall be truly weighed at a place as near to the pit mouth as is reasonably practicable.

Provided that nothing in this section shall preclude the owner, agent or manager of the mine from agreeing with the persons employed in the mine that deductions shall be made in respect of stones or substances other than the mineral contracted to be gotten, which shall be sent out of the mine with the mineral contracted to be gotten, or in respect of any tubs, baskets or hutches being improperly filled in those cases where they are filled by the getter of the mineral or his drawer, or by the person immediately employed by him; such deductions being determined in such special mode as may be agreed upon between the owner, agent or manager of the mine on the one hand, and the persons employed in the mine on the other, or by some person appointed in that behalf by the owner, agent or manager, or (if any check weigher is stationed for this purpose as hereinafter mentioned), by such person and such check weigher, or in case of difference by a third person to be mutually agreed on by the owner, agent or manager of the mine on the one hand, and the persons employed in the mine on the other, or in default of agreement appointed by a chairman of a court of quarter sessions within the jurisdiction of which any shaft of the mine is situate.

(2.) If any person contravenes or fails to comply with, or permits any person to contravene or fail to comply with, this section, he shall be guilty of an offence against this Act: and in the event of any such contravention or non-compliance by any person whomsoever, the owner, agent and manager of the mine shall each be guilty of an offence against this Act, unless he proves that he had taken all reasonable means by publishing and to the best of his power enforcing the provisions of this section to prevent the contravention or non-compliance.

(3.) Where it is proved to the satisfaction of a Secretary of State, in the case of any mine or class of mines employing not more than thirty persons under-ground, to be expedient that the persons employed therein should, upon the joint representation of the owner or owners of any such mine or class of mines and the said persons, be paid by any method other than that provided by this Act, such Secretary of State may if he think fit, by order allow the same either without conditions or during the time and on the conditions specified in the order.

13. (1.) The persons who are employed in a mine, and are paid according to the weight of the mineral gotten by them, may, at their own cost, station a person (in this Act referred to as "a check weigher") at each place appointed for the weighing of the mineral, and at each place appointed for determining the deductions in order that he may on behalf of the persons by whom he is so stationed take a correct account of the weight of the mineral or determine correctly the deductions as the case may be.

(2.) A check weigher shall have every facility afforded to him for enabling him to fulfil the duties for which he is stationed, including facilities for exam-ining and testing the weighing machine, and checking the tareing of tubs and trams where necessary; and if at any mine proper facilties are not afforded to a check weigher as required by the section, the owner, agent and manager of the mine shall each be guilty of an offence against this Act, unless he proves that he had taken all reasonable means to enforce to the best of his power the requirements of this section.

(3.) A check weigher shall not be authorized in any way to impede or inter-rupt the working of the mine, or to interfere with the weighing, or with any of the workmen or with the management of the mine ; but shall be authorized only to take such account or determine such deductions as aforesaid, and the absence of a check weigher from the place at which he is stationed shall not be a reason for interrupting or delaying the weighing or the determination of deductions at such place respectively, but the same shall be done or made by the person appointed in that behalf by the owner, agent or manager, unless the absent check weigher had reasonable ground to suppose that the weighing or the determination of the deductions, as the case may be, would not be pro-ceeded with : Provided always, that nothing in this section shall prevent a check weigher giving to any workman an account of the mineral gotten by him, or information with respect to the weighing, or the weighing machine, or the tareing of the tubs or trams, or with respect to the deductions or any other matter within the scope of his duties as check weigher, so always, nevertheless, that the working of the mine be not interrupted or impeded.

(4.) If the owner, agent or manager of the mine desires the removal of a check weigher on the ground that the check weigher has impeded or inter-rupted the working of the mine, or interfered with the weighing, or with any of the workmen, or with the management of the mine, or has at the mine to the detriment of the owner, agent or manager done anything beyond taking such account determining such deductions or giving such information as aforesaid, he may complain to a court of summary jurisdiction, who, if of opinion that the owner, agent or manager shows sufficient primâ facie ground for the removal of the check weigher, shall call on the check weigher to show cause against his removal.

(5.) On the hearing of the case the court shall hear the parties, and, if they think that at the hearing sufficient ground is shown by the owner, agent or manager to justify the removal of the check weigher, shall make a summary order for his removal, and the check weigher shall thereupon be removed, but without prejudice to the stationing of another check weigher in his place.

(6.) The court may in every case make such order as to the costs of the procedings as the court may think just.

(7.) If in pursuance of any order of exemption made by a Secretary of State, the persons employed in a mine are paid by the measure or guage of the material gotten by them, the provisions of this Act shall apply in like manner as if the term "weighing" included measuring and gauging, and the terms relating to weighing shall be construed accordingly.

(8.) If the person appointed by the owner, agent or manager to weigh the mineral impedes or interrupts the check weigher in the proper discharge of his duties, or improperly interferes with or alters the weighing machine or the tare in order to prevent a correct account being taken of the weighing and tareing he shall be guilty of an offence against this Act.

14. (1.) Where a check weigher has been appointed by the majority, ascertained by a ballot, of the persons employed in a mine who are paid according to the weight of the mineral gotten by them, and has acted as such, he may recover from any person for the time being employed at such mine and so paid his proportion of the check weigher's wages or recompense, notwithstanding that any of the persons by whom the check weigher was appointed may have left the mine or others have entered the same since the check weigher's appointment, any rule of law or equity to the contrary notwithstanding.

(2.) It shall be lawful for the owner or manager of any mine, where the majority of the before-mentioned persons, ascertained as aforesaid, so agree, to retain the agreed contribution of the persons so employed and paid as aforesaid for the check weigher, notwithstanding the provisions of the Acts relating to truck, and to pay and account for the same to the check weigher.

15. (1.) The Weights and Measures Act, 1878, shall apply to all weights, balances, scales, steelyards and weighing machines used at any mine for determining the wages payable to any person employed in the mine according to the weight of the mineral gotten by him, in like manner as it applies to weights, balances, scales, steelyards and weighing machines used for trade.

(2.) An inspector of weights and measures appointed under the said Act shall once at least in every six months inspect and examine in manner directed by the said Act the weights, balances, scales, steelyards and weighing machines used or in the possession of any person for use as aforesaid at any mine within his district; and shall also make such inspection and examination at any other time in any case where he has reasonable cause to believe that there is in use at the mine any false or unjust weight, balance, scale, steelyard or weighing machine.

(3.) The inspector shall also inspect and examine the measures and gauges in use at the mines within his district; but nothing in this section shall prevent or interfere with the use of the measures or guages ordinarily used at the mine.

(4.) An inspector may, for the purposes of this section, without any authorization from a justice of the peace, exercise at or in any mine, as respects all weights, measures, scales, balances, steelyards and weighing machines used or in the possession of any person for use at or in that mine, all such powers as he could exercise, if authorized in writing by a justice of the peace, under section forty-eight of the Weights and Measures Act, 1878, with respect to any such weights, measures, scales, balances, steelyards and weighing machines as therein mentioned; and all the provisions of that section, including the liability to penalties, shall apply to such inspection.

(5.) The inspector of weights and measures shall not, in fulfilling the duties required of him under this section, impede or obstruct the working of the mine.

SINGLE SHAFTS.

16. (1.) After the commencement of this Act, the owner, agent or manager of a mine shall not employ any person in the mine, or permit any person to be in the mine for the purpose of employment therein, unless the following conditions respecting shafts or outlets are complied with, that is to say,—

a. There must be at least two shafts or outlets, with which every seam for the time being at work in the mine shall have a communication, so that such shafts or outlets shall afford separate means of ingress and egress available to the persons employed in every such seam, whether the shafts or outlets belong to the same mine or to more than one mine:

b. Such shafts or outlets must not at any point be nearer to one another than fifteen yards; and there shall be between such two shafts or outlets a communication not less than four feet wide and three feet high, and in the case of communications made after the commencement of this Act between shafts or outlets, not less than four feet high.

c. Proper apparatus for raising and lowering persons at each such shaft or outlet shall be kept on the works belonging to the mine; and such apparatus if not in actual use at the shafts or outlets, shall be constantly available for use.

(2.) Every owner, agent and manager of a mine who acts in contravention of or fails to comply with this section shall be guilty of an offence against this Act.

(3.) Any of Her Majesty's superior courts, whether any other proceedings have or have not been taken, may, on the application of the Attorney General, prohibit by injunction the working of any mine in which any person is employed, or is permitted to be for the purpose of employment, in contravention of this section, and may award such costs in the matter of the injunction as the court thinks just; but this provision shall be without prejudice to any other remedy permitted by law for enforcing the provisions of this Act.

(4.) Written notice of the intention to apply for such injunction in respect of any mine shall be given to the owner, agent or manager of the mine not less than ten days before the application is made.

17. No person shall be precluded by any agreement from doing such acts as may be necessary for providing a second shaft or outlet to a mine, where

the same is required by this Act, or be liable under any contract to any penalty or forfeiture for doing such acts as may be necessary in order to comply with the provisions of this Act with respect to shafts or outlets.

18. The foregoing provisions of this Act with respects to shafts or outlets shall not apply—

i. In the case of a new mine being opened—

   a. to any working for the purpose of making a communication between two or more shafts; or

   b. to any working for the purpose of searching for or proving minerals;

so long as not more than twenty persons are employed below ground at any one time in the whole of the different seams in connection with a single shaft or outlet: nor

ii. To any proved mine so long as it is exempted by order of a Secretary of State on the ground either—

   a. that the quantity of mineral proved is not sufficient to repay the outlay which would be occasioned by sinking or making a second shaft or outlet, or by establishing communication with a second shaft or outlet, in any case where such communication existed and has become unavailable; or

   b. that the workings in any seam of the mine have reached the boundary of the property or the extremity of the mineral field of which that seam is a part, and that it is expedient to work away the pillars already formed in course of the ordinary working, notwithstanding that one of the shafts or outlets may be cut off by so working away the pillars of that seam;

and so long as not more than twenty persons are employed below ground at any one time in the whole of the different seams in connection with a single shaft or outlet; nor

iii. To any mine—

   a. while a shaft is being sunk, or an outlet being made; or

   b. one of the shafts or outlets of which has become, by reason of some accident, unavailable for the use of the persons employed in the mine;

so long as the mine is exempted by order of a Secretary of State, and as the conditions (if any) annexed to the order of exemption are duly observed. The provision in this Act requiring the two shafts or outlets of a mine to be separated by a distance of not less than fifteen yards shall not apply to any mine which is provided with two shafts sunk before the first day of January one thousand eight hundred and sixty-five but at that time separated by a distance of less than ten feet, or commenced to be sunk before the commencement of this Act but separated by a distance of more than ten feet and less than fifteen yards.

The foregoing provisions of this Act as to the dimensions of the communication between two shafts or outlets shall not apply to any mine or class of mines so long as the same is exempted therefrom by order of a Secretary of State by reason of the thinness of the seams or other exigencies affecting that mine or class of mines, and so long as the conditions (if any) annexed to the order of exemption are duly observed.

DIVISION OF MINE INTO PARTS.

19. (1.) Where two or more parts of a mine are worked separately, the owner, agent or manager of the mine may give notice in writing to that effect to

the inspector of the district, and thereupon each such part shall, for all the purposes of this Act, be deemed to be a separate mine.

(2.) If a Secretary of State is of opinion that the division of a mine in pursuance of this section tends to lead to evasion of the provisions of this Act, or otherwise to prevent the carrying of this Act into effect, he may object to the division by notice served on the owner, agent or manager of the mine ; and the owner, agent or manager, if he declines to acquiesce in such objection, may, within twenty days after receipt of the notice, send a notice to the inspector of the district stating that he declines so to acquiesce, and thereupon the matter shall be determined by arbitration in manner provided by this Act ; and the date of the receipt of the last-mentioned notice shall be deemed to be the date of the reference.

CERTIFICATED MANAGERS.

20. (1.) Every mine shall be under a manager, who shall be responsible for the control, management, and direction of the mine, and the owner or agent of every such mine shall nominate himself or some other person to be the manager of such mine, and shall send written notice to the inspector of the district of the manager's name and address.

(2.) A person shall not be qualified to be a manager of a mine unless he is for the time being registered as the holder of a first class certificate under this Act.

(3.) If any mine is worked for more than fourteen days without there being such a manager for the mine as is required by this section, the owner, and agent of the mine shall each be liable to a fine not exceeding fifty pounds, and to a further fine not exceeding ten pounds for every day during which the mine is so worked.

Provided that—

a. The owner of the mine shall not be liable to any such fine if he proves that he had taken all reasonable means by the enforcement of this section to prevent the mine being worked in contravention of this section ;

b. If for any reasonable cause there is for the time being no manager of a mine qualified as required by this section, the owner or agent of the mine may appoint any competent person not holding a certificate under this Act to be manager, for a period not exceeding two months for such longer period as may elapse before such person has an opportunity in the district wherein the mine is situate of obtaining by examination a certificate under this Act, and shall send to the inspector of the district a written notice of the manager's name and address, and of the reason for his appointment ; and

c. A mine in which not more than thirty persons are employed below ground shall be exempt from the provisions of this section, unless the inspector of the district, by notice in writing served on the owner or agent of the mine, requires that it be under the control of a manager.

21. (1.) In every mine required by this Act to be under the control of a certificated manager, daily personal supervision shall be exercised either by the manager, or by an under-manager nominated in writing by the owner or agent of the mine.

(2.) Every person so nominated must hold either a first class or second class certificate under this Act, and shall, in the absence of the manager, have the same responsibility, and be subject to the same liabilities as the manager under this Act; but the nomination of an under manager shall not affect the personal responsibility of the manager under this Act.

22. A contractor for mineral, or person employed by such a contractor, is not eligible for the post of manager or under-manager under this Act.

23. (1.) There shall be two descriptions of certificates of competency under this Act (i), first class certificates, that is to say, certificates of fitness to be manager; and (ii) second class certificates, that is to say, certificates of fitness to be under-manager; but no person shall be entitled to a certificate under this Act unless he shall have had practical experience in a mine for at least five years.

(2.) For the purpose of granting in any part of the United Kingdom, to be from time to time defined by an order of a Secretary of State, certificates of competency for the purposes of this Act, examiners shall be appointed by a board consisting of—

a. Three persons being owners of mines in the said part of the United Kingdom; and

b. Three persons employed or who have been employed in or about any mine in the said part of the United Kingdom, not being owners, agents or managers of a mine; and

c. Three persons practising as mining engineers, agents or managers of mines, or coal viewers in the said part of the United Kingdom; and

d. One inspector under this Act.

(3.) The members of the board shall be appointed and may be removed by a Secretary of State, and shall hold office during his pleasure.

24. (1.) The proceedings of each board shall be in accordance with the rules contained in schedule one to this Act.

(2.) Each board shall from time to time appoint examiners, not being members of the board, except with the consent of the Secretary of State, to conduct the examinations in the part of the United Kingdom for which the board acts, of applicants for certificates of competency under this Act, and may from time to time make, alter and revoke rules as to the conduct of such examinations and the qualifications of the applicants, so, however, that in every such examination regard shall be had to such knowledge as is necessary for the practical working of mines in that part of the United Kingdom, and that the examination and qualifications of applicants in second class certificates shall be suitable for practical working miners.

(3.) Each board shall make from time to time to a Secretary of State a report of their proceedings, and of such other matters as a Secretary of State may from time to time require.

25. A Secretary of State may from time to time make, alter and revoke rules as to the places and times of examinations of applicants for certificates of competency under this Act, the number and remuneration of the examiners, and the fees to be paid by the applicants, so that the fees do not exceed those specified in schedule two to this Act. Every such rule shall be observed by every board appointed under this Act to which it applies.

26. (1.) A Secretary of State shall deliver to every applicant who is duly reported by the examiners to have passed the examination satisfactorily, and to have given satisfactory evidence of his sobriety, experience, ability and general good conduct, such a certificate of competency as the case requires. The certificate shall be in such form as a Secretary of State from time to time directs.

(2.) A register of the holders of such certificates shall be kept by such person and in such manner as a Secretary of State from time to time directs.

27. If at any time representation is made to a Secretary of State by an inspector or otherwise, that any manager or under-manager holding a certificate under this Act is by reason of incompetency or gross negligence unfit to discharge his duties, or has been convicted of an offence against this Act, the Secretary of State may, if he think fit, cause inquiry to be made into the conduct of the manager or under-manager, and with respect to every such inquiry the following provisions shall have effect:

(1.) The inquiry shall be public, and shall be held at such place as the Secretary of State may appoint by such county court judge, metropolitan police magistrate, stipendiary magistrate, or other person or persons, as may be directed by the Secretary of State, and either alone or with the assistance of any assessor or assessors named by the Secretary of State:

(2.) The Secretary of State shall, before the commencement of the inquiry, furnish to the manager or under-manager a statement of the case on which the inquiry is instituted:

(3.) Some person appointed by the Secretary of State shall undertake the management of the case:

(4.) The manager or under-manager may attend the inquiry by himself, his counsel, solicitor, or agent, and may, if he thinks fit, be sworn and examined as an ordinary witness in the case:

(5.) The person or persons appointed to hold the inquiry, in this Act referred to as the court, shall, on the conclusion of the inquiry, send to the Secretary of State a report containing a full statement of the case, and the opinion of the court thereon, and such report of, or extracts from the evidence, as the court may think fit:

(6.) The court shall have power to cancel or suspend the certificate of the manager or under-manager, if it finds that he is by reason of incompetency or gross negligence, or of his having been convicted of an offence against this Act, unfit to discharge his duty:

(7.) The court may, if he thinks fit, require a manager or under-manager to deliver up his certificate, and if any manager or under-manager fails, without sufficient cause to the satisfaction of the court, to comply with such requisition, he shall be liable to a fine not exceeding one hundred pounds. The court shall hold a certificate so delivered until the conclusion of the investigation, and shall then either restore, cancel or suspend the certificate according to its judgment on the case:

(8.) The court shall have for the purpose of the inquiry, all the powers of a court of summary jurisdiction, and all the powers of an inspector under this Act:

(9.) The court may also, by summons signed by the court, require the attendance of all such persons as it thinks fit to summon and examine for the purpose of the inquiry, and every person so summoned shall be allowed such expenses as would be allowed to a witness attending on subpœna before a court of record; and in case of dispute as to the amount to be allowed, the same shall be referred by the court to a master of one of Her Majesty's superior courts, who, on request signed by the court, shall ascertain and certify the proper amount of such expenses.

28. (1.) The court may make such order as it thinks fit respecting the costs and expenses of the inquiry, and such order shall, on the application of any party entitled to the benefit thereof, be enforced by any court of summary jurisdiction as if such costs and expenses were a fine imposed by that court.

(2.) The Secretary of State may, if he thinks fit, pay to the person or persons constituting the court, including any assessors, such remuneration as he may with the consent of the Treasury appoint.

(3.) Any costs and expenses ordered by the court to be paid by a Secretary of State, and any remuneration paid under this section, shall be paid out of moneys provided by Parliament.

29. (1.) Where a certificate of a manager or under-manager is cancelled or suspended in pursuance of this Act, a Secretary of State shall cause the cancellation or suspension to be recorded in the register of holders of certificates.

(2.) A Secretary of State may at any time, if it is shown to him to be just so to do, renew or restore, on such terms as he thinks fit, any certificate which has been cancelled or suspended in pursuance of this Act, and cause the renewal or restoration to be recorded in the register aforesaid.

30. Whenever any person proves to the satisfaction of a Secretary of State that he has, without fault on his part, lost or been deprived of any certificate granted to him under this Act, the Secretary of State shall, on payment of such fee, if any, as he may direct, but not exceeding the fee specified in schedule two to this Act, cause a copy of the certificate to which the applicant appears by the register to be entitled, to be made out and certified by the person who keeps the register, and delivered to the applicant; and any copy which purports to be so made and certified as aforesaid shall have all the effect of the original certificate.

31. (1.) All expenses incurred by a Secretary of State with the concurrence of the Treasury in carrying into effect the provisions of this Act with respect to certificates of competency shall be defrayed out of moneys provided by Parliament.

(2.) All fees payable by the applicants for examination for or for a copy of a certificate under this Act shall be paid into the receipt of Her Majesty's Exchequer in such manner as the Treasury may from time to time direct, and be carried to the Consolidated Fund.

32. Every person who commits any of the following offences; that is to say,

(1.) Forges, or counterfeits, or knowingly makes any false statement in any certificate of competency under this Act, or in any certificate of service granted under this Act or any Act repealed by this Act, or any official copy of any such certificate; or

(2.) Knowingly utters or uses any such certificate or copy which has been forged or counterfeited or contains any false statement; or

(3.) For the purpose of obtaining for himself or any other person, employment as a certificated manager or under-manager, or the grant renewal or restoration of any certificate under this Act, or a copy thereof either

　　a. makes or gives any declaration, representation, statement or evidence which is false in any particular, or

　　b. knowingly utters, produces, or makes use of any such declaration, representation, statement or evidence, or any document containing the same,
shall be guilty of a misdemeanor, and be liable on conviction to imprisonment for a term not exceeding two years, with or without hard labor.

RETURNS, PLAN, NOTICES, AND ABANDONMENT.

33. (1.) On or before the twenty-first day of January in every year the owner, agent or manager of every mine shall send to the inspector of the district on behalf of a Secretary of State a correct return, specifying, with respect to the year ending on the preceeding thirty-first day of December, the particulars contained in the form in schedule three to this Act, or in such other form as may from time to time be prescribed in lieu of that form by a Secretary of State : Provided that in the case of any mine which is not required by this Act to be under the control of a certificated manager, a return shall not be required of the particulars contained in Part B. of the said form unless or until a Secretary of State otherwise prescribes.

(2.) Forms for the purpose of the returns required by this section shall from time to time, on application, be furnished by the inspector of the district on behalf of the Secretary of State.

(3.) The Secretary of State may publish the aggregate results of the returns made under this section with respect to any particular county or inspector's district, or any large portion of a county or inspector's district, and so much of any individual return as does not relate to the quantity of mineral gotten or wrought, but the portion of any individual return relating to the quantity of mineral gotten or wrought shall not be published without the consent of the person making the return, or of the owner of the mine to which it relates; and no person except an inspector or Secretary of State or any body of commissioners incorporated by Act of Parliament for the drainage of mines, and authorized to assess and levy rates in respect of minerals gotten from such mines, shall be entitled, without such consent, to see such portion as aforesaid of any individual return.

(4.) Every owner, agent or manager of a mine who fails to comply with this section or makes any return which is to his knowledge false in any particular shall be guilty of an offence against this Act.

34. (1.) The owner, agent or manager of every mine shall keep in the office at the mine an accurate plan of the workings of the mine, showing the workings up to a date not more than three months previously, and the general direction and rate of dip of the strata, together with a section of the strata sunk through, or if that be not reasonably practicable, a statement of the depth of the shaft, with a section of the seam.

(2.) The owner, agent or manager of the mine shall, on request at any time of an inspector under this Act, produce to him at the office at the mine such plan and section, and shall also on the like request mark on such plan and section the then state of the workings of the mine ; and the inspector shall be entitled to examine the plan and section, and for official purposes only to make a copy of any part thereof respectively.

(3.) If the owner, agent or manager of any mine fails to keep, or wilfully refuses to produce or allow to be examined, the plan and section aforesaid, or wilfully withholds any portion thereof, or wilfully refuses, on request, to mark thereon the state of the workings of the mine, or conceals any part of those workings, or produces an imperfect or inaccurate plan or section, he shall (unless he shows that he was ignorant of the concealment, imperfection or inaccuracy) be guilty of an offence against this Act; and further, the inspector may by notice in writing (whether a penalty for the offence has or has not been inflicted) require the owner, agent or manager to cause an accurate plan and section, showing the particulars hereinbefore required, to be made within a reasonable time at the expence of the owner of the mine. Every such plan must be on a scale of not less than that of the Ordnance Survey of twenty-five inches to the mile or on the same scale as the plan for the time being in use at the mine.

(4.) If the owner, agent or manager fails within twenty days after the requisition of the inspector, or within such further time as may be allowed by a Secretary of State, to cause such plan and section to be made as hereby required, he shall be guilty of an offence against this Act.

35. (1.) Where in or about any mine, whether above or below ground, either—

i. loss of life or any personal injury whatever to any person employed in or about the mine occurs by reason of any explosion of gas, or of any explosive, or of any steam boiler; or

ii. loss of life or any serious personal injury to any person employed in or about the mine occurs by reason of any accident whatever,

the owner, agent or manager of the mine shall, within twenty-four hours next after the explosion or accident, send notice in writing of the explosion or accident and of the loss of life or personal injury occasioned thereby to the inspector of the district on behalf of a Secretary of State, and shall specify in the notice the character of the explosion or accident and the number of persons killed or injured respectively.

(2.) Where loss of life or serious personal injury has immediately resulted from an explosion or accident, the place where the explosion or accident occurred shall be left as it was immediately after the explosion or accident, until the expiration of at least three days after the sending of such notice as aforesaid of such explosion or accident, or until the visit of the place by an inspector, whichever first happens, unless compliance with this enactment would tend to increase or continue a danger or would impede the working of the mine.

(3.) Where any personal injury, of which notice is required to be sent under this section, results in the death of the person injured, notice in writing of the death shall be sent to the inspector of the district on behalf of a Secretary of State within twenty-four hours after such death comes to the knowledge of the owner, agent or manager.

(4.) Every owner, agent or manager who fails to act in compliance with this section shall be guilty of an offence against this Act.

36. In any of the following cases, namely,

i. Where any working is commenced for the purpose of opening a new shaft for or a seam of any mine ;

ii. Where a shaft or seam of any mine is abandoned or the working thereof discontinued ;

iii. Where the working of a shaft or a seam of any mine is recommenced after any abandonment or discontinuance for a period exceeding two months ; or

iv. Where any change occurs in the name of any mine or in the name of the owner, agent or manager of any mine to which this Act applies, or in the principal officers of any incorporated company which is the owner of a mine ; the owner, agent or manager of the mine shall give notice thereof to the inspector of the district within two months after the commencement, abandonment, discontinuance, recommencement, or change, and if such notice is not given the owner, agent or manager shall be guilty of an offence against this Act.

37. (1.) Where any mine is abandoned or the working thereof discontinued at whatever time the abandonment or discontinuance occurred, the owner thereof, and every other person interested in the minerals of the mine, shall cause the top of every shaft and every side entrance from the surface to be and to be kept securely fenced for the prevention of accidents :

Provided that—

i. Subject to any contract to the contrary, the owner of the mine shall, as between himself and any other person interested in the minerals of the mine, be liable to carry into effect this section, and to pay any costs, charges and expenses incurred by any other person interested in the minerals of the mine in carrying this section into effect :

ii. Nothing in this section shall exempt any person from any liability under any other Act, or otherwise.

(2.) If any person fails to act in conformity with this section, he shall be guilty of an offence against this Act.

(3.) No person shall be precluded by any agreement from doing, or be liable under any contract to any damages, penalty or forfeiture for doing such acts as may be necessary in order to comply with the provisions of this section.

(4.) If any occupier of land or other person wilfully obstructs the owner of a mine or other person interested as aforesaid in doing any such acts, he shall be guilty of an offence against this Act.

(5.) Any shaft or side entrance which is not fenced as required by this section, and is within fifty yards of any highway, road, footpath, or place of public resort, or is in open or uninclosed land, shall be deemed to be a nuisance within the meaning of section ninety-one of the Public Health Act, 1875.

38. (1.) Where any mine or seam is abandoned, the owner of the mine or seam at the time of its abandonment, shall, within three months after the abandonment, send to a Secretary of State an accurate plan showing the boundaries of the workings of the mine or seam up to the time of the abandonment, and the position of the workings with regard to the surfaces, and the general direction and rate of dip of the strata, together with a section of the strata sunk through, or if that is not reasonably practicable, a statement of the depth of the shaft, with a section of the seam. Every such plan must be on a scale of not less than that of the ordnance survey of twenty-five inches to the mile, or on the same scale as the plan used at the mine at the time of its abandonment.

(2.) The plan and section shall be preserved under the care of the Secretary of State; but no person, except an inspector under this Act, shall be entitled, without the consent of the owner of the mine or seam, to see the plan when so sent until after the expiration of ten years from the time of the abandonment.

(3.) The owner aforesaid shall also, within three months of the abandonment of the mine or seam, send to the inspector of the district, on behalf of a Secretary of State, a correct return specifying, with respect to the period which has elapsed since the expiration of the year covered by the last annual return made under this Act, the particulars required in that return; and the provisions of this Act with respect to the said annual return shall apply to the return so sent.

(4.) If the owner of a mine or seam fails to comply with this section, he shall be guilty of an offence against this Act, and be liable to a fine not exceeding thirty pounds.

(5.) A complaint or information of an offence under this section may be made or laid at any time within six months after abandonment of the mine or seam, or after service on the owner aforesaid of a notice to comply with the requirements of this section, whichever last happens.

INSPECTION.

39. (1.) A Secretary of State may from time to time appoint any fit persons to be inspectors (under whatever title he may from time to time fix) of mines, and assign them their duties, and may award them such salaries as the Treasury may approve, and may remove any such inspector: Provided always, that in the appointment of inspectors of mines in Wales and Monmouthshire among candidates, otherwise equally qualified, persons having a knowledge of the Welsh language shall be preferred.

(2.) Notice of the appointment of every such inspector shall be published in the London *Gazette*.

(3.) Every such inspector is referred to in this Act as an inspector, and the inspector of a district means the inspector who is for the time being assigned to the district or portion of the United Kingdom with reference to which the term is used.

(4.) Any person appointed or acting as inspector under the Metalliferous Mines Regulation Act, 1872, if directed by a Secretary of State to act as an inspector under this Act, may so act, and shall be deemed to be an inspector under this Act.

(5.) The salaries of the inspectors and the expenses incurred by them or by a Secretary of State in the execution of this Act shall continue to be paid out of moneys to be provided by Parliament.

40. Any person who practises or acts as or is a partner of any person who practises or acts as a land agent or mining engineer, or as a manager, viewer

24

agent or valuer of mines, or arbitrator in any difference arising between
owners, agents or managers of mines, or is otherwise employed in or about any
mine, or is a miner's agent or a mine owner (whether the mine is one to
which this Act applies or not), shall not act as an inspector of mines under
this Act, and no inspector shall be a partner or have any interest direct or in-
direct in any mine in the district under his charge.

41. An inspector under this Act shall have power to do all or any of the
following things; namely,

i. To make such examination and inquiry as may be necessary to ascertain
whether the provisions of this Act relating to matters above ground or below
ground are complied with in the case of any mine :

ii. To enter inspect and examine any mine, and every part thereof, at all
reasonable times by day and night, but so as not to impede or obstruct the
working of the mine :

iii. To examine into and make inquiry respecting the state and condition
of any mine, or any part thereof, and the ventilation of the mine, and the
sufficiency of the special rules for the time being in force in the mine, and all
matters and things connected with or relating to the safety of the persons
employed in or about the mine or any mine contiguous thereto, or the care
and treatment of the horses and other animals used in the mine :

iv. To exercise such other powers as may be necessary for carrying this
Act into effect.

Every person who wilfully obstructs any inspector in the execution of his
duty under this act, and every owner, agent and manager of a mine who
refuses or neglects to furnish to the inspector the means necessary for making
any entry, inspection, examination, or inquiry under this act, in relation to the
mine, shall be guilty of an offence against this Act.

42. (1.) If in any respect (which is not provided against by any express provision of this Act, or by any special rule) any inspector finds any mine, or any
part thereof, or any matter, thing or practice in or connected with any such
mine, or with the control, management, or direction thereof by the manager to
be dangerous or defective, so as in his opinion to threaten or tend to the
bodily injury of any person, he may give notice in writing thereof to the owner,
agent or manager of the mine, and shall state in the notice the particulars in
which he considers the mine or any part thereof, or any matter, thing or practice, to be dangerous or defective, and require the same to be remedied; and
unless the same be forthwith remedied shall also report the same to a Secretary of State.

(2.) If the owner, agent or manager of the mine objects to remedy the matter
complained of in the notice he may, within ten days after receipt of the notice,
send his objection in writing, stating the grounds thereof, to a Secretary of
State ; and thereupon the matter shall be determined by arbitration in manner
provided by this Act ; and the date of the receipt of the objection shall be
deemed to be the date of the reference.

(3.) If the owner, agent or manager fail, when no objection is sent as aforesaid, to comply with the requisition of the notice within ten days after the expiration of the time for objection, or when there has been an arbitration to comply with the award within the time fixed by the award, he shall be guilty of an

offence against this Act, and the notice and award shall respectively be deemed to be written notice of the offence.

Provided that the court, if satisfied that the owner, agent or manager has taken active measures for complying with the notice or award, but has not, with reasonable diligence, been able to complete the works, may adjourn any proceedings taken before them for punishing the offence, and if the works are completed within a reasonable time, no penalty shall be inflicted.

(4.) No person shall be precluded by any agreement from doing, or be liable under any contract to any penalty or forfeiture for doing, such acts as may be necessary in order to comply with the provisions of this section.

43. Every inspector of a district under this Act shall make an annual report of his proceedings during the preceding year to a Secretary of State, which report shall be laid before both Houses of Parliament.

44. Where in any mine an explosion or accident has caused loss of life or personal injury to any person, a Secretary of State may at any time direct an inspector to make a special report with respect to the explosion or accident.

45. Where it appears to a Secretary of State that a formal investigation of any explosion or accident and of its causes and circumstances is expedient, the Secretary of State may direct such investigation to be held, and with respect to any such investigation the following provisions shall have effect :

(1.) The Secretary of State may appoint a competent person to hold the investigation, and may appoint any person or persons possessing legal or special knowledge to act as assessor or assessors in holding the investigation.

(2.) The person or persons so appointed (hereinafter called the court) shall hold the investigation in open court, in such manner and under such conditions as the court may think most effectual for ascertaining the causes and circumstances of the explosion or accident, and enabling the court to make the report in this section mentioned.

(3.) The court shall have for the purpose of the investigation all the powers of a court of summary jurisdiction when acting as a court in hearing informations for offences against this Act, and all the powers of an inspector under this Act, and in addition the following powers; namely,

a. Power to enter and inspect any place or building the entry or inspection whereof appears to the court requisite for the said purpose :

b. Power, by summons signed by the court, to require the attendance of all such persons as it thinks fit to call before it and examine for the said purpose, and for that purpose to require answers or returns to such inquiries as it thinks fit to make :

c. Power to require the production of all books, papers and documents which it considers important for the said purpose :

d. Power to administer an oath and require any person examined to make and sign a declaration of the truth of the statements made by him in his examination :

(4.) Persons attending as witnesses before the court shall be allowed such expenses as would be allowed to witnesses attending before a court of record; and in case of dispute as to the amount to be allowed, the same shall be referred by the court to a master of one of Her Majesty's superior courts, who on request, signed by the court, shall ascertain and certify the proper amount of the expenses :

(5.) The court holding an investigation under this section shall make a report to the Secretary of State, stating the causes of the explosion or accident and its circumstances, and adding any observations which the court thinks right to make :

(6.) All expenses incurred in and about an investigation under this section (including the remuneration of any person appointed to act as assessor) shall be deemed to be part of the expenses of the Secretary of State in the execution of this Act.

(7.) Any person who without reasonable excuse (proof whereof shall lie on him) either fails, after having had the expenses (if any) to which he is entitled tendered to him, to comply with any summons or requisition of a court hold-ing an investigation under this section, or prevents or impedes the court in the execution of its duty, shall for every such offence be liable to a fine not exceed-ing ten pounds, and in the case of a failure to comply with a requisition for making any return or producing any document shall be liable to a fine not exceeding ten pounds for every day that such failure continues.

46. The Secretary of State may cause any special report of an inspector or any report of a court under this part of this Act to be made public at such time and in such manner as he may think fit.

ARBITRATION.

47. With respect to arbitrations under this Act, the following provisions shall have effect :

(1.) The parties to the arbitration are in this section deemed to be the owner, agent or manager of the mine on the one hand, and the inspector of mines (on behalf of the Secretary of State) on the other :

(2.) Each of the parties to the arbitration may, within fourteen days after the date of the reference, appoint an arbitrator.

(3.) No person shall act as arbitrator or umpire under this Act who is employed in or in the management of or is interested in the mine to which the arbitration relates :

(4.) The appointment of an arbitrator under this section shall be in writing, and notice of the appointment shall be forthwith sent to the other party to the arbitration, and shall not be revoked without the consent of that party :

(5.) The death, removal or other change in any of the parties to the arbitra-tion shall not affect the proceedings under this section :

(6.) If within the said fourteen days either of the parties fails to appoint an arbitrator, the arbitrator appointed by the other party may proceed to hear and determine the matter in difference, and in that case the award of the single arbitrator shall be final :

(7.) If before an award has been made any arbitrator appointed by either party dies or becomes incapable to act, or for seven days refuses or neglects to act, the party by whom such arbitrator was appointed may appoint some other person to act in his place ; and if he fails to do so within seven days after notice in writing from the other party for that purpose, the remaining arbitrator may proceed to hear and determine the matter in difference, and in that case the award of the single arbitrator shall be final:

(8.) In either of the foregoing cases where an arbitrator is empowered to act singly, on one of the parties failing to appoint, the party so failing may, before the single arbitrator has actually proceeded in the arbitration, appoint an arbitrator, who shall then act as if no failure had occurred:

(9.) If the arbitrators fail to make their award within twenty-one days after the day on which the last of them was appointed, or within such extended time (if any) as may have been appointed for that purpose by both arbitrators under their hands, the matter in difference shall be determined by the umpire appointed as hereinafter mentioned:

(10.) The arbitrators, before they enter on the matter referred to them, shall appoint by writing under their hands an umpire to decide on points on which they may differ:

(11.) If the umpire dies or becomes incapable of acting before he has made his award, or refuses to make his award within a reasonable time after the matter has been brought within his cognizance, the persons or person who appointed such umpire shall forthwith appoint another umpire in his place:

(12.) If the arbitrators refuse or fail or for seven days after the request of either party neglect to appoint an umpire, then on the application of either party an umpire may be appointed by the chairman of the general or quarter sessions of the peace, within the jurisdiction of which the mine or any shaft of the mine is situate:

(13.) The decision of every umpire on the matters referred to him shall be final.

(14.) If a single arbitrator fails to make his award within twenty-one days after the day on which he was appointed, the party who appointed him may appoint another arbitrator to act in his place:

(15.) Arrangements shall whenever practicable be made for the matter in difference being heard at the same time before the arbitrators and the umpire:

(16.) The arbitrators and the umpire or any of them may examine the parties and their witnesses on oath, and may also consult any counsel engineer or scientific person whom they may think it expedient to consult:

(17.) The payment, if any, to be made to any arbitrator or umpire for his services shall be fixed by the Secretary of State, and together with the costs of the arbitration and award shall be paid by the parties or one of them according as the award may direct. Such costs may be taxed by a master of one of Her Majesty's superior courts, who, on the written application of either of the parties, shall ascertain and certify the proper amount thereof. The amount, if any, payable by the Secretary of State shall be paid as part of the expenses of inspector under this Act. The amount, if any, payable by the owner, agent or manager may in the event of non-payment be recovered in the same manner as fines under this Act:

(18.) Every person who is appointed an arbitrator under this section shall be a practical mining engineer, or a person accustomed to the working of mines, and every person who is appointed an umpire under this section shall be a county court judge, a police or stipendiary magistrate, a recorder of a borough, or a registrar of a county court, but when an award has been made under this section the arbitrator or umpire who made it shall be deemed to have been duly qualified as provided by this section.

CORONERS.

48. With respect to coroners' inquests on the bodies of persons whose death may have been caused by explosions or accidents in or about mines, the following provisions shall have effect:

(1.) When a coroner holds an inquest on the body of any person whose death may have been caused by any explosion or accident, of which notice is required by this Act to be given to the inspector of the district, the coroner shall adjourn the inquest unless an inspector, or some person on behalf of a Secretary of State, is present to watch the proceedings:

(2.) The coroner, at least four days before holding the adjourned inquest, shall send to the inspector for the district notice in writing of the time and place of holding the adjourned inquest:

(3.) The coroner, before the adjournment, may take evidence to identify the body, and may order the interment thereof:

(4.) If an explosion or accident has not occasioned the death of more than one person, and the coroner has sent to the inspector of the district notice of the time and place of holding the inquest at such time as to reach the inspector not less than twenty-four hours before the time of holding the same, it shall not be imperative on him to adjourn the inquest in pursuance of this section, if the majority of the jury think it unnecessary so to adjourn: ·

(5.) An inspector shall be at liberty at any such inquest to examine any witness, subject nevertheless to the order of the coroner:

(6.) Where evidence is given at an inquest at which an inspector is not present of any neglect as having caused or contributed to the explosion or accident, or of any defect in or about the mine appearing to the coroner or jury to require a remedy, the coroner shall send to the inspector of the district notice in writing of such neglect or defect:

(7.) Any person having a personal interest in or employed in or in the management of the mine in which the explosion or accident occurred shall not be qualified to serve on the jury empannelled on the inquest; and it shall be the duty of the constable or other officer not to summon any person disqualified under this provision, and it shall be the duty of the coroner not to allow any such person to be sworn or to sit on the jury:

(8.) Any relative of any person whose death may have been caused by the explosion or accident with respect to which the inquest is being held, and the owner, agent or manager of the mine in which the explosion or accident occurred, and any person appointed by the order in writing of the majority of the workmen employed at the said mine, shall be at liberty to attend and examine any witness, either in person or by his counsel, solicitor, or agent, subject nevertheless to the order of the coroner.

Every person who fails to comply with the provisions of this section shall be guilty of an offence against this Act.

PART II.

General Rules.

49. The following general rules shall be observed, so far as is reasonably practicable, in every mine :

Rule 1. An adequate amount of ventilation shall be constantly produced in every mine to dilute and render harmless noxious gases to such an extent that the working places of the shafts, levels, stables, and workings of the mine, and the travellling roads to and from those working places shall be in a fit state for working and passing therein.

In the case of mines required by this Act to be under the control of a certificated manager, the quantity of air in the respective splits or currents shall at least once in every month be measured and entered in a book to be kept for the purpose at the mine.

Rule 2. Where a fire is used for ventilation in any mine newly opened after the passing of this Act, the return air, unless it be so diluted as not to be inflammable, shall be carried off clear of the fire by means of a dumb drift or airway.

Rule 3. Where a mechanical contrivance for ventilation is introduced into any mine after the commencement of this Act, it shall be in such position and placed under such conditions as will tend to ensure its being uninjured by an explosion.

Rule 4. A station or stations shall be appointed at the entrance to the mine, or to different parts of the mine, as the case may require; and the following provisions shall have effect :

i. As to inspection before commencing work :—

A competent person or competent persons appointed by the owner, agent or manager for the purpose not being contractors for getting minerals in the mine shall, within such time immediately before the commencement of each shift as shall be fixed by special rules made under this Act, inspect every part of the mine situate beyond the station or each of the stations, and in which workmen are to work or pass during that shift, and shall ascertain the condition thereof so far as the presence of gas ventilation, roof and sides, and general safety are concerned.

No workman shall pass beyond any such station until the part of the mine beyond that station has been so examined and stated by such competent person to be safe.

The inspection shall be made with a locked safety-lamp, except in the case of any mine in which inflammable gas has not been found within the preceding twelve months.

A report specifying where noxious or inflammable gas, if any, was found present, and what defects (if any) in roofs or sides, and what (if any) other source of danger were or was observed, shall be recorded without delay in a book to be kept at the mine for the purpose, and accessible to the workmen, and such report shall be signed by, and so far as the same does not consist of printed matter shall be in the handwriting of the person who made the inspection.

For the purpose of the foregoing provisions of this rule, two or more shifts succeeding one another without any interval are to be deemed to be one shift.

ii. As to inspection during shifts :—

A similar inspection shall be made in the course of each shift of all parts of the mine in which workmen are to work or pass during that shift. but it shall not be necessary to record a report of the same in a book : Provided that in the case of a mine worked continuously throughout the twenty-four hours by a succession of shifts, the report of one of such inspections shall be recorded in man ner above required.

Rule 5. A competent person or competent. persons appointed by the owner, agent or manager for the purpose, shall, once at least in every twenty-four hours, examine the state of the external parts of the machinery, the state of the guides and conductors in the shafts, and the state of the head gear, ropes, chains, and other similar appliances of the mine which are in actual use both above ground and below ground, and shall once at least in every week examine the state of the shafts by which persons ascend or descend ; and shall make a true report of the result of such examination, and every such report shall be recorded without delay in a book to be kept at the mine for the purpose, and shall be signed by the person who made the inspection.

Rule 6. Every entrance to any place which is not in actual use or course of working and extension, shall be properly fenced across the whole width of the entrance, so as to prevent persons inadvertently entering the same.

Rule 7. If at any time it is found by the person for the time being in charge of the mine, or any part thereof, that by reason of inflammable gases prevailing in the mine, or that part thereof, or of any cause whatever, the mine or that part is dangerous, every workman shall be withdrawn from the mine or part so found dangerous, and a competent person appointed for the purpose shall inspect the mine or part so found dangerous, and if the danger arises from inflammable gas shall inspect the mine or part with a locked safety-lamp ; and in every case shall make a true report of the condition of the mine or part ; and a workman shall not, except in so far as is necessary for inquiring into the cause of danger or for the removal thereof, or for exploration, be readmitted into the mine, or part so found dangerous, until the same is stated by the person appointed as aforesaid not to be dangerous. Every such report shall be recorded in a book which shall be kept at the mine for the purpose, and shall be signed by the person who made the inspection.

Rule 8. No lamp or light other than a locked safety-lamp shall be allowed or used—

a. In any place in a mine in which there is likely to be any such quantity of inflammable gas as to render the use of naked lights dangerous ; or

b. In any working approaching near a place in which there is likely to be an accumulation of inflammable gas.

And when it is necessary to work the coal in any part of a ventilating district with safety-lamps, it shall not be allowable to work the coal with naked lights in another part of the same ventilating district situated between the place where such lamps are being used and the return air-way.

Rule 9. Wherever safety-lamps are used. they shall be so constructed that they may be safely carried against the air current ordinarily prevailing in that part of the mine in which the lamps are for the time being in use, even though such current should be inflammable.

Rule 10. In any mine or part of a mine in which safety-lamps are required by this Act or by the special rules made in pursuance of this Act to be used—

i. A competent person appointed by the owner, agent or manager for the purpose, shall, either at the surface or at the appointed lamp station, examine every safety-lamp immediately before it is taken into the workings for use, and ascertain it to be in safe working order and securely locked; and such lamps shall not be used until they have been so examined and found in safe working order and securely locked:

ii. A safety-lamp shall not be unlocked except either at the appointed lamp station or for the purpose of firing a shot, in conformity with the provisions hereinafter contained:

iii. A person, unless he has been appointed either for the purpose of examining safety lamps or for the purpose of firing shots, shall not have in his possession any contrivance for opening the lock of any safety-lamp.

iv. A person shall not have in his possession any lucifer match or apparatus of any kind for striking a light, except within a completely closed chamber attached to the fuse of the shot.

Rule 11. Where safety-lamps are required to be used, the position of the lamp stations for lighting or re-lighting the lamps shall not be in the return air.

Rule 12. Any explosive substance shall only be used in the mine below ground as follows:

a. It shall not be stored in the mine:

b. It shall not be taken into the mine, except in cartridges in a secure case or canister containing not more than five pounds:

> Provided, that on the application of the owner, agent or manager of any mine, the Secretary of State may by order exempt such mine from so much of this rule as forbids taking an explosive substance into the mine except in cartridges.

c. A workman shall not have in use at one time in any one place more than one of such cases or canisters:

d. In the process of charging or stemming for blasting, a person shall not use or have in his possession any iron or steel pricker, scraper, charger, tamping rod, or stemmer, nor shall coal or coal dust be used for tamping:

e. No explosive shall be forcibly pressed into a hole of insufficient size, and, when a hole has been charged, the explosive shall not be unrammed, and no hole shall be bored for a charge at a distance of less than six inches from any hole where the charge has missed fire:

f. In any place in which the use of a locked safety-lamp is for the time being required by or in pursuance of this Act, or which is dry and dusty, no shot shall be fired except by or under the direction of a competent person appointed by the owner, agent or manager of the mine, and such person shall not fire the shot or allow it to be fired until he has examined both the place itself where the shot is to be fired and all contiguous accessible places of the same seam within a radius of twenty yards, and has found such place safe for firing:

g. If in any mine, at either of the four inspections under Rule 4 recorded last before a shot is to be fired, inflammable gas has been reported to be present in the ventilating district in which the shot is to be fired, the shot shall not be fired—

(1.) Unless a competent person, appointed as aforesaid, has examined the place where gas has been so reported to be present, and has found that such gas has been cleared away, and that there is not at or near such place sufficient gas issuing or accumulated to render it unsafe to fire the shot ; or

(2.) Unless the explosive employed in firing the shot is so used with water or other contrivance as to prevent it from inflaming gas, or is of such a nature that it cannot inflame gas :

h. If the place where a shot is to be fired is dry and dusty, then the shot shall not be fired unless one of the following conditions is observed, that is to say—

(1.) Unless the place of firing and all contiguous accessible places within a radius of twenty yards therefrom are at the time of firing in a wet state from thorough watering or other treatment equivalent to watering, in all parts where dust is lodged, whether roof, floor, or sides; or

(2.) In the case of places in which watering would injure the roof or floor, unless the explosive is so used with water or other contrivance as to prevent it from inflaming gas or dust, or is of such a nature that it cannot inflame gas or dust :

i. If such dry and dusty place is part of a main haulage road, or is a place contiguous thereto, and showing dust adhering to the roof and sides, no shot shall be fired there unless—

(1.) Both the conditions mentioned in sub-head (*h*) have been observed ; or

(2.) Unless such one of the conditions mentioned in sub-head (*h*) as may be applicable to the particular place has been observed, and moreover all workmen have been removed from the seam in which the shot is to be fired, and from all seams communicating with the shaft on the same level, except the men engaged in firing the shot, and such other persons, not exceeding ten, as are necessarily employed in attending to the ventilating furnaces, steam boilers, engines, machinery, winding apparatus, signals, or horses, or in inspecting the mine :

k. In this Act "ventilating district" means such part of a seam as has an independent intake commencing from a main intake air course, and an independent return air-way terminating at a main return air course; and "main haulage road" means a road which has been, or for the time being is, in use for moving trams by steam or other mechanical power :

l. Where a seam of a mine is not divided into separate ventilating districts the provisions in this Act relating to ventilating districts shall be read as though the word "seam" were substituted for the words "ventilating district : "

m. So much of this rule as requires the explosive substance taken into the mine to be in cartridges, and so much of the provisions of sub-head (*f*) as relates to a dry and dusty place, and the provisions (*g*), (*h*), (*i*), (*k*) and (*l*) shall not apply to seams of clay or stratified ironstone which are not worked in connection with any coal seam, and which contain no coal in the working.

Rule 13. Where a place is likely to contain a dangerous accumulation of water, the working approaching that place shall not at any point within forty yards of that place exceed eight feet in width, and there shall be constantly kept at a sufficient distance, not being less than five yards in advance, at least one bore-hole near the centre of the working, and sufficient flank bore holes on each side.

Rule 14. Every underground plane on which persons travel, which is self acting or worked by an engine windlass or gin, shall be provided (if exceeding thirty yards in length) with some proper means of communicating distinct and definite signals between the stopping places and the ends of the plane, and shall be provided in every case, with sufficient man-holes for places of refuge, at intervals of not more than twenty yards, or if there is not room for a person to stand between the side of a tub and the side of the plane, then (unless the tubs are moved by an endless chain or rope) at intervals of not more than ten yards.

Rule 15. Every road on which persons travel underground where the load is drawn by a horse or other animal shall be provided, at intervals of not more than fifty yards, with sufficient man-holes, or with places of refuge, and every such place of refuge shall be of sufficient length, and at least three feet in width, between the wagons running on the road and the side of such road. There shall be at least two proper travelling ways into every steam-engine room and boiler gallery.

Rule 16. Every man-hole and every place of refuge shall be constantly kept clear, and no person shall place anything in any such man-hole or place of refuge.

Rule 17. Every travelling road on which a horse or other draught animal is used underground shall be of sufficient dimensions to allow the horse or other animal to pass without rubbing against the roof or timbering.

Rule 18. The top of every shaft which for the time being is out of use, or used only as an air shaft, shall be and shall be kept securely fenced.

Rule 19. The top and all entrances between the top and bottom, including the sump, if any, of every working, ventilating or pumping shaft shall be properly fenced, but this shall not be taken to forbid the temporary removal of the fence for the purpose of repairs or other operations, if proper precautions are used.

Rule 20. Where the natural strata are not safe, every working or pumping shaft shall be securely cased, lined or otherwise made secure.

Rule 21. The roof and sides of every travelling road and working place shall be made secure, and a person shall not, unless appointed for the purpose of exploring or repairing, travel or work in any such travelling road or working place which is not so made secure.

Rule 22. Where the timbering of the working places is done by the workmen employed therein, suitable timber shall be provided at the working place, gate end, pass bye, siding or other similar place in the mine convenient to the workmen, and the distance between the sprags or holing props where they are required shall not exceed six feet or such less distance as may be ordered by the owner, agent or manager.

Rule 23. Where there is a downcast and furnace shaft to the same seam, and both such shafts are provided with apparatus in use for raising and lowering persons, every person employed in the mine shall, on giving reasonable notice, have the option of using the downcast shaft.

Rule 24. In any mine which is usually entered by means of machinery, a competent male person not less than twenty-two years of age shall be appointed for the purpose of working the machinery which is employed in lowering and raising persons therein, and shall attend for that purpose during the whole time that any person is below ground in the mine.

Where any shaft, plane, or level is used for the purpose of communication from one part to another part of a mine, and persons are taken up or down or along such shaft, plane, or level by means of any engine, windlass, or gin, driven or worked by steam or any mechanical power, or by an animal, or by manual labor, the person in charge of such engine, windlass, or gin, or of any part of the machinery, ropes, chains, or tackle connected therewith must be a competent male person not less than eighteen years of age.

Where the machinery is worked by an animal, the person under whose direction the driver of the animal acts, shall for the purposes of this rule, be deemed to be the person in charge of the machinery.

Rule 25. Every working shaft used for the purpose of drawing minerals or for the lowering or raising of persons shall, if exceeding fifty yards in depth, and not exempted in writing by the inspector of the district, be provided with guides and some proper means of communicating distinct and definite signals from the bottom of the shaft and from every entrance for the time being in use between the surface and the bottom of the shaft to the surface, and from the surface to the bottom of the shaft and to every entrance for the time being in use between the surface and the bottom of the shaft.

Rule 26. If in any mine the winding apparatus is not provided with some automatic contrivance to prevent overwinding, then the cage, when men are being raised, shall not be wound up at a speed exceeding three miles an hour after the cage has reached a point in the shaft to be fixed by the special rules.

Rule 27. A sufficient cover overhead shall be used for every cage or tub employed in lowering or raising persons in any working shaft, except where the cage or tub is worked by a windlass, or where persons are employed at work in the shaft, or where a written exemption is given by the inspector of the district.

Rule 28. A single linked chain shall not be used for lowering or raising persons in any working shaft or plane except for the short coupling chain attached to the cage or tub.

Rule 29. There shall be on the drum of every machine used for lowering or raising persons, such flanges or horns, and also if the drum is conical, such other appliances as may be sufficient to prevent the rope from slipping.

Rule 30. There shall be attached to every machine worked by steam, water, or mechanical power, and used for lowering or raising persons, an adequate break or breaks, and a proper indicator (in addition to any mark on the rope) showing to the person who works the machine the position of the cage or tub in the shaft.

If the drum is not on the crank shaft, there shall be an adequate break on the drum shaft.

Rule 31. Every fly-wheel and all exposed and dangerous parts of the machinery used in or about the mine shall be and shall be kept securely fenced.

Rule 32. Each steam boiler, whether separate or one of a range shall have attached to it a proper safety valve, and also a proper steam gauge and water gauge, to show respectively the pressure of steam and the height of water in each boiler.

Rule 33. A barometer and thermometer shall be placed above ground in a conspicuous position near the entrance to the mine.

Rule 34. Where persons are employed underground, ambulances or stretchers, with splints and bandages, shall be kept at the mine ready for immediate use in case of accident.

Rule 35. No person · shall wilfully damage, or without proper authority remove or render useless, any fence, fencing, man-hole, place of refuge, casing, lining, guide, means of signalling, signal, cover, chain, flange, horn, break, indicator, steam gauge, water gauge, safety-valve, or other appliance or thing provided in any mine in compliance with this Act.

Rule 36. Every person shall observe such directions with respect to working as may be given to him with a view to comply with this Act or the special rules in force in the mine.

Rule 37. The books mentioned in these rules shall be provided by the owner, agent or manager, and the books, or a correct copy thereof, shall be kept at the office at the mine, and any inspector under this Act, and any person employed in the mine or any one having the written authority of any inspector or person so employed, may at all reasonable times inspect and take copies of and extracts from any such books; but nothing in these rules shall be construed to impose the obligation of keeping any such book or a copy thereof for more than twelve months after the book has ceased to be used for entries therein under this Act.

Any report by this Act required to be recorded in a book may be partly in print (including lithograph) and partly in writing.

Rule 38. The persons employed in a mine may from time to time appoint two of their number or any two persons, not being mining engineers, who are practical working miners, to inspect the mine at their own cost, and the persons so appointed shall be allowed once at least in every month, accompanied, if the owner agent or manager of the mine thinks fit, by himself or one or more officers of the mine, to go to every part of the mine, and to inspect the shafts, levels, planes, working places, return air-ways, ventilating apparatus, old workings, and machinery. Every facility shall be afforded by the owner, agent and manager, and all persons in the mine for the purpose of the inspection, and the persons appointed shall forthwith make a true report of the result of the inspection, and that report shall be recorded in a book to be kept at the mine for the purpose, and shall be signed by the persons who made the inspection ; and if the report state the existence or apprehended existence of any danger, the owner, agent or manager shall forthwith cause a true copy of the report to be sent to the inspector of the district.

Rule 30. No person not now employed as a coal or ironstone getter shall be allowed to work alone as a coal or ironstone getter in the face of the workings until he has had two years' experience of such work under the supervision of skilled workmen, or unless he shall have been previously employed for two years in or about the face of the workings of a mine.

50. Every person who contravenes or does not comply with any of the general rules in this Act, shall be guilty of an offence against this Act; and in the event of any contravention of or non-compliance with any of the said general rules in the case of any mine to which this Act applies, by any person whomsoever, the owner, agent and manager shall each be guilty of an offence against this Act, unless he proves that he had taken all reasonable means, by publishing and to the best of his power enforcing the said rules as regulations for the working of the mine, to prevent such contravention or non-compliance.

SPECIAL RULES.

51. (1.) There shall be established in every mine such rules (referred to in this Act as special rules) for the conduct and guidance of the persons acting in the management of such mine or employed in or about the mine as, under the particular state and circumstances of such mine, may appear best calculated to prevent dangerous accidents, and to provide for the safety, convenience and proper discipline of the persons employed in or about the mine.

(2.) Such special rules, when established, shall be signed in duplicate by the inspector who is inspector of the district at the time the rules are established, and shall be observed in and about every such mine (including any extension thereof) in the same manner as if they were enacted in this Act.

(3.) If any person who is bound to observe the special rules established for any mine, acts in contravention of or fails to comply with any of them, he shall be guilty of an offence against this Act, and also the owner, agent and manager of such mine shall each be guilty of an offence against this Act unless he proves that he had taken all reasonable means, by publishing and to the best of his power enforcing the rules as regulations for the working of the mine, so as to prevent such contravention or non-compliance.

52. (1.) The owner, agent or manager of every mine shall frame and transmit to the inspector of the district, for approval by a Secretary of State, special rules for the mine within three months after the commencement of this Act, or within three months after the commencement (if subsequent to the commencement of this Act) of any working for the purpose of opening a new mine or of renewing the working of an old mine.

(2.) The proposed special rules, together with a printed notice specifying that any objection to the rules on the ground of anything contained therein or omitted therefrom may be sent by any of the persons employed in the mine to the inspector of the district, at his address, stated in the notice, shall, during not less than two weeks before the rules are transmitted to the inspector, be posted up in like manner as is provided in this Act respecting the publication of special rules for the information of persons employed in the mine, and a certificate that the rules and notice have been so posted up shall be sent to the inspector with two copies of the rules, signed by the person sending the same.

(3.) If the rules are not objected to by the Secretary of State within forty days after their receipt by the inspector, they shall be established.

53. (1.) If the Secretary of State is of opinion that the proposed special rules so transmitted, or any of them, do not sufficiently provide for the prevention of dangerous accidents in the mine, or for the safety or convenience of the persons employed in or about the mine, or are unreasonable, he may, within forty days after the rules are received by the inspector, object to the rules, and propose to the owner, agent or manager in writing any modifications in the rules by way either of omission, alteration, substitution or addition.

(2.) If the owner, agent or manager does not, within twenty days after the modifications proposed by the Secretary of State are received by him, object in writing to them, the proposed special rules, with those modifications, shall be established.

(3.) If the owner, agent or manager sends his objection in writing within the said twenty days to the Secretary of State, the matter shall be referred to arbitration under this Act, and the date of the receipt of the objection by the Secretary of State shall be deemed to be the date of the reference, and the rules shall be established as settled by an award on arbitration.

54. (1.) After special rules are established under this Act in any mine, the owner, agent or manager of the mine may from time to time propose in writing to the inspector of the district, for the approval of a Secretary of State, any amendment of the rules or any new special rules, and the provisions of this Act with respect to the original special rules shall apply to all such amendments and new rules in like manner, as nearly as may be, as they apply to the original rules.

(2.) A Secretary of State may from time to time propose in writing to the owner, agent or manager of the mine any new special rules, or any amendment of the special rules, and the provisions of this Act with respect to a proposal of a Secretary of State for modifying the special rules transmitted by the owner, agent or manager of a mine shall apply to all such new special rules and amendments in like manner, as nearly as may be, as they apply to the proposal.

55. If the owner, agent or manager of any mine makes any false statement with respect to the posting up of the rules and notices, he shall be guilty of an offence against this Act; and if special rules for any mine are not transmitted within the time limited by this Act to the inspector for the approval of a Secretary of State, the owner, agent and manager of such mine shall each be guilty of an offence against this Act, unless he proves that he had taken all reasonable means, by enforcing to the best of his power the provisions of this Act, to secure the transmission of the rules.

56. An inspector under this Act shall, when required, certify a copy which is shown to his satisfaction to be a true copy of any special rules which for the time being are established under this Act in any mine, and a copy so certified shall be evidence (but not to the exclusion of other proof) of such special rules and of the fact that they are duly established under this Act and have been signed by the inspector.

57. For the purpose of making known the provisions of this Act and the special rules to all persons employed in and about each mine, an abstract of this Act supplied, on the application of the owner, agent or manager of the mine, by the inspector of the district on behalf of a Secretary of State, and a correct copy of all the special rules shall be published as follows:

(1.) The owner, agent or manager of the mine shall cause the abstract and copy of the rules, with the name of the mine and the name and address of the inspector of the district, and the name of the owner or agent and of the manager appended thereto, to be posted up in legible characters, in some conspicuous place at or near the mine, where they may be conveniently read by the persons employed; and so often as the same become defaced, obliterated or destroyed, shall cause them to be renewed with all reasonable despatch:

(2.) The owner, agent or manager shall supply a printed copy of the abstract and the special rules gratis to each person employed in or about the mine who applies for a copy at the office at which the persons immediately employed by the owner, agent, or manager are paid:

(3.) Every copy of the special rules shall be kept distinct from any rules which depend only on the contract between the employer and employed:

In the event of any non-compliance with the provisions of this section by any person whomsoever, the owner, agent and manager shall each be guilty of an offence against this Act; but the owner, agent or manager of such mine shall not be deemed guilty if he proves that he had taken all reasonable means, by enforcing to the best of his power the observance of this section, to prevent such non-compliance.

58. Every person who pulls down, injures, or defaces any abstract, notice, proposed special rules, or special rules when posted up in pursuance of the provisions of this Act, or any notice posted up in pursuance of the special rules, shall be guilty of an offence against this Act.

PART III.

SUPPLEMENTAL.

Legal Proceedings.

59. (1.) Every person employed in or about a mine, other than an owner, agent or manager, who is guilty of any act or omission which in the case of an owner, agent or manager would be an offence against this Act, shall be deemed to be guilty of an offence against this Act.

(2.) Every person who is guilty of an offence against this Act for which a penalty is not expressly prescribed, shall be liable to a fine not exceeding, if he is an owner, agent or manager or under-manager, twenty pounds, and if he is any other person, two pounds, for each offence; and if an inspector has given written notice of any such offence, to a further fine not exceeding one pound for every day after such notice that such offence continues to be committed.

60. Where a person who is an owner, agent, manager or under-manager of or a person employed in or about a mine is guilty of any offence against this Act which, in the opinion of the court that tries the case, is one which was reasonably calculated to endanger the safety of the persons employed in or about the mine, or to cause serious personal injury to any of such persons, or to cause a dangerous accident, and was committed wilfully by the personal act, personal default, or personal negligence of the person accused, such person shall be liable, if the court is of opinion that a fine will not meet the circumstances of the case, to imprisonment, with or without hard labor, for a period not exceeding three months.

61. (1.) All offences under this Act not declared to be misdemeanors, and all fines under this Act, and all money and costs by this Act directed to be recovered as fines, may be prosecuted and recovered in manner directed by the Summary Jurisdiction Acts before a court of summary jurisdiction.

(2.) Proceedings for the removal of a check weigher shall be deemed to be a matter on which a court of summary jurisdiction has authority by law to make an order in pursuance of the Summary Jurisdiction Acts; and summary orders under this Act may be made on complaint before a court of summary jurisdiction in manner provided by the Summary Jurisdiction Acts.

62. In every part of the United Kingdom the following provisions shall have effect:

i. Any complaint or information made or laid in pursuance of this Act shall (save as otherwise expressly provided by this Act) be made or laid within three months from the time when the matter of the complaint or information arose:

ii. Any person charged with any offence under this Act, may, if he thinks fit, be sworn and examined as an ordinary witness in the case:

iii. The court shall, if required by either party, cause minutes of the evidence to be taken and preserved.

63. If any person feels aggrieved by any conviction made by a court of summary jurisdiction on determining any information under this Act, by which conviction imprisonment or a fine amounting to or exceeding one half the maximum fine, is adjudged, he may appeal therefrom to a court of quarter sessions in manner provided by the Summary Jurisdiction Acts.

64. If it appears that a boy or girl was employed on the representation of his or her parent or guardian that he or she was of the age at which his or her employment would not be in contravention of this Act, and under the belief in good faith that he or she was of that age, or that a person has worked alone as a coal or iron-stone getter on his representation that he has had two years' experience of such work under the supervision of skilled workmen, or that he has been previously employed for two years in or about the face of the workings of a mine, and under the belief in good faith that he has had such experience or has been so previously employed, the owner, agent or manager of the mine and employer shall be exempted from any penalty, and the parent or guardian or the person who has so worked alone, as the case may be, shall, for the misrepresentation, be deemed guilty of an offence against this Act.

65. No prosecution shall be instituted against the owner, agent, manager or under manager of a mine for any offence under this Act, not committed

personally by such owner, agent, manager or under manager, which can be prosecuted before a court of summary jurisdiction, except by an inspector or with the consent in writing of a Secretary of State; and in the case of any offence of which the owner, agent, manager or under manager of a mine is not guilty if he proves that he had taken all reasonable means to prevent the commission thereof, an inspector shall not institute any prosecution against such owner, agent, manager or under manager, if satisfied that he had taken such reasonable means as aforesaid. No prosecution shall be instituted against a coroner for any offence under this Act except with the consent in writing of a Secretary of State.

66. Where the owner, agent or manager of a mine has taken proceedings under this Act against any person employed in or about a mine in respect of an offence committed under this Act, he shall, within twenty-one days after the hearing of the case, report the result thereof to the inspector of the district.

67. In Scotland the following provisions shall have effect:

(1.) The court of summary jurisdiction when hearing and determining an information or complaint shall be the sheriff:

(2.) All jurisdictions, powers and authorities necessary for the court of summary jurisdiction under this Act are hereby conferred on that court:

(3.) Every person found liable under this Act by a court of summary jurisdiction in any fine, or to pay any money or costs by this Act directed to be recovered as fines, shall be liable in default of immediate payment to be imprisoned for a term not exceeding three months, and the conviction and warrant may be in the form of No. 3 of Schedule K of the Summary Procedure Act, 1864:

(4.) Any fine exceeding fifty pounds shall be recovered and enforced in the same manner in which any penalty due to Her Majesty under any Act of Parliament may be recovered and enforced:

(5.) An appeal shall not lie from any conviction made by a sheriff, save to the next circuit court, or where there are no circuit courts, to the High Court of Justiciary at Edinburgh, in the manner prescribed by such of the provisions of the Act of the twentieth year of the reign of King George the Second, chapter forty-three, and any Acts amending the same, as relate to appeals in matters criminal, and by and under the rules, limitations, conditions and restrictions contained in the said provisions.

68. (1.) Nothing in this Act shall prevent any person from being indicted or liable under any other Act or otherwise to any other or higher penalty or punishment than is provided for any offence by this Act, so, however, that no person be punished twice for the same offence.

(2.) If the court before whom a person is charged with an offence under this Act think that proceedings ought to be taken against such person for such offence under any other Act or otherwise, the court may adjourn the case to enable such proceedings to be taken.

69. A person who is the owner, agent or manager of any mine, or a miner or miner's agent, or the father, son or brother, or father-in-law, son-in-law, or brother-in-law, or such owner, agent or manager, or of a miner or miner's agent, or who is a director of a company being the owner of a mine, shall not,

except with the consent of both parties to the case, act as a court or member of a court of summary jurisdiction in respect of any offence under this Act.

70. Where a fine is imposed under this Act for neglecting to send a notice of any explosion or accident or for any offence against this Act which has occasioned loss of life or personal injury, a Secretary of State may (if he thinks fit) direct such fine to be paid to or distributed among the persons injured, and the relatives of any persons whose death may have been occasioned by the explosion, accident or offence, or among some of them.

Provided that—

i. Such persons did not in his opinion occasion or contribute to occasion the explosion or accident, and did not commit and were not parties to committing the offence :

ii. The fact of the payment or distribution shall not in any way affect or be receivable as evidence in any legal proceeding relative to or consequential on the explosion, accident, or offence.

Save as aforesaid—

All fines recovered in England or Scotland under this Act shall be paid into the receipt of Her Majesty's Exchequer, and shall be carried to the Consolidated Fund ;

All fines recovered in Ireland under this Act shall be applied in manner directed by the Fines Act (Ireland), 1851, and any Act amending the same.

MISCELLANEOUS.

71. If any question arises (otherwise than in legal proceedings) whether a mine is a mine to which this Act or the Metalliferous Mines Regulation Act, 1872, or any other Act 'for the time being in force and relating to metalliferous mines applies, the question shall be referred to a Secretary of State, whose decision thereon shall be final.

72. Any order of or exemption granted by a Secretary of State under this Act may be made, and from time to time revoked, or altered by a Secretary of State, either unconditionally or subject to such conditions as he may see fit, and shall be signed by a Secretary of State or under secretary or assistant under secretary.

73. All notices under this Act shall (unless expressly required to be in print) be in either writing or print (including lithograph), or partly in writing and partly in print (including lithograph), and all notices and documents required by this Act to be served or sent by or to an inspector may be either delivered personally, or served and sent by post by a prepaid letter ; and, if served or sent by post, shall be deemed to have been served and received respectively at the time when the letter containing the same would be delivered in the ordinary course of post ; and in proving such service or sending it shall be sufficient to prove that the letter containing the notice was properly addressed and put into the post.

74. Section thirty-eight of the Public Health Act, 1875 (which relates to privy accommodation for any house used as a factory or building in which both sexes are employed), shall apply to the portions of a mine which are above ground, and in which girls and women are employed, in like manner as if it

were herein re-enacted with the substitution of "those portions of the mine" for the house in the said section mentioned.

75. In this Act, unless the context otherwise requires,—

"Mine" includes every shaft in the course of being sunk, and every level and inclined plane in the course of being driven, and all the shafts, levels, planes, works, tram-ways, and sidings, both below ground and above ground, in and adjacent to and belonging to the mine:

"Shaft" includes pit:

"Plan" includes a correct copy or tracing of any original plan:

"Owner," when used in relation to any mine, means any person or body corporate who is the immediate proprietor or lessee, or occupier of any mine, or of any part thereof, and does not include a person or body corporate who merely receives a royalty, rent, or fine from a mine, or is merely the proprietor of a mine subject to any lease, grant, or license for the working thereof, or is merely the owner of the soil, and not interested in the minerals of the mine; but any contractor for the working of any mine, or any part thereof, shall be subject to this Act in like manner as if he were an owner, but so as not to exempt the owner from any liability:

"Agent," when used in relation to any mine, means any person appointed as the representative of the owner in respect of any mine, or of any part thereof, and as such superior to a manager appointed in pursuance of this Act:

"Secretary of State" means one of Her Majesty's Principal Secretaries of State:

"The Treasury" means the Commissioners of Her Majesty's Treasury:

"Boy" means a male under the age of sixteen years:

"Girl" means a female under the age of sixteen years:

"Woman" means a female of the age of sixteen years or upwards.

76. In the application of this Act to Scotland—

(1.) The term "Attorney General" means the Lord Advocate:

(2.) The term "injunction" means interdict:

(3.) The term "misdemeanor" means "crime and offence":

(4.) The term "chairman of quarter sessions" means the sheriff of the county:

(5.) The term "sheriff" includes sheriff substitute:

(6.) The term "attending on subpœna before a court of record" means attending on citation the Court of Justiciary:

(7.) The auditor of the sheriff court of the county or district of a county in which any inquiry takes place shall perform the duties of a master of one of the superior courts under this Act:

(8.) "County court judge, police magistrate, stipendiary magistrate, recorder or registrar of a county court" means a sheriff or sheriff substitute:

(9.) Notices of explosions, accidents, loss of life or personal injury shall be deemed to be sent to the inspector of the district on behalf of the Lord Advocate:

(10.) Sections forty-one and sixteen of the Public Health (Scotland) Act, 1867, shall respectively be substituted for sections thirty-eight and ninety-one of the Public Health Act, 1875.

(11.) The term "public elementary school" means State-aided school.

Nothing in this Act shall affect any provision in the Education (Scotland) Acts, 1872 to 1883.

77. In the application of this Act to Ireland,—

a. The expression "the Summary Jurisdiction Acts" means, as regards the Dublin metropolitan police district, the Acts regulating the powers and duties of justices of the peace and of the police of that district, and elsewhere, in Ireland, the petty sessions (Ireland) Act, 1851, and the Acts amending the same.

b. In hearing and determining a charge under this Act, a court of summary jurisdiction elsewhere than in the Dublin metropolitan police district, shall be constituted of two or more justices of the peace or of a resident magistrate, with or without other justices, sitting in petty sessions; and a resident magistrate means a magistrate appointed pursuant to the Act of the session of the sixth and seventh years of the reign of King William the Fourth, chapter fourteen:

c. Sections forty-eight and one hundred and seven of the Public Health (Ireland) Act, 1878, shall respectively be substituted for sections thirty-eight and ninety-one of the Public Health Act, 1875.

d. The expression "police or stipendiary magistrate" means resident magistrate:

"Master of one of Her Majesty's Superior Courts" means a taxing master of the High Court of Justice in Ireland:

"Registrar of a county court" means clerk of the peace:

"London *Gazette*" means Dublin *Gazette:*

"Attorney-General" means Attorney-General for Ireland:

"Chairman of quarter sessions" means county court judge.

TRANSITORY PROVISIONS AND REPEAL.

78. The persons who at the commencement of this Act are acting as inspectors under the Acts hereby repealed, and the boards for appointing examiners for managers' certificates under those Acts, shall continue to act in the same manner, and generally to be in the same position, as if they had been respectively appointed under this Act.

79. All orders made by a Secretary of State under any Act repealed by this Act, which are in force immediately before the commencement of this Act, shall be deemed to have been made under this Act; and all certificates of competency or of service granted under any Act repealed by this Act which are in force immediately before the commencement of this Act, shall be deemed to be first-class certificates granted under this Act; and the register of holders of certificates, and the other registers which at the commencement of this Act are kept in pursuance of the Acts hereby repealed, shall be deemed to be registers or parts of registers kept in pursuance of this Act.

80. (1.) A certificate of service shall be granted by a Secretary of State to every person who satisfies him either that before the passing of this Act he

was exercising, and has since that date exercised, or that he has at any time within five years before the passing of this Act for a period of not less than twelve months exercised, functions substantially corresponding to those of an under manager in a mine.

(2.) Every such certificate of service shall contain particulars of the name, place, and time of birth, and the length and nature of the previous service of the person to whom the same is delivered, and a certificate of service may be refused to any person who fails to give a full and satisfactory account of the particulars aforesaid, or to pay such registration fee as the Secretary of State may direct, not exceeding that mentioned in the Second Schedule to this Act.

(3.) A certificate of service granted under this section shall have the same effect for the purposes of this Act as a second class certificate of competency granted under this Act.

81. The special rules which at the commencement of this Act are in force under any Act hereby repealed in any mine shall continue to be the special rules in such mine until special rules are established under this Act for such mine, and while they so continue shall be of the same force as if they were established under this Act.

82. The provisions of this Act shall not—

a. Prevent a boy under the age of twelve years who, before the commencement of this Act, is lawfully employed in any mine below ground from continuing to be employed in a mine; nor

b. Prevent a boy or girl who, before the commencement of this Act, is lawfully employed above ground in connection with any mine from continuing to be employed above ground in connection with a mine; nor

c. Prevent a competent male person above the age of eighteen years who before the commencement of this Act is lawfully employed in working the machinery used for lowering and raising persons in a mine from continuing to be so employed; in like manner and subject to the same provisions and regulations as before the commencement of this Act, and the provisions of the Acts repealed by this Act, with respect to the employment of such boy or girl or competent male person shall continue to apply accordingly.

83. Any enactment or document referring to any Act repealed by this Act, or to any enactment thereof, shall be construed to refer to this Act, and to the corresponding enactments thereof.

84. The Acts described in Schedule Four to this Act are hereby repealed.

Provided that this repeal shall not affect any exemption granted, or other thing done or suffered before the commencement of this Act; and all offences committed and penalties incurred and proceedings commenced before the commencement of this Act may be punished, recovered, continued and completed in the same manner as if this Act had not passed.

SCHEDULES.

SCHEDULE ONE.

PROCEEDINGS OF BOARD FOR EXAMINATIONS.

(1.) The board shall meet for the despatch of business, and shall from time to time make such regulations with respect to the summoning notice place, management and adjournment of such meetings, and generally with respect to the transaction and management of business, including the quorum at meetings of the board, as they think fit, subject to the following conditions:—

a. Any regulations made by the board constituted under the Acts repealed by this Act, and in force at the commencement of this Act, shall continue in force till repealed or altered by the board.

b. An extraordinary meeting may be held at any time on the written requisition of three members of the board addressed to the chairman;

c. The quorum to be fixed by the board shall consist of not less than three members;

d. Every question shall be decided by a majority of votes of the members present and voting on that question;

e. The names of the members present, as well as those voting upon each question, shall be recorded;

f. No business shall be transacted unless notice in writing of such business has been sent to every member of the board seven days at least before the meeting.

(2.) The board shall from time to time appoint some person to be chairman, and one other person to be vice-chairman.

(3.) If at any meeting the chairman is not present at the time appointed for holding the same, the vice-chairman shall be the chairman of the meeting, and if neither the chairman nor vice-chairman shall be present, then the members present shall choose some one of their number to be chairman of such meeting.

(4.) In case of an equality of votes at any meeting, the chairman for the time being of such meeting shall have a second or casting vote.

(5.) The appointment of an examiner may be made by a minute of the board signed by the chairman.

(6.) The board shall keep minutes of their proceedings, which may be inspected or copied by a Secretary of State, or any person authorized by him to inspect or copy the same.

SCHEDULE TWO.

TABLE OF MAXIMUM FEES TO BE PAID IN RESPECT OF CERTIFICATES.

First Class Certificate.

By an applicant for examination   .   .   Two pounds.
For copy of certificate   .   .   .   Five shillings.

Second Class Certificate.

By an applicant for examination   .   One pound.
For copy of certificate   .   .   Two shillings and sixpence.

MINING LAWS OF THE KINGDOM OF PRUSSIA.

THE regulation of coal mines in the kingdom of Prussia is governed by special ordinances under the authority of the general mining law of the kingdom, passed June 24th, 1865. These special ordinances are issued by the duly appointed mining authorities of each district into which the kingdom is divided, and vary but little in their provisions. The following regulations are in force in the three circuits of Breslau, Bonn and Dortmund, and are based upon the regulations, consisting of twelve articles, laid down by the chief mining office of Breslau.

I. Provides for the protection of the surface in the interest of personal safety and of public traffic.

II. Safety of the miners—Fixes the thickness of the pillars at 20 meters (65 feet 7 inches) measured at right angles to the boundary line. Limits the extraction of brown coal deposits to a height of 5 meters (16 feet 5 inches) at one time.

III. Hauling or hoisting.—Forbids the hauler or hoister to stand, sit or lie on the wagons or cages; regulates the distance between wagons at not less than 15 meters (49 feet 4 inches) on inclines, and 10 meters (32 feet 11 inches) on level tracks; provides for the safety of the men during the filling of the wagons and cages, and for locking contrivances on the hoisting gear in shafts, protection against the dropping of materials down the shaft, also for efficient signalling apparatus in shafts and slopes, and secure grips, clutches brakes, etc.

IV. Ladder or man-ways, and hoisting of miners.—Every underground mine is to be provided with two separate man-ways or means of egress, which must be apart at least 20 meters (65 feet 10 inches) for their entire length, and permit of complete isolation at each end, the termination of such man-ways to have a central location in the mine, and the miner to be permitted to enter and leave the mine only through such man-ways. All man or ladder-ways to be lined and isolated in a secure manner when forming part of a shaft used for hoisting or hauling, and hoisting or hauling to be stopped during the use of such man-ways by the miners. The inclination of ladder-ways not to exceed 80 degrees, and all ladder-ways to be provided with resting places every 10 meters.

Hoisting of miners is only allowed by special permission of the chief officer and after inspection by the district surveyor. In case inclined shafts are used for the hoisting of miners, such shafts must be provided with isolated ladder-ways, single or double, in accordance with the character of the shaft.

VENTILATION.

General Regulations.—All mines must be provided with regular ventilation precautions, and in such a way that all parts of the mine are in a proper state to be entered and worked.

All entries to parts of mines, which shall not be worked for a longer period than eight days, and parts of mines in which foul gas is to be feared, shall be closed by special arrangements, and the entrance to such parts by miners is forbidden. Upon the request of the district surveyor, a ventilation plan has to be prepared and continued, showing at any time the whole system of ventilation and all parts thereof.

All necessary information concerning the ventilation, especially as to the number of distinct splits into which the mine has been divided and all changes from the original ventilation plan have to be inserted in the mine plan.

The approved mine plan and every alteration thereof have to be registered in the mine book.

The ventilation with a fire kibble is forbidden.

The ventilation of mines by furnace is only permitted in case of special consent from the district surveyor.

Every mine has to be provided with at least two safety-lamps of a pattern approved by the district surveyor.

All mines have to be tested for fire-damp by the district surveyor or by a deputy appointed by him, and the intervals between such tests are fixed by the district surveyor.

The mine superintendent is required to report to the district surveyor at once on the first appearance of fire-damp, also any reappearance of it after a long interval, and all important circumstances connected therewith. For such mines the following regulations are applied:

The intake and the outlet of air must pass through different mine openings. Exceptions therefrom need the special permit of the district surveyor, who has a right to cancel the permission at any time.

The section of the air-ways is dependent upon the quantities of air necessary for the ventilation of the whole mine, including the different splits, calculated upon a velocity of 240 meters per minute for the fresh air current, and of 360 meters for the return air current.

The principal air-way to have a section of at least 3 square meters, the second class air-ways of at least 2 square meters, and the crosscuts at least 1 square meter in the clear.

Smaller sections may be permitted by the chief officer in exceptional cases.

REGULATIONS FOR FIRE-DAMP MINES.

For mines, and such parts of mines as are ventilated by separate air splits, in which fire-damp has been shown by means of a safety-lamp, separate regulations and precautions have to be instituted by the mine superintendent, subject to the approval of the chief mining officer.

The ventilation of fire-damp mines must be sufficient to prevent the accumulation of fire-damp under ordinary circumstances, and to keep all parts of the mine constantly in a safe condition to be entered and worked. The mine superintendent is required to watch the ventilation closely, to provide for a regular and sufficient air circulation for all mine operations, and to adopt proper precautions, according to circumstances. It is his duty to test such precautions, as may have been taken by his subordinates or deputies in urgent cases, and plainly to approve or to change the same.

Special air plans are to be prepared in fire-damp mines. Ventilation by natural draught and through the chimneys of the boiler plant is insufficient.

The use of ventilating furnaces is permitted only on condition that the furnace be fed with fresh air and the safe egress of the fireman be provided for, and that (ignition) of the fire-damp by the furnace gas is prevented. The quantity of fresh air per minute for a fire-damp mine is to be at least 2 cubic-meters for each man, of the largest force working underground, and a horse is counted to be equal to four men.

The ventilators are to be of such dimensions, as will supply if necessary at least 25 per cent. more than this minimum. Exceptions therefrom are only allowed by the chief mining officer.

All fire-damp mines must have stations for the measurement of the air currents. Such stations to be given on the working plan and on the ventilation plan of the mine.

Drill-holes for the accomplishment of air communication are permitted under condition to enlarge the same promptly.

In whole as well as in parts—the ventilation is to be so arranged that the fresh air from the surface is carried down to the working places by the shortest route, while the divided air currents are returned through the compartments or chambers.

Downward ventilation of working mines—excepting in inclined drifts—is only permitted upon special consent from the district surveyor, and can be revoked at any time.

Rising drifts and road levels longer than 15 meters cannot be worked without special ventilation.

Air currents, which are not to be used again can be carried downward upon permission from the district surveyor.

Only so many working places can be supplied by one air current, as will leave the air at the last point still of the required purity. Air currents, which are charged with foul air to any extent are to be returned by the shortest route, without entering any other working place.

Shafts, cross-cuts and drifts must either be run parallel in pairs, or air brattices have to be carried along. The distance of the working-face from the last (cross-heading) or from the air brattice must not exceed 20 meters for level workings. In case there is fire-damp at such working faces, the brattice must be brought forward close up to the working places. The inclination of boards or chambers shall not exceed one in one hundred.

The ventilation of very foul working places has to be accomplished by means of separate ventilation—with compressed air or blowing cylinders or other suitable apparatus. Hand ventilators must always be located in fresh air. With hand-suction ventilators the discharge pipe must be carried into the return air way. Blowing hand ventilators must be located at the last open cross-heading in the fresh-air current and at that side from which the fresh air enters. The use of hand-ventilators in fire-damp mines is only permitted upon an order of the mine superintendent, and such order has to be recorded in the mine book.

All air-ways that are not in use, must be closed air-tight and in a durable manner.

Air-doors are to be self-closing. In places where a good air lock is necessary or where there is much traffic, double doors are required, of which one is always closed. Gates not needed to be taken down.

Changes in the arrangements for the air regulation shall not be made without order from the mine superintendent. Mine overseers and miners are compelled to report any damage to air brattices, etc., to the mine superintendent or to the nearest foreman. The lighting of combustible gas purposely is forbidden.

The escape of fire-damp from old workings must be prevented by ventilation or closing off. In all headings near old workings or where the accumulation of fire-damp may be expected, trial bore-holes must be driven.

Regular mining shall not be carried on before the air-way is cut through to the upper level, excepting in cases where downward ventilation has been permitted.

Every fire-damp mine must be provided with an efficient supervision of every part of the ventilation system. Upon request of the district surveyor special foremen must be engaged for this purpose.

Every working place must be tested for fire-damp before the miners are permitted to enter, except in case of changing shift. In case such tests show fire-damp in the workings these workings must be closed, necessary precautions be taken at once, and only opened again by special permission from the mine superintendent.

All miners and laborers must be withdrawn from the endangered workings in case of stoppage or interruption of the ventilation, and must not be allowed to resume work until a careful test has shown the safety of the workings, such permission to rest only with the mine superintendent.

The miner is required to close the workings as soon as dangerous accumulations of fire-damp are noticed, to withdraw from such places, warn his fellow miners, and report the case to the nearest mine foreman.

Smoking is forbidden in fire-damp mines.

BLACK DAMP MINES.

In all mines in which spontaneous combustion of coal is to be feared, efficient precautions must be taken against mine fires and especially the air circulation through old workings must be prevented.

The construction of dams in mine fires and the opening of burning mines or parts thereof is only permitted when an efficient gang of men with the necessary apparatus for rescue is at hand.

All mine workings, especially shafts and slopes, which are not connected with other workings carrying fresh air, must be examined for black damp (with a burning light) by a mine foreman or a reliable miner before the mining gang enters the mine.

Miners are not allowed to go to work unless the safety of the workings has been established.

LIGHTING.

V. The connecting and independent parts of shafts, slopes, sumps, self-acting inclined planes and galleries, in which machine-hauling takes place and also all brakes have to be lighted while in operation (by separate and stationary lamps) in case daylight does not reach those places.

All traffic and communication without miners' lamps is forbidden in mines which are neither lighted by daylight nor stationary lamps.

Every miner and official underground is required—if not otherwise ordered—to carry a tinder box for the purpose of relighting his lamp.

Open workings as well as surface structures are to be lighted during the night in such a manner, that the workmen can easily perceive and avoid any danger.

For all fire-damp mines the use of open lights underground is forbidden. Only safety-lamps and incandescent electric lights may be used. But in the fresh air intake in shafts and at pit-heads the open light may be used. The use of open lights in return air-ways and shafts needs the written permission of the district inspector.

Safety-lamps must be of a pattern approved by the district inspector.

Safety-lamps must be provided and kept in order by the mine owner.

Safety-lamps are to be numbered with running numbers and each miner shall always receive the same number, except in case of repairs or a change in the arrangement.

A.—EXPLOSIVES.

General Regulations.—The name of those mine foremen who have to attend to the reception, transport, storage, and distribution of explosives and fuse, and who attend to making up cartridges, are to be entered in the mine book and posted up in the miners' room.

Only reliable men over twenty-one years of age shall be employed in the transportation, storage, and distribution of explosives and making up cartridges, and the use of open lamps and smoking are forbidden during the transport and distribution of explosives and also in the storage rooms.

It is also forbidden to carry away from the mine any explosives or fuse given out.

The use of pure nitroglycerine and uncompressed gun-cotton is prohibited.

In the use of compressed gun-cotton and similar explosives the regulations designated for nitroglycerines are to be in force.

B.—THE PURCHASE OF EXPLOSIVES.

Only a mine owner or his representatives may purchase of explosives and fuse for use in a mine, and these must obtain the same either from the manufacturer or from warehouses licensed by the police. And upon the district inspector's request they must show that they have complied with this regulation.

Miners are compelled to obtain their supply of explosives and fuse exclusively from the mine owners by whom they are employed.

Blasting-powder shall be obtained only in packages or cartridges; nitroglycerine only in cartridges. If making up is necessary—such has to be done on the surface under proper supervision, and in structures designated for this purpose, which latter must have no connection with other buildings.

C.—STORAGE.

The storage rooms above ground must be licensed by the police. The district inspector must be informed of the police permit.

Special powder-chambers must be provided underground for the distribution of explosives to the miners, which chambers shall not contain more than 300 kilograms at one time. These powder-chambers must be distant at least 30 meters from each other, and at least 50 meters from all man-ways, hauling roads, and shafts, and shall have no direct connection with the same. The entrance and exit must be arranged, so that the men entering and leaving cannot meet each other.

Distribution-rooms may be arranged in exceptional cases and upon a written permit from the district inspector above ground, but this officer has the right to withdraw this permit at any time. The quantity of explosives in such rooms above ground must not exceed the daily need of the mine by more than 50 kilograms.

The temperature of the powder-chambers, below ground, in which dynamite is kept, must not be below 8° Celsius (+6½° Réaumur) and not 50° Celsius (+40° Réaumur).

Frozen nitroglycerine must not be worked with solid tools and must not be used for blasting, or given out in such a state.

Nitroglycerine, commencing to decompose (which can be perceived by the pungent smell and the appearance of a reddish brown gas), shall not be used for blasting. It must be burned in open fires, above ground, and under the supervision of a mine foreman.

Percussion caps must not be kept unlocked nor in the same room with the explosives.

Rooms in which explosives are stored shall neither be entered with open light nor is smoking permitted in the same.

The powder-chambers must contain two divisions, separated from each other and provided with locks, one division to serve for the distribution of explosives and the other for the storage of the same.

In powder-chambers the distribution-room must be entered with a lantern, which is secured against breaking by a strong gauze of brass wire. The lighting of this room by means of lanterns located outside, is also permitted, but the same must be sufficiently protected against damage from the outside.

Inside storage-rooms receive their light only through the open door of the distribution-room, and may be entered only by the mine foreman and overseers intrusted with the distribution of explosives and the workmen engaged in their transportation, but only barefoot or with felt shoes over their common shoes.

All nails, entirely or partly on the inner wall of the powder-rooms, must be of copper, zinc or wood, the keys and the bolt of the door locks of brass or copper. In general all iron work must be lined with copper or zinc-plates wherever it can come in contact with other iron work or may be walked over, the door-sills to be of wood and the floors of both divisions to be covered with hair-covers.

The powder-rooms are to be locked in such a way, that no stranger can open the same without using force. On the outside of the locks are to be placed, the words: "*Notice: Explosives,*" in a clearly visible manner.

D.—TRANSPORTATION OF EXPLOSIVES.

The carriage of explosives from the storage-rooms to the powder-chambers, and to the distribution-rooms above ground must be in the original boxes or kegs of the factory and under the supervision of a foreman or mine overseer.

For the transport of the boxes or kegs containing dynamite or nitroglycerine to their destination underground, such boxes or kegs must be placed in a second box of wood, which is filled up with saw-dust, tow, hair-covers or similar substances, and these boxes are provided with handles of rope, leather, or similar materials. The boxes to be locked, carried and hung in that way.

Explosives of a total weight of more than 5 kilograms have to be transported separately near all shafts and mine-structures as well as underground.

The workmen engaged in the carriage of explosives have to notify persons in their neighborhood by calling out "*Powder comes.*" Workmen, who transport explosives, are not allowed to carry lamps or lanterns. Two men must always be employed for the transport of explosives weighing more than 25 kilograms.

Fuse, caps, etc., must not be transported along with explosives.

The engine tender and the filler at the pit-head must be notified before explosives are carried in the shaft.

The engine tender must lower slowly and prevent the cage from jarring. The filler has to remove the explosives carefully from the cage and turn them over to the persons designated.

Laborers must use closed vessels for the transport of powder from the powder chamber and the distribution rooms above ground to the working places, and also for the return of the unused explosives. Only closed sheet-iron boxes shall be used for the transport of explosives of the nitro-glycerine class.

E.—DISTRIBUTION OF EXPLOSIVES.

In distributing explosives the vessels containing them must be opened only by authorized persons and only for the purpose of taking out explosives for immediate use.

The daily consumption of each working place is to be fixed by the foreman and is to be inserted in the distribution book.

The distribution has to take place only in the distribution room of the powder-chambers, which have to be in conformity with regulations set forth under C. The door to the inner room has to be closed.

The opening of the boxes or kegs containing explosives has to be effected with a wooden or brass wedge smeared with tallow, and a wooden mallet.

The distribution of explosives is only permitted for the purpose of blasting, and only in the common interest of the whole mining shift.

All explosives, not consumed during the shift, have to be returned to the distribution-foreman after the shift is ended, and in the same vessels used for their transportation, the vessel to bear the number of the working-gang, or else the same have to be turned over to the foreman of the following gang for use at the heading in case the first gang is relieved.

F.—BLASTING.

A driller has to be designated as foreman for each gang of miners who are blasting. The gang-foreman is appointed by the mine superintendent ; he must be reliable and thoroughly familiar with such work. He is responsible for carrying out the regulations for shot-firing. Other members of such gangs have to obey his orders unhesitatingly.

The distributed supply of explosives, fuse and caps, shall under no circumstances be taken to the working place, but shall be kept in the closed transport-vessel, in a locked box, standing in a safe place designated by the mine foreman. This box is opened only by the gang foreman when necessary and is closed again immediately.

Priming cartridges used with dynamite and other blasting materials shall not be kept on hand, but must be prepared as wanted by the insertion of cap and fuse.

Powder must be used only in form of cartridges. Well glued paper or other material which will not ignite is to be used for the manufacture of the cartridges.

Tamping must not be done with coal, but with soft stone, which will not strike fire, or with clay. It is forbidden to drive the cartridges in by force.

The use of iron tamping bars, and of a sponge and oiled paper instead of a sulphur wick are forbidden.

Smoking is forbidden during the manufacture of the cartridges, and while charging and firing of the blasts.

The one who fires the shot has to warn persons working in the vicinity with the call "*It burns*," before the charge is fired.

Extra precautions have to be taken when necessary against the effects of the blast.

The working place shall not be entered again for ten minutes after firing, in case the shot has missed, or that the explosive has burnt away without explosion.

Boring out or firing of shots, which have missed, is forbidden, as is also the deepening of holes left standing.

G.—BLASTING IN FIRE-DAMP MINES.

Blasting in fire-damp mines or in places which contain fire-damp is prohibited.

This prohibition extends also over all parts of the same mine, which have close connection with places containing fire-damp, until the mine superintendent has found the several working places and places connected with them are free of fire-damp.

In places where experience has proven the formation of inflammable coal dust, the use of powder or other slow acting explosives for blasting is forbidden, even when no fire-damp is present.

This prohibition is extended to such mine chambers as are on the same airsplit.

Before firing a shot, it must be established immediately before firing by careful examination with the safety-lamp, that there is no accumulation of fire-damp within a distance of 20 meters.

COAL-CUTTING.

The undercutting of loose and easy falling materials is forbidden.

The undercut faces must be secured by props or by pillars left in place.

A reliable man has to watch during the work of undercutting, where these precautions cannot be taken, and to give notice of any sign of giving way, when the workmen must leave the undercut stope at once.

All workings in front of which hauling and other labor takes place, must be examined carefully, at the beginning of each shift and after the noon rest, by a foreman or reliable workman appointed by him.

In case dangerous materials are discovered, all operations have to cease until the removal of the same.

The drawing of mine timber in of coal mines is only permitted under the supervision of a mine foreman or competent overseer, and only under circumstances which allow of the detection of movements in the hanging wall.

In brown coal mines the removing of timber may be done only by a miner experienced in such work.

Mines from which the timber has been removed, must be closed against entrance.

It is prohibited to mine coal in such mines.

LABOR.

Males of less than sixteen years of age, or females under eighteen years, shall not be allowed to work on the windlass, or with hand carts on inclined roads or in dragging carts by a strap across the neck.

Every working mine must have arrangements showing the number and sex of the employees.

The mine owner or his representative must inform the district inspector of these arrangements and receive his permit ; he has also to publish the duties of the mine foreman and laborers connected with the execution of these arrangements, by hanging the same in the miners' room.

Every working place in the mine must be inspected by a foreman at least once in every shift.

In all mines in which there is a temperature of more than 25° Celsius, thermometers must be provided, and observed regularly at the places designed by the district inspector, and laborers shall not work longer than six hours in a temperature of 30° Celsius or over in underground workings.

Workmen, who have not served at least one year as apprentice under the supervision of an experienced miner or hewer, shall not be employed as hewer independently.

A longer working than the common shift time, shall not be permitted to workmen of a mine or dressing works, if the health and life of other workmen is dependent upon their activity (such as engine-man, boiler-fireman, tender of ventilating furnaces, filler, bank man, etc.).

There must be a change house and a room for roll call which can be heated, at every mine.

An Extract of all important regulations must be posted in the mine room. (For mines employing Polish workmen, this extract must be published also in the Polish language.)

Care must be taken that workmen who cannot read are instructed as to regulations pertaining to their labors.

The mine owner or his representative is responsible for the execution of this regulation.

CONCLUDING ARTICLE.

Entrance to mines, shaft-houses and rooms containing engines and boilers is permitted only to persons holding permits, and employees. The mine superintendent must provide such persons with an experienced guide. This prohibition against visitors must be posted up.

Intoxicated or sick persons, or imbeciles, who, for these reasons may endanger their own or other lives, shall not be allowed in mines.

Nobody shall interfere with the arrangements for the security of the mines, the lives of workmen or the protection of the surface, neither shall any one change, or render ineffective such arrangements without the permission of the mine superintendent.

The pages of the mine book, ordered by the general mining law, shall be numbered, and the district inspector shall certify to their number.

The violation of these police regulations shall be punished by a fine of 150 marks, according to § 208 of the general mining law, provided, however, that the existing laws do not impose a more severe punishment.

The above police regulations take effect on April 1, 1888.

The general mine office can, upon application, grant reasonable time for the execution of the necessary arrangements set forth in these regulations.

SUPPLEMENT.

MINING LAWS OF KANSAS.

The text of the act to regulate mines and the mining of coal that has recently passed the Legislature reads as follows:

SECTION 1. It shall be unlawful for any mine owner, lessee or operator of coal mines in this state employing miners at bushel or ton rates or other quantities to pass the output of coal mined by said miners over any screen or other device, which shall take any part from the value thereof, before the same shall have been weighed and duly credited to the employee sending the same to the surface and accounted for at the legal rate of weights as fixed by the laws of Kansas.

SEC. 2. The weighman employed at any mine shall subscribe an oath or affirmation before a justice of the peace or other officer, authorized to administer oaths, to do justice between employer and employee, and weigh the output of coal from the mines in accordance with the provision of Section 1 of this act. Said oath or affirmation shall be kept conspicuously posted in the weigh office, and any weigher of coal or other person so employed who shall knowingly violate any provisions of the act shall be deemed guilty of a misdemeanor, and upon conviction thereof shall be punished by a fine of not less than $25.00 nor more than $100 for each offence, or by imprisonment in the county jail for not over 30 days, or both, as the court may decree.

SEC. 3. Any person or persons having or using scales, for the purpose of weighing the output of coal mines, so arranged or constructed that fraudulent weighing may be done thereby, or who shall knowingly resort to or employ any means whatsoever by reason of which such coal is not correctly weighed and reported, in accordance with the provisions of this act, shall be deemed guilty of a misdemeanor and be subject to a fine of from $200 to $500 and to 60 days in the county jail, or both.

SEC. 4. Any provisions, contract or agreement between mine owners or operators thereof and the miners who are employed therein, whereby the provisions of Section 1 of this act is waived, modified or annulled, shall be void and of no effect, and the coal sent to the surface shall be weighed in accordance with the provisions of this act, and right of action shall not be invalidated by reason of any contract or agreement.

SEC. 5. The provisions of this act shall also apply to the class of workers in mines known as loaders, engaged in mines where the mining is done by machinery. Wherever the workmen are under contract to load coal by the bushel, ton or quantity, it shall be settled for in accordance with this act.

SEC. 6. All miners and other laborers in any mines shall be paid in lawful money once at least in every fifteen days, after the first day of May, 1889.

SEC. 7. Whenever any mine owner, lessee or contractor, or operator of coal mines in this state shall fail to pay any of their employees in accordance with Section 6, then a penalty for such failure shall be attached as follows : A sum equivalent to ten per cent. of each day's wages or salary so earned for each day's payment is withheld after the expiration of the fifteen days, specified in Section 6 of this act, such penalty to attach for each day except Sundays and legal holidays, until the full amount of wages is paid. This act goes into effect May 1st, 1889.

THE AMENDED COLORADO MINE INSPECTION LAW.

THE following is the act passed by the Legislature creating a Mine Inspector, and dividing the State into Inspection Districts :

SECTION 1. That for the purpose of facilitating the examination and inspection of metalliferous mines within the State of Colorado, the State shall be divided into three metalliferous mining districts ; the counties composing said districts being as follows :

District No. 1—Shall include the counties of Routt, Larimer, Weld, Logan, Grand, Gilpin, Clear Creek, Jefferson, Arapahoe, Douglas, Elbert, El Paso, Washington, Boulder.

District No. 2—Shall include the counties of Eagle, Summit, Pitkin, Lake, Park, Chaffee, Mesa, Delta, Gunnison, Fremont, Pueblo, Custer, Bent, Garfield, Huerfano, Sagauche.

District No. 3—Shall include the counties of Montrose, San Miguel, Ouray, Dolores, San Juan, Hinsdale, Rio Grande, La Plata, Archuleta, Conejos, Costilla, Las Animas.

SEC. 2. For the purpose of securing an efficient and thorough inspection of metalliferous mines within the State of Colorado and to provide for an adequate force therefor, the Governor shall appoint by and with the consent of the Senate, one mine inspector of metalliferous mines of Colorado, who with consent and approval of the Governor, shall appoint three assistant inspectors of metalliferous mines, and each assistant inspector shall be a resident of the district to which he is appointed. The inspector and assistants so appointed shall hold their office for the term of two years from the date of their appointment, or until their successors are appointed and qualified. The first appointment hereunder shall be made on or before the 1st day of April, 1889, and in case of the removal, resignation or death of either the inspector or assistants, the vacancy shall be filled by appointment by the Governor in case of the inspector and by the inspector of mines in the case of the assistant for the unexpired term only of the position or positions so made vacant.

SEC. 3. No person shall be appointed inspector or assistant inspector who is not a citizen of the United States and of the State of Colorado, and unless he has a practical knowledge of the best methods of working, ventilating and timbering mines; and he must have had an experience of at least five years in mining in the metalliferous mines of this State.

SEC. 4. Before entering upon the discharge of their duties, the inspector shall give a bond to the State in the sum of five thousand dollars ($5,000), and each assistant inspector shall give bond to the State in a sum of two thousand five hundred dollars ($2,500), to be approved by the Governor, conditioned on the faithful performance of their duties, respectively. Said bond shall be deposited with the Secretary of State.

SEC. 5. The inspector or the assistant inspector, or either of them, shall not act as manager or agent or lessee for any mining or other corporation during his term of office, but shall give his whole time and attention to the duties of the office to which he has been appointed. He shall on receipt of any reliable information relating to the health and safety of the workmen employed in any metalliferous mine in the State, instruct the assistant inspector of that district to examine and report to him the condition of such mine; the mine owner, agent, manager or lessee shall have the right of appeal to the inspector on any differences that may arise between such parties and the assistant inspector; on receipt of notice of any accident in any mine, whether fatal or not, he shall personally inquire into the cause of such accident. On receipt of a report from any assistant inspector of any mine, he shall issue a notice to the owner, agent, manager or lessee of such mine, of what changes or additions are necessary to insure the health and safety of the workingmen employed in such mine. He shall order the assistant inspectors of the different districts to inspect and report on any mines in their districts whenever he considers such inspection necessary, or receives a notice from any person that the health or safety of the workingmen require such inspection, and he shall not be required to give notice to any owner, agent, manager or lessee of the time when such inspection will be made. He shall see that the provisions and requirements provided for in this act are faithfully observed and obeyed, and that the penalties of the law be enforced, and that all existing laws consistent with this act be enforced.

SEC. 6. It shall be the duty of each assistant inspector to report to the inspector the names and locations of all the metalliferous mines in operation in his district, and to collect and report all the data possible in regard to the manner of working the mine, whether by shaft, tunnel, incline or otherwise. It shall be his duty to examine and report the condition of the hoisting machinery, engines, boilers, whims, cages, cars, buckets, ropes and chains used in the mine; also the appliances used for the extinguishing of fires. He shall examine and report upon the manner and method of working, and timbering the shafts, drifts, inclines, stopes, winzes, tunnels and upraises, through which persons pass to and fro while engaged in their daily labor. He shall examine and report upon all exits from the mine, and how the mine is ventilated; and also how and where all explosives and inflammable oils and supplies are stored; he shall also report on the system of signals used in the mine. He shall state in his report what changes or additions are necessary to ensure the health and safety of the workingmen in and about the mine. He shall be subject to the orders of the inspector, and shall make inspection and report on mines whenever ordered to do so by the inspector.

SEC. 7. Every owner, agent, manager or lessee of any metalliferous mine in this State shall admit the inspector or his assistants to such mine on the exhibition of his certificate of appointment, for the purpose of making the examination and inspection provided for in this act, whenever the mine is in active operation, and render any necessary assistance for such inspection ; but said inspector or his assistants shall not unnecessarily obstruct the working of said mine. Upon the refusal of the owner, agent, manager or lessee to admit the inspector or his assistants to such mine, such owner, agent, manager or lessee shall be subject to a fine of not less than fifty dollars ($50) nor more than five hundred dollars ($500).

SEC. 8. If the inspector, his assistants, or either of them, shall reveal any information in regard to ore bodies, chutes or deposits of ore, or location, course or character of underground workings, or give any information or opinion respecting any mine obtained by them in making such inspection, upon conviction thereof he or they shall be removed from office and fined in a sum of not less than one hundred dollars ($100) nor more than five thousand dollars (5,000).

SEC. 9. The inspector and his assistants shall exercise a sound discretion in the enforcement of this act, and if they shall find any matter, thing or practice in or connected with any metalliferous mine to be dangerous or defective, so as to, in their opinion, threaten or tend to the bodily injury of any person, the inspector or his assistants shall give notice in writing thereof to the owner, agent, manager or lessee of such mine, stating in such notice the particulars in which he considers such mine or part thereof, or practice, to be dangerous or defective, and order the same to be remedied.

SEC. 10. In case the owner, agent, manager or lessee after written notice being duly given, does not conform to the provisions of this act, or disregards the requirements of this act, or any of its provisions or lawful order of the inspector or any of his assistants made hereunder, any court of competent jurisdiction may, on application of the inspector of mines, by civil action in the name of the State of Colorado, enjoin or restrain the owner, agent, manager or lessee from working the mine until it is made to conform to the provisions of this act ; and such remedy shall be cumulative, and shall not affect any other proceedings against such owner, agent, manager or lessee, authorized by law for the matter complained of in such action.

SEC. 11. Any owner, agent, manager or lessee having charge of or operating any metalliferous mine, whenever loss of life or serious accident shall occur, connected with the working of such mine, shall give notice immediately and report all facts thereof to the mine inspector, who shall investigate and ascertain the causes and make a report, which report shall be filed in his office for future reference.

SEC. 12. The inspector shall have an office in the city of Leadville, Lake county, to be furnished by the Secretary of State, in which he shall carefully keep all records of mine examinations, showing the date of examination, condition in which the mines are found, manner and method of working, the extent to which the laws are obeyed and what recommendations, if any, were ordered by the inspector and his assistants. He shall collate and embrace all information he can in his biennial report to the Governor of Colorado on or before December 15th of each year. Said report shall contain the number of mines visited, number of mines in operation, and the number of miners employed therein. It shall also contain the number and cause of accidents, fatal and non-fatal, that may have occurred in and about the mine. This and all other pertinent information shall be embodied in the report. All instruments, books and memoranda pertaining to the office shall be the property of the State, and shall be delivered to his successor in office.

SEC. 13. The inspector of metalliferous mines shall receive a salary of three thousand five hundred dollars ($3,500) per year, and ten cents per mile for mileage actually and necessarily travelled in the discharge of his official duties, said mileage not to exceed one thousand dollars ($1,000) in any one year, to be paid monthly by the State Treasurer out of any moneys appropriated for that purpose, on the certificate of said state inspector of metalliferous mines, showing services rendered and the amount thereof, and on presentation of such certificate to the State Auditor by the person entitled thereto, he shall issue his warrant for the amount thereof, to be paid out of any appropriation, as aforesaid. He is hereby authorized to procure such instruments and stationery from time to time as may be necessary to the proper discharge of his duties under this act, at the expense of the State, which shall be paid by the State Treasurer upon accounts duly certified by him and audited by the proper department of the State.

SEC. 14. The assistant inspector or inspectors shall each receive a salary of fifteen hundred dollars ($1,500) per year and ten cents per mile mileage for the number of miles actually and necessarily travelled while in the discharge of his duties, said mileage not to exceed five hundred dollars ($500) in any one year, which is to be paid monthly in like manner and form as prescribed in the previous section relating to the payment of the metalliferous mine inspector.

SEC. 15. The neglect or refusal by the inspector or his assistants to perform the duties or requirements of this act shall be deemed a misdemeanor, and shall be punished by a fine of not less than $100, nor more than $500, and all fines collected under the provisions of this act shall be paid into the general fund of the treasury of the State.

SEC. 16. The Governor shall have the power at any time to summarily remove from office the inspector or any assistant inspector for incompetency, inefficiency, neglect of duty or abuse of the privileges of his office.

SEC. 17. All acts and parts of acts not consistent with this act are hereby repealed.

Approved April 1st, 1889.

INDEX.

409

"THE BEST MINING PAPER IN THE WORLD."

THE ENGINEERING AND MINING JOURNAL

COAL

EDITORS :

RICHARD P. ROTHWELL, C.E., M.E.,
ROSSITER W. RAYMOND, Ph.D., M.E.

CONTRIBUTORS:

THE MOST EMINENT ENGINEERS AND METALLURGISTS IN EVERY PART OF THE WORLD.

The value of the mineral products of the United States in 1883 was \$591,659,931, or greater than that of all other countries in the world combined.

The skill and knowledge acquired in effecting this vast production are recorded in the pages of THE ENGINEERING AND MINING JOURNAL, which for nearly a quarter of a century has been not only the leading but practically the only paper in America devoted to the Engineering Arts of Mining and Metallurgy, and the marketing of mineral products.

Can any one in the whole world who is interested in the production, manufacture or trade in mineral products afford to be ignorant of the latest American practice and the character and values of these products?

THE ENGINEERING AND MINING JOURNAL combines Science and Practice, Technology and Trade. It furnishes that information that has practical money value to the Miner, the Engineer, the Metallurgist, the Chemist and Geologist, as well as to the Mechanic, the Metal Worker, the Merchant, the Investor and the Banker.

SUBSCRIPTION PRICE, including postage :

Weekly Edition (which includes the Export Edition), for the United States, Mexico and Canada, \$4 per annum; \$2.25 for six months; all other countries in the Postal Union, \$5.

Monthly Export Edition, all countries, \$2.50 gold value per annum.

THE SCIENTIFIC PUBLISHING CO., PUBLISHERS,

P. O. Box 1833.   **27 Park Place.**
NEW YORK.

Facts Concerning the Use of Judson Powder in Mining Anthracite and Bituminous Coal.

IT is generally believed that only black powder can be used for coal mining, and that no explosive containing nitro-glycerine in any proportion can be employed because of the expense and greater waste of coal which it is assumed would result.

As a matter of fact, Judson Powder, which contains a small percentage of nitro-glycerine, has been regularly used, in increasing quantities, for more than eight years at mines in the Hazleton District of Pennsylvania.

Critical tests made at the Cross Creek Colliery, under the direction of the Hon. E. B. Coxe, prove that Judson Powder, although of higher price than black powder, is nevertheless more economical to use.

Instead of making more fine coal, as was at first feared by some, the opposite has been found to be the case; less small coal being made with Judson than with black powder.

The cap which is required to explode the Judson was objected to at first, but we know of no accident happening with either the caps or powder during eight years' constant use; on the contrary, competent miners rate the Judson as safer than common blasting powder, since sparks or flame from miners' lamps will not explode it ; a lighted lamp may be thrown into a package of Judson Powder without danger.

Users notice that the smoke from Judson Powder is much less than that from black powder, which makes it possible to quickly and thoroughly inspect the walls after making a blast, so that the miner is enabled to better guard against the fatal falls of top coal which are so common.

We refer to our customers for confirmation of our claims as to safety, economy and power. For further particulars address

SMALL & SCHRADER, Gen. Agts.,
245 BROADWAY, NEW YORK.

THE
Jeffrey Manufacturing Company
COLUMBUS, OHIO,

MANUFACTURERS OF

THE JEFFREY ELECTRIC COAL MINING MACHINE.

Electric Generators, Electric Motors, Cars, Electric Mine Drills, Electric Power Pumps, Electric Fans.

COMPRESSED AIR COAL MINING MACHINE.

Power Drills, Chain Belting, Elevating and Conveying Machinery.

SEND FOR CATALOGUE.

AIR
CO·MPRESSORS

THE NORWALK IRON WORKS CO.
SOUTH NORWALK, CONN.